Dynamics of American Democracy

Dynamics of American Democracy

Partisan Polarization, Political Competition, and Government Performance

Edited by
Eric M. Patashnik and Wendy J. Schiller

University Press of Kansas

Published by the University Press of Kansas (Lawrence, Kansas 66045), which was organized by the Kansas Board of Regents and is operated and funded by Emporia State University, Fort Hays State University, Kansas State University, Pittsburg State University, the University of Kansas, and Wichita State University

Library of Congress Cataloging-in-Publication Data

Names: Patashnik, Eric M., editor. | Schiller, Wendy J., 1964- editor.
Title: Dynamics of American democracy : partisan polarization, political competition, and government performance / edited by Eric M. Patashnik and Wendy J. Schiller.
Description: Lawrence : University Press of Kansas, 2020.
Identifiers: LCCN 2020013201
ISBN 9780700630004 (cloth)
ISBN 9780700630011 (paperback)
ISBN 9780700630028 (epub)
Subjects: LCSH: Political culture—United States. | Polarization (Social sciences)—Political aspects—United States. | Divided government—United States. | Government accountability—United States. | Political participation—United States. | Two-party systems—United States. | United States—Politics and government—Public opinion.
Classification: LCC JK1726 .D96 2020 | DDC 306.20973—dc23
LC record available at https://lccn.loc.gov/2020013201.

British Library Cataloguing-in-Publication Data is available.

Printed in the United States of America

10 9 8 7 6 5 4 3 2 1

The paper used in this publication is recycled and contains 30 percent postconsumer waste. It is acid free and meets the minimum requirements of the American National Standard for Permanence of Paper for Printed Library Materials Z39.48-1992.

Contents

Acknowledgments

This book originated in Mitch Julis's encouragement that we bring together leading scholars and practitioners to consider the performance of the American political system. We wish to thank the Julis-Rabinowitz family for its generous support of this project.

We would like to thank the Watson Institute for International and Public Affairs and the Department of Political Science at Brown University for hosting the conference where initial versions of the essays in this book were presented. We appreciate the support of Watson director Ed Steinfeld and Watson events manager Christine Kilgus. We also would like to thank Ian Shapiro and Margaret Weir for their participation at the conference.

We thank David Congdon at University Press of Kansas for all his support for the project.

An earlier version of chapter 4 was published as Frances Lee, "The 115th Congress and Questions of Party Unity in a Polarized Era," *Journal of Politics* 80, no. 4: 1464–1473.

Introduction

Eric M. Patashnik and Wendy J. Schiller

In this book, we set out to address the challenges to contemporary American democracy. Our investigation looks beneath the surface of current events to examine the twenty-first-century forces that are reshaping democratic politics in the United States and around the world. These forces include ideological polarization and political "tribalism"; rapid demographic, economic, and technological change; the influence of online news and social media; and the increasing importance of public attitudes about gender and race.

A central focus of the book is the performance of US political parties in connecting citizens to leaders, promoting problem-solving, and ensuring democratic responsiveness and accountability. Although the advent of social media and the renewal of protest politics have reduced the capacity for party leaders to control the public agenda, conflict over government policy is still structured through political parties. Today, we take it for granted that all Democrats and all Republicans stand unified in opposition to each other on ideas about the federal government's role in addressing issues such as health care, income inequality, and climate change. Yet it was not that long ago that Democrats and Republicans could work across the partisan aisle to enact major policies such as the Elementary and Secondary Education Act, the Clean Air Act, Immigration Reform, and Infrastructure Investment. Senators from the Deep South would work together with senators from the Northeast and Northwest in these policy areas on a regular basis.

While some observers argued then that such fluidity across partisan lines was good for policymaking, many others argued that it undermined democratic accountability and government performance because it made it harder for voters to assign credit or blame to one party for policy outcomes.

To bring necessary clarity to the voters, the American Political Science Association published a famous report in 1950 that advocated for stronger political parties, stating, "The party system that is needed must be democratic, responsible and effective—a system that is accountable to the public, respects and expresses differences of opinion, and is able to cope with the great problems of modern government" (APSA 1950, 17).

It took a long time, but party reformers eventually got their wishes in many respects. While bipartisanship has not disappeared from Capitol Hill, the two major parties are far more cohesive than they were during the 1950s, 1960s, and 1970s. Candidates today increasingly run for the House and the Senate as members of unified party teams. The parties today are increasingly composed of groups with different social identities and have distinct geographical bases. The Democrats today perform increasingly well among highly educated professionals and minorities who live in upscale and ethnically diverse coastal cities and university towns. The Republicans perform better among less educated workers who live in whiter, more rural areas and in outlying suburbs. Individual leaders still matter a great deal in national politics, but parties (and their networks of donors, affiliated interest groups, and base supporters) are increasingly the prime movers.

Voters today are becoming a mirror image of the distinct partisanship among legislators by sorting into two sides and fighting exclusively for their team during election season. Political scientists have observed that voters no longer split their electoral voting across parties as they once did, and incumbents are less safe than they used to be because they cannot rely on crossover voting in their district anymore (Jacobson 2015). The presidency has also been become more polarizing and has been elevated to a level of power and prominence in American politics well beyond past eras.

The rise of Fox News, MSNBC, and Facebook, Twitter, and other social media outlets can reinforce this "team" mentality and, in doing so, undermine the elite consensus required to sustain a common public sphere, giving rise to conflicting partisan narratives about current events. As opposed to past decades, where there was a relatively small and narrow echo chamber for these partisan sentiments, internet technology, cable news, and social media have expanded such that there are almost no limits on sources of information about politics. With fewer shared sources of information and fewer accepted filters for legitimizing that information, it is harder and harder for Democratic and Republican voters to agree on common facts about politics and policy outcomes.

Despite fulfilling the reform pleas of fifty years ago, the more responsible and ideologically structured party system has not succeeded in promoting more effective governance. Instead of competing over which party can deliver policy solutions that reach the largest number of voters in need, politicians spend much of their time casting blame on the other side. From healthcare and the environment to economic mobility and college accessibility, government does not work to deliver its best on the behalf of voters.

The essays in this volume focus on the core reasons for why a "more responsible party system" has failed to deliver better results. We have gathered some of the nation's leading scholars of US politics, public policy, and public opinion together with business practitioners who are working to reform the US political process. Their individual and collective contributions demonstrate the vast changes that the American democracy has experienced over the past few decades. The authors try to explain how these changes have occurred and identify the consequences they have produced, all in the context of a political and information age that is distinctly different from any time that has come before it.

In part 1, we begin with a focus on the effect that entrenched polarization, now commonly referred to as "tribal politics," has on bipartisan cooperation and compromise. Many current observers of politics and policy argue that such polarization stands in the way of a more productive and responsive political system and, by extension, government. In chapter 1, James A. Morone explores the historical development of the powerful themes of race and ethnicity in the American party system from the early 1800s through the present day. He argues that use of "us vs. them" is embedded in the fabric of American political development and has been a large part of the division between the two major parties but that it has become much more pronounced in recent years. In chapter 2, Matt Grossmann argues that the long timeline for policy enactment runs headlong into the short-term interest of political parties in winning elections. This misalignment reinforces polarization and contributes to limited substantive achievement. Conservatives, seeking to limit government action, focus on maintaining power to block new (or scale back recent) policy initiatives, while liberals continually seek to broaden their issue agenda. Without a resolution of the tension between the continuously expanding policy reach of government and intense ideological polarization, the parties will continue prolonged warfare, with occasional bursts of liberal policymaking leading to conservative backlashes and limited policy results.

In part 2, three leading congressional scholars write about political institutions and government performance and their interactions with the party structure. In chapter 3, Sarah A. Binder builds on her book *Stalemate* (2003) as well as David Mayhew's *Divided We Govern* (1991) to address congressional gridlock and policymaking since World War II. She examines whether and how intense partisanship shapes the potential for bipartisan agreement, both inside Congress and with the president, on the issues that comprise the federal agenda. Binder argues that polarization today undercuts the legislative productivity of majority parties in periods of unified party control of Congress and the White House, because the opposition party has an incentive to exploit their parliamentary rights, such as insisting on sixty votes in the Senate on most amendments. In chapter 4, Frances E. Lee presents an alternative view to the general trends that Binder identifies and builds on the theme of partisan versus bipartisan lawmaking using data on party cohesion in House and Senate roll-call voting in the 115th Congress. This chapter discusses why and how the Republican majority secured votes by members of the minority party to pass key legislation, which runs counter to the expectations of party competition under polarization. Lee proposes that scholars may be overestimating the extent to which majority parties can afford to shut out the minority in policymaking because majority members experience district and state-level pressures to deliver legislation. In chapter 5, Nolan McCarty provides a deep dive into how polarization affects the operation of our federal system and state-level policy activity and identifies how it has reduced the capacity for policymaking at the federal level. He argues that the declining capacity of the US Congress and the executive to produce legislation and address policy needs will influence the relative power of the federal and state governments. As policy enactments diminish at the federal level and policy needs stay the same or grow larger, states are increasingly addressing these needs without federal action, which on the surface appears to be a corrective to the lack of responsiveness by the national government. However, McCarty also argues that polarization may have the effect of pushing states farther away from each other on policy dimensions along partisan lines, especially as states adopt different policies in the same issue domains, such as health care, abortion, and gun control.

Part 3 includes four chapters that explore how public opinion and political behavior reflect and reinforce the divisions that exist in a polarized era. In doing so, these chapters provide original and important insights into what voters know, how they judge parties, and how they evaluate governments. In chapter 6, Kristin Kanthak uses American National Election Studies (ANES) data to explore how "negative partisanship" (the tendency of some voters to form their opinions based on their opposition to the party they dislike) affects factors that may be related to satisfaction with democracy, such as trust in government. Examining government at the state level, she finds that when government is controlled by the opposite party of respondents, they exhibit less trust in government generally; the more active that government is, the more intense the level of distrust. She warns that increasing polarization at all levels of government threatens to erode trust in government. In chapter 7, John Sides, Michael Tesler, and Lynn Vavreck assess the role of attitudes toward gender and how it interacts with partisanship to influence electoral choices. They find that there is a stronger relationship between sexist attitudes and women's vote choice in 2018 than in 2016, but they find no difference in the correlation between sexist attitudes and vote choice for men. They argue that the effect of the #MeToo movement combined with feelings toward Donald Trump may be intensifying partisan differences along a new dimension in electoral choices for 2020 and beyond.

In chapter 8, Samara Klar and Yotam Shmargad study the effects of social media's algorithmic sorting of the news on political attitudes and evaluations. Using an experiment with automatic sorting of news stories that are fed to individuals on their social media pages, this chapter demonstrates how the placement of the story, combined with how well it lines up with the individual's ideological positions, affects subsequent political evaluations. Because news stories that are given "likes" more frequently rise to the top of a news feed, social media's use of popularity-based algorithms exacerbates selective exposure. In chapter 9, Deborah J. Schildkraut, Jeffrey M. Berry, and James M. Glaser use an original data set of Twitter political elites who are measured along liberal and conservative lines, and their followers' tweets and replies, to measure variation in levels of engagement and civility according to ideology. In doing so, they assess whether there is a difference between liberals and conservatives as to their willingness to engage in conflict with the other side and how uncivil they are in their use of language. They find that liberals are more conflict avoidant than conservatives on Twitter but that ideology was not associated with the levels of "toxicity" contained in users' tweets.

In part 4, we include two essays that address the inadequacies of the American party system and propose possible reforms. In chapter 10, CEO Katherine M. Gehl and business administration professor Michael E. Porter apply economic concepts and tools to diagnose the problems of American democracy.

Drawing an analogy between the economic competition between firms over profits and market share, on the one hand, and political competition over votes and power, on the other, Gehl and Porter argue that competition in the US politics "industry" is highly imperfect and unhealthy. Indeed, they argue that Democrats and Republicans behave as a "duopoly." Rather than competing over which party can better serve average voters by delivering outcomes for their benefit, the authors contend that the two parties jointly control the terms of competition to serve their own interests and those of primary voters, special interests, and donors.

They argue that parties create and reinforce partisan divisions, avoid finding common ground, and strategically keep conflicts alive to generate interest among their partisan bases. As a result, the preferences of ordinary voters (and nonvoters) are ignored frequently and many important national challenges go unaddressed.

Gehl and Porter argue that the fundamental solution is to restore healthy political competition and strengthen democratic accountability through reforms. They propose the elimination of partisan primaries and would instead allow the top five vote-getters from a single nonpartisan ballot to advance to the general election. They would also replace plurality voting and instead use "ranked choice" voting with instant runoff in general elections to prevent candidates who are opposed by a majority of voters from winning office. Each of these reforms echoes similar efforts from the past, such as the McGovern-Fraser Commission, to give voters more say over their choice of candidates in both primaries and the general elections. Gehl and Porter's reform strategy stands as the latest in a long line of attempts to bring power over nominations for elected office, and the elections themselves, closer to the people.

In chapter 11, Lee Drutman, William A. Galston, and Tod Lindberg argue that a third party might provide just the type of competition that Gehl and Porter seek to produce more effective representation but that the obstacles facing third-party emergence are formidable. They use public opinion data from Pew, Gallup, ANES, and their own VOTER Survey to measure public support for third parties and to understand what it would take to enable third parties to succeed. They find that there is general support for alternatives to the two existing major parties but that voters say they would prefer a multiparty system, not necessarily just an additional "third" major party. At the same time, they find that most voters do not grasp how much procedural reform would have to take place to enable third-party success and have little grasp of the way our politics would change under a multiparty system. Moreover, even if a third party were to emerge, it is not clear from the data that most voters would switch their party allegiance away from their current political party. The three authors also do something unusual in that they conclude the chapter with their individual views on solutions to the marginalization of third parties and prospects for their success.

In part 5, we turn to a discussion of Donald Trump's impact on the Republican Party and the cementing of executive-centered partisanship. In chapter 12, Nicholas F. Jacobs and Sidney M. Milkis reflect on the evolution of American politics during the Trump presidency and on the implications for executive power of his effective takeover of the Republican Party. One lesson of the chapter is that present-day parties are so weak as public-regarding, problem-solving institutions that they cannot withstand the efforts of a single aggressive politician to use them for his own self-advancement; some may argue that the Senate's failure to convict Trump in the impeachment proceedings, or even to call witnesses, reflects this weakness. Jacobs and Milkis argue that Trump's success in redefining aspects of the Republican Party to mirror his personal policy objectives is not a new development. Rather it is the culmination of a decades-long reorientation within both major parties interacting with the rise of an executive-centered party system.

Finally, our conclusion takes stock of the findings of the volume and assesses potential paths forward for the party system in American politics. The world looks a lot different now than it did in 1950, when political scientists called for strengthening parties to promote better government, and in most ways, it is a freer, more open, and more equal democracy than when they wrote. In spite of all the tremendous progress the American democracy has made since then, observers of American politics appear to be more worried about the state of the democracy than ever before. To conclude this volume, we assess and summarize the findings of our authors' research and reflect on how these developments in American politics may, or may not, bring us to a place of more responsive and effective government.

REFERENCES

American Political Science Association. "Toward a More Responsible Two-Party System: A Report of the Committee on Political Parties." *American Political Science Review*, Supplement 44, no. 3 (1950): v–96.

Binder, Sarah A. *Stalemate: Causes and Consequences of Legislative Gridlock.* Washington, DC: Brookings Institution, 2003.

Jacobson, Gary C. "It's Nothing Personal: The Decline of the Incumbency Advantage in US House Elections." *Journal of Politics* 77, no. 3 (2015): 861–873.

Mayhew, David R. *Divided We Govern.* New Haven, CT: Yale University Press, 1991.

PART ONE

A Historical Perspective on Today's Tribal Politics

CHAPTER 1

The Rise of Tribal Politics in Historical Perspective

James A. Morone

American politics has grown increasingly partisan, moving beyond spirited competition to a kind of fury that can best be tagged as tribal.[1] The two parties—once ideological cousins with plenty of overlap in the middle—now reflect different worlds. As polarization grows, both party leaders and their followers stake out very different positions. On policy issues, like the environment, where there was little disagreement between the parties twenty years ago, the parties now take radically different perspectives. Moreover, partisanship has spilled beyond politics and policies. Republican Party members call Democrats "immoral" and "lazy," and Democrats fire back with "closed-minded" and "dishonest." Where's the ideal place to live? Among Democrats, 46 percent chose cities; among Republicans, 4 percent. On dating apps, people even spurn romance with partners from the opposite party—and that's just as well, since six out of ten parents would be unhappy about their children marrying someone from across the political divide (up from 4 percent in more quiescent times).[2]

Today, no one gives voice to fierce partisan animosity quite like President Donald Trump, who seemed to egg on violence at his rallies. Pointing to black protesters being hustled out of one venue, he told the cheering crowd, "They used to treat them very, very rough," or, still more directly, at another rally, "Knock the crap out of them" and "I'd like to punch him in the face." When white nationalists murdered members of a Jewish synagogue in Pittsburgh or mailed bombs to liberal Democrats across the nation, in October 2018, the White House—from press secretary right up to vice president—were in the extraordinary position of denying that murder and attempted murder were the president's fault (quoted in Sides et al. 2018, 2).

The fierce partisanship has spread and touches—many would say menaces—every aspect of government. "We are appalled by the current state of politics in America," write two congressional veterans from either side of the aisle. When we arrived in Washington, "Congress was both fun and productive." Now it's all gridlock and scorched earth. "The Republicans grew radical," adds a longtime Republican staffer (political scientists call it "asymmetrical polarization"—one side going to extremes). And the Democrats, he continued, are hesitant, lost, clueless (Davis et al. 2014, 2–3; see also Lofgren 2012 and Hacker and Pierson 2006).

Is all this doom-mongering anything new? Or are sharp political elbows, gridlock, and jeremiads about awful government long and familiar traditions in American politics? After all, nothing that Donald Trump had jeered or tweeted on the 2016 campaign trail is any nastier than the broadsides launched during the very first contested election of 1800 between Thomas Jefferson and John Adams, who was described as a "hideous hermaphroditical character who has neither the force nor firmness of a man, nor the gentleness and sensibility of a woman." And the violence? Historian Joanne Freeman recently totaled up seventy fights with fists or weapons in and near the House and Senate Chambers between 1830 and 1860. Of that long list, only one is widely remembered, but it went far beyond anything we have seen in recent times: Congressman Preston Brooks (D-SC) pummeled abolitionist Senator Charles Sumner (R-MA), striking him some thirty times with a cane as his colleague Laurence Keitt (D-SC) stopped anyone from interfering. It took Sumner three years to recover from his wounds. Brooks resigned from Congress, became a hero, was unanimously reelected, and collected dozens of new gold-headed canes from his admirers. And is Congress (or Federalism, for that matter) more "broken" today than it was in the golden bipartisan 1950s when, year after year, Congress failed to break filibusters and legislate the most basic rights for civil rights marchers braving terrible state-sponsored brutality? (see Morone 2020, chaps. 2 and 4; on fistfights in Congress, see Freeman 2018).

In this chapter, I suggest how the present partisan warfare reflects long-standing patterns in American political history. Yes, every feature we lament today has a long American legacy: white supremacy, nativism, populism, voter suppression, and the rest. Is there anything new in the present politics? Yes, again. The difference is that the old patterns have come together today in new and unprecedented ways. In the past, no party embraced both racial justice and immigrant rights—the positions were long spread out between parties or party factions. The result: party politics long diffused tribal conflicts; today, it amplifies them.

This chapter explores what the history of American partisanship tells us about the current state of American politics and speculates about what we might do to rescue contemporary politics and policy from the tribal war between "us and them." We begin with a kind of partisan baseline: the very first contested election.

ON THE SHOULDERS OF SLAVES: THE FIRST ELECTION CAMPAIGN

The founders knew that parties and competition were wrong. Good leaders, they thought, should rise above partisanship or self-interest and simply do what was right. Washington pleaded for unanimity as factions tore up his cabinet; he devoted his Farewell Address—by far his most celebrated piece of writing—to warning the country against the "horrible," "baneful," "frightful despotism" of party spirit. Jefferson, as usual, managed the most quotable summation: "The last degradation of a free and moral agent. If I could not get to heaven but with a party, I would not go there at all" (Washington 1796).[3]

Partisan conflict was wrong, but what could they do? By 1800, each side (the Federalists led by Alexander Hamilton and John Adams and the Democratic-Republicans led by James Madison and Thomas Jefferson) believed that the other side would wreck American democracy.[4] Each party denied it was a party while it plunged into a no-holds-barred partisan campaign. In the process, they offer a very rough baseline for the critical dimensions in partisan politics. Four important themes mark that distant campaign. Each offers a rough early variation of a partisan perennial that runs through American history right to the present.

The Constitution and the Vote

The Constitutional Convention never established voting rules, much less a right to vote. Instead, the founders passed the job to the states. Of course, they dreamt up the electoral college. But who would select or elect those electors? This was left to the states. And down in the states, the ruling majorities immediately measured the existing rules by a simple criterion: did they boost their party's chance to win? In 1800, seven (out of seventeen) states either fiddled with the rules or seriously debated doing so.

In Virginia, for example, Jefferson had stoutly supported choosing electors district by district—that, after all, was more sensitive to the voice of the people. Now he had changed his mind. In a letter to governor James Monroe, he commented on the folly of permitting Adams to take one of the Commonwealth's electoral votes (as he had done in the previous election of 1796). Virginia smoothly switched to winner take all, which guaranteed Jefferson all twenty-four electors. Massachusetts and New Hampshire flipped the vote from the public (meaning white men with property) to the more reliably Federalist legislatures. In New York, Hamilton and the Federalists crushed their rival's plan to pry the vote from the Federalist legislature and vest it in the people, voting by districts—until the Federalists unexpectedly lost control of the legislature and shamelessly turned around and pressed Governor John Jay to do precisely what they had previously rejected (he quietly declined). Pennsylvania's divided government fought so long and so hard about the voting rules that Jefferson expected the Keystone State to miss the election altogether (Jefferson 1896, 429–434; for a summation of voting machinations, see Larson 2007).

State control set off the scramble to tilt the rules in 1800. Once that scramble went into motion, it never ended—right down to the present day. The American electoral process has few set rules and, more dramatically, no right to vote. Over time, eight amendments regulating elections never created national rules. Or rights.

For example, the Seventeenth Amendment is usually described simply as providing for the direct election of senators. But it does not actually guarantee anyone a ballot. Take a closer look at who actually gets to vote directly for their senator: "Those with the qualifications requisite for the electors of the most numerous branch of the State legislatures." In 1913, that meant white men only in North Carolina or Georgia; the Seventeenth Amendment granted women the right to vote for senators in Montana and Utah but not in New York and Texas. The partisan manipulation of the rules continued through the years—repeatedly tangled up, as it was in the young republic, with controlling immigration and African Americans (Lichtman 2018; Keyssar 2000).

Wild Irishmen and French Refugees

In 1800, the parties clashed over refugees and immigrants. Democratic-Republicans embraced them (and were none too punctilious about whether they were eligible to vote as they thrust ballots into their hands). Federalists feared the newcomers as a disruptive, even revolutionary, influence and pushed through Alien Acts to curb their influence. The most controversial of the three Acts gave the executive branch the power to hunt down dangerous aliens and deport them without constitutional protections or judicial process. At the same time, Sedition Acts forbade the rising newspapers from criticizing the government (which they had been doing with great gusto). Each side blamed the other for putting the American experiment at risk—by fostering anarchy (as the Federalist charged) or by suppressing free speech (as the Democratic-Republicans responded).

What we remember is Jefferson and his followers standing up to Alien and Sedition acts that were tinged with autocracy. However, to the Federalist mind, the Democratic-Republicans were leading the new country into a bloody anarchy like the French Revolution (which the Jeffersonians unabashedly admired). Remember, the Constitution was little more than a decade old and had not yet sunk deep roots in law or politics.

The Alien and Sedition Acts posed a fundamental political choice that divided the society at the time: proper hierarchical order versus robust free speech. The basic choice was deeply entangled with the refugees who had fled nations like Ireland, France, and Haiti as revolutions and counterrevolutions sent people fleeing for the United States. The newcomers—often fired up with fervor inspired by the French Revolution—provoked questions about the nature of the country right from the start.

Race

At the same time, questions of race and slavery rattled Americans and have now been strangely forgotten. The election of 1800 fired up that early American contradiction: shouts for liberty in a society that protected slavery. Beginning in 1791, slaves successfully rebelled in the French colony of Saint-Domingue (now Haiti) and, over the next decade, repulsed Spanish, English, and French efforts to pluck the island and restore slavery. The rebellion had a profound effect on American society: it generated horror among American slaveholders; it kindled hope in American slave quarters; it produced waves of refugees who arrived at American ports (dragging along their slaves) with breathless new tales of the rebellion; and, for the next century, it produced the seminal text for white supremacists—endlessly repeating the horrors of Haiti.

Moreover, the Adams administration, long criticized for its Alien and Sedition Acts, made an alliance with the former slaves. Adams himself met with representatives of the Haitian regime, pushed a trade bill through Congress, and dispatched three naval vessels to intervene in the fighting. All of this horrified the Jeffersonians. Jefferson himself wrote sourly to Madison as the trade legislature squeaked through thanks to the Federalist majority: "We may expect, therefore, black crews, supercargoes & missionaries thence into Southern states; and when the leven begins to work . . . we have to fear it" (Jefferson 1896, 305).

That "leven" erupted just as the states were voting for president in 1800. The largest slave rebellion in Virginia history filled the newspapers: Gabriel and a large number of followers (twenty-six were eventually put to death) planned to seize Richmond and declare their freedom. The closing month of the election campaign saw each party make the same claim: the slave rebellion was a terrible vindication of what they had been saying all along.

The endless declaiming about equality and rights, charged the Federalists, had seduced slaves into believing they too should be free. This was what French notions of liberty inevitably brought down on a society. What did the Adams administration expect, retorted the Democratic-Republicans, when they crossed the race line and signed treaties with rebellious slaves in Haiti?

In the end, Jefferson and the Democratic-Republicans won, and their triumph created a more democratic and a more open nation—except on racial matters, where the United States turned more authoritarian. With Jefferson's election, the United States joined the Europeans and cut off Haiti for three generations. President Abraham Lincoln, no longer bound to a slave holder foreign policy, finally restored relations in 1862. An "empire of liberty," comments historian Douglas Egerton, "would have been better served by the reelection of John Adams [in 1800]" (Egerton 2002, 309).

In Sum

The Federalists notoriously quashed free speech, harshly regulated immigrants, and kept people without property away from the ballot box. At the same time, they blithely ignored the color line in pursuing their foreign policy interests (most importantly, sticking it to the French). By modern standards, the Federalists showed real flashes of enlightenment about racial matters. They entered into an alliance with the rebellious slaves led by Toussaint Louverture. On the other side, the Republicans stoutly defended immigrants and threw open the vote to men without property. However, they were the primary party of slavery and drew a harsh line on any interaction with the breakaway island.

There was one final race twist to the 1800 campaign. When Jefferson won, the Federalist newspapers did the math and began to howl over the three-fifths rule (which, in allocating seats in the House and electoral college votes added three-fifths of the slave population to the free citizens). "We have proved, by numerical calculation," ran one widely reprinted article in a Federalist newspaper, "*that a majority of the freeman* of the United States have *really* elected Mr. Adams to the Presidency." The United States, it continued, would now "elevate to the presidential chair, two citizens who . . . ride into the TEMPLE OF LIBERTY upon the s*houlders of slaves*" (*Mercury and New England Palladium* 1801, 2).

To be sure, the Federalists faded not just because slavery biased the rules, which it did, but because their aristocratic vision was out of time, lost in a raucous new age. The artisans in New York and Philadelphia would latch onto the Democratic-Republican vision as heartily as the slaveholders of Virginia. The slavery issue that had so entangled the delegates at the Constitutional Convention remained the most important issue for eighty years. The complaints that followed the election of 1800 proved prophetic. Then, later, and now, the most intense battles about the voting rules would cluster around the race line.

THE PATTERNS

Even at the dawn of partisan politics, we can recognize the first stirrings of intense themes that would evolve to the present day: race, immigration, and fiddling with the rules. We might even see, in this election, a distant intimation of populism. While only about 4 percent of the population voted in 1800, the populists rising out of the West ninety years later would identify Jefferson as their inspiration. More precisely, the parties' philosophies in 1800 matched the conservative, moralistic, hierarchical, Federalists against the more popular, more republican, Democratic-Republicans who, like all future populists, were highly critical toward financial elites.

Immigration, Race . . .

What is striking about these old themes is the way they fell into politics. The Federalists were unabashed elitists who restricted the franchise to men with property. They rejected the rabble and tried to bar the Irish and other noisy newcomers from politics. In states like New York, however, they had no objections to black voters who met the property qualification; and in the Adams administration, they were ready to assist the former slaves in Haiti. In short, the conservative party was, by the standards of the day, sympathetic to one liminal group on the margin of power, free black men, while they were keen to suppress another liminal group, the immigrants.

On the other side, the Democratic-Republicans were more far more sympathetic to common men and embraced the immigrants. In fact, for the next six decades, the Democratic Party platforms would routinely twit their conservative rivals (first Whigs, then Republicans) for being latter-day nativists stamped in the Federalists' mold and reflecting the spirit of the Alien and Sedition laws. In contrast, the Democrats cheered the immigrants and escorted them into politics. The Democrats would eagerly strike down property qualifications. But the rise of the common man, under Democratic tutelage, meant the repression of the African American. As voting rights spread, the states began to ban black voting under any circumstance.

Note the pattern, for it would last the roughly 140 years that the conservative parties were judicious about race. They would offer a home to abolitionists and, later, radical Republicans and African Americans. But they also were the primary locus of nativism. They embraced one group on the margins of power and rejected another.

The Democrats, in contrast, embraced immigrants. The Irish and the Germans grew to be important constituents. But, North and South, they stuck to states' rights, which enabled the party to house white supremacy. Democrats, before the Civil War, generally defended slavery; during the war, they ferociously opposed emancipation, and after the war, they would unabashedly turn into the party of white supremacy.

Slavery and immigration both stirred riots in the cities and fistfights in Congress. But these disputes did not easily map onto party politics. The conservative parties included abolitionists (as well as Southern conservatives) and nativists; the more popular Democrats recruited most of the immigrants—and most of the white supremacists.

To put it in more contemporary terms, the parties had not sorted themselves in tribal terms. As the parties moved out from under Washington's taboo and became an unabashed feature of American politics, early proponents celebrated just this feature of organized political life. Parties, by pursing plums (or jobs) would calm the internecine issues, like slavery, that kept rising to the surface (Van Buren 1827).

What has changed? This diffusion of tribal issues lasted until the current party era. In a long, slow process that began with the election of 1932, the tectonic plates began to shift. The Democrats slowly became the party of people on the margins of power—African Americans, immigrants, and others (including, in the 1970s, gender activists seeking equal rights).

On the other side, the Republicans slowly became the white people's party. Today, to take just one of many indicators of this trend, the Democratic caucus in Congress is roughly one-third white men; the Republicans, in contrast, are almost 90 percent white men. Those numbers are not far off from the party breakdown in the presidential vote. What this adds up to is simple and dramatic: parties, which once muffled tribal battles, now amplify them. In a system where the Constitution failed to clarify rules and rights, the politics of identity collide with party politics in increasingly powerful ways.

. . . And Bashing the Feds

This racial sorting helps illuminate the more familiar ideological sort. From the very start, the party of white supremacy opted for states' rights over national authority. The conservatives—the Federalists, the Whigs, the Republicans—were eager to use national power to improve the nation: build roads, dredge canals, erect universities. But they always ran into the same roadblock.

Former president John Quincy Adams, who became an irascible, antislavery congressman from Boston, summed up the problem when he furiously wrote to his constituents that "Slavery stands aghast at the prospective promotion of general welfare" (Adams 1842; see also "City of Washington" 1840, 3). More than a half century later, Democrat William Jennings Bryan made the same complaint of his own party, which resisted his populist proposals because, "You are afraid your Jim Crow laws against the negroes will be abolished by the general government. As if your personal objection to riding with negroes should interfere with great national reform" (quoted in Kazin 2006, 147). One striking feature of nineteenth-century debates is the link that Adams identified: concern for racial hierarchy blocked federal government action whenever it might possibly imply a danger to slavery, or later, to white supremacy.

The Patterns Change

During the New Deal, the alignments changed and slowly reordered American politics. The Democratic Party shucked off states' rights and became the party of active government, the party of labor, and the party of black Americans (all first visible by the 1932 election). And then it expanded these bases by becoming the party of women's rights (in the 1970s) and the pro-immigration party (clearly visible by 2000). Moreover, the politics of civil rights, immigration, and gender equality were all framed by the civil rights template.

During the same long period, conservatives in the Republican Party finally defeated their own Northeastern moderates (who went down as they lost the black vote to the new Democrats). Republicans became the party of states' rights and resistance to the federal government and the home of white voters and housed those who were skeptical about both civil rights and immigration. In short, the parties had sorted themselves out, not just by ideology but by the deepest tribal issues running through American history. With groups on the margins of power all in one party, the politics that once muffled these deep conflicts now aggravated them.

The lynchpin of all the changes was, as always, the politics of race. A close look suggests that changes in the race line occurred far sooner than told by the usual story—it was already in motion in the 1930s. Once the racial politics changed, other powerful forces, like populism and a dread of government, fell slowly into a pattern around racial politics.

THE RACE LINE AND HOW IT CHANGED

Race, more than anything else, stirs up passion, riots, and violent reactions of "us versus them." Notice, again, how partisan politics has, traditionally, intersected with race. It was always the more conservative party that made a place for civil rights. The abolitionists went into the Whig and, later, Republican Parties. On the other hand, populist movements boosting the common man—the Jeffersonians and Jacksonians and, eventually, the Populists of the 1890s—tended to get entangled with a brutish white supremacy.

The Search for Cross-Racial Alliances—and the Populism on Both Sides

President Andrew Johnson sneered at Frederick Douglass and the black leaders who had come to talk about securing black voting rights after the Civil War. "The poor white and the negro have always been enemies," he insisted. "Throw them together at the ballot box and a race war would begin." No, said this lifelong Democrat (chosen as Lincoln's running mate to project unity after the Civil War), as long as he was president, the federal government would not interfere with the states' right to determine who votes.[5] And it certainly wouldn't subject white voters to having to vote next to black men. W. E. B. Du Bois, would comment that Johnson had "all the narrowness and ignorance of a certain class of whites who have always looked upon the colored races as out of the pale of humanity" (Du Bois 1992, 248). Still, Du Bois recognized the reaction as an integral feature of poor, uneducated, white society: their whiteness gave them status. Political leaders preserved their apartheid by constantly warning that social reforms would result in a radical loss of white status—a point that Tocqueville had also shrewdly noticed by 1835 (De Bow 1860, 9–10; see also Morone 2020, chap. 4).

In a typical expression of the argument, an influential Southern editor put it this way as the Civil War loomed: In the North, the poor white worker stands on the very lowest rung of the social ladder. In contrast, his Southern brother, "has ascended several steps" and "can look down upon those who are beneath him [meaning black people, slave or free] at an infinite remove." No one tells the white man in the South that the Declaration of Independence "refers equally to the negro as himself," or that black free men will vote alongside him, or that black children will sit next to his in school or work at the very same job and on and on down the long list until, inevitably, a warning about how slavery (and later apartheid) protected his daughters from interracial sex. The argument summed up a powerful urge with a long and bitter American life: status, freedom, and even dignity comes from occupying a preferred place in the racial hierarchy.

Against this, American political parties have a long and rarely successful tradition of trying to construct interracial coalitions. The abolitionist movement, from the late 1820s to the Civil War, tried to build a cross-racial (and for that matter, cross-gender) coalition for basic human rights. They never made much progress in finding allies, though never was a group more successful at getting its issue on the agenda. The Republicans who rose up in the 1850s fiercely opposed the extension of slavery, but only the most radical joined the abolitionists in proposing racial equality or the right to vote for free blacks. In fact, few Republicans had any clear plan for the slaves themselves. Democrats like Stephen Douglas (D-IL) constantly mocked Lincoln and his party by asking if they were proposing racial equality—a proposition that Lincoln constantly denied (Lincoln 1953, vol. 3, 11, 56, 105).

After the Civil War, however, black voting rights briefly seemed to intimate a new alliance: the Republican Party combined African Americans and white race liberals, at least in parts of the former Confederacy where black citizens comprised a majority or near majority. The Fifteenth Amendment seemed to make it possible. But the amendment did not lodge a right to vote into the Constitution. Instead, it simply barred states from abridging the vote on account of race. A stronger version would have finally affirmed voting rights and prohibited restrictions like poll taxes or literacy tests. It fell short in Congress because Northerners wanted to bar Irish voters and Westerners wanted to bar Chinese American voters. Even the weaker version of the amendment helped incite a reign of terror, and its convenient (nativist-inspired) built-in loopholes eventually enabled the restoration of white supremacy—beginning in Mississippi in 1890 and quickly spreading through the Southern states (Morone 2018).

The Populist movement in the early 1890s also tried to forge the cross-racial alliance in the South. They would throw off the reign of Southern oligarchs by connecting poor Southerners, white and black. "You are kept apart," declared Georgia's Tom Watson, so "that you may be separately fleeced of your earnings" (Watson 1892, 545). The Populists reached right back to Republican Reconstruction hopes three decades earlier: link white and black voters to overthrow the Southern powers. What they encountered was, once again, intimidation, riots, and killing.

For example, a Populist cross-racial alliance broke through and managed to win North Carolina state offices in 1894 and then expanded their hold in 1896. The backlash, in 1898, brought something extremely rare in American history: a violent coup. As the white leader (and future mayor) of Wilmington, the state's largest city, put it the day before the 1898 election: "You are Anglo Saxons. You are armed and prepared and you will do your duty. . . . Go to the polls tomorrow, and if you find the negro out voting, tell him to leave the polls, and if he refuses, kill him." The threats were followed by the all too familiar: a white mob, organized by a local militia, ran through the black quarter killing, burning, and driving the middle class out of town. They forced Republican leaders to resign their posts and replaced them, by blood and acclamation, with leaders dedicated to white supremacy (Morone 2020, chap. 5).

Two long traditions: First, the struggle to disrupt the dominant political order by creating a political coalition that reaches across the race line. The great civil rights tradition of the 1950s and 1960s stands in that long historical legacy. Second, violent, angry, disruptive backlash. Both traditions invoke American populism; both the interracial alliance that took North Carolina, for example, and the violent backlash against them can be counted as Populist motions. The counter currents led Southern historian C. Vann Woodward to note that historians, at some moments, approach Populism as "the root of all good in democracy" and, at others, "the root of all evil" (Woodward 1993, 147).

Listening to Donald Trump shouting "punch him in the face" and barnstorming the country with tales of rapists and terrorists in a migrant "caravan" reflects the latter. But it should not make us forget the former, the long hard efforts of challenging the status quo by reaching across the race line. The overarching question for our parlous time: is there a way to make that interracial connection in a stable way, in a way that does not unleash the tribal demons?

How the Black Vote Turned Democratic

After the Civil War, the African American vote was reliably Republican. Until the turn of the century, Republicans tried, with diminishing vigor, to protect their voters. But by the turn of the century, fortified by Western states coming into the union (as Republicans), the party had given up that difficult fight. Republican president William Howard Taft intoned a long eulogy for civil rights, right at the start of his inaugural address in 1909: "There was a time when northerners who sympathized with the negro . . . sought to give him suffrage," said Taft, but "the movement proved to be a failure." Black Americans "may well have our profound sympathy," he continued, and "personally, I have not the slightest race prejudice," but the sad fact is that "race feeling is so widespread and so acute" that appointing African Americans to office or protecting their right to vote would "do more harm than good." Black Republicans, of course, had no alternatives and stuck with the Republicans because the Democrats remained the party of white supremacy—Taft's Democratic successor, Woodrow Wilson, permitted the segregation of the major federal agencies, the Treasury and the Post Office (where scandalized Democrats revealed that white women were working under the supervision of black men and quickly shoved the latter out of office).

The Great Migration of African Americans out of the South changed the calculations. As black men and women moved north, they suddenly had the disruptive power of the ballot again and local Democratic politicians began to recruit them. African Americans went into the national party in three great waves, what might be called the Franklin Roosevelt (1936), the Harry Truman (1948), and the Martin Luther King Jr. (1965) surges.

The motion became clear in 1936 when the Democrats established a national campaign committee to win the Northern black vote—and dramatically succeeded. One syndicated columnist expressed the conventional wisdom as the 1938 midterms approached: "If the Republican Party expects to continue as a going concern it seems essential to recover lost ground with the Negroes of the North" (Kent 1936).[6] Of course, continued the conventional wisdom, this should not be difficult to do. In case no one noticed, the Southern segregationists ran the Democratic Party. The conventional wisdom in the 1930s was that black voters were being duped into the party of segregation, whose members could not be anything more than "sham friends" to African Americans (Kent 1940, 8).

Contemporary reconstructions suggest that party affiliation among African Americans split evenly between the Democrats and the Republicans after 1936. The second great step in the move to the Democratic Party came during the 1948 election when the Democrats read the polls and went all in on civil rights. At a raucous Democratic Party Convention, the party faithful embraced a far-reaching, ardently contested civil rights plank—and precipitated a bolt of Dixiecrats, who ran Strom Thurmond (D-SC) for president in the hopes of throwing the election into the House and reasserting Southern control over what had been their party. After that election, black identification with the Democratic Party rose to roughly 60 percent. And then it leapt up to close to 90 percent after the 1964 passage of the Civil Rights Act.

Each stage in the process brought two other important ramifications: First, the moderate, Northeast Republicans (known later as Rockefeller Republicans) also needed those African American votes, and as those votes migrated to the Democratic Party, the moderates went down to defeat and slowly vanished from the Republican Party. Second (and relatedly), as the Democrats embraced civil rights, the white Southern Democrats looked elsewhere—first bolting and voting independent (in 1948), then slowly making their way into a Republican Party that was losing its moderate wing and turning to its right: anti-government, pro states' rights, and fierce opposition to federal government support for civil rights. The Barry Goldwater campaign, in 1964, illuminated the new alignment. Goldwater based his campaign on personal liberty—he had voted against the Civil Rights Act of 1964 to halt the rise of big government. But he did not say a word as the segregationists and white supremacists clambered aboard his campaign. From the start, Republicans had to grapple with a fatal entanglement: the fight against federal power all mixed in with the protection of white privilege. As I shall suggest below, the challenge for the Republicans, after Trump, will be to finally, fully separate those two passions, which (recall John Quincy Adams) have been intertwined since the early nineteenth century.

This historical reconstruction of black partisanship breaks with the traditional story in two big ways. First, in popular memory, the fight for civil rights sprang up on a city bus in Montgomery, Alabama, when Rosa Parks courageously refused to move. However, the tectonic plates of black activism, Southern reaction, and shifting coalitions began rumbling all the way back in the 1930s. The classic civil rights movement of the 1950s and 1960s was the heroic breakthrough in a battle that had already been raging for decades. The savvy Lyndon Johnson allegedly signaled the great transformation as he signed the Civil Rights Bill with his famous quip, "there goes the south." More recent work, in both history and political science, sets the clock way back. The changes that burst into prominence in the mid-

1950s had been rumbling through American society since the 1930s; the tectonic plates of race and party shifted across more than three decades. The Northern black vote began going to the Democratic Party early in the New Deal. And, on the other side, historians of the South have demonstrated that white supremacy quickly learned the lesson of a new era: racial epithets lost the rest of the country, while calling for liberty and denouncing the federal government (and its welfare machine) won allies. The conservatives in the Republican Party, as it fought down the moderates in the Northeast, welcomed the former Democrats from the South. The massive resistance to racial equality (and federal intrusion) began not in the 1950s, in response to blockbuster decisions like *Brown v. Board of Education,* but decades earlier, in response to the New Deal. This is not to diminish the formidable "classic" civil rights era but to appreciate the new context of a racial conflict that included discrimination up North as well as segregation in the South, that spanned more than three decades, and that encountered even more (and deeper) resistance than in the usual narrative.[7]

Second, historians have recently emphasized the segregationist choke hold on New Deal policy. As Ira Katznelson puts it in his monumental book, *Fear Itself: The New Deal and the Origins of Our Time,* the New Deal coalition looked like an alliance between South Africa (apartheid) and Sweden (liberal social policy), and largely dominated by the white supremacists. All true. But a wider historical gaze shows how that unhappy alliance was part of a remarkable transformation. African Americans climbed into the party of white supremacy (in 1936), pushed for brash new racial policies, and by the end of the New Deal (in 1948) were sending segregationists bolting out of the Democratic convention and running their own Dixiecrat candidate.[8]

The racial changes altered American politics. But the full force of change—the Trump-force winds—came as the racial politics mixed with the politics of immigration.

THE POLITICS OF STRANGERS AND HOW THEY EVOLVED

Racial politics has always been complicated by immigration. As noted above, the Democratic Party had a long tradition of embracing European immigrants. This is no surprise: early refugees were Democrats fleeing from counterrevolutions or crackdowns in France and Ireland and arrived with Jeffersonian principles. As late as 1856, the Democratic Party platform was still cheering immigrants and pounding the long-defunct Federalists (and their heirs): "Every attempt to abridge the privilege of becoming citizens and the owners of soil among us, ought to be resisted with the same spirit which swept the alien and sedition laws from our statute-books" (Morone 2020, 11).

In the 1850s, California's Democrats denounced the Massachusetts Republicans for erecting higher barriers to immigrant voting than for black voting. But they were hardly purists: they themselves were eager to suppress the Chinese population. For a long time, the racial binary—us versus the other—helped Democrats make a strange sense of immigration: black and Asian Americans were "other" and out. The Irish morphed into white people ("us") and were to be protected; Northern Italians were "us," Southern Italians, flourishing stilettos, were dark, dangerous, and "them." In short, the Democrats were the party of immigrants as long as they were, or became, white.

Scrambling the Parties

That simple connection—Democrats and white immigrants—grew far more complicated toward the end of the nineteenth century. The number of immigrants rose. By the 1870s, 2.8 million immigrants had arrived in the United States. Then came a great leap, to 5.2 million (in the 1880s) and then up to 8.8 million (in the 1900s). By 1890, the percentage of people born abroad tipped in at 14.8 percent of the population, still the all-time high. Beyond the sheer numbers were what seemed to be their strange origins: "Greeks, Italians, Poles, Hungarians, Jews," complained one senator, "Syrians, Portuguese, Magyars." The unfamiliar immigrants ran into a familiar barrage: these people came from inferior countries, they were the wrong race, they practiced dangerous religions, they refused to assimilate, they would drag America down (Morone 2020, chap. 5).

By the turn of the century, the immigration issue had scrambled the simple party alignment. Conservative Republicans began to fret about the Anglo-Saxon American culture. Representative Henry Cabot Lodge, the very first individual to win a political science degree from Harvard University, brought his erudition to the subject: "Not only is our immigration changing in point of race, but . . . it [is] deteriorating." Lodge led the charge for controls, latching at first onto the Northern Republican standard, literacy tests—now to be applied to immigrants at American ports. For the next decade and beyond, Lodge championed the restriction in an effort to staunch the inflow of inferior blood.[9]

Organized labor joined the Lodge campaign. It bitterly opposed the Chinese and grew increasingly agitated about big business manipulating immigrants. The newcomers offered the corporations an army of cheap labor and strikebreakers. Business contracted with foreigners to undercut native workers (or so the union leaders thought). The predictable results: lower wages and less bargaining power. Eventually, unions pressed against the open door. Terrence Powderly, who headed the Knights of Labor, endorsed restrictions in 1896 and the AFL threw its support behind the literacy test in 1897. Tom Watson crudely summed up their perspective: "The treacherous manufacturing interests . . . dumped . . . the scum of creation on us." Why? Because "they wanted cheap labor and they didn't care a curse . . . [about] the consequence of their heartless policy" (Magliocca 2011, 38–39).

On the other side, the coalition supporting immigration was just as unusual. George Washington Plunkitt, a rascally Tammany Hall politician, published a day from his diary: "Attended the funeral of an Italian as far as the ferry. Hurried back to make appearance at the funeral of a Hebrew constituent." And on went Plunkitt, down his international checklist. "A man born in Germany can settle down and become a good New Yorker"—the pinnacle of patriotism in Plunkitt's book. "Why, even a Jap or Chinaman can become a New Yorker." The urban machines in the Northeast and Midwest cheerfully mobilized the ethnic voters. Plunkett's enemies were natives, the rural "hayseed legislators up in Albany" who attacked the sources of Tammany power—corruption, spoils, and immigrants (see Riordan 1963, chaps. 23 [Hebrew], 10 [New Yorkers], and 5 [Albany]).

By the late 1890s, American industry needed workers and was also fighting for open immigration. The National Board of Trade opposed the literacy test. The National Association of Manufacturers organized a pro-immigration lobby. California growers even pushed against the racial tide and tried to win a suspension of Chinese exclusion. When the economy was strong, business saw its bottom line reflected in a plentiful labor supply—and never mind the alleged glories of the Anglo-Saxon race.

The peculiar coalitions faced off. The WASPs and the workers met the bosses and the business leaders. Note the implications for party politics: each party was split on the immigration issue. Immigration set off a raucous culture war. But the parties did not amplify it. They could not do so, for they were each internally divided on the matter.

Restrictions Win

Over time, slowly but surely, the advantage slipped away from the champions of the open door. It took almost a half century to muscle limitations through the checks and balances of American government. Four different presidents vetoed literacy tests, for example. But restrictions slowly began to add up: In 1882, the Chinese Exclusion Act banned new workers and barred the Chinese from becoming citizens (except, of course, for the few that were born on American soil and were protected by the Fourteenth Amendment). The bans were strengthened multiple times until, in 1906, Congress banned all Asian people. When that offended Japan, the Theodore Roosevelt administration negotiated a deal: the United States pledged not to bar Japanese immigrants, and the Japanese government promised not to send any. Eventually, Congress muscled full immigration quotas into place with the Emergency Quota Act of 1921. By 1924, when more permanent limits were put in place, the quotas were tied to national populations back in 1890—a way of restricting the newer groups.

In 1892, as the Populists gathered in St. Louis for their national convention, 579,000 people arrived on American shores. Fifteen years later, in 1907, that number had risen to 1.3 million. A quarter century later, as Franklin Roosevelt took the oath of office, the number of newcomers had dwindled to just 23,000.

THE PARTY PATTERNS OLD AND NEW

Notice, again, how race and immigration played against party politics—traditionally and today. This section summarizes the argument and then moves forward to the present.

Through the entire nineteenth century, Democrats stood as the party of white supremacy. At the same time, they championed immigration (as long as the newcomers were white or could be reconstructed as white). In direct contrast, conservative parties (Federalists, Whigs, Republicans) were the party of nativists—as the Democrats never tired of pointing out. However, insofar as anyone stood up for African Americans, the conservative parties did. Each of these issues stimulated riots, murder, fistfights in Congress, culture wars, and stuffed ballot boxes. But for the most part, they were not amplified by the parties themselves. The party alignments on these tribal issues—with slavery and race, on the one hand, and immigration, on the other—kept the issues apart.

In antebellum America, the parties also tried to diffuse the corrosive slavery issue itself. This was how the champions of unabashed mass parties, like Martin Van Buren, sold their idea to the Southern leaders they were recruiting in the 1820s. Moreover, the fight against slavery was further limited by the need to find Southern votes. The Whigs found themselves with the difficult task of holding together Southern planters and New England abolitionists ready to bolt to a third party. In the end, the slavery issue proved too difficult and broke both parties. The Whigs split along sectional lines after 1852 and were not able to nominate a presidential candidate after that; the Democrats split during the 1860 campaign and nominated two candidates, one for the North and one for the South.

By the time Franklin Roosevelt and the Democrats came back into power and began to rebuild the party coalition (the Democrats elected just two men to the White House between 1856 and 1932), these battles seemed like truly ancient history. The race issue seemed to have been quietly put aside—the Republicans, as we've seen, had long ago stopped making trouble over it. And immigration had been choked off with the end of large-scale immigration. To be sure, nativism would flare up against the Japanese in the West, Mexicans in the Southwest, and Jews in the Northeast; but it was not a major axis of political conflict between the parties. The culture wars seemed to have fallen quiet. The problem was the Great Depression.

But even as the old issues seemed silent, the tectonic plates were in motion. African Americans were on the move. They began to leave the rural South and head north, a great migration that would run on for five decades. Once they were up North, black men and women engaged dazzling new ideas—like Marcus Garvey's Pan-African nationalism. They would organize, participate, and eventually make their way into the Democratic Party. As they did so, they re-created the same conundrum—and the same perilous opportunity—that had faced the populists, and before them, the Whigs: how to run a party precariously balanced between white Southern voters intent on racial repression and reformers committed to racial justice?

With that sea change, the politics described above—the rise of a Democratic Party increasingly committed to civil rights—slowly came into motion. The final step in what Katherine Tate calls a "concordance" between black politics and Democratic Party policies was set into motion by the well-known events of the 1960s: the Civil Rights Act, the Voting Rights Act, the Goldwater campaign, the Nixon Southern strategy. By the 1980s, the parties were flatly and explicitly divided by race.

And then they divided again by immigration. After President John Kennedy was murdered, President Johnson pushed to reopen the golden door. Congress casually passed the Hart-Celler Act repealing the immigration quotas first set in 1921. The sponsors promised that nothing would change: "Our cities will not be flooded with a million immigrants annually," said Senator Ted Kennedy, "the ethnic mix of this country will not be upset." "This bill we sign today," agreed President Johnson sitting in the shadow of the Statue of Liberty, "is not a revolutionary bill. It does not affect the lives of millions" (Johnson 1965, vol. 2, entry 546, 1037–1040).

The immigration reform was introduced, debated, and understood as another, relatively minor civil rights bill. The opposition came almost entirely from Southern Democrats now fighting a rearguard action for white supremacy. The consequences took two generations to fully emerge. But they can be seen stirring in the terms of the debate back in 1965.

African Americans had sorted into the Democratic Party. Over time, immigrants followed them. In contrast to the black vote, the Republicans divided over immigrants. George H. W. Bush handily won the (relatively small) Asian vote in 1992; George W. Bush worked to bring the Latino vote into the party (winning 40 percent in 2004); the Republican "autopsy" after 2012 focused, again, on the Latino vote. But these impulses were overwhelmed by the anti-immigrant voice stirring within the party. After the 2016 election, Speaker Paul Ryan marveled at the unexpected Trump sweep: "We won more seats that anyone expected" because "Donald Trump heard a voice in this country that no one else heard" (Schwartz 2016). This voice was, more than anything else, a full nativist blast against immigrants. It was, once again, in full cry as the Republicans expanded their grip on the Senate in the 2018 midterm.

Observers had long debated the role racial animosity and white status anxiety had played in contemporary party politics. The numbers themselves lined up more and more clearly across the twenty-first century. Counting votes, members of Congress, public opinion, and party identification all yielded the same conclusion: the Republican Party had become the party of white voters who were anxious about immigration, skeptical of civil rights politics, and ready for populist bluster. It was, finally, Donald Trump who gave the constituency its tag: white identity politics.

On the other side, Democrats attracted people of color along with a minority of white voters. This kind of cross-racial dynamic has always eluded racial reformers. But a new dynamic appears to be at work: the new generation of immigrants were not splitting into the old racial binary, black versus white. They did not seem to follow the move documented by Du Bois and assert their whiteness. Or perhaps the jumpy nativism of the present day—inflected with memories of 9/11 and carefully curated fears of terrorism—simply barred entire groups from slipping into whiteness, even if they wished to do so. Trump managed to hear (and blast) that white anxiety.

Spurning such a broad category may very well produce an unexpected (and, to nativists, an unwelcome) break with the long legacy of futility in interracial coalitions. As long as immigrants from Asia and Latin America do not melt into whiteness like the generations before them, the nonwhite percentage of the electorate continues to grow by roughly two percent for every presidential election cycle. The census bureau projects a majority-minority nation by midcentury. While that projection is disputed—and never mind the distribution of the population across states or the jagged electoral rules—the numbers of people who identify as white steadily diminishes. A rising new coalition reconstructs one of the political parties and, in the intermediate run, bids to change American politics. Put simply, a coalition that includes the vast majority of African Americans, a solid majority of immigrants, and a minority of reform-minded whites now begins to add up. Put bluntly, there are voting numbers there that never existed in the past.

But in the short run, the consequences are fire and fury. For the first time, race and immigration line up with partisan politics. And now—again, this is unprecedented—it is the rich people's party that offers a home to white status in both the South and the North. This is an old Southern tradition: the party of the planters offered poor whites a roaring, populist, racial status. The antebellum planter move is now writ large across the nation. It developed slowly, over time, in gestures and dog whistles, until now. The election of President Trump and his capture of the Republican Party now give the racial divisions a central place in the partisan debate.

What are the consequences of a party system that amplifies the culture wars? We are learning, day by day. However, add these deep cleavages to parties that are already sorted by ideology and by place of residence (urban-rural) and we have a politics that is more ferocious than anything that the United States has experienced since the Civil War.

LESSONS FROM THE PAST, PROSPECTS FOR THE FUTURE

Reformers thinking about the future ought to bear in mind a simple historical reality: politics is always in flux. Today's rock-solid certainties will sound positively quaint tomorrow. You can mark the rate of change simply by checking an election map from a generation ago. In 1988, for instance, when Michael Dukakis was running against George H. W. Bush, Democrats knew that they would win West Virginia (now the single reddest state with more than two out of three voters picking Trump in 2016) and that they had almost no chance in California (now bright blue, but, back then, it had gone Democratic just once in the past nine presidential elections). We usually process politics in two-year stanzas—extrapolating the future from the last midterm election. But a longer view reminds us how small, steady changes add up. Power shifts, the economy changes, groups drift out of old coalitions, new alignments emerge, and blue regions run to red—and vice-versa.

Consider three reforms to address the partisan furies of the present.

Secure the Vote

The single most important reform to leap out of America's partisan history is this: secure the right to vote. For everyone. Automatically. Register every American when she turns eighteen. No caveats. No paperwork. No convoluted residency tests. Today, technology makes it possible to identify voters without ID cards—much less the rigamarole of taking two different days to register and cast a ballot.

There's more we can do. Elections—national, state, and local—ought to be held on the same day. Why, for example, does Chicago vote for mayor in the frozen middle of February during the off years between midterm and presidential elections? So only the most faithful party members will bother, of course. In fact, we should consider an even stronger position: *require* voting, as countries such as Belgium and Australia already do.

Turning more people out to vote might just lower the political temperature. In 2016, nonvoters in forty-four states outnumbered those who cast votes for either candidate. With plenty of barriers to voting, only the most intense partisans turn out. A larger electorate would require the true believers to rally their neighbors now lingering on the sidelines. Less committed partisans may very well be open to, well, less partisan arguments. As John Dewey famously put it, "The cure for the ailments of democracy is more democracy."[10]

There is one problem with this suggestion. The whole idea of turnout has itself grown partisan. Democrats piously press for voting rights, expand access to the ballot in blue states, and coast to office amid high turnout. Of course, they do. Low turnout voters—young people, Latina Americans, Asian Americans, people with low incomes—all lean blue. Republicans, by contrast, do exactly what the Democrats did for so many generations, especially in the South. They win, in many places, by squeezing down the vote.

The vote suppressors make the same arguments in every era. Voting should be reserved for the better informed, for those with more at stake (like the wealthy), and for those who are willing to take the trouble. People who recite these old arguments don't know that they are echoing a long, violent tradition of racial repression. It was the argument of white supremacy in the South, the cry against Spanish speakers in California, the charge again Irish voters in New England. And it continues to do the same work today.

But Republicans ought to reconsider for a more important reason. In the long-term, it will be impossible to suppress turnout enough to bar the growing numbers of multiracial and young voters. A million new voters come online each year—either young people turning eighteen or immigrants naturalizing. Both groups trend heavily Democratic. In the long run, the Republicans (and the republic itself) will prosper only if the party finds a way, once again, to appeal to these populations. Remember, politics is always in flux. Every one of these Democratic groups once tilted Republican. In the long run, conversion will be more successful than suppression. And suppression strong enough to maintain control would be the end of popular government.

The Task for Democrats: Confront Inequality

Throughout American history, there has always been a party or a faction that defended the common person against the money power—usually, the Democrats. In the 1890s, the Populists bequeathed the Democrats a bold version for modern times. Forty years later, President Franklin Roosevelt refined it into his four freedoms and his economic bill of rights. Government owed each person the basics—food, shelter, health care, security, and a decent shot at the American dream.

On the campaign trail, during the worst economy since the Great Depression, candidate Barack Obama resurrected the old Democrats' communal dream. At one campaign stop, a large, muscular man with a shaved head and anti-government principles (soon famous as Joe the Plumber) challenged Obama about taxes. Obama responded with a powerful restatement of the populist creed: "My attitude is that if the economy's good for folks from the bottom up, it's gonna be good for everybody. If you've got a plumbing business, you're gonna be better off if you've got a whole bunch of customers who can afford to hire you, and right now everybody's so pinched that business is bad for everybody and I think when you spread the wealth around, it's good for everybody" (quoted in Associated Press 2008). Republicans pounced on the line "spread the wealth around" and branded Obama a socialist. Obama stuck to the trusty canon. The parties each laid a clear principle face up before the electorate: positive freedom and the power of collective action to lift everyone versus the primacy of the markets, low taxes, and limited government.

But when Obama's "spread the wealth" entered the halls of power, the message turned murky and the populist call to champion the little guy morphed into a search for managerial efficiency. The signature move of the new Democrat (connecting the Democratic presidents of the last half century—Jimmy Carter, Bill Clinton, and Barak Obama) sets aside the ambitious Populist agenda ("spread the wealth around") and reaches for expertise and good government to lift us beyond partisanship and politics. The shift in perspectives rattled through President Obama's first inaugural: "The question we ask today is not whether our government is too big or too small, but whether it works . . . where the answer is yes, we intend to move forward. Where the answer is no, programs will end. And those of us who manage the public's dollars will be held to account, to spend wisely, reform bad habits, and do our business in the light of day, because only then can we restore the vital trust between a people and their government" (Obama 2009). The clarion calls to share, to spread the wealth, and to lift the poor all vanished—displaced by pledges of efficiency. The president promised to manage wisely; he called for reforming not the rampant inequality of a roaring gilded age but government's "bad business habits."

During the Great Depression of the 1930s, the Democrats built their half-century majority by squarely addressing this issue of rich and poor. Then, during the Johnson years, there was a smashup: the politic of lifting up the common person ran into racial furies. The white majority came to see "spreading the wealth around" as spending "our" money on "those" people. As the majority of whites abandoned the Democrats amid the tumult of the 1960s and 1970s, there were no longer enough votes to keep the New Deal vision intact. Now, as we head toward what may become a majority-minority nation, the votes just might be there (*Wilmington Semi-Weekly* 1898, 8).

The problem grows. Both inequality and poverty have created havoc across all kinds of communities: rural as much as urban, white as well as Latino, Asian, and black. The fading American dream destabilizes our politics and depresses entire areas. Of course, every generation updates its populism for the times. Democrats ought to find a new way to champion the old dream. As FDR put it in his first inaugural address: "These dark days will be worth all they cost us if they remind us that our true purpose is to minister . . . to our fellow man" (Roosevelt 1933).

How should contemporary Populists face up to the problem of inequality? Democrats across the party spectrum ought to make that long-neglected question their urgent business and begin a debate within the party about what such a program will look like.

The Challenge for Republicans

From the early nineteenth century, the party of racial repression has gone by the same name: states' rights. It has been a party vehemently opposed to federal government action. This puts Barry Goldwater conservatives in an agonizing spot: they view Federal government imperialism as a road to serfdom. But white supremacists have long been among their most vehement allies.

As a presidential candidate, Goldwater simply looked the other way. From Richard Nixon (the Southern strategy) through Ronald Reagan (launching his campaign calling for states' rights in Philadelphia, Mississippi) to George H. W. Bush (Willie Horton), the Republicans used racial winks and dog whistles to round up votes while denying racial malice and pursuing conservative policies and, off and on, efforts to limit federal action.[11]

The Trump era makes the silent treatment—fight the government, say nothing about white identity, accept help from whatever traveler joins your coalition—morally dangerous. Perhaps it was always so. Calling all conservative intellectuals: it is time to build a small government coalition without the racism. White supremacy has always hated federal action. Now, it's time to build a conservatism without those passionate (but toxic) partners.

Young conservatives may be especially eager to start the operation. It's one way they can rescue the party from the grandparents and connect it to the young. What's more, as Republicans make inroads among African Americans, Latinos, or Asians, the tribal passions will begin to ebb—differences of principle and policy will stop firing up differences of tribal identity.

Impossible? Not for those who take a longer historical view. Ethnic and racial politics are always changing—alliances shift, attitudes develop, opinions turn. After all, what could be more unlikely than the great tribal change of the twentieth century: black voters entered a party run by segregationists. The reasons why are relevant to reformers seeking new coalitions in any generation: Local party leaders recruited them, allies organized with them, Democratic policies appealed to them, and their own party took them for granted.

NOTES

1. This article is drawn from my forthcoming book, *Republic of Wrath: How American Politics Turned Tribal from George Washington to Donald Trump* (New York: Basic, 2020). I am grateful to Eric Patashnik, Wendy Schiller, Margaret Weir, and the other authors in this volume for valuable comments.

2. Political scientists have registered increasing alarm at the state of partisanship. Consider three stages in the arc: David Mayhew's classic, *Divided We Govern*, celebrated divided government, suggesting it did not impair effective governance. As measures of partisanship rose, Frances Lee suggested the close competition between the parties—either could win it all in any election—eroded cooperation and undermined effective governance; see Lee, *Beyond Ideology: Politics, Principles, and*

Partisanship in the U.S Senate. Similarly, Thomas E. Mann and Norman J. Ornstein lamented the growing breakdown in Congress, in *The Broken Branch: How Congress Is Failing America and How to Get It Back on Track.* Finally, a more recent spate of books reads the Trump election as an indicator of an American identity crisis, entangled in the political parties. See, especially, John Sides, Michael Tesler, and Lynn Vavreck, *Identity Crisis*; Lilliana Mason, *Uncivil Agreement*; and Alan Abramowitz, *The Great Alignment.*

On the public opinion data, see Pew Research Center, "What Republicans and Democrats Say about Each Other." Survey conducted March 2–28 and April 5–May 2, 2016. On intermarriage, see Lynn Vavreck, "A Measure of Identity: Are You Married to Your Party?" *New York Times*, January 30, 2017, A3.

3. The address—really a letter published in newspapers—is often thought to be a statement of isolationism in foreign policy. It is not that. The real theme (and passion) in this powerful letter is a warning against the spirit of division between parties and regions. In an effort to keep Washington above the fray, the document is routinely attributed to Alexander Hamilton, who did, indeed, write two separate drafts, but comparing all five drafts of the address shows how Washington was very much in charge of the speech. Thomas Jefferson to Frances Hopkinson, Paris, March 13, 1789, vol. 6, 278.

4. A word about party names: The Jeffersonians generally referred to themselves as Republicans. Later, they came to be called Democrats, the same name by which the party is known today. Historians have tidied things up by calling the Jeffersonians "Democratic-Republicans," though the party members did not use the term themselves. On the other side, the Federalist Party soon vanished and most members (and their attitudes) drifted into the Whig Party, in the 1830s, and, from there, to the Republicans, in the mid-1850s. Of course, the nineteenth-century parties look very different from their twenty-first-century counterparts, but by the election of 1856, the two major parties were the Democrats and the Republicans.

5. The meeting is famously described in "Reply of the Colored Delegation to the President," February 7, 1866, Frederick Douglass, *Selected Speeches and Writings*, 1999, 586–589.

6. Kent was a syndicated columnist who began as a Democrat and turned intensely against the New Deal. Like many other columnists, he was incredulous about the black vote going to "sham friends" in the Democratic Party.

7. This scholarly literature resetting the clock is now voluminous. In political science, I especially admire and was influenced by Schickler 2016, Ware's *The Democratic Party Heads North, 1877–1962* (2006), and Mickey *Paths Out of Dixie* (2015) and, in history, Kruse's White Flight (2005).

8. Morone, Republic of Wrath, chapter 5. A fuller account would include labor. The rise of the CIO pushed the Democrats to the left and also welcomed the alliance with black voters. A classic example of policies making politics.

9. See Honorable Henry Cabot Lodge, "Lynch Law and Unrestricted Immigration," *North American Review* 152 (1891): 602–612. Quoted at 603, 608.

10. I concluded my first book, *The Democratic Wish*, by criticizing this quote from Dewey. But partisanship has brought me round to his perspective.

11. For a more detailed and nuanced statement of this point, see Morone, *Republic of Wrath*, chapter 8.

REFERENCES

Abramowitz, Alan. *The Great Alignment*. New Haven, CT: Yale University Press, 2018.

Adams, John Quincy. *Address of John Quincy Adams to his Constituents, of the Twelfth Congressional District at Braintree, September 17, 1842*. Boston, MA: J. H. Eastburn, Printer, 1842.

"City of Washington." *Washington Globe*, February 6, 1840, 2.

Davis, Tom, Martin Frost, Richard Cohen, and David Eisenhower. *The Partisan Divide: Congress in Crisis*. Campbell, CA: FastPencil, 2014.

De Bow, James Dunwoody Brownson. *The Interest in Slavery of the Southern Non-Slaveholder*. Charleston, SC: Evans and Cogswell, 1860.

Douglass, Frederick. *Selected Speeches and Writings*. Chicago, IL: Lawrence Hill, 1999.

Du Bois, W. E. B. *Black Reconstruction in America*. New York: Athenaeum, 1992.

Egerton, Douglas R. "The Empire of Liberty Reconsidered." In *The Revolution of 1800: Democracy, Race and the New Republic*, ed. James Horn, Jan Ellen Lewis, and Peter Onuf, 309–330. Charlottesville: University of Virginia Press, 2002.

Freeman, Joanne. *The Field of Blood: Violence in Congress and the Road to Civil War*. New York: Farrar, Straus, and Giroux, 2018.

Hacker, Jacob, and Paul Pierson. *Off Center*. New Haven, CT: Yale University Press, 2006.

Jefferson, Thomas. *The Writings of Thomas Jefferson*. Ed. Thomas Ford. New York: Putnam, 1896.

"Joe the Plumber Becomes Focus of Debate," Associated Press, October 15, 2008, https://www.youtube.com/watch?v=PUvwKVvp3-o.

Johnson, Lyndon. *Public Papers of the Presidents of the United States: Lyndon B. Johnson, 1965*. Volume 2, entry 546. Washington, DC: Government Printing Office, 1965

Katznelson, Ira. *Fear Itself: The New Deal and the Origins of Our Time*. New York: Liveright, 2014.

Kazin, Michael. *A Godly Hero: The Life of William Jennings Bryan*. New York: Knopf, 2006.

Kent, Frank. "The Parties and the Poll Tax." *News Journal*, May 15, 1940, 8.

———. "The Great Game of Politics." *Los Angeles Times*, December 16, 1936, 14.

Keyssar, Alexander. *The Right to Vote*. New York: Basic, 2000.

Kirk, Reverend J Allen. *A Statement of the Facts Concerning the Bloody Riot in Wilmington, N.C.: Bloody Riot Perpetrated upon the Helpless and Inoffensive Negro*. Wilmington, NC, Thursday, November 10, 1898.

Kruse, Kevin. *White Flight*. Princeton, NJ: University of Princeton Press, 2005.

Larson, Edward J. *A Magnificent Catastrophe: The Tumultuous Election of 1800, America's First Presidential Campaign.* New York: Free, 2007.

Lee, Frances. *Beyond Ideology: Politics, Principles, and Partisanship in the U.S Senate.* Chicago: University of Chicago Press, 2009.

"Let Us Heed the Lesson." *Wilmington Semi-Weekly Messenger,* August 26, 1898, 8.

Lichtman, Alan. *The Embattled Right to Vote in America: From the Founding to the Present.* Cambridge, MA: Harvard University Press, 2018.

Lincoln, Abraham. *The Collected Works of Abraham Lincoln.* Ed. Roy Basler. New Brunswick, NJ: Rutgers University Press, 1953.

Lodge, Henry Cabot. "Lynch Law and Unrestricted Immigration." *North American Review* 152 (1891): 602–612.

Lofgren, Mike. *The Party Is Over: How Republicans Went Crazy, Democrats Became Useless, and the Middle Class Got Shafted.* New York: Penguin, 2012.

Magliocca, Gerard. *The Tragedy of William Jennings Bryan.* New Haven, CT: Yale University Press, 2011.

Mann, Thomas E., and Norman J. Ornstein. *The Broken Branch: How Congress Is Failing America and How to Get It Back on Track.* New York: Oxford University Press, 2006.

Mason, Lilliana. *Uncivil Agreement: How Politics Became Our Identity.* Chicago: University of Chicago Press, 2018.

Mayhew, David. *Divided We Govern.* New Haven, CT: Yale University Press, 2005.

Mickey, Robert. *Paths Out of Dixie: The Democratization of Authoritarian Enclaves in America's Deep South.* Princeton, NJ: University of Princeton Press, 2015.

Morone, James. *Republic of Wrath: How American Politics Turned Tribal from George Washington to Donald Trump.* New York: Basic, 2020.

———. "Why the Right to Vote Is Not a Right." *New York Times Sunday Book Review,* September 16, 2018, 15.

———. *The Democratic Wish.* New Haven, CT: Yale University Press, 1998.

Obama, Barack. Inaugural Address. Washington, DC. January 20, 2009.

Pew Research Center: US Politics and Policy, "Partisanship and Political Animosity in 2016—What Republicans and Democrats Say about Each Other." June 22, 2016.

"A Plain Fact." *Mercury and New England Palladium,* Boston, January 21, 1801, 2.

Riordan, William. *Plunkitt of Tammany Hall: A Series of Very Plain Talks on very Practical Politics Recorded by William Riordan.* New York: St. Martin's, 1963.

Roosevelt, Franklin. First Inaugural Address. Washington, DC, Saturday, March 4, 1933.

Schickler, Eric. *Racial Realignment: The Transformation of American Liberalism, 1932–1965.* Princeton, NJ: Princeton University Press, 2016.

Schwartz, Ian "Paul Ryan: 'Trump heard a voice out in this country that no one else heard.'" November 6, 2016. Real Clear Politics: https://www.realclearpolitics.com/video/2016/11/09/paul_ryan_trump_heard_a_voice_out_in_this_country_that_no_one_else_heard.html.

Sides, John, Michael Tesler, and Lynn Vavreck. *Identity Crisis.* Princeton, NJ: Princeton University Press, 2018.

Tocqueville, Alexis de. *Democracy in America.* New York: Doubleday, 1969.

Van Buren, Martin. Papers of Martin Van Buren. 1827. Washington, DC: National Archives, 2016.

Vavreck, Lynn. "A Measure of Identity: Are You Married to Your Party?" *New York Times,* January 30, 2017, A3.

Ware, Alan. *The Democratic Party Heads North, 1877–1962.* New York: Cambridge University Press, 2006.

Washington, George. "Farewell Address." *American Daily Advertiser,* September 19, 1796, 1.

Watson, Tom E. "The Negro Question in the South." *Arena* 6 (1892): 540–550.

Woodward, C. Vann. *The Burden of Southern History.* Baton Rouge: Louisiana State University Press, 1993, 147.

CHAPTER 2

Incremental Liberalism or Prolonged Partisan Warfare

Matt Grossmann

With unified Republican control of government after a campaign of big promises, some expected a major transformation of government in 2017. But despite Donald Trump's claim to "have accomplished more than almost any administration," the agenda of the 115th Congress was limited, and the record of achievements was paltry. To give full credit, they did pass a major tax overhaul, cutting corporate taxes (and shifting individual income tax burdens toward those who itemize). In the session's final days, they also passed criminal justice reform and a farm bill. But after spending months focused on repealing the Affordable Care Act, they gave up when they could not secure votes in the Senate to advance any plan. On the budget, they agreed only to break the budget control caps and extend funding of all kinds. Legislating mostly grinded to a halt in 2018. Progress then slowed even further into the 116th Congress; it began amid the longest-ever government shutdown, which produced no additional agreement, and was marked mainly by impeachment.

The modest output and limited policy debates make a stark contrast to the vitriolic hyperventilation of the American campaign trail over the last few cycles, where everything was said to be at stake. Control of the House, Senate, and the presidency are now regularly in the balance—with the parties alternating in control of each; but rather than moderating to attract the median voter, the two parties are now presenting very different visions of government and society. For voters, partisanship is now a more central and emotionally charged identity than ever before. It is (not coincidentally) more closely tied to many other group affiliations and issue positions.

Swing voters do still exist—but they swing wildly against the party in power. The last productive Congress, the 111th under full Democratic control in 2009–2010, was met with a massive electoral backlash that returned control to the Republicans. And in 2018, Republicans paid the electoral cost for their more limited but still historically conservative and unpopular record.

Given the charged nature of our politics, why are the policy stakes so low? And is there anything that can break the cycle of crazed politics and gridlocked policymaking? I argue that our current conflicts hide a fundamental mismatch between our programmatic parties and our institutions built for arduous consensus-building. The historical solution was incremental liberalism: government would slowly take on new tasks over time, driven by Democratic demands but modified by Republicans' conservative skepticism. As that era fractures, it is difficult to see a way out of hyperbolic conflict combined with low-achievement policymaking.

The mismatch is multifaceted. American elections are nationalized and closely divided, with two ideologically and socially sorted parties forced to share power. This fits poorly with American institutions, which were designed for broad agreement and evolved to incorporate issue area expertise and compromise among competing interests as government took on more roles. This electoral-policymaking disconnect makes partisan polarization more likely, as parties focus on winning or holding power by opposing the other party. But it also breeds limited substantive achievement, because the sides have neither enough power to easily legislate on their own nor much incentive to compromise over policy.

These dynamics do not have equal consequences for the two-sided American political system. Conservatives are less interested in new government action and thus less fazed by gridlock. They focus on maintaining power to block new initiatives or scale back recent programs. This agenda is unpopular, but they are able to sell their supporters on a broader restoration of past government and society that is unachievable in practice (but seemingly always just around the corner). Democrats need government to act to achieve their myriad goals, but they disagree on how best to respond to intransigent Republicans. Some say only fundamental institutional reforms, like a national popular vote and remaking the Senate, will work. Others seek to emulate conservatives in hardball tactics at all costs, remaking an ideologically committed left. Still others seek to broaden debates beyond government programs, hoping to find a new agenda that might gain wide support.

This chapter reviews how the country got to this point and why Americans are stuck in this predicament. I point to the long-running role of a tacit compromise between the sides: policies addressed Democratic goals through Republican means. Democrats led policymaking but usually focused on a few narrow issues at a time, areas where they were willing to compromise to achieve results. Republicans' conservative critiques forced revisions to Democratic proposals to make them more ideologically compatible: the format of American policy thus incentivized private actors, decentralized implementation to states and localities, and avoided direct spending and regulation. Without a return to these two historic roles, the parties seem bound to continue their prolonged warfare, where gridlock reigns until Democrats occasionally gain full control of government—when they are bound to overshoot with a burst of liberal policymaking and again be met with a large conservative backlash. There is no easy way out of this quandary.

POLARIZED, NATIONALIZED, AND CLOSE ELECTORAL COMPETITION

Most accounts of contemporary political dysfunction look back to the middle of the twentieth century as a period of relative success and policy consensus. But American politics of that era was, of course, an anomaly in many ways. The Democratic Party included a segregationist Southern wing that was skeptical of its leadership. The Republican Party was uncompetitive in congressional elections for decades. And both parties left considerable room for ideological and regional divisions as well as diversity in issue priorities. Voters were used to splitting tickets and rewarding incumbents for federal largesse and service—not simply voting for one's team.

Since then, electoral politics have undergone four revolutionary changes: (1) elite policy polarization with mass affective polarization, (2) social and ideological sorting into two distinct parties, (3) nationalization of elections and voter concerns, and (4) persistently close national competition. Each has reinforced polarized and gridlocked policymaking.

First, the Democratic and Republican Parties in Congress have moved apart on all measures of legislative voting, with the most commonly used data (DW-Nominate) showing Democrats moving from the center to the center-left from the 1960s to the 1970s and then moving slowly further left (as they lost their most conservative Southern white representatives) as the Republicans moved more abruptly to the right from the late 1970s onward. Cosponsorships have also divided by party over time, with less and less crossover in appeals across bills and topic areas (Neal 2018).

Although there has been some debate over the extent to which partisans in the public have polarized, the evidence against this polarization shows only that partisans are not growing more extreme in their ideological self-placements or their opinions on specific policy issues (Fiorina 2017). This stability has not deterred the steady lining up of policy issue positions with partisanship, making for fewer partisans with mismatched views on public policy issues like abortion, guns, or the environment (Abramowitz 2018). Partisans have also increasingly adopted different views on racial discrimination and gender roles and attitudes toward social groups (Tesler 2016). All of this has contributed to the strong rise of negative partisanship, with Republicans increasingly disliking the Democratic Party and vice versa (Abramowitz and Webster 2016). Ideological polarization among party leaders has fueled this pattern in the public, often called "affective polarization" (Rogowski and Sutherland 2016). Our dislike of the out-party is now tied to emotional distaste and feeling socially distant to opposing partisans, even objecting to partisan intermarriage (Iyengar and Westwood 2015). Elites have thus polarized on policy positions while the public has polarized on emotional loyalties.

Second, conservatives have sorted into the Republican Party while liberals have sorted into the Democratic Party, leaving few ideological dissenters in either party. Even those self-labeling as "slightly liberal" or "slightly conservative" have mostly found the closer associated political party. Voters who did not choose the appropriate party based on a prior ideological identification mostly did the opposite: changing ideology to match their party. Republicans also like the social groups "conservatives" more and "liberals" less than did their prior generations—with Democrats increasingly taking the opposite view. Partisans even now share their broader views of society and their thinking habits with one another (Oliver and Wood 2018). As a result, more citizens can now place the parties correctly on an ideological spectrum and identify major differences between them. Even those who pay the least attention to politics and have no attachment to either political party can today see the same big differences between the parties that only the strongest and most aware partisans of the 1960s saw (Smidt 2017). As a result, even the unattached are often no longer undecided or ambivalent between the parties or candidates.

Partisans have also sorted socially, with Republicans now overwhelmingly white and Christian (and increasingly male) and Democrats now made up of more racial or religious minorities and women (Mason 2018). Voters' views of the parties are increasingly tied to these social identities, with voters perceiving the other party in terms of its most stereotypical voters; those who harbor the strongest attachments to their party's dominant identities maintain the most positive feelings about their own party. Geographic areas at all levels have now segregated more by partisanship, so that voters are more likely to be surrounded by those who agree with them politically in cities, counties, and states (Hopkins 2017). Partisans even vary more in their consumer cultures and product purchases, with nearly any social decision—from car purchases to restaurant meals—now serving as a valid partisan signal (Hetherington and Weller 2018).

All of this is tied to the third related trend: nationalization. American political decisions, including votes for state and local office, are increasingly tied to views of national political figures (especially the president) and national issues. Even as voters know that state and local government actions are important to them, they pay far less attention to state and local issues, in large part because they rely increasingly on national media that covers politics through a Washington lens—if they follow any political media at all (Hopkins 2018). Americans are forgetting their governors' names, even as they still know national figures like the vice president. Nationalization has made voters less likely to split their tickets for national and state offices. And when the smaller group of remaining swing voters disapprove of the president's party, they also take it out on aligned state leaders. In fact, Americans now use their view of the president far more than their view of state government even in considering candidates for state legislature (Rogers 2016).

The political parties thus maintain less distinct regional reputations, with Democratic politicians in the South and Republicans in the Northeast disappearing. The Democrats have fewer pro-life or pro-gun candidates to offer Red State voters, while the Republicans have few moderates to offer Blue State voters. Candidates increasingly run on their national party's reputation and brand name; voters notice, failing to give opposition party candidates a chance to differentiate themselves from the national party. Nationalization was, in part, a deliberate strategy by Republicans, who wanted to sell a conservative vision to what they perceived as a conservative nation, and Democrats, who wanted to kick out Southern conservatives and expand their issue agenda (Rosenfeld 2017). It further increased even in 2018, when four Red State Democratic incumbent senators lost despite a national Democratic partisan wave.

Polarized and national politics have worked out better for the Republicans. The conservative movement knew that converting the already conservative South to the party could lead to a national majority—and they pursued that regional conversion vigorously. Republican leaders in Congress, especially Newt Gingrich, also championed the nationwide cause of firm opposition to undermine the longtime Democratic leadership. Hardline Republicans rose to power and took control of the caucus just in time for

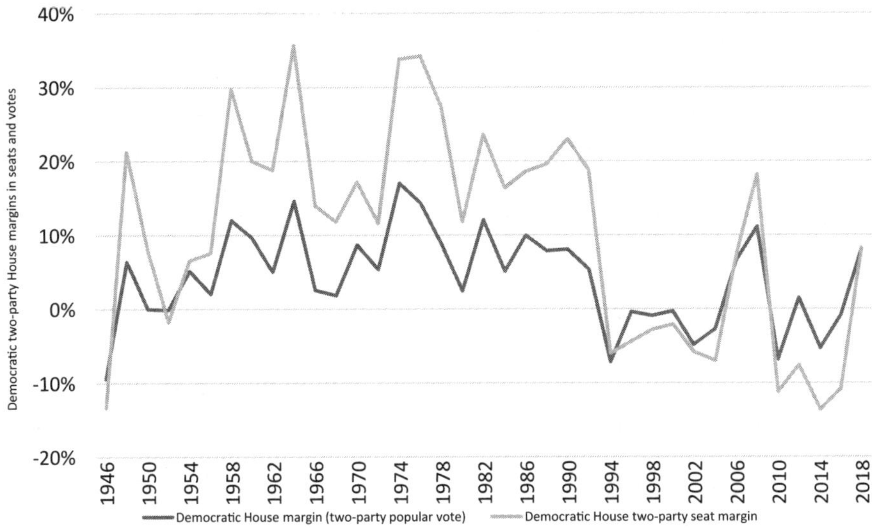

Figure 2.1: Democratic Two-Party House Margins in Seats and Votes. *Source*: Author's calculations, updated from Vital Statistics on Congress, Brookings Institution. Data available at https://www.brookings.edu/multi-chapter-report/vital-statistics-on-congress/

the party to win control of the House of Representatives (Kornacki 2018). Gingrich's obstructionist tactics and abrasive media style later made their way to the Senate through members that had previously served with him in the House (Theriault 2008). Because the Democrats relied on Red State Senate representation, nationalized politics made it harder for the party to win a majority of seats; their candidates carried the baggage of the national party. Along with nationalization, increasing Democratic concentration in urban areas—combined with consecutive losses in multiple redistricting cycles in state governments—also reversed the traditional geographic advantage that Democrats held in the House. Whereas they had previously garnered a higher proportion of seats than national votes for decades, Democrats now needed a large popular vote majority to win control (as the party became increasingly uncompetitive in rural areas).

Figure 2.1 illustrates these trends. Whereas Democrats maintained a large House seat majority with a modest popular vote advantage from the 1960s to the early 1990s, they regularly lost the majority starting in 1994 and no longer maintained an advantage in translating votes into seats. Both the popular vote and the battle for control of the chamber remained close, with Republicans advantaged in the seat count (with the exception of the

2008 election). Democrats won an average of 61 percent of seats (on 53 percent of national votes) from 1960 to 1992. Since 1994, they have averaged 48 percent of both seats and votes (Brookings Institution 2018).

Republicans, who had held the House for only four years between 1935 and 1994, controlled the House for twenty of the prior twenty-four years before losing control in 2018. They had held the Senate for only eight years between 1935 and 1994 but have held control for sixteen of the last twenty-six years (though their largest margin has been ten seats). Since 1994, the average party margin in the Senate has been seven seats (counting independents, who caucus with Democrats).

Polarized, well-sorted, and nationalized politics produced perennial close presidential elections as well. The presidency has alternated between Democrats and Republicans since 1952, with George H. W. Bush's 1992 victory standing as the only third consecutive term for either party. The most recent "landslide" presidential election, Barack Obama's 2008 victory, was only a seven-percentage-point margin despite a large national recession (compare that to twenty-three-percentage-point margins for Richard Nixon in 1972 and Lyndon Johnson in 1964 and eighteen percentage points for Ronald Reagan in 1984). Four of the last seven presidential elections have produced a minority popular vote winner—including two with a split decision between the popular vote and the Electoral College vote.

This close national competition has encouraged the congressional political parties to dedicate increasing time and resources to messaging and campaigning and relatively fewer resources to policymaking (Lee 2016). The parties have pursued more show votes, procedural hardball, and position taking for the media, knowing that the next election victory or loss could come soon. They have less incentive for bipartisan compromise and more incentive to highlight differences, even on policy issues where there is a popular position in the middle (Fiorina 2017).

Both public opinion and election results have moved thermostatically—against the ideological direction of policymaking (Wlezien 1995). This means that the public becomes more liberal when policy is more conservative and vice versa, swinging back and forth electorally as each party overshoots on policy in its preferred ideological direction (Erikson, MacKuen, and Stimson 2002). Figure 2.2 illustrates two trends in public opinion standardized and averaged across many poll questions (see Stimson 2004). The overall policy mood measures how often citizens agree with the liberal position on a policy question (out of all those who took a liberal or conservative position). The second includes only opinions on questions related to the overall size and scope of government. Citizens are consistently more likely

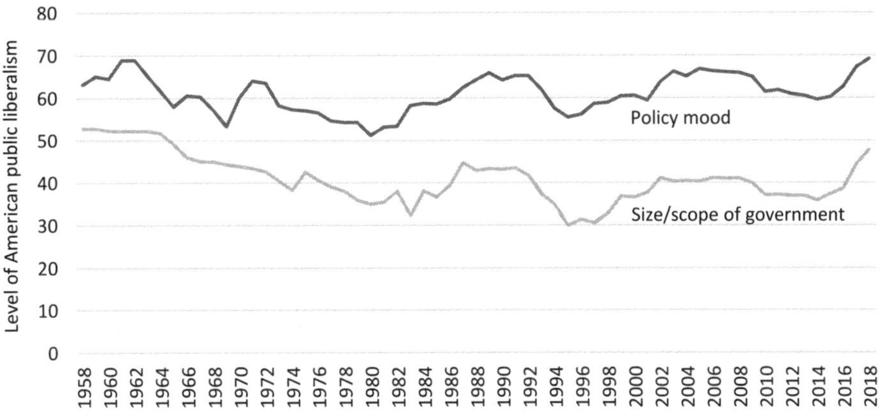

Figure 2.2: American Public Liberalism over Time. *Source*: Author's calculations from James Stimson's policy mood measures (and a subset). Data available at http://stimson.web.unc.edu/data/.

to give liberal answers on specific policy questions compared to broad sentiments about government, but both move together over time against the party in power and their policy changes. The largest recent conservative shifts came in the initial years of the Clinton and Obama administrations, with Trump's initial years producing a large shift leftward.

Because of close recent national elections, these backlashes have lately been large enough to switch congressional majorities. The two years since the 1960s when Democrats were most successful in passing liberal policies, namely, 1993 and 2009, were met with the two largest electoral shifts against them in the national House vote (Grossmann 2018). The conservative policymaking of Trump's first two years was likewise followed by a large shift toward the Democrats.

With the electorate polarized and sorted into national partisan and ideological coalitions of roughly equal size, both parties are bound to remain competitive. But the smaller remaining swing vote still shifts abruptly from left to right—usually to voice opposition to the governing majority. We are thus left with a very temperamental middle between two easily polarized sides.

THE DECLINE OF STEADY COMPROMISE POLICYMAKING

Despite no mention of parties in the Constitution, they developed quickly in response to the majoritarian needs of legislators and political candidates (Aldrich 2011). With plurality single-member districts, a presidential system, and no regional parties, the United States retains the lowest number of effective parties in the democratic world—consistently only two. But unlike a parliamentary system, it is difficult to meld this two-party competition with our policymaking institutions. National government separates the executive and legislative functions but gives each branch checks on the other. Bicameralism, with the strongest upper chamber in the democratic world, creates additional conflicts and forces compromises (Ryan 2018).

Congress has repeatedly changed its institutions to alter the balance of power between backbench legislators, party leaders, and committee chairs, but most rules reforms have been compromises that balance multiple interests and are layered on top of one another, increasing complexity (Schickler 2001). Reforms have included both supermajoritarian requirements, such as the Senate filibuster, and exceptions to those rules, such as the budget reconciliation process; but both are typically employed as compromises among rival centers of power (Reynolds 2017).

The most significant trend in rules has been to empower party leaders over committees, starting with the post-Watergate internal reforms of the Democratic caucus that deposed conservative committee chairs and empowered the party caucus in chair selection (Rohde 1991). They were eventually amplified by a newly empowered Republican majority, which concentrated power in the Speaker (Polsby 2005). The result is a disempowering of expertise and interest accommodation in committees, with more power flowing through party leaders.

Congressional institutions still usually require building wide consensus. Historically, most major legislation was passed in the House and Senate with two-thirds majorities—including majorities of both parties (Mayhew 2005; Krehbiel 1998). These patterns continue despite polarization: majority parties are now even a bit worse at passing their agendas without bipartisan support, with both landmark laws and less important actions still mostly passing with broad majorities (Curry and Lee 2019). This has been necessary to avert gridlock, with slowly built compromises among major party leaders, pivotal centrists, and committee chairs. Even after passage, major legislation can be reversed or later scaled back if it does not involve multiple interests and ensure alignment with their incentives (Patashnik 2014); legislators thus seek large enacting coalitions to ensure sustainability. When they are forced to share power in periods of divided government, the parties have reacted by each producing their own policy agenda (Binder 2003). What does pass is therefore a more limited subset of what each party seeks to achieve. There is more disappointment on both sides, though successful actions are mostly still bipartisan.

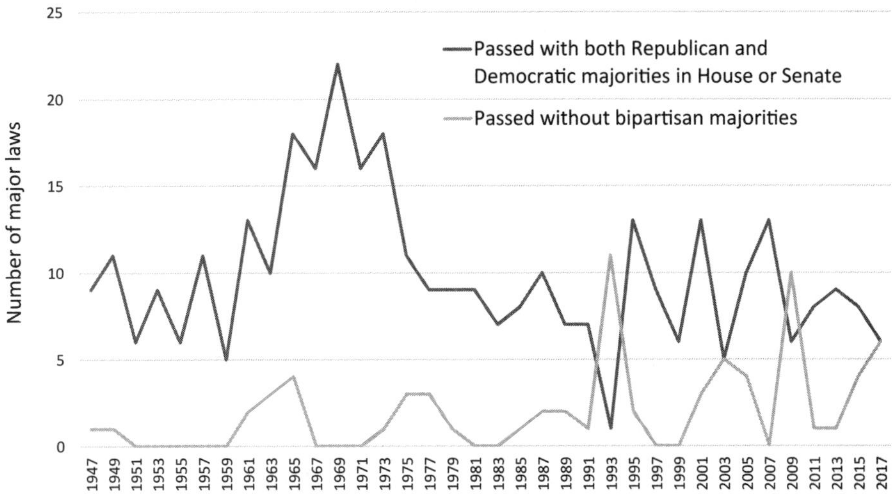

Figure 2.3: Major Laws Passed with and without Support from Bipartisan Majorities. *Source*: Author's calculations, compiled and updated from David Mayhew's lists. Data available at http://campuspress.yale.edu/davidmayhew/datasets-divided-we-govern/.

Figure 2.3 illustrates these trends in bipartisan policymaking and their exceptions. It tracks the number of major laws (tracked by Mayhew 2005) that passed with majorities of each party in in at least one chamber and the number that passed with only a majority of Democrats or a majority of Republicans. When Congress was most active in the 1960s and 1970s, it was mostly passing bipartisan laws. Since 1993, it has begun to pass more major laws on party-line votes. In 1993 and 2009 (the two congresses preceding Democrats' biggest electoral losses), Democratic congresses actually passed more partisan than bipartisan laws. Many of these laws were also subject to relentless and immediate efforts to repeal or reform them.

The dominant trend since the 1960s has been partisan and ideological polarization, with each party relinquishing moderates and moving away from the ideological center; incumbents have shifted opinions away from the center or been replaced by newly elected and more extreme members (McCarty, Poole, and Rosenthal 2006). The political parties were already divided on economic policy issues but became increasingly divided on civil rights, immigration, and foreign policy (Lapinski 2013). The block of conservative Southerners, who had allied with Republicans in the conservative coalition to block civil rights laws but also served as centrists on economic policy for the decades between the late 1930s and the 1970s (Caughey 2018), slowly disappeared. The Republican Party, meanwhile, shifted abruptly rightward with the elections of 1978 and 1980 and never looked back.

Even one-party rule had usually involved minority parties in crafting major and minor legislation, but that changed in the 1990s and 2000s. The Democratic majority in 1993 passed a series of bills with overwhelming Democratic support and almost no support from Republicans. The new Republican majority in 1995 followed up with party-line votes on its agenda outlined in the Contract with America in the preceding election. Despite a vitriolic impeachment battle, there was a return to bipartisanship on legislation in the late 1990s. George W. Bush also gained some support from Democrats on his signature legislative achievements: tax cuts, education reform, prescription drug coverage, homeland security, and the Iraq War. But his second term was more partisan and less legislatively successful. Barack Obama's presidency was highly partisan from the very beginning, with Democrats passing major legislation with almost no Republican support in health care, financial reform, equal pay, economic stimulus, community service, and student loans.

Despite the partisan bursts of 1993, 2009, and 2017, sustained and successful lawmaking has been difficult. The bursts were met with immediate backlashes. In the past, policymakers had been able to sustain policymaking even in the face of public and electoral resistance. From 1961 to 1976, in a period I have labeled "The Long Great Society," American policymaking underwent a "big bang" across branches and policy areas, vastly expanding the size and scope of government with bipartisan support (Grossmann 2014). The period also featured a "Great Issue Expansion," with Congress addressing more issues with more resources, enabled by an expanded central and committee staff and a matching expansion of think tanks, advocacy groups, and lobbyists able to supplement legislative capacity (Baumgartner and Jones 2015). But the golden age of congressional policymaking came to an end in the 1980s, with committee staff and policymaking hearings going into decline despite a sustained large issue agenda.

The increasingly crowded legislative calendar was often dedicated to renewals of prior legislation, with Congress facing regular deadlines of expiring provisions but less able to meet them over time (Adler and Wilkerson 2013). Even the Farm Bill, the most regular comprehensive legislation Congress approves, has been caught up in regular partisan fights in recent years and postponed for postelection action. Increasingly intransigent hardline factions, like the House Freedom Caucus, have refused to move forward on even consensus legislation in the hopes of influencing other legislation that is a higher priority (Bloch Rubin 2017). Total congressional lawmaking has been limited, with Congress passing a lower percentage of bills introduced and a lower total number of resolutions and laws in the 2010s (National Journal 2018). Government shutdowns and debt ceiling crises have become more commonly used as partisan leverage.

The Senate, which traditionally featured more bipartisan folkways, has also disrupted policymaking with partisanship. Its nomination review powers have been increasingly contested, with recent Supreme Court, lower court, and executive branch nominees all facing party line votes after decades of wide bipartisan support. Procedural hardball has amped up, involving filibuster reforms, reconciliation for traditional legislation, and even the postponing of any consideration of President Obama's Supreme Court nominee to enable a postelection appointment.

DIFFERENT IMPLICATIONS FOR LIBERALS AND CONSERVATIVES

The roots of congressional change stem from the reform period of the 1970s, which was led by liberals who sought to make Congress more responsive to interest groups and constituency demands (Zelizer 2004). But that does not mean it has been beneficial to liberals; instead, the reforms coincided with the end of the expansion of the size and scope of government and eventually empowered Republicans to pursue a more forthright conservative agenda (Zelizer 2012).

Conservatives are less interested in government action to address social problems. They tend to focus instead on maintaining power to block new initiatives or attack programs and policies most vulnerable to reversal. As a result, Republican issue agendas are smaller, their legislative achievements are less extensive, and their policy discussion is less frequent and specific (Grossmann and Hopkins 2016). Republican politicians less often voice disappointment with gridlock and occasionally say they proactively support less lawmaking and want to pass fewer laws.

They are able to sell this vision to their supporters because the Republican electorate is also less motivated by—and less united around—legislative policy proposals. Republicans benefit from consistent public opinion pluralities regarding conservative self-identification and views of the size and role of government, the speed of social change, the importance of national tradition, and support for America's interests in the world. But they simultaneously lack public support for their specific proposals on economic, social, and foreign policy issues (Ellis and Stimson 2012). Republicans are thus more comfortable as an opposition party that works against new interventions and sells supporters on a restoration of traditional American values.

The ideological direction of policymaking is usually liberal; Congress passes far more policies that expand government than contract it, a pattern that is common around the world (Grossmann 2014). Social issue policy also tends to move in a liberal direction as society evolves its social norms. Yet the Republican Party is the world's only center-right party to avoid acquiescing to the growth of the welfare state and government intervention in the economy. Instead, they claim to oppose these roles but still make few (unpopular) efforts to actually overturn the inherited policy order.

In measures of congressional polarization, the Republicans thus show up as repeatedly moving rightward further than Democrats are moving leftward. Their move is also national, whereas most of the Democratic move is accounted for by the replacement of white Southern conservatives with Republicans and racial minorities. But since most policy proposals debated and passed expand government's role, their move has not necessarily meant conservative retrenchment. Policy has moved significantly rightward since 1981 on taxes, but that has been accompanied by slow expansions of government into new areas. The size of government has also grown, with larger deficits whenever taxes are lowered and fail to keep up.

With a choice between gridlock and liberal policymaking, Republicans are relatively better off with gridlock. Especially since their control also brings changes to executive and court appointments, they may be able to achieve their goals without much legislating. They have also been able to lower and redirect taxes under three of their last four presidents, so they also have enough of an agenda to sell to conservative interest groups and their allies in the business community. For conservatives who accept their inability to scale back the size and role of government or reverse the direction of social change, the current disconnect between electoral politics and policymaking produces a reasonable outcome: the power to slow liberalism and retain authority.

Republicans have a large conservative media infrastructure to sell whatever achievements they do accomplish and convince their supporters of constant threats from the left (Hemmer 2016). With their advantage in talk radio, their success in online story distribution, and especially the soaring ratings of the Fox News channel (Martin and Yurukoglu 2017), they have been able to achieve a consolidated American right, even without an extensive achievable agenda. They also developed a prominent set of think tanks to produce constant research in support of their ideological predilections, challenging each new liberal proposal and ostensible problem in need of government intervention (Stahl 2016) while also communicating actively through the media to undermine the old system of assumed-to-be neutral expertise (Medvetz 2012).

Conservative parties worldwide, which tend to represent traditional economic elites, need a broader religious and nationalist social base to compete in democratic elections; even then, they tend to be skeptical of democratizing reforms and face threats of losing power to lower classes on the left or being overrun by nativist elements on the right (Ziblatt 2017). As a result, they must balance strong conservative institutions with a mass base less tied to their policy agenda. It is not uncommon for parties on the right to pursue upper-class economic policy interests but depend on the symbolic power of the flag and the cross. Although the Republican Party divorces its policymaking and campaigning more than other center-right parties, the disconnect is endemic to conservative politics.

Liberals, meanwhile, are caught in a more difficult dilemma. They gained power within a party that was a coalition of social groups, each seeking distinct government actions (Grossmann and Hopkins 2016). Democratic electoral victories were also traditionally more reliant on "bringing home the bacon" to serve district interests and to a nonideological image as a problem solver for local communities (Shafer and Johnston 2009). Nationalized politics with fewer achievements may not be as good for a party built on real policy beneficiaries.

Democratic constituencies are now expressing a growing list of concerns and forwarding an even larger menu of policy proposals. With a diversifying electorate, evolving social demands, and increasingly difficult-to-solve problems (such as climate change and economic inequality), Democrats are constantly pressed to forward new initiatives despite their shrinking power. Their supporters still expect tangible results. It is not clear, however, that they can achieve more of their expanding agenda, especially without a major electoral backlash. Even if they do have some success, they may achieve a lower share of their activists' and constituencies' wish lists. Even during their last two periods of great policy success, 1993–1994 and 2009–2010, they left a lot of proposals and problems on the table. They also compromised on their major initiatives to satisfy interest groups and try to dampen conservative opposition.

Liberals have pursued quite different responses to this situation. Some have elaborated new visions of institutional reform, from changes in voting rules and campaign finance to swifter legislative policymaking (Weiser and Bannon 2018). Others seek to emulate conservatives, with some even forthrightly arguing "it's time to fight dirty" (Faris 2017) and many other Democrats seeing merit in heretofore extreme-sounding proposals like expanding the Senate and packing the Supreme Court (Sargent 2018). Trump's election also brought forth an increasingly rancorous debate over whether Democrats should abandon the "identity politics" concerns of women and minorities (Lilla 2017) or broaden their agenda to new issues like open immigration and abandoning mass incarceration. The trouble for Democrats is the need both to hold white working-class voters and to motivate youth and minority participation simultaneously, which may be difficult.

Unfortunately for Democrats, these are mostly theoretical debates about what to do assuming they can regain full control of government. To get to that point, they will have to hang on to many Republican-leaning states—and win more of them. During the Trump administration, Democrats are highly energized and have mobilized a variety of causes via protests and constituent pressure—even stimulating record new candidacies and fundraising. But the movement is diverse: women and minorities are prizing descriptive representation; some candidates are advancing messages to win back Trump voters while others try to expand on Clinton's new suburban coalition; and the left is mobilizing alongside traditional Democratic Party groups. The diverse and divisive 2020 presidential nomination process dominated Trump-era discussions; few candidates voiced interest in working with Trump on achieving anything in the interim.

If Democrats do ascend to power, they will immediately face trade-offs about what to prioritize, including institutional reforms or substantive policy (problems less acute for Republicans' more limited agenda). They will also face pressure from more relentless activism but also from vulnerable legislators uninterested in pursuing the full panoply of liberal policy goals at once. Meanwhile, the Republicans will do what they do best: foment rebellion over Democratic proposals, characterizing them as moves on the slippery slope toward socialism and remaking America (Skocpol and Williamson 2012). It is not clear why that strategy could not work again next time.

THE OLD COMPROMISE: INCREMENTAL LIBERALISM TEMPERED BY CONSERVATISM

There was a historical solution to the competition between asymmetric parties. It did not make for optimal policy and it may not be able to make a fulsome resurgence, but it is nonetheless worth reviewing to have a clear sense of exactly what has been lost. In short, American policymaking used to pursue Democratic goals through Republican means. Democrats led policymaking to address the practical needs of their constituencies, but they methodically worked through the long list, focusing on a few narrow compromises at a time. Republicans and some Democrats raised conservative ideological objections to each new initiative but also aided in occasional bipartisan compromises (Grossmann 2014). These included policy tools that incentivized the participation of private actors such as companies and nonprofits. They also decentralized the implementation to states and localities, often expanding the financial role of the federal government but leaving decisions to implementers away from Washington. The compromises also avoided direct spending where possible, using tax credits and deductions instead of appropriations. Rather than directly regulating businesses and individuals, they also tried to use incentives to stimulate change and compliance. Compromises on policy tools, exceptions, and implementation were common.

As a result, American public policy stands out in the world for multiple design peculiarities (Grossmann and Hopkins 2016). Social benefits are much more likely to be delivered by employers and private providers at a higher total cost (Hacker 2002). The United States relies far more, and increasingly over time, on state and local employees to carry out federal priorities (Baumgartner and Jones 1993). Our government also employs myriad contractors and grantees to carry out government functions, accounting for all of the growth in government since the 1960s and making for a privatized government unprecedented in worldwide comparisons (Light 2018). And we rely disproportionately on tax credits and deductions (with more precedent in the world) to advance social goals.

These policy designs were not always forced by Republicans. Democrats avoided upsetting American public and elite opinion by preemptively compromising on the format of policy as long as it achieved some of their goals, leading to objections that they often sought to compromise with themselves. These concessions often made for jury-rigged proposals that stimulated complaints about complexity, with critics alleging that simpler systems would have gained more support. But these were real efforts to minimize opposition to expansions in government's role.

Two recent examples under Obama show that the process was still in motion but lacked the ability to encourage bipartisan cooperation. First, Obama's economic stimulus package was composed of about one-third tax cuts, a traditional Republican priority. Another one-fifth of the package was few-strings-attached funding to state governments, another conservative policy format. Still more was spent on infrastructure projects that Republicans claimed to support. But even with a faltering economy, the initiative did not gain their support; it was a large expansion in government advanced by a Democratic president, after all. The minimization of direct federal spending, however, did sway wavering moderate senators (even influencing Arlen Spector's decision to switch parties) and endear the proposal to strange bedfellow interest groups like the US Chamber of Commerce.

Second, the Affordable Care Act's two main systems for coverage expansion, Medicaid and subsidized insurance exchanges, were supposed to be set up by state governments. But many states fell back on the federal backstop, healthcare.gov, and refused to expand Medicaid (after the Supreme Court overruled conditioning all Medicaid funding on expansion). The legislation, which became known as Obamacare, also incorporated tax credits, did not substantially alter the private provision of health care, and gave new business to private sellers of health insurance. But it still gained little Republican interest. Some Democrats are now calling for a simpler—and far more expensive—plan to substantially lower the eligibility age of Medicare to provide government-paid and -managed coverage. But that means sacrificing interest group endorsements that enable passage. The prior decision to preemptively compromise did bring on the critical support of the health insurance industries along with the wider business community, and it forced substantially less upheaval on existing health plans and providers. As a result, it may turn out to be surprisingly stable—with more states joining the Medicaid expansion over time.

Both of these initiatives did constitute large and diverse expansions of government responsibility that advanced long-term Democratic goals, so it is not that surprising that they failed to generate Republican buy-in. Prior presidents had more often reached over to the other side's list of key priorities to advance some of them, so much so that the second Bill Clinton administration was actually to the right of the first George W. Bush administration in terms of policy achievements (Grossmann 2014). Clinton advanced banking deregulation, tax cuts, and housing and regulatory reforms. Bush prioritized education spending, campaign finance reform, industry regulation, and Medicare expansion. Before Trump, Republican presidents usually had advanced some liberal initiatives to accompany their conservative priorities: civil rights, taxes, and regulation under H. W. Bush; transportation, job training, and immigration under Reagan; voting rights, employment benefits, natural resource management, and pensions under Ford; and social benefits, public jobs, environmental protection, and local assistance under Nixon.

Trump's embrace of only his own party's limited agenda has been unprecedented. Despite a few fleeting claims that he was excited to work with "Chuck and Nancy" on their initiatives and repeated claims that he wanted to reverse his own decisions on issues like health care and the Deferred Action for Childhood Arrivals (or Dreamers) program—not to mention dozens of postponed versions of "infrastructure week"—he never seriously advanced a major Democratic initiative. The Republican Congress, seeing little potential help from Democrats on tax reform or Obamacare repeal, also mostly drafted and negotiated their proposals within the party. They did manage bipartisan bills to address opioid addiction and criminal justice, but they were mostly symbolic acts that contained little funding and aligned national regulations and state efforts.

Does it have to remain that way? Trump's partisanship is strong, but his off-the-cuff comments suggest he harbors few true philosophical objections to Democratic priorities. A liberal-conservative coalition of interest groups and senators succeeded in passing criminal justice reform with his support, even though its less punitive aims directly contradicted his "law and order" campaign rhetoric. But even in an unlikely conciliatory scenario, Democrats would also have to prioritize a few achievable policy goals, be willing to compromise on the format, and embrace working with Trump to achieve them. We may not even get a chance to pursue a return to the historical norm until the next presidency.

PROLONGED PARTISAN WARFARE AHEAD

It seems most likely that our current combination of partisan rancor and limited policy action will remain for the foreseeable future. It is understandable that Democrats would want to avoid pursuing less-effective policy half-measures when Republicans are no longer willing to join the effort. When it comes to challenges like climate change or income inequality, which would likely require very large liberal government interventions to move the needle, Democrats are increasingly developing broad policy proposals that have even less hope for advancement in Congress. And it is similarly reasonable that a party opposed to further government intervention and unwilling to embrace social change would decide to avoid teaming up with their rivals to advance those very goals. But without a return to the tacit compromise that Democrats get to direct new government action to limited priorities and Republicans get to force an adaption of the format to be more in line with traditional American policy tools, there may not be another solution to nationalized and polarized politics between asymmetric sides.

Instead, the parties are likely to keep at their prolonged war of procedural one-upmanship and media-driven public charades. If full government retrenchment and social restoration are off the table (as they are around the world, with center-right parties usually acquiescing), the current system is working reasonably well for Republicans. Their electoral messages and policymaking strategies do not match, but that may be an advantage given how divorced contemporary campaigns are from realistic policy discussions. Republicans have been able to remain electorally competitive—even dominant in state governments—without shifting their rightward march. The Trump administration, though full of daily distractions and discomfort even for the most ardent supporters of his brand of politics, has accumulated the most conservative policy record in generations through unabashed plodding in administrative agencies, conservative ascendance in the judiciary, and a legislative record that prioritized major tax cuts without advancing liberal priorities.

Democrats unwilling or unable to change the current trajectory are betting on occasional bursts of liberal policymaking after near-perfect electoral conditions. Since the last large Democratic majority was built on the largest recession since the Great Depression—and was immediately dismembered two years later—it could be a significant wait. Perhaps next time will be different, and their policy successes will not be met with a large conservative backlash. But the historical record suggests a regularity to how the public reacts when Democrats' bottled-up legislative program bursts into action with successive leftward moves—and the results are not pretty for them.

The modest policy stakes of the 2018 election were quite divorced from the frightening electoral campaign. Neither party expected to achieve much in Congress, and each began 2019 with low expectations. Neither advanced any potential major compromises with the opposition. Instead, they are each developing new and more extreme proposals without any plan for enactment, including some that are nonstarters even for their own party leaders. And policy overall was quite secondary to the permanent campaigning, with the 2020 cycle beginning immediately after 2018. Democrats say democracy itself is on the ballot and that they must stop Trump at all costs. Republicans say the nation could disintegrate in the face of rising socialism—or even after the next refugee caravan. Our loud, vindictive campaigns mask the limited policymaking potential of either party but do broadcast their only remaining agreement: that compromise is dead.

The public theater obscures some remaining policymaking potential, where legislating often occurs behind the scenes and out of the media spotlight. The parties reached agreement on an opioid bill, a farm bill, and a criminal justice reform in the 115th Congress, along with smaller changes to intellectual property law, financial regulation, sex-trafficking enforcement, ocean protection, and water resources projects. They even passed sanctions on Russia and agreed to government funding parameters, despite those issues being the product of high-profile fights. For the most part, however, the important deals were made out of the public eye, often the product of intentional efforts to depoliticize issues by bipartisan teams. Despite a long government shutdown over border wall funding, their $6 billion disagreement within a more than $4-trillion-dollar budget was hardly a large breach with no hope of closure.

Perhaps the sides will recognize that there is a path back to sanity in government, one that was modeled for decades and has not lost support in the American public. Government can take on a few additional roles at a time, after prioritizing problems and evaluating the feasibility of solutions and their compatibility with existing institutions. After considerable negotiation, proposals can scale down their ambitions, limit their disruption of existing policy, and meld onto our decentralized, non-statist system of public-private partnerships. Those kinds of proposals may not be enough to address liberal policy goals, such as reducing the rise in global temperature or decreasing the gap between rich and poor, so it is understandable that they would hope for a new kind of politics and alternative institutions. But hope does nothing to change the very real institutional constraints. Incremental liberalism does not make for optimal policy or beautiful sausage making, but it does reconcile Americans' long-standing endorsement of both liberal policy goals and conservative ideological objections.

Slow, pragmatic, and compromised governance is not a great campaign bumper sticker. In an era of socially sorted and polarized partisans who believe that the other side is made up of different people with distinct views of the nation, it is especially hard to sell. But liberals should recognize that, in the traditional system of incremental liberalism, they were gaining ground in a long war of attrition, one policy at a time. And conservatives should realize that they were also winning the wider war over American self-definition: the United States is not (and likely never will be) a socialist country that undermines its traditions. Policymakers used to leave the campaign trail, come to Washington, and get about the business of policymaking within this consensus—without making every battle the one to end them all. We remain far from that today, but perhaps the stalemate and the fury will subside once the dismal results become clear.

REFERENCES

Abramowitz, Alan I. *The Great Alignment: Race, Party Transformation, and the Rise of Donald Trump.* New Haven, CT: Yale University Press, 2018.

Abramowitz, Alan I., and Steven Webster. "The Rise of Negative Partisanship and the Nationalization of US Elections in the 21st Century." *Electoral Studies* 41, no. 2 (2016): 12–22.

Adler, E. Scott, and John Wilkerson. *Congress and the Politics of Problem Solving.* New York: Cambridge University Press, 2013.

Aldrich, John. *Why Parties? The Origin and Transformation of Political Parties in America.* 2nd ed. Chicago: University of Chicago Press, 2011.

Baumgartner, Frank R., and Bryan D. Jones. *The Politics of Information: Problem Definition and the Course of Public Policy in America.* Chicago: University of Chicago Press, 2015.

———. *Agendas and Instability in American Politics.* Chicago: University of Chicago Press, 1993.

Bloch Rubin, Ruth. *Building the Bloc: Intraparty Organization in the US Congress.* New York: Cambridge University Press, 2017.

Brookings Institution. Vital Statistics on Congress. 2018. Online: https://www.brookings.edu/multi-chapter-report/vital-statistics-on-congress/.

Caughey, Devin. *The Unsolid South: Mass Politics and National Representation in a One-Party Enclave.* Princeton, NJ: Princeton University Press, 2018.

Curry, James M., and Frances E. Lee. "Non-Party Government: Bipartisan Lawmaking and Party Power in Congress." *Perspectives on Politics* 17, no. 1 (2019): 47–65.

Ellis, Christopher, and James Stimson. *Ideology in America.* Cambridge: Cambridge University Press, 2012.

Erikson, Robert S., Michael B. Mackuen, and James A. Stimson. *The Macro Polity.* New York: Cambridge University Press, 2002.

Faris, David. *It's Time to Fight Dirty: How Democrats Can Build a Lasting Majority in American Politics.* New York: Melville House, 2017.

Fiorina, Morris. *Unstable Majorities: Polarization, Party Sorting, and Political Stalemate.* Stanford: Hoover Institution Press, 2017.

Grossmann, Matt. "Voters Like a Political Party Until It Passes Laws." 2018. FiveThirtyEight. Online: https://fivethirtyeight.com/features/voters-like-a-political-party-until-it-passes-laws/.

———. *Artists of the Possible: Governing Networks and American Policy Change Since 1945.* New York: Oxford University Press, 2014.

Grossmann, Matt, and David Hopkins. *Asymmetric Politics: Ideological Republicans and Group Interest Democrats.* New York: Oxford University Press, 2016.

Hacker, Jacob. *The Divided Welfare State: The Battle over Public and Private Social Benefits in the United States.* New York: Cambridge University Press, 2002.

Hemmer, Nicole. *Messengers of the Right: Conservative Media and the Transformation of American Politics.* Philadelphia: University of Pennsylvania Press, 2016.

Hetherington, Marc, and Jonathan Weiler. *Prius or Pickup? How the Answers to Four Simple Questions Explain America's Great Divide.* New York: Houghton Mifflin Harcourt, 2018.

Hopkins, Daniel. *The Increasingly United States: How and Why American Political Behavior Nationalized.* Chicago: University of Chicago Press, 2018.

Hopkins, David A. *Red Fighting Blue: How Geography and Electoral Rules Polarize American Politics.* New York: Cambridge University Press, 2017.

Iyengar, Shanto, and Sean Westwood. "Fear and Loathing across Party Lines: New Evidence on Group Polarization." *American Journal of Political Science* 59, no. 3 (2015): 690–707.

Krehbiel, Keith. *Pivotal Politics: A Theory of US Lawmaking.* Chicago: University of Chicago Press, 1998.

Lapinski, John S. *The Substance of Representation: Congress, American Political Development, and Lawmaking: Congress, American Political Development, and Lawmaking.* Princeton, NJ: Princeton University Press, 2013.

Lee, Frances. *Insecure Majorities: Congress and the Perpetual Campaign.* Chicago: University of Chicago Press, 2016.

Light, Paul C. *The Government-Industrial Complex: The True Size of Government, 1984–2018.* New York: Oxford University Press, 2018.

Lilla, Mark. *The Once and Future Liberal: After Identity Politics.* New York: HarperCollins, 2017.

Martin, Gregory, and Ali Yurukoglu. "Bias in Cable News: Persuasion and Polarization." *American Economic Review* 107, no. (2017): 2566–2599.

Mason, Liliana. *Uncivil Agreement: How Politics Became Our Identity.* Chicago: University of Chicago Press, 2018.

Mayhew, David. *Divided We Govern: Party Control, Lawmaking, and Investigations, 1946–2002.* 2nd ed. New Haven, CT: Yale University Press, 2005.

McCarty, Nolan, Keith T. Poole, and Howard Rosenthal. *Polarized America: The Dance of Ideology and Unequal Riches.* Cambridge, MA: MIT Press, 2006.

Medvetz, Thomas. *Think Tanks in America.* Chicago: University of Chicago Press, 2012.

National Journal. *Congressional Productivity.* 2018. Online: https://www.nationaljournal.com/md/653624/congressional-productivity.

Neal, Zachary. "A Sign of the Times? Weak and Strong Polarization in the US Congress, 1973–2016." *Social Networks.* 2018. Online: https://www.sciencedirect.com/science/article/pii/S0378873317303039.

Oliver, Eric, and Thomas Wood. *Enchanted America: How Intuition and Reason Drive Our Politics.* Chicago: University of Chicago Press, 2018.

Patashnik, Eric. *Reforms at Risk: What Happens After Major Policy Changes Are Enacted.* Princeton, NJ: Princeton University Press, 2014.

Polsby, Nelson W. *How Congress Evolves: Social Bases of Institutional Change.* New York: Oxford University Press, 2004.

Reynolds, Molly. *Exceptions to the Rule: The Politics of Filibuster Limitations in the US Senate.* Washington, DC: Brookings Institution, 2017.

Rhode, David W. *Parties and Leaders in the Postreform House.* Chicago: University of Chicago Press, 1991.

Rogers, Steven. "National Forces in State Legislative Elections." *Annals of the American Academy of Political and Social* Science. 2016. Online: http://journals.sagepub.com/doi/abs/10.1177/0002716216662454.

Rogowski, Jon, and Joseph Sutherland. "How Ideology Fuels Affective Polarization." *Political Behavior* 38, no. 2 (2016): 485–508.

Rosenfeld, Sam. *The Polarizers: Postwar Architects of Our Partisan Era.* Chicago: University of Chicago Press, 2017.

Ryan, Josh M. *The Congressional Endgame: Interchamber Bargaining and Compromise.* Chicago: University of Chicago Press, 2018.

Sargent, Greg. *An Uncivil War: Taking Back Our Democracy in an Age of Trumpian Disinformation and Thunderdome Politics.* New York: Custom House, 2018.

Schickler, Eric. *Disjointed Pluralism: Institutional Innovation and the Development of the US Congress.* Princeton, NJ: Princeton University Press, 2001.

Shafer, Byron, and Richard Johnston. *The End of Southern Exceptionalism: Class, Race, and Partisan Change in the Postwar South.* Cambridge, MA: Harvard University Press, 2009.

Skocpol, Theda, and Vanessa Williamson. *The Tea Party and the Remaking of Republican Conservatism.* New York: Oxford University Press, 2012.

Smidt, Corwin. "Polarization and the Decline of the American Floating Voter." *American Journal of Political Science* 61, no. 2 (2017): 365–381.

Stahl, Jason. *Right Moves: The Conservative Think Tank in American Political Culture since 1945.* Chapel Hill: University of North Carolina Press, 2016.

Stimson, James. *Tides of Consent: How Public Opinion Shapes American Politics.* New York: Cambridge University Press, 2004.

Tesler, Michael. *Post-Racial or Most-Racial? Race and Politics in the Obama Era.* Chicago: University of Chicago Press, 2016.

Theriual, Sean. *The Gingrich Senators: The Roots of Partisan Warfare in Congress.* New York: Oxford University Press, 2013.

Weiser, Wendy, and Alicia Bannon. *Democracy: An Election Agenda for Candidates, Activists, and Legislators.* New York: Brennan Center for Justice, 2018. https://www.brennancenter.org/publication/democracy-election-agenda-2018.

Wlezien, Christopher. "The Public as Thermostat: Dynamics of Preferences for Spending." *American Journal of Political Science* 39, no. 4 (1995): 981–1000.

Zelizer, Julian E. *Governing America: The Revival of Political History.* Princeton, NJ: Princeton University Press, 2012.

———. *On Capitol Hill: The Struggle to Reform Congress and Its Consequences, 1948–2000.* Cambridge: Cambridge University Press, 2004.

Ziblatt, Daniel. *Conservative Parties and the Birth of Democracy.* New York: Oxford University Press, 2017.

PART TWO

Political Institutions and Government Performance

CHAPTER 3

Legislative Stalemate in Postwar America, 1947–2018

Sarah A. Binder

The single most important thing we want to achieve is for President Obama to be a one-term president.

—Senate Minority Leader Mitch McConnell (R-KY)

Nearly two years after the election of President Barack Obama and a Democratic Congress in 2008, Senate Republican leader Mitch McConnell of Kentucky on the eve of the 2010 midterm elections declared his party's top goal: prevent Obama from securing a second term. McConnell failed to block Obama's reelection. But Republicans retook the House in 2010 and the Senate in 2014, and Donald J. Trump captured the White House in 2016. McConnell's strategy—keeping GOP fingerprints off Democratic initiatives and blocking much of their agenda after 2010—limited Democrats' accomplishments and helped to propel Republicans back to power.

Obama's relationships with Democratic and Republican Congresses over the course of eight years in office—as well as President Trump's three years with a Republican and then a split-party Congress—provide windows into the politics of legislating in polarized times. Under Obama, Republicans' bare-knuckles strategy, which reflected and fueled ideological and partisan polarization, largely undermined Democrats' capacity to govern after Democrats lost control of the House in the 2010 midterm elections, producing some of the least productive Congresses since World War II. Under Trump, a fractured GOP majority was largely unable to leverage unified control of government and barely advanced its policy agenda through Congress. In this chapter, I review the forces that shape Congress's legislative capacity, explore the politics of stalemate during the Obama and early Trump years, and reflect on evolving legislative dynamics of the long postwar era.

DYNAMICS OF LAWMAKING, IN THEORY

Publication of David Mayhew's *Divided We Govern* in 1991 marks the origins of the contemporary study of congressional-presidential relations and their effect on Congress's legislative performance. Highlighting questions about the effects of political parties on Capitol Hill, Mayhew brought systematic evidence to bear in testing claims about the effect of divided party control on Congress and the president's ability to generate landmark laws. *Divided We Govern* followed decades of works by presidential and legislative scholars perplexed and frustrated by the periods of divided party government that prevailed after World War II. Between 1897 and 1954, divided party control of government occurred 14 percent of the time; between 1955 and 1990, two-thirds of the time. As prominent political scientist V. O. Key in the 1960s summed up the state of our knowledge of the impact of party, "Common partisan control of executive and legislature does not assure energetic government, but division of party control precludes it" (Key 1964, 688). Decades later, scholars continued to call for a new theory of coalitional government to explain how Congress and the president could secure major policy change in the presence of divided government (e.g., Sundquist 1988–1989).

In *Divided We Govern,* Mayhew tackles the challenge by asking a simple question about Congress's performance in the postwar era: "Were many important laws passed?" (Mayhew 1991, 36). Mayhew sought to test for the effect of divided party control on the level of lawmaking. He identified landmark laws in a two-stage process that combined contemporary judgments about the significance of Congress's work each session with policy specialists' retrospective judgments about the importance of legislation. Mayhew then generated a comprehensive list of landmark laws enacted in each Congress between 1946 and 1990, which was subsequently updated online through 2016. Mayhew then tested whether the presence of divided government reduced the number of major laws enacted each Congress.

Mayhew concluded that party control is inconsequential in shaping a president's legislative accomplishments: not much more gets done when a single party controls both ends of Pennsylvania Avenue than under divided party control. Mayhew absolved divided government as a cause of legislative inaction and then attempted to disentangle other influences that could shape congressional performance. Some of those forces—including legislators' electoral incentives—pointed toward constancy in the record of lawmaking. In other words, the ever-present incentive to secure reelection could limit variation in Congress's legislative performance over time. But Mayhew instead pointed to alternative sources of variation to explain changes over time in Congress's level of legislative activity. Most importantly, Mayhew argued that broad shifts in the public mood (such as the rise and fall of a taste for activist government), presidents' electoral cycles, and issue coalitions that cut across the left-right divide could help us to account for variation in Congress's productivity during the postwar era.

Mayhew's counterintuitive finding produced a healthy debate about the forces that undergird the legislative records of Congress and the president. One prominent theoretical response to Mayhew's work was Keith Krehbiel's *Pivotal Politics* (Krehbiel 1998). Krehbiel introduced a new theoretical framework for conceptualizing the conditions that foster lawmaking by the two branches. Krehbiel's key contribution was the concept of legislative and presidential "pivots" engaged in a "pivotal politics" game—institutional actors endowed with key procedural rights within a stylized legislative game (see also Brady and Volden 1998).

Krehbiel's book argued that constitutional and extra-constitutional institutional rules create "pivotal" players on whom collective choice depends. In the congressional context, the collective choice at stake is the formulation of public law. Focusing on the presidential veto and the Senate filibuster, Krehbiel argued that the cloture and veto pivots drove the likelihood of major policy change. Any policy located between these pivots (the "gridlock interval") cannot be changed, assuming that legislative politics follows along a single dimension and that lawmakers' votes and presidential positions reflect their sincere preferences over policy. In other words, legislative stalemate can occur even in the presence of a president and a congressional majority that favors policy change.

The pivotal politics theory has important implications for understanding the conditions under which Congress and the president agree on major policy change. Most importantly, the theory suggests that policy outcomes must be consistent with the views of the supermajority pivots of the legislature. For example, with a conservative president and bicameral congressional majority, efforts to move policy substantially to the right would be blocked by a liberal filibuster pivot. Senate Democrats in 2005, for instance, blocked Republican president George W. Bush's push to privatize Social Security. Threatening to filibuster, Democrats prevented the proposal from moving forward—even though Republicans controlled both branches of government. According to the pivotal politics model, right-of-center status quos would also remain unchanged when conservatives controlled both branches: a conservative president would veto any movement left of the policy and the veto would be sustained by the veto pivot. Under the theory, major policy change is likely only when elections alter the alignment of pivotal players or major exogenous shocks make existing policy untenable. Crises, such as the terrorist attacks of September 11, 2001, are a prime example. Despite split party control of Congress in the fall of 2001, President Bush succeeded in securing bipartisan support for most of the legislative measures he sought in retaliation against the perpetrators of 9/11.

Noticeably, the pivotal politics model does not include a role for political parties. Legislators are individual utility maximizers, rather than partisans seeking the party's collective electoral or policy goals. Parties are aggregations of individuals rather than players endowed with formal agenda-setting or -blocking rights. One of the model's nice features is that it helps to explain why unified party control often fails to produce major policy change. Failure to secure the support of the filibuster pivot has hamstrung many a majority party, including Democrats under President Bill Clinton in 1993 when he sought a large stimulus bill and Republicans under President George W. Bush in 2005 when he pushed to privatize Social Security. *Pivotal Politics* also helps to explain the challenges faced by President Obama's Democratic majority in 2010 after the loss of its filibuster-proof Senate majority, requiring compromise with the Republicans, for example, to write the Dodd-Frank Act that revamped the financial regulatory system.

The model also suggests that legislative gridlock will occur in periods of divided government, for instance, with a Republican-controlled Congress and a Democrat in the White House. In this scenario, a conservative congressional majority's effort to move policy to the right would be thwarted by a left-side filibuster pivot, as well as by a left-side presidential veto. The veto pivot, whose vote would be necessary to override the president's veto, is also unlikely to prefer the conservative majority's proposed policies. For example, Republican efforts in 2015 to repeal Obamacare and Dodd-Frank and to authorize construction of the Keystone pipeline faltered in the face of Democratic threats to filibuster and Obama vetoes.

The broader implication of both the Mayhew and Krehbiel models is that policy change is likely only when large, bipartisan coalitions agree that major change is necessary to resolve public problems. Moreover, Krehbiel's model helps to account for other empirical regularities identified by Mayhew, including the "honeymoon" effect that helps new presidents to secure major policy change. The pivotal politics model suggests that gridlock would indeed be broken if a new president pushes major change when he inherits extreme status quo policies that are out of step with both his views and those of new congressional majorities.

In the two decades since the publication of *Pivotal Politics*, other legislative scholars have challenged Mayhew and Krehbiel's nonpartisan accounts by building theories that expect there to be party influence over the shape of policy outcomes. In my own work on gridlock, discussed below, I suggest that both interbranch and intrabranch conflict—conditioned by partisan and institutional forces—shape the prospects for major legislative change (Binder 2003). First, I show that the degree of partisan polarization matters: ideologically distant, cohesive parties make harder both the crafting of large bipartisan majorities and the harnessing of public support necessary for durable policy change. Second, I suggest that intrabranch conflict is a subtle barrier to legislative action, showing that bicameral differences within a party limit Congress's legislative capacity. Other scholars, such as Frances Lee (2016), suggest that policy deadlock ensues in electorally competitive eras: opposition parties have few incentives to negotiate agreements if they believe they will recapture control of both branches in the near future. Messaging rather than legislating becomes the order of the day. Taken together, such accounts suggest that electoral, partisan, and institutional forces collectively shape the prospects for legislating in polarized times. More often than not, when bipartisan agreement is out of reach, the parties opt to campaign on issues rather than take credit for new laws.

PATTERNS IN POSTWAR LAWMAKING

To measure legislative deadlock, I isolate salient issues on the nation's agenda and then determine the legislative fate of each issue in each Congress (for details, see Binder 2003, chap. 3). The result is a ratio of failed measures to all issues on the agenda for each Congress. The measure nicely captures past episodes of Congress's legislative performance. Lyndon Johnson's Great Society Congress is the most productive of the postwar period; the 2013–2014 Obama Congress (in which Republicans drove the government to shut down and to nearly default on its debt), the most deadlocked. Such assessments comport with historical and contemporary coverage of Congress and the president's postwar performance.

In *Stalemate*, I identify every policy issue on the legislative agenda based on the issues discussed in the unsigned editorials in the *New York Times*. Using the level of *Times* attention to an issue in any given Congress as an indicator of issue salience, I locate for each Congress between the Eightieth

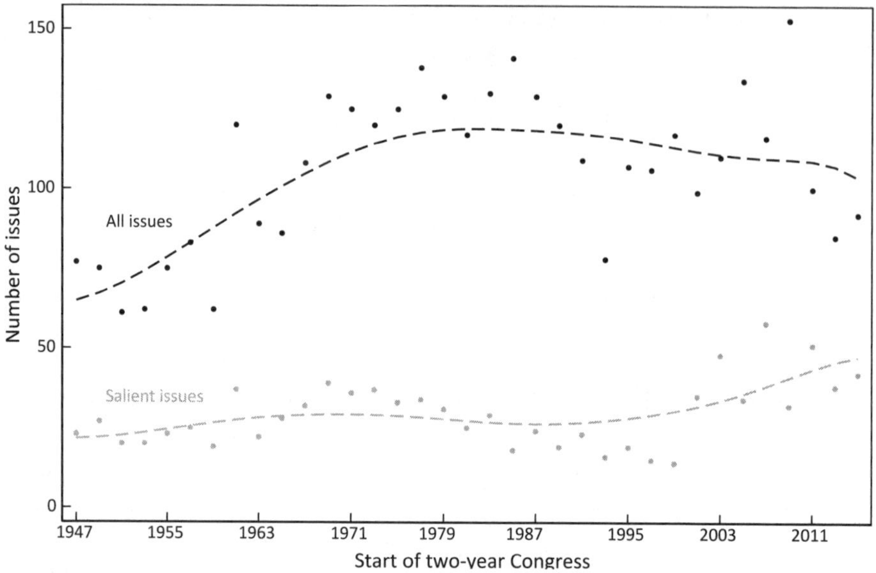

Figure 3.1: Number of Issues on the Legislative Agenda, 1947–2016. *Source:* Binder (2003, 2014), as updated by author.

(1947–1948) and the 114th (2015–2016) the most salient issues on the legislative agenda. I then turn to news coverage and congressional documents to determine whether or not Congress and the president took legislative action in that Congress to address each salient issue. The measurement strategy produces a denominator of every major legislative issue raised by elite observers of Capitol Hill and a numerator that captures Congress's record in acting on those issues. The resulting gridlock score captures the percentage of agenda items left in limbo at the close of each Congress.

Figure 3.1 displays the size of the policy agenda through 2016.[1] Looking first at the smoothed trend line in the total number of legislative issues mentioned each Congress in the *Times* editorials ("All issues"), the size of the overall agenda increases as expected with the arrival of large liberal majorities during the mid-1960s and stays at this expanded level through the advent of the civil rights, environmental, and women's movements of the 1970s. Only in later years do we see a slight increase in the size of the agenda, no doubt reflecting both later efforts to renew the spate of landmark laws of the earlier, activist period and newer issues brought to the fore by the war on terror, global climate change, and so on.

The trend in the number of salient issues is more eye-catching. The overall size of the agenda increases only incrementally over the most recent decade, but the number of salient issues rises markedly in the most recent Congresses. Possibly the recent rise in deadlock has helped to fuel expansion of the agenda: big issues remain unsolved and thus recur on the nation's agenda in the following years. Failure to address reform of immigration law, entitlement programs, and the tax code, for example, likely helped to increase the number of salient issues on the agenda during the Obama years. Moreover, a spate of new issues in the past decade likely caught the attention of the *Times*' editorial writers, including homeland security, global warming, cyber security, US wars in Iraq and Afghanistan, the onset of financial crisis, and the worst economy since the Great Depression.

Five features stand out in patterns of legislative deadlock on salient issues (figure 3.2). First, the frequency of deadlock rises steadily over time. Perceptions that Congress struggles more today than it did decades ago hit the mark. Second, the direst claims about congressional performance during the Obama administration are true. Despite a remarkably productive Congress in 2009 and 2010, when Obama enjoyed a filibuster proof, 60-vote majority in the Senate for several months, most of the Obama years are marked by record levels of deadlock. By this measure, the 113th Congress appears to be the "worst Congress ever"—at least since the series begins after the end of World War II. In fairness, the title should be shared with the last Congress of the Clinton administration in 1999–2000 and with the dismal 112th Congress (2011–2012). In all three Congresses, lawmakers and the president deadlocked on almost three-quarters of the most salient issues on the agenda. It's no surprise that public approval of the 113th Congress bottomed out at 7 percent when legislative stalemate closed down nonessential parts of the federal government for three weeks. Only after securing Senate control in 2014 did Senate Majority Leader Mitch McConnell (R-KY) vow to show voters that they could entrust Republicans with power (Min and Burgess 2015). Indeed, gridlock eased in 2015 and 2016: Congress and the president addressed several salient policy issues: revamping education laws, bolstering highway funding, and reforming Medicare payment systems.

Third, caution is in order when comparing recent Congresses. Some of the issues considered "successfully" addressed today might not have previously been seen as legislative accomplishments. For example, Congress and the president traditionally fund federal highway construction for multiyear periods. Following expiration of highway programs in 2009, however, it took more than thirty short-term extensions of the highway program before

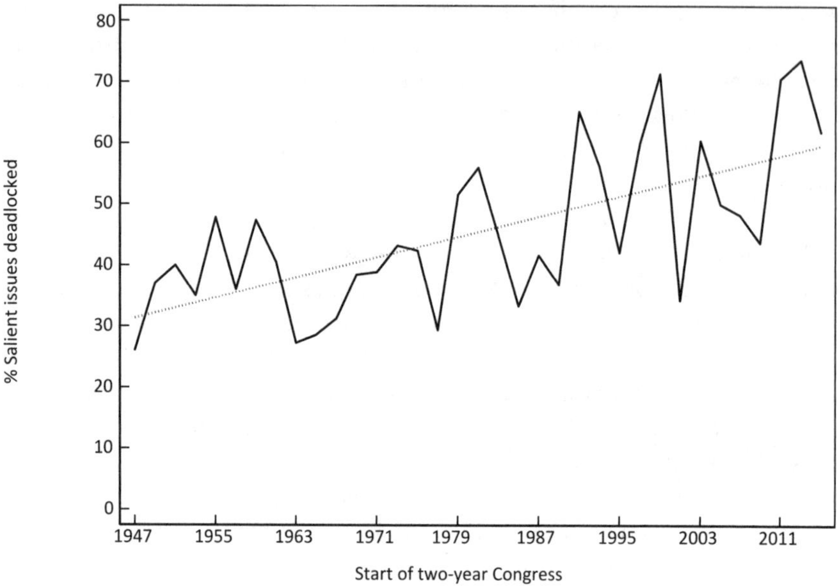

Figure 3.2: Frequency of Legislative Gridlock, 1947–2016. *Source*: Binder (2003, 2014), as updated by author.

the two parties finally agreed to a fully funded, multiyear bill late in 2015. Two-week extensions seem like obvious failed efforts to reauthorize highway spending. But what about the two-year highway bill adopted in 2012 that fell four years short of the traditional six-year bill? I consider that highway bill as a success, even though the bill punted on funding highway construction after the first two years. Lawmakers did not resolve the financial impasse until late in the fall of 2015 when legislators raided the capital surplus of the Federal Reserve to replenish the highway trust fund (Rubin 2015). Similarly, Congress and the president reached an agreement to raise the government's debt limit in the summer of 2011 that included creation of a special committee to generate more than a trillion dollars in federal savings. I consider the 2011 deficit reduction package to be a legislative "success," even though the resulting "Super Committee" deadlocked. The frequency of deadlock in the Obama years likely underestimates the challenges of legislating in highly polarized times.

Fourth, President Obama's first Congress from 2009 to 2010 (111th Congress) achieved a substantially greater share of its agenda than Congress's performances over the previous decade (with the exception of the 9/11 Congress). But the 111th Congress fell far shy of the records of unified Democratic Congresses under President Johnson's Great Society. Granted, the 111th Congress was nearly thirty points more productive than the Obama Congresses that followed, overhauling the health care and financial regulatory systems and enacting landmark stimulus measures in the wake of the financial crisis. But the widely-heralded 111th Congress still left a hefty list of issues in limbo, including proposals to revamp secondary education programs and address global warming, gun ownership, and immigration reform. Even with control of the White House and large Democratic majorities, Obama's party struggled to surmount barriers to major policy change.

Fifth, a brief look at the 107th Congress's performance in the wake of the attacks of September 11, 2001, is instructive. Overall, the 107th Congress (with unified Republican control of both branches for just a few months early in 2001) was fairly productive, stalemating on just one-third of the policy agenda in 2001 and 2002. But lawmakers' capacity to make deals was directly shaped by the events of 9/11. Eight of the thirty-five salient issues on the agenda that Congress addressed stemmed directly from the attacks of September 11. And on those eight issues, Congress and the president mustered a perfect record: they enacted the Patriot Act, wrote the Authorization for the Use of Military Force, addressed the needs of 9/11 victims, and more. Even on less salient issues stemming from September 11, congressional deadlock was extraordinarily rare, with just a single issue left in legislative limbo.

Still, cooperative spirit was short-lived. If we exclude the issues related to the terrorist attacks, Congress and the president deadlocked on just under half of their salient policy issues. Congress appears to have retained the capacity to act swiftly when some crises occur, as also evidenced by Congress's October 2008 bailout of Wall Street after the Federal Reserve and Treasury allowed Lehman Brothers to go under just weeks before. However, legislative unity dissipates when Congress turns its attention back to its normal policy agenda. Moreover, not every crisis spurs action. Despite overwhelming majorities in favor of tougher limits on gun purchases after the mass killing of schoolchildren in Newtown, Connecticut, in 2012, Congress and the president failed to enact any changes to gun ownership laws. Measures considered in the Democratic-controlled Senate failed to surpass the sixty-vote threshold agreed to by both parties for adopting any proposal regulating guns, and a GOP-controlled House showed little interest in legislating new controls on gun ownership.

EXPLAINING LEGISLATIVE DEADLOCK

In my initial study of legislative stalemate, spanning the Truman through Clinton administrations, unified party control of Congress and the White House significantly bolstered Congress's legislative performance. In contrast, split party control of Congress and the White House empowered opposition parties to block policy measures they opposed, generating higher levels of stalemate during periods of divided government. Still, more matters than just party control. First, stalemate was more frequent when Congress's political center was smaller.[2] The emergence of polarized political parties, even before the Bush and Obama presidencies, complicated the challenge of building coalitions capable of overcoming Capitol Hill veto points. Second, bicameral policy differences complicated the formation of winning coalitions, even in periods of unified party control.[3] Although electoral and policy differences between the branches tend to garner the most attention in Washington, bicameral policy differences also appear to undermine lawmakers' legislative capacity. Certainly the 2010 and 2012 congressional elections—handing control of the House to Republicans while keeping the Senate and White House in Democratic hands—generated bicameral conflict that contributed to record levels of deadlock after Obama's first two years in office.

When I expand my purview beyond the initial *Stalemate* study to include the sixteen years of the George W. Bush and Obama administrations, I find that partisan polarization remains consequential.[4] Declining moderation—controlling for party control, bicameral conflict, and the state of the federal budget—still generates more frequent bouts of deadlock.[5] With moderation at barely one-tenth of its postwar high, nearly 75 percent of salient issues were mired in deadlock in 2013 and 2014. Regardless of whether we view polarization as a function of ideological differences, strategic disagreement by partisans seeking electoral advantage, or a mix of the two, the results are clear: when ideological or electoral incentives yield intensely partisan behavior, lawmakers and the president struggle to find broadly palatable, bipartisan solutions to the range of problems they face (Gilmour 1995). Counter to the expectations of the American Political Science Association's classic 1951 statement, *Towards a More Responsible Party System,* loyal, cohesive parties undermine rather than facilitate problem-solving in Congress.

In contrast, the impact of party control on legislating over the longer period appears attenuated. On average, once we control for the polarized nature of today's parties, we find that unified governments are hardly more productive than divided ones. To be sure, unified Democratic control of government after the election of 2008, coupled with a short-lived filibuster proof Senate majority of sixty Democratic senators, yielded major legislative dividends in 2009 and 2010: Congress and the president crafted the Affordable Care Act, rewired the nation's financial sector in the Dodd-Frank Wall Street Reform Act, advanced major arms control, and dumped the military's "Don't ask, don't tell" policy, among other accomplishments. But the impact of unified party control more generally over the longer period is harder to detect.

Why does it seem that unified party control has lost its firepower? The recent, rising proclivity of opposition party senators to insist on sixty votes for adoption of most amendments and measures likely undermines the legislative power of majority parties in periods of unified party control (see Smith 2014). For example, increased minority party exploitation of its parliamentary rights would help to explain the litany of legislative measures left in limbo after Senate Democrats lost their filibuster-proof majority in the winter of 2010, as well as the heavy load of measures left undone at the close of the Republican-led 108th Congress (2003-2004). Rising polarization—as well as increased electoral competition (Lee 2016)—increases the incentives for the opposition party to insist on sixty votes, undermining the traditional power of unified party control in driving legislative agreements. It could well be that Mayhew's focus on crosscurrents that run within the parties also helps to explain why Congress now seems no more productive in unified than divided periods. But why such crosscurrents might be more pressing today than in the past years seems tough to explain in today's more intensely polarized era.

The updated data also suggest that bicameral differences no longer diminish the prospects for lawmaking. That said, my measure of bicameral differences (which taps the level of discord when the chambers review decisions of House-Senate conference committees) is itself a victim of rising partisanship: Congress rarely goes to conference anymore to resolve bicameral disagreements. The sharp decline in conferencing partially reflects the overall decline in major lawmaking in Congress. But it also reflects the increased centralization of decision-making in Congress: leaders and staff are more likely to negotiate deals behind closed doors rather than the typically more open forum of a conference committee under the guidance of committee chairs. Avoiding conference also precludes the need to build a supermajority to defeat a filibuster of the motion to go to conference. Whatever the reason, the measure no longer offers a robust way to capture the degree of bicameral conflict. In short, the model likely underestimates the impact of bicameral disagreement on Congress's ability to solve problems. After all, we know that the two chambers have taken markedly different approaches to numerous salient issues in recent years, including climate change, reform of immigration laws, and repeal of Obamacare and Dodd-Frank. Summed up, electoral, partisan, and institutional forces systematically influence the prospects for major change in Washington, indelibly shaping the legislative interactions of Congress and the president.

LESSONS FROM THE OBAMA YEARS

The relationship between the Obama White House and Congress illustrates the difficulties of governing in a polarized era: the Constitution forces the branches of government to share power, but political and institutional forces today complicate the parties' ability to resolve differences. These lessons offered by the Obama presidency remind us about the power and limits of unified party control of government, as well as the fragility of the concept of bipartisanship in polarized times. Still, the Obama years also remind us that the parties often retain incentives to cooperate despite the intensity of partisan competition in Washington—suggesting a limited but important capacity for deal-making, even in a polarized era.

To understand the governing challenges faced by the Obama administration, I return to Senator McConnell's vow to make Obama a one-term president. McConnell waited until the fall of 2010 to declare his party's goal. But his party's strategy colored all eight years of the Obama administration. As McConnell stated that fall: "We worked very hard to keep our fingerprints off of these proposals, because we thought—correctly, I think—that the only way the American people would know that a great debate was going on was if the measures were not bipartisan. When you hang the "bipartisan" tag on something, the perception is that differences have been worked out, and there's broad agreement that that's the way forward" (as cited in Klein 2016). As political analyst Ezra Klein (2016) summed up McConnell's strategy, "Bipartisanship isn't a function of the ideas in a policy proposal; it's a function of whether the minority party signs on to a policy proposal."

Seeking to derail Obama's proposals, House and Senate GOP leaders cajoled rank and file Republicans to resist collaborating and negotiating with Democrats on most salient measures (see Mann and Ornstein 2016). To do otherwise would signal GOP acceptance of Obama's initiatives—if not his presidency. Even on must-pass measures, such as annual spending bills and the periodic requirement that Congress raise the government's legal borrowing limit, GOP leaders stalled until the last minute, hoping brinkmanship would afford them leverage. What's more, Republican-aligned media (such as Fox News) and other organizations (such as Heritage Action, the activist arm of the conservative Heritage Foundation think tank) pressed Republicans to resist Obama's proposals by threatening to cooperate with Democrats by supporting a primary challenge on the lawmaker's right flank.

McConnell's strategy paid dividends for Republicans. First, GOP tactics limited the power of unified party control to deliver substantial policy gains to the party in power. During Obama's first two years in office, Republicans largely refused to cooperate with the Democrats' efforts to stimulate the economy in the wake of the worst financial crisis since the Great Depression of the 1930s, to rewire the nation's financial regulatory system, and to revamp the nation's health-care system. Their strategy left Democrats to cobble mostly partisan coalitions for the most salient problems on the agenda—exposing them to charges of partisan maneuvering and overreach, even when Democrats adopted proposals that Republicans had previously championed. For example, Democrats based Obamacare largely on "RomneyCare," the health-care model adopted in Massachusetts by future 2012 Republican presidential nominee, Mitt Romney. Similarly, in crafting the Dodd-Frank Wall Street Reform Act, Democrats adopted key proposals from the GOP, including the proposal to require the Federal Reserve to dedicate a steady stream of funding to finance the new Consumer Financial Protection Bureau. Despite their genesis in GOP ideas, both programs were relentlessly attacked by Republicans after enactment—generating legislative efforts to repeal them and legal challenges to their constitutionality.

Second, McConnell's strategy surely contributed to Democrats' 2010 loss of the House and 2014 loss of the Senate. Taking advantage of an increasingly partisan electorate—one that often favors Republicans in off-year elections—Republicans recruited a cadre of Tea Party–inspired and other political newcomers who successfully nationalized the midterm elections as referenda on Obama's record. To be sure, fermenting Republican opposition among the electorate also put the party's leadership in the grassroots' crosshairs. Speaker John Boehner (R-OH) and House Majority Leader Eric Cantor (R-VA) both lost their jobs: Cantor lost his primary election in 2014, and Boehner resigned in the face of a right-wing revolt inside his party conference in 2015. Still, the party's opposition to Obama eventually empowered Republicans to take back control of both branches of government, ending a short-lived experiment in Democratic control of government.

Third, McConnell's ploy also empowered Republicans to influence the ideological contour of the Supreme Court even when their party was shut out of the White House. McConnell extended his tactic of resolute opposition to Obama by refusing to allow Senate consideration of the president's pick for the Supreme Court after the sudden death of conservative justice Antonin Scalia early in 2016. Most Republicans running for reelection in 2016—even those facing voters in states won by Obama in 2012—supported the GOP's refusal to consider or vote on the nomination of US Court of Appeals judge Merrick Garland for the Supreme Court, even though Garland had previously received support from conservative Senate Republicans. Democrats highlighted Republicans' brazen disregard for advice and consent in their widespread unwillingness to even meet with the president's nominee. Although Republicans claimed that the Senate typically refrains from considering Supreme Court nominees during a presidential election year, neutral observers suggested their claims were historically inaccurate and constitutionally suspect (as fact-checked by Carroll 2016). McConnell's actions raised the strong possibility that future Supreme Court vacancies might only be filled when the president's party controls the Senate.

Still, McConnell's strategy was not entirely cost-free, especially in the realm of advice and consent. Repeated GOP filibusters of executive and judicial branch nominees in 2013 convinced Democrats to curtail filibusters of any nominee save for the Supreme Court—in Senate parlance, known as "going nuclear." The immediate spark was a set of Republican filibusters against three Obama nominees to the DC Court of Appeals in 2013. Some Republicans opposed the nominees on ideological grounds; others admitted that they sought to stop Obama from adding Democratic judges to a circuit evenly balanced with both parties' appointees. More broadly, the battle reflected years of partisan frustration: Democrats added up GOP efforts to block Obama's agenda and his picks for prime appointments and collectively lit the fuse. Democrats went nuclear through a series of procedural motions that created a new interpretation of Senate rules: only fifty-one votes (rather than sixty) would now be required to cut off debate and bring a nomination to an up or down vote. McConnell deemed Majority Leader Harry Reid's action a "power grab," calling it "a sad day in the history of the Senate" (as quoted in Kane 2013).

By going nuclear, Senate Democrats empowered the president to more fully fill the ranks of the executive branch and the federal courts. Before the Senate went nuclear at the end of 2013, roughly thirty nominees had been confirmed to the federal trial and appellate courts. One year later, the

Senate had confirmed nearly one hundred nominees who had either been pending when Democrats went nuclear or were nominated afterward. Overall, the Senate confirmed 90 percent of the president's judicial nominees in the 113th Congress—a success rate last achieved in the late 1980s. After Republicans took back control of the Senate in the elections of 2014, the GOP-led Senate ground advice and consent for Obama nominees to a near halt.

Finally, winning back control of the Senate in 2014 led McConnell to revise his playbook for the final two years of the Obama administration. With control of Congress in GOP hands and a wide-open race for the White House approaching in 2016, McConnell adopted a minimally more constructive legislative stance, telling his colleagues that the party needed accomplishments to run on in 2016. "I don't want the American people to think that if they add a Republican president to a Republican Congress, that's going to be a scary outcome. I want the American people to be comfortable with the fact that the Republican House and Senate is a responsible, right-of-center, governing majority," McConnell noted late in 2014 (as cited in Kane 2015).

Toward that end, Republicans in 2015 came to the negotiating table to resolve long-stalemated problems in health, education, and the economy. Among other deal-making, the two parties resolved the annual "doc fix" cliffhanger that required changes to Medicare reimbursement formulas, overhauled the long-expired No Child Left Behind education law, negotiated a two-year budget deal to prevent scheduled cuts in domestic and defense funding, and provided long-term funding for federal highway and mass transit programs. In each of these bipartisan bargains, both parties brought to the table their most preferred policies, often crafting "win-win" deals that combined the top priorities of both parties (Binder and Lee 2015). For example, to finally resolve the "doc fix" stalemate, lawmakers matched Republicans' preference for Medicare cuts with Democrats' desire to expand funding for community health programs. Both parties gained from coming to the negotiating table. Of course, McConnell encouraged resolution of these long-stalled proposals to ensure that Senate Republicans running for reelection in blue states in 2016 would have a record to run on—confirming as always the power of electoral prospects to condition governing strategies. Although the 2016 elections diminished GOP margins in both chambers, Republicans kept control of Congress and returned the White House to the GOP.

LESSONS FROM THE TRUMP YEARS

McConnell's strategy might have aided the election of Donald Trump in 2016: undermining Obama legislative record fueled public dissatisfaction with Washington and with Democrats' capacity to solve public problems. In that sense, McConnell's strategy succeeded: the return of unified GOP control for the first time since 2006 promised Republicans a straight course to achieve the GOP's right-of-center agenda, including cutting taxes, repealing Obamacare, and paring back government regulation of the economy. Assisted by Democrats' ban on filibustering most presidential nominations, Republicans stood poised at the outset of 2017 to reverse Obama's policy legacy.

Ironically, Trump's election threw a wrench in McConnell's expectation of a center-right governing majority. To be sure, many of Trump's priorities overlapped with those of conservatives—including tax cuts, deregulation, repeal of Obamacare, and confirming conservative judges to the federal bench. But major components of Trump's electoral appeal were ideologically at odds with the views of "establishment" conservative lawmakers: protectionism over free trade, fiscal stimulus instead of austerity, saving rather than cutting entitlements, threatening in place of strengthening ties with international allies, and embracing instead of challenging Russian leader Vladimir Putin. After the November 2016 elections and into early 2017, tensions amongst GOP elites aired publicly as Trump assembled his administration and some Republicans staked out positions that challenged his priorities.

The Republican Congress achieved a middling record before losing control of the House in the 2018 midterm elections. On popular issues with Democratic support, Congress and Trump made progress: lifting spending caps on both domestic and defense spending in a two-year budget deal, paring back of some Dodd-Frank financial regulations, increasing funding to address the opioids crisis, and imposing new sanctions on Russia and North Korea. Beyond those generally popular, bipartisan solutions, however, Republicans struggled to advance their agenda (Curry and Lee 2019). They even occasionally put up road blocks to the president's agenda, opposing funding for the border wall, pushing the administration to end its family separation policy at the border, and hemming in the president's ability to remove troops from South Korea, among other limits.

In the face of extreme partisan differences and a slim Senate majority, Republicans discovered the limited firepower of unified party control in polarized times. On most other major issues, Republicans struggled to legislate. GOP difficulties encouraged Republicans to find ways to legislate without the need for Democratic votes. First, they cut parliamentary corners in ways that limited the blocking power of Senate Democrats, for instance, lowering the threshold to a simple majority to cut off debate on Supreme Court nominations (Binder 2018). Second, they exploited laws that banned filibusters, thereby allowing Republicans to move by majority vote. For example, Republicans deployed the Congressional Review Act (CRA) to reverse more than a dozen Obama-era rules by majority vote. Such action allowed Republicans to make a down payment on their vow to deregulate energy, financial, and other sectors. But given the limited applicability of the CRA, Republicans scarcely dented the Obama administration's broader regulatory gains. To be sure, agencies headed by Trump appointees made dozens of moves to deregulate across the environmental, energy, banking, and other sectors, but litigation tied up vast numbers of those efforts in federal court. More broadly, Trump largely proved unable beyond landmark tax cuts to exploit his legislative majorities to secure more of his agenda.

Viewed more broadly, efforts to bend the rules can limit the policy reach of ambitious majorities. The most visible illustration occurred when Republicans avoided a Democratic filibuster by exploiting the Congressional Budget Act to attempt repeal of the Affordable Care Act (ACA). Tough limits on the use of the Act's "reconciliation" rules complicated Republicans' pursuit of their agenda. Divisions within the GOP—coupled with parliamentary constraints known as the "Byrd Rule" embedded in the Budget Act—foiled the GOP push to repeal and replace the ACA. Procedural rules also affected the breadth and durability of Republican tax cuts in 2017: Republicans gave permanent tax cuts to the wealthy and corporations while sun-setting reductions for the middle class. This decision undercut the political value of tax cuts on the campaign trail in the 2018 midterms. Unwilling to make the sorts of concessions necessary to secure any Democratic votes, Republicans engineered remarkably unpopular tax cuts. That said, slim majorities confirmed record numbers of conservative judges to the federal bench. Early in Trump's fourth year in office, about a third of the new Trump-appointed appellate and district court judges replaced jurists appointed by Democratic presidents (Wheeler 2020). Republicans also confirmed two conservative Supreme Court justices after McConnell led his Republican colleagues to ban Supreme Court filibusters.

Republicans on Capitol Hill do not shoulder all of the blame for their stunted policy success. At the end of his second year in office, Trump proved an undisciplined and historically unpopular president. His weak approval generated leeway for Democratic and Republican lawmakers to resist his policy overtures. The problem was not strictly the president's poor command of policy detail. Equally (or perhaps more) problematic for Republicans: lawmakers could not trust the president to stick to his policy pronouncements. Trump, for example, declared the House ACA repeal bill "mean"—even after celebrating House passage in 2017 in a Rose Garden event. Democrats targeted centrists who voted for the bill (as well as conservatives more broadly) during midterm campaigns for supporting an unpopular bill. (Some lost their 2018 races even after voting against the bill.) Similar scenarios played out when the president vowed to curtail gun ownership after the mass school shooting in Parkland, Florida, and protect Deferred Action for Childhood Arrivals (DACA) "Dreamers." After televised statements, Trump quickly retreated and blamed Democrats for the ensuing stalemate. Given disagreements within the Republican Party—even in a period of polarization and intense partisanship—Trump's inability to pave the way forward on contested policy squandered any further policy gains for the Republican Congress.

Democrats' capture of the House in the 2018 midterm elections ushered in split party control of Congress. On cue, the splintered branches and Congress stalemated over funding the government, precipitating a record-long government shutdown that began in December 2018 and lasted well into January after Democrats took up House gavels. Remarkably, Trump took credit for the shutdown, thinking that closing the government would force Congress to better fund his campaign-promised border wall. Ultimately, Trump backed down and the government opened without a congressional commitment to fund the wall. But frustrated by bipartisan resistance in both chambers, Trump secured billions for his border wall by invoking the National Emergencies Act—allowing the administration to divert previously appropriated funds for military construction projects. As lawmakers and the public discovered, supermajorities in both chambers are necessary to protect Congress's core power of the purse.

Apart from a bipartisan budget deal that burst spending caps on both domestic and defense spending in the summer of 2019, Congress and the president failed to agree on most other issues. One exception was passage of the United States-Mexico-Canada trade deal, a top priority of the Trump administration. House Democrats insisted on significant amendments, and GOP lawmaker and the White House eventually folded to their demands. Otherwise, the more common pattern consisted of the Democratic House—but not the GOP Senate—passing major bills, such as to lower prescription drug prices, reform the nation's electoral laws, and address climate change. As of early in Trump's fourth year in office, such measures piled up on the Senate's doorstep with little chance of enactment.

More dramatically, Congress and the president focused their attention at the end of 2019 and early 2020 on Democrats' effort to impeach the president. After the Republican-led Senate acquitted President Trump, the president embarked on a retribution tour, ordering the firing of impeachment witnesses who testified against him and all but interfering in several highly salient federal criminal prosecutions of both perceived friends and perceived enemies. In the immediate wake of impeachment in early 2020, few expected the president to engage in any significant legislative efforts in the run-up to the 2020 presidential election. The contrast to the aftermath of Bill Clinton's impeachment is instructive, though limited. Clinton explicitly apologized to the public for the transgressions that provoked his impeachment by the GOP-led House. But his impeachment took place in an entirely different electoral context: the country was two years out from the next election, and the Constitution precluded Clinton from running again. Of course, both the Clinton and Trump impeachments took place in a period of historically high gridlock in the postwar era, so few expected that either president would end his term after impeachment with any remarkable legislative achievements.

CONCLUSION

It is difficult to turn the ship of state in postwar American national politics. Bipartisan agreement is necessary to overcome innumerable veto points in our constitutional system and is tough to build, especially in today's era of intensely polarized and competitive political parties. To be sure, policy change can occur despite congressional inaction and is often termed "policy drift": for example, blocking change in the law setting a federal minimum wage undermines the minimum wage because the law does not index the benefit for inflation (Patashnik 2015). More broadly, the alignment of partisan and institutional interests necessary to circumvent barriers to change complicates efforts to resolve even widely recognized problems, from underinvestment in the nation's infrastructure to the high cost of prescription drugs. And even past successful efforts to address public problems can suffer from deferred maintenance: "Existing policies require upkeep and maintenance if they are to continue to function well" (Mettler 2016, 369).

That said, the broader conditions that challenge Congress predate the Trump presidency. Intensely polarized and competitive parties, often facing internal rifts, help to diminish the legislative capacity of our national legislature. Half-measures, second bests, and just-in-time legislating—or no action at all—are now the norm. To be sure, unified party control retains some punch. But its firepower has diminished as Congress has polarized into competing partisan teams. Perhaps, as Mayhew suggests, partisan thrusts have always been challenged by crosscutting currents. But with the rise in polarized and competitive parties over the past quarter century come more cohesive opposition parties often intent on depriving legislative majorities of policy victories, a dynamic that no doubt underlies the broad rise in legislative deadlock over the postwar era. Regardless of why stalemate is rising, these legislative difficulties have been costly—both to the long-term fiscal health of the country and to citizens' trust in government. Even if the parties' political incentives eventually compel them to meet more often at the bargaining table, regenerating public trust remains a difficult task for the future.

NOTES

1. Binder (2014, 20–22) explains the methodological challenges encountered in updating the dataset.

2. To capture legislative moderation, I built a measure of the size of the political center based on voting scores generated by Keith Poole and Howard Rosenthal's NOMINATE system. As detailed in Binder (2003), I determined the number of "moderate" legislators in each chamber each Congress and divided the percentage of moderates by the ideological distance between the two chamber parties. I then averaged both chamber's moderation to create a single moderation score for each Congress. I define "moderate" as a legislator whose first dimension DW-NOMINATE ideological score places him or her closer to the ideological median of the chamber than to her or his own party's median. Dividing by party distance helps to distinguish Congresses both by the size and by the relative location of the political center. For instance, a Congress with a small political center coupled with ideologically proximate parties would score stronger on the "moderation" scale than a Congress with a small political center but ideologically distant parties. Because of changes in the availability of DW-NOMINATE scores after 2014, I use DW-NOMINATE for the 80th–113th Congress (1947-2014) and Common Space NOMINATE scores for the 114th Congress (2015-2016). The correlation of Common Space and DW-NOMINATE scores is quite high, although the two measures make different theoretical assumptions about the stability of lawmaker voting scores over time. Overall, the correlation of my measure of moderation (which falls with a rise in polarization) and a simple polarization score (distance between the party medians only using Common Space scores) is -0.9.

3. To capture the policy distance between the two chambers, I identified all conference reports considered by both the House and the Senate in each Congress and determined the percentage of each chamber that voted in support of each report.

To measure bicameral policy distance, I calculated the difference in chamber support for each report and generated a mean disagreement score for each Congress. The measure varied from a low of just 2 percent in the early 1950s to a high of more than 10 percent in the mid-1990s.

4. Results available from the author.

5. Budgetary situation is measured as the size of surplus or deficit as a percentage of federal outlays each year. See Office of Management and Budget, "Historical Tables," accessed November 8, 2018: https://www.whitehouse.gov/omb/historical-tables/.

REFERENCES

Binder, Sarah A. "Dodging the Rules in Trump's Republican Congress." *Journal of Politics* 80, no. 4 (2018): 1454–1463.

———. "Polarized We Govern." *Governance Studies Strengthening American Democracy Series* 86 (May 2014): accessed November 4, 2018: http://www.brookings.edu/research/papers/2014/05/27-polarized-we-govern-congress-legislative-gridlock-polarized-binder.

———. *Stalemate.* Washington, DC: Brookings Institution, 2003.

Binder, Sarah A., and Frances E. Lee. "Making Deals in Congress," in *Solutions to Political Polarization in America*, ed. Nathaniel Persily. New York: Cambridge University Press, 2015.

Brady, David, and Craig Volden. *Revolving Gridlock.* Boulder, CO: Westview, 1998.

Carroll, Lauren. "Mitch McConnell Exaggerates 'Tradition' of not Confirming Election Year Supreme Court Nominees." *Politifact* (March 22, 2016): accessed November 8, 2018: http://www.politifact.com/truth-o-meter/statements/2016/mar/22/mitch-mcconnell/mitch-mcconnell-exaggerates-tradition-not-confirmi/.

Curry, James, and Frances E. Lee. "Non-Party Government: Bipartisan Lawmaking and Party Power in Congress." *Perspectives on Politics* 17, no. 1 (2019): 47–65.

Gilmour, John. *Strategic Disagreement: Stalemate in American Politics.* Pittsburgh: University of Pittsburgh Press, 1995.

Kane, Paul. "New Senate Majority Leader's Main Goal for GOP: Don't Be Scary." *Washington Post*, January 4, 2015.

———. "Reid, Democrats Trigger 'Nuclear' Option; Eliminate Most Filibusters on Nominees." *Washington Post*, November 21, 2013.

Kessler, Glenn. "When Did McConnell Say He Wanted to Make Obama a 'One-Term President'?" *Washington Post.* September 25, 2012.

Key, V. O. *Politics, Parties and Pressure Groups.* New York: Ty Crowell, 1964.

Kim, Seung Min, and Burgess Everett. "McConnell Vows Ambitious Agenda in Treacherous 2016." *Politico*, November 14, 2015: accessed November 5, 2018: https://www.politico.com/story/2015/12/mitch-mcconnell-senate-2016-216695.

Klein, Ezra. "Obamacare Didn't Pave the Way for Donald Trump. The GOP's Response to It Did." Vox.com. March 9, 2016: accessed November 8, 2018: http://www.vox.com/policy-and-politics/2016/3/9/11182590/obamacare-donald-trump.

Krehbiel, Keith. *Pivotal Politics.* Chicago: University of Chicago Press, 1998.

Lee, Frances E. *Insecure Majorities: Congress and the Perpetual Campaign.* Chicago: University of Chicago Press, 2016.

Mann, Thomas E., and Norman J. Ornstein. *It's Even Worse Than It Looks.* Rev. ed. New York: Basic, 2016.

Mayhew, David R. "Datasets and Materials: Divided We Govern." Accessed November 4, 2018: http://campuspress.yale.edu/davidmayhew/datasets-divided-we-govern.

———. *Divided We Govern.* New Haven, CT: Yale University Press, 1991.

Mettler, Suzanne. "The Policyscape and the Challenges of Contemporary Politics to Policy Maintenance." *Perspectives on Politics* 14, no. 2 (2016): 369–390.

Patashnik, Eric M. "Paul Pierson's Dismantling the Welfare State: A Twentieth Anniversary Reassessment: Introduction." *P.S. Political Science & Politics* 48, no. 2 (2015): 267–269.

Rubin, Gabe. "Fed Is a 'Piggy Bank' for Highway Bill." *Morning Consult,* December 2, 2015. Accessed November 4, 2018: http://morningconsult.com/2015/12/fed-is-a-piggy-bank-for-highway-bill/.

Smith, Steven S. *The Senate Syndrome: The Evolution of Procedural Warfare in the Modern US Senate.* Norman: University of Oklahoma Press, 2014.

Sundquist, James L. "Needed: A Political Theory for the New Era of Coalition Government in the United States." *Political Science Quarterly* 103 (Winter 1988–1989): 613–635.

Wheeler, Russell. "Judicial Appointments in Trump's First Three Years: Myths and Realities." FixGov. January 28, 2020. Brookings Institution. Accessed February 15, 2020: https://www.brookings.edu/blog/fixgov/2020/01/28/judicial-appointments-in-trumps-first-three-years-myths-and-realities/.

CHAPTER 4

Challenges of Measuring Party Unity in a Polarized Era: The 115th Congress

Frances E. Lee

And to the majority, especially to our returning members, I want to say, "This is a once-in-a-lifetime opportunity." This is the kind of thing that most of us only dream about. I know—because I used to dream about it. The people have given us unified government.

—House Speaker Paul Ryan, "Speaker Ryan's Opening Day Address to the House," January 3, 2017

In his opening day speech, House Speaker Paul Ryan (R-WI) told his fellow Republicans in the 115th Congress that they had been given a once-in-a-lifetime opportunity. Ryan's optimism certainly seemed justified. At the time, the Republican majority in the House (241R–194D) was the largest it had been in unified government since 1925, and the party's Senate majority, albeit thin (52R–48D), afforded more maneuvering room than it had possessed under President George W. Bush in 2001. Republicans in the 115th Congress would seemingly be able to legislate over even total Democratic opposition. Yet the legislative record of the 115th Congress (2017–2018) fell well short of the party's ambitions.

This chapter will first examine the basis for Republican optimism about achieving transformative policy change in the 115th Congress. Namely, the party had a broad-ranging, detailed agenda plan, as well as an established record of party cohesion sufficient to carry legislation even over unified Democratic opposition. The chapter will then take stock of the party's successes and failures, examining where and why Republicans struggled to deliver on their legislative agenda. The narrow Senate majority, well short of the sixty votes necessary to overcome Democratic filibusters, was a key structural obstacle. On some agenda priorities, Republicans were forced to back down from provisions they wanted to enact in order to move legislation through the sixty-vote Senate. But on many of the party's failed agenda items, Republicans were unable to enact legislation because of disunity within their own ranks, not because they were blocked by Democrats' capacity to wield the Senate filibuster. Reviewing the record of the 115th Congress, internal Republican disunity was at least as important a limitation on Republican agenda success as Democratic Party–controlled veto points.

More broadly, I argue that the Republican Party in 2017–2018 was less well-positioned to deliver on its agenda than it appeared because roll-call voting data tends to exaggerate party unity, especially in the contemporary era. Roll-call votes offer limited insight into intraparty disagreement for two key reasons. First, many important policy questions that divide the majority party are poorly represented in the roll-call agenda. In an era when parties caucus much more frequently, a great deal of intraparty deliberation happens outside public view. Deep fissures among Republicans have been evident in other ways, including in leadership turmoil, party factionalism, primary challenges, and news coverage of intraparty dissent.

Second, congressional roll-call votes are used for purposes beyond legislating. In recent years, the roll-call record has been rife with messaging votes that members (1) knew would have no effect on public policy but that (2) affect party image-making. Members' votes on messaging bills are subject to different considerations than their votes on bills that might actually result in law. A roll-call record containing a large share of messaging votes offers a flawed measure of members' policy positions or a party's capacity for cohesion on important legislation.

Taken together, the 115th Congress invites scholars to reexamine their reliance on measures of members' preferences based on roll-call votes. The limited legislative success of Republicans in 2017–2018 makes more sense in light of alternative measures pointing to significant intraparty disagreement on policy and priorities.

REPUBLICAN UNITY AS MEASURED BY ROLL-CALL VOTES

Shortly after his ascent to the speakership in October 2015, Ryan assembled a series of task forces to develop a policy agenda aimed at turning the GOP from an "opposition" party into a "proposition" party. Unveiled in the summer of 2016, the Better Way platform encompassed a sweeping blueprint for a new majority party in control of unified government.[1] When Re-

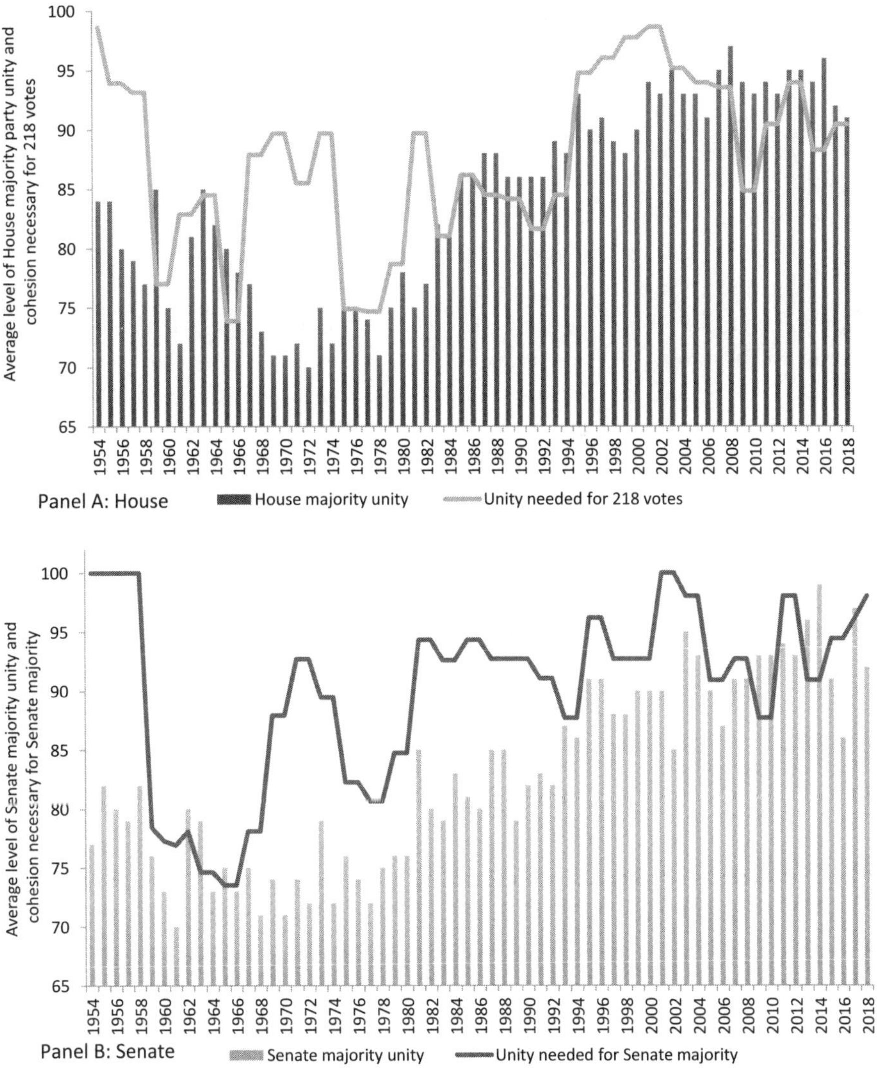

Figure 4.1: Majority Party Cohesion Necessary for Chamber Majorities, 1954–2018. *Source*: Brookings Institution; Congressional Quarterly.

publicans won unified government control in the 2016 elections, they already had a policy agenda in place, positioning the party to move forward quickly. At the Republican retreat in January 2017, President Trump declared, "This Congress is going to be the busiest Congress we've had in decades, maybe ever" (Wagner 2017).

Furthermore, Republican cohesion on roll-call votes would suggest a party ready to move forward on its agenda in lockstep. Figure 4.1 sets party cohesion in the contemporary Congress in the context of all majority parties since 1953. The only Senate majority more unified than the 2017 Republicans (averaging 97 percent cohesion) was the Democratic majority in 2014 (averaging 99 percent cohesion). At 92 percent, the House majority party in 2017–2018 continued the extraordinarily high levels of majority party cohesion maintained since 2000.

Even high levels of party cohesion, however, may not be sufficient to yield a chamber majority. A majority party with a narrow margin of control must marshal very high levels of party cohesion to carry legislation over unified minority party opposition. Since 1994, margins of control in the House and the Senate have been thin compared to the previous postwar era.

Taking into account variation in majority size, the heavy lines in figure 4.1 display the level of cohesion necessary for majority parties to put up a chamber majority from within their own ranks for each Congress since 1953,[2] along with bars showing the majority party's average level of party cohesion each year. As is evident in Panel A, mean House majority party unity has rarely been sufficient to yield a chamber majority without cross-party help. The Democrats of the 1960s and 1970s almost never reached the bar, despite their large majorities. Democrats of the late 1980s had begun to achieve the necessary cohesion before they lost the House majority. Republicans between 1996 and 2005 were highly cohesive, but because their majorities were so thin, they still usually needed some help from Democrats to reach a House majority. But since 2006, majority party cohesion would routinely yield a House majority without any minority party assistance. By this measure, the House Republican Party of the 115th Congress should have been capable of regularly putting up 218 votes without any support from Democrats.

Panel B displays the same data series for the Senate.[3] Of course, the Senate does not operate by majority rule, and so on many measures even a 100 percent unified majority party cannot carry the day. But for those votes on which a simple majority could decide the outcome (Reynolds 2017a), Republicans in 2017 regularly possessed the necessary cohesion to muster a Senate majority without help (as did the Democratic majorities of 2009–2010 and 2013–2014). After the loss of an Alabama Senate seat in January 2018, Republican cohesion fell short of the party unity necessary to pass measures without any minority party support in the 2nd session of the 115th Congress.

In short, Republicans of the 115th Congress had a well-developed policy agenda, unified party control of national government, and a track record of strong party cohesion. Although they would have to deal with a mercurial president whose positions were out of step with party orthodoxy in key ways (Nelson 2018) and the loss of a Senate seat in 2018, Republicans seemingly stood in a strong position to notch major policy achievements.

LEGISLATIVE ACCOMPLISHMENTS OF THE 115TH CONGRESS IN CONTEXT

"'This is our plan for 2017,' said [House Speaker Paul] Ryan, waving a copy of his 'Better Way' policy agenda. 'Much of this you can do through budget reconciliation'" (Weyl 2016). By planning to execute much of the party's agenda via budget reconciliation, Speaker Ryan indicated that House Republicans would proceed, if necessary, without any bipartisan support. Following through on this plan, Republicans passed two budget resolutions and two budget reconciliation bills in 2017.

But by the close of the 115th Congress, Republicans had completed only a fraction of the "Better Way" agenda (see Edwards 2018; Pearson 2017). Table 4.1 benchmarks the 115th Congress's legislative enactments against the agenda items designated as priorities by the majority party leadership. This list of twelve agenda priorities was compiled from the action items mentioned in the opening Congress speeches of Speaker Ryan and Majority Leader Mitch McConnell (R-KY), as well as from the measures slotted into the bill numbers reserved for the majority leadership of the House and Senate. Although immigration policy does not appear in leaders' opening Congress speeches or among the leadership-reserved bills, I also included immigration as a Republican priority considered in the 115th Congress because it was featured in the "Better Way" agenda and was the subject of bills negotiated by party leaders in both House and Senate in 2018.[4] This list of twelve priorities encompasses just a narrow slice of the agenda priorities appearing in the lengthy "Better Way" agenda, most of which never received consideration in the 115th Congress.

THE REPUBLICAN MAJORITY'S AGENDA FAILURES

Out of twelve agenda items in table 4.1, Republicans failed to pass any legislation on five of them. The most spectacular failure occurred on the drive to repeal and replace Obamacare, the party's foremost legislative priority. Republican disunity was on clear display throughout the effort. House Republicans' repeal-and-replace bill (H.R. 1628) initially had to be pulled

Table 4.1: Republican Agenda Priorities, 115th Congress (2017–2018)

Agenda Item	Outcome	Explanation (Path to Success or Cause of Failure)
Obamacare repeal and replacement	Failed	**Intraparty disunity**: The House passed an Obamacare repeal and replace bill (H.R. 1628), but the Senate was unable to clear one, despite the use of budget reconciliation procedures that prohibited filibusters.
Domestic spending cuts	Failed	**Intraparty disunity**: The House passed H.R. 3, rescinding $15 billion in budget authority. But the Senate declined to move forward owing to the opposition of two Republican senators, depriving Senate Republicans of a majority.
Reform agency rulemaking	Failed	**Intraparty disunity**: The House passed H.R. 5 reforming the rulemaking process, but the Senate declined to advance a companion bill from committee.
End taxpayer funding of abortion	Failed	**Intraparty disunity**: The House passed H.R. 7 prohibiting qualified health plans under the ACA from covering abortions, but the Senate did not consider a similar measure.
Immigration reform and border security	Failed	**Intraparty disunity**: Both the House and the Senate considered measures negotiated by Republican leaders to reform immigration and enhance border security. No measure could gain a chamber majority.
Rollback of financial regulations (Dodd-Frank)	Partial success	**Bipartisan support, likely forced by Senate cloture**: Republicans sought broad rollbacks of the 2010 Dodd-Frank reforms, including the House Republicans' far-reaching H.R. 10, but to win Senate approval for S. 2155, they settled for narrow legislation exempting community and regional banks from more stringent regulatory oversight. The resulting legislation passed with Democratic support in both chambers, but a majority of Democrats voted no.

Farm bill	Partial success	**Bipartisan support, likely forced by Senate cloture**: Senate Republicans sought a broadly bipartisan bill, while House Republicans initially passed a partisan bill by a narrow margin (H.R. 2). In the end, House Republicans had to back down on all of their controversial provisions, including work requirements for food stamp recipients. The final legislation passed with overwhelming bipartisan support.
FAA reauthorization	Partial success	**Bipartisan support**: To secure House passage (H.R. 4), Republicans had to drop their bid to privatize air traffic control. The legislation passed both chambers with overwhelming bipartisan margins.
Tax cuts/tax reform	Clear success	**Rolled the minority party**: Using budget reconciliation, House and Senate Republicans were able to push their signature achievement, the Tax Cuts and Jobs Act (H.R. 1), into law without a single Democratic vote in either the House or the Senate.
Obama administration rules rollback	Clear success	**Rolled the minority party**: Under the Congressional Review Act, Republicans were able to roll back fourteen Obama-era regulations on party-line votes.
Opioid crisis response	Clear success	**Bipartisan support sought from the outset**: Both parties wanted to take action on opioids, and the final bill (H.R. 6) was an omnibus combining numerous measures sponsored by members of both parties. The legislation cleared both chambers with overwhelming bipartisan support.
Water resources development	Clear success	**Bipartisan support sought from the outset**: Republicans sought to pass a bipartisan water resources development reauthorization as part of their broad efforts on "infrastructure." The measure (S. 3021) passed with almost unanimous support in both chambers.

from the floor because of a lack of votes. A revised version of the bill narrowly cleared the House in May (217–213), with twenty Republicans voting in opposition.[5] Senate Republican leaders were not able to marshal sufficient votes for their version of repeal-and-replace, the Better Care Reconciliation Act, which never came up for a formal vote. As a last ditch effort, Senate leaders brought a scaled back "skinny repeal" bill to the floor—mainly as a vehicle to continue negotiations with the House—but even this measure failed due to the defections of three Republican senators.[6] In the end, the repeal-and-replace effort had consumed the first nine months of 2017 and was finally abandoned in late September, after Republicans could not marshal support for a last-ditch effort spearheaded by Senators Lindsey Graham (R-SC) and Bill Cassidy (R-LA). With Republicans employing streamlined reconciliation procedures requiring only simple majority support for passage, the party's failure to enact legislation repealing and replacing Obamacare stemmed from insufficient intraparty consensus, not Democratic-controlled veto points.

Republicans also had to abandon their effort to reduce domestic discretionary spending. The first two Trump administration budgets proposed sweeping spending cuts to domestic programs but were treated as dead on arrival in Congress. Rather than cuts, expenditures on domestic programs were raised by 10 percent under the two-year budget agreed to in 2018.[7] Because reconciliation procedures cannot be employed to pass appropriations legislation, the bipartisan deal to increase discretionary spending is attributable to Democrats' ability to use the filibuster to achieve negotiating leverage. But under the Congressional Budget and Impoundment Control Act of 1974, a majority party is empowered to pass rescissions via simple majority vote in both the House and the Senate. Republicans took up such a measure, a $15 billion package of domestic spending cuts, and narrowly passed it in the House (H.R. 3).[8] However, the Senate rejected the rescissions package (48Y–50N) on a procedural vote, with two Republican senators, Richard Burr (R-NC) and Susan Collins (R-ME), voting no.[9] Thus, Republicans' failure to pass any legislation cutting domestic discretionary spending in the 115th Congress must be chalked up to intraparty dissent as much as to Democratic resistance.

Disagreement between House and Senate Republicans on policy priorities was a source of intraparty friction that also resulted in agenda failure. After the House passed a sweeping reform of agency rulemaking (H.R. 5), no Senate committee moved to advance a companion measure. Similarly, the Senate did not act upon the House-passed bill prohibiting qualified health plans under the Affordable Care Act from covering abortion (H.R. 7). Even though it would have been difficult or impossible for Republicans to muster sixty votes for Senate cloture on abortion or agency rulemaking legislation, I could not find evidence that anticipation of Democratic filibusters induced Senate Republicans to hold back on these issues. Given the likely need to win over Senator Susan Collins (R-ME) or Senenator Lisa Murkowski (R-AK), both supporters of abortion rights, Senate Republicans had strong reason for pessimism about getting even majority support for H.R. 7. Both rulemaking reform and abortion rights are sufficiently controversial within Senate Republican ranks to make these House bills a heavy lift for Senate passage.

On immigration, the Republican Party in both the House and the Senate was in general disarray. Even though immigration reform and enforcement issues appeared as priorities on the "Better Way" agenda, Republican leaders were reluctant to bring up the issue in the 115th Congress because of disunity in the party's ranks. The issue came up in the Senate only after a three-day government shutdown in February 2018 when Democrats succeeded in forcing a vote on the fate of the young undocumented "Dreamers."[10] The three resulting Senate votes exposed divisions within the Senate Republican Party on immigration issues, indicating that between four and eight Republican senators favored a narrow border-wall-for-Dreamers deal proposed by Minority Leader Chuck Schumer (D-NY) and fourteen Republican senators opposed the broader immigration reform plan supported by the Trump administration. No Senate proposal could reach sixty votes, but Republicans were well short of unanimity on any one of them.

Likewise, House Republican leaders capitulated to pressure to bring up immigration legislation when a discharge petition drive to force the issue came within two signatures of success. The result was two roll-call votes that similarly exposed divisions on the issue within the House Republican conference. Forty-one House Republicans defected from the hardline proposal favored by House judiciary chair Bob Goodlatte (R-VA).[11] Only about half of House Republicans would support the proposal their own party leaders had negotiated with Republican moderates.[12] At the conclusion of the debate, Representative Jeff Denham (R-CA) said, "What was obvious today is that Republicans cannot pass a 218 Republican [immigration] bill" (Siegel and Parkinson 2018).

From these cases, it is clear that Republicans were far short of intraparty consensus, even on the select few agenda priorities they took up for consideration. Despite the party's impressive roll-call voting cohesion statistics, the failures of Republicans to pass a number of their agenda items in the 115th Congress resulted from intraparty disagreement rather than Democratic veto players.

THE REPUBLICAN MAJORITY'S CLEAR AGENDA SUCCESSES

Of the twelve agenda items in table 4.1, Republicans achieved four clear successes. By "clear success," I mean legislation was enacted without Republicans having to significantly scale back their stated policy ambitions along the way.

The major legislative achievement of the 115th Congress was the Tax Cuts and Jobs Act (TCJA). The TCJA (H.R. 1) sharply and permanently lowered tax rates for corporations, dramatically reduced taxes on the foreign profits of US companies, limited and eliminated many tax deductions for individuals while raising the standard deduction, exempted more taxpayers from the alternative minimum tax and the estate tax, and temporarily lowered individual income tax rates. The TCJA included two other top Republican Party priorities: opening the Arctic National Wildlife Refuge to oil and natural gas drilling and abolishing the Affordable Care Act's individual mandate. Enacted via budget reconciliation procedures, the TCJA passed over the opposition of all Democrats in both the House and the Senate.

In addition to the TCJA, Republicans achieved a second clear agenda victory in a series of regulatory rollbacks of agency rules adopted in the last sixty days of the Obama administration. Using the streamlined procedures of the Congressional Review Act prohibiting Senate filibusters, Republicans overturned fourteen agency rules on party-line votes without support from Democrats.[13]

Republicans also achieved two other clear agenda successes on the strength of broad, bipartisan majorities: a water resources development bill, and a response to the opioid crisis (H.R. 6). The SUPPORT for Patients and Communities Act was a modest measure bundling together many smaller measures sponsored by both Republicans and Democrats that did not commit any large-scale or long-term funding to opioid addiction treatment. Although a leadership priority originally introduced as H.R. 8, the water resources development bill that was enacted (S. 3021) was routine legislation authorizing new Army Corps projects and studies. Both of these bills achieved what Republicans set out to do, but one could hardly point to them as major partisan policy achievements.

The CRA agency rule roll-backs and the TJCA were the only two clear agenda successes Republicans achieved over the opposition of a majority of Democrats in both the House and the Senate. Put differently, Republicans won only two clear victories in the 115th Congress with the party-line votes that Speaker Ryan anticipated when he told reporters that the party could enact much of the Better Way agenda through budget reconciliation (Weyl 2016).

THE REPUBLICAN MAJORITY'S PARTIAL AGENDA SUCCESSES

Among the agenda items in table 4.1, Republicans achieved three partial successes: a roll-back of financial regulations, a farm bill, and a reauthorization of the Federal Aviation Authority. In each of these cases, Republicans had to back down from controversial positions to enact legislation.

In passing the Economic Growth, Regulatory Relief, and Consumer Protection Act (EGRRCPA; S. 2155), the 115th Congress exempted community banks from stringent regulatory oversight but left in place the regulations that had been imposed on larger financial institutions. The legislation did not accomplish the Dodd-Frank repeal Republicans had sought. "I wish it did gut Dodd-Frank," said House financial services chair Jeb Hensarling (R-TX) of the legislation. "It didn't" (Warmbrodt 2018). The EGRRCPA won a significant block of bipartisan support, though most Democrats in both House and Senate voted against it.[14] Likewise, the 115th Congress successfully reauthorized farm programs (H.R. 2) but only after stripping out provisions that would have imposed new work requirements on food stamp recipients. The result was that the Farm Bill contained no "entitlement reform" or noteworthy conservative policy victories.

The 115th Congress also enacted a reauthorization of the Federal Aviation Authority (FAA; H.R. 4) but only after jettisoning privatization of the nation's air traffic control system, a priority for both the Trump administration and House Transportation and Infrastructure Committee Chairman Bill Shuster (R-PA).

Two of these partial successes likely stemmed from Democrats' control of the Senate cloture veto point. To pass the Farm Bill and the EGRRCPA, Republicans had to win enough Democratic support to impose Senate cloture. Democratic support came at the price of the more sweeping reforms Republicans sought in these two cases. But in the case of the third partial success, the FAA reauthorization, air traffic control privatization was sufficiently controversial to be dropped even before the House passed its bill.

OVERVIEW OF REPUBLICAN ACHIEVEMENTS IN 2017–2018

Taken together, Republican achievements in the 115th Congress were limited, partial, and stymied as much by intraparty dissent as by Democratic opposition. Very few of the policies outlined in the Better Way agenda were even considered at all. Of those that were, only two clear Republican victories were passed over Democratic opposition (the TCJA and the CRA rollbacks). With the exception of the immigration policy drives, the Republican Party did not make further efforts at single-party legislating in 2018. Indeed, the party did not even mount another attempt to use the budget reconciliation process.

In failing on five of its twelve agenda priorities (42 percent), the majority party of the 115th Congress achieved a rather ordinary result. The previous four Congresses with unified government and newly elected presidents (the 103rd, 107th, 109th, and 111th) failed to act on just under half (46 percent; 25/54) of the majority party's stated agenda priorities (Curry and Lee 2019). Of these four Congresses, the 109th (2005–2006) had the best success rate, succeeding to some extent on two-thirds of Republican agenda priorities. With a similar flop on a high-profile drive to reform health insurance markets, the 103rd Congress (1993–1994) under President Bill Clinton bears notable resemblance to the 115th Congress. In sum, despite unified Republican control and strong party cohesion on roll-call votes, the 115th Congress was still relatively gridlocked on legislation. Furthermore, as shown by the data in table 4.1, a significant share of policy gridlock in 2017–2018 stemmed from intraparty dissent, rather than minority party veto players.

LIMITATIONS OF ROLL-CALL-BASED MEASURES OF PARTY UNITY

Despite its overall voting cohesion, the Republican Party hardly marched in lockstep to enact a sweeping policy agenda after winning unified party control in 2016. This fact poses a question: are Republicans really as unified as their voting cohesion suggests?

Republicans' roll-call behavior stands at odds with other ways of gauging party unity. If one followed the news, rather than looking to congressional votes, the post-2010 Republican Party in Congress does not appear unified, at all. Starting in 2011, news coverage of Congress was rife with accounts of intra-Republican policy disputes and power struggles. Figure 4.2 tracks the frequency of news stories covering intraparty factionalism among both Republicans and Democrats since 2005. Before 2010, factionalism among Republicans and Democrats received similar amounts of attention, both during George W. Bush's second term and Barack Obama's first Congress.[15] After 2010, however, news outlets published many more stories on internal conflict in the congressional GOP. Accounts of Republican strife began to appear with increased frequency just after Republicans regained control of Congress in the 2010 midterms. From 2011 to 2017, there were fully ten times as many news stories about intra-Republican Party conflict as about intra-Democratic Party conflict.

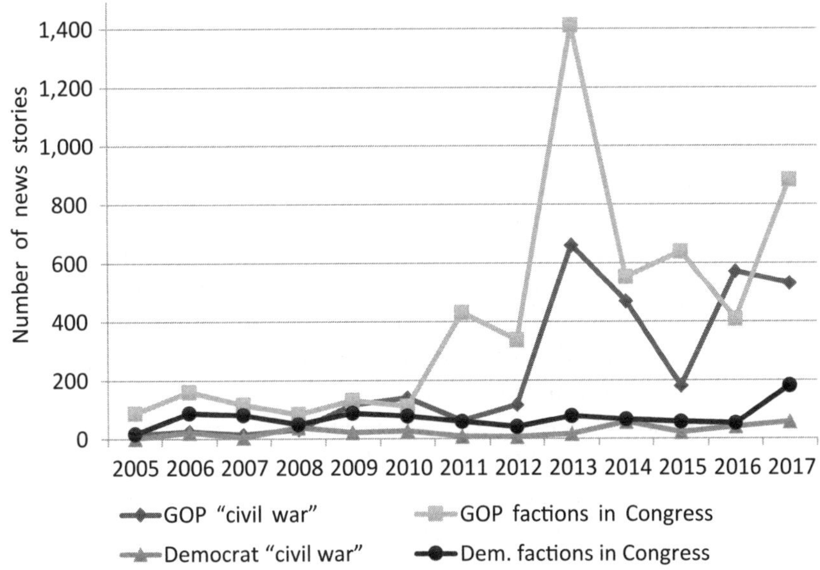

Figure 4.2: News Stories about Intra-Party Conflict, 2005–2017. The Nexis Uni news database was searched for: (Congress AND Republican w/5 factions); (Congress AND Democrat w/5 factions); ("Republican civil war" OR "GOP civil war"); ("Democrat! civil war").

Another indicator of disunity in Republican ranks was turmoil in the party's leadership. House Speaker John Boehner (R-OH) regularly struggled to unify Republicans on legislation, particularly on must-pass bills to raise the debt limit or fund the government (Sinclair 2016a, 62–68). No leadership struggle comparable to Boehner stepping down under pressure had occurred in the House for a century (Jenkins and Stewart 2015). Although Speaker Ryan was more successful, at times, in managing intraparty divisions, his decision to retire from Congress undoubtedly reflected frustration with leading a fractious Republican Party.

Between 2011 and 2018, Republican leaders in both chambers took withering fire from conservative groups and activists. The extent and harshness of this intraparty criticism stands out from the recent norm and from Democratic leaders' experience. Boehner faced such pervasive and persistent criticism that in 2014, one conservative activist was quoted as saying, "There are not enough curse words in the English language to describe how movement conservatives think of John Boehner" (McLaughlin 2014). Criticism reached a fever pitch in October 2017 after the Senate failed to repeal Obamacare, when several conservative groups held a press conference to demand the ouster of Senate Majority Leader Mitch McConnell. On numerous occasions after 2011, conservative groups, such as Heritage Action and Club for Growth, rallied against legislation supported by Republican leaders. Heritage Action even actively opposed the House leadership's first attempt to repeal and replace Obamacare in 2017.[16]

Activist groups' criticisms of Republican leaders were accompanied by an unusual number of ideological challenges to Republican incumbents in congressional primaries. According to an analysis by Boatright (2014, 4), "The number of ideological challenges [to congressional incumbents] . . . increased steadily over the past five election cycles. This is entirely due to challenges within the Republican Party."

In short, news coverage of partisan in-fighting, leadership struggles, and outside activist challenges to party leadership and incumbents all point to a contemporary Republican Party riven by conflict; meanwhile, data on roll-call voting cohesion throughout this whole period paint a picture of a party in near lockstep agreement. These divergent indicators raise questions as to whether roll-call votes offer a reliable measure of party unity. Below, I will discuss two reasons for concern about the capacity of roll-call based measures to accurately gauge intraparty policy agreement, particularly in recent Congresses.

SELECTION BIAS IN MEASURING PARTY UNITY FROM ROLL-CALL VOTES

Roll-call votes do not occur on the whole range of policy questions that arise in US national politics (Clinton and Lapinski 2008). Instead, the roll-call record is selected endogenously, and a variety of strategic considerations shape its construction (e.g., Carrubba and Gabel 2008; Egar 2016). Most importantly, party leaders both in the United States and elsewhere prefer, if possible, to avoid questions that divide their parties internally (Cox and McCubbins 2004).

Changes in congressional processes offer reason to suspect that roll-call votes present a more biased indicator of party unity than in the past. First, contemporary House and Senate leaders censor votes via procedural tools more than their predecessors did. Nearly all important bills considered in the House in recent years have come to the floor under restrictive rules, a rare practice before the late 1980s (Sinclair 2016b). The first session of the 115th Congress set a new record for restrictions on amending, with most rules (55 percent) permitting no amendments at all (Thorning 2018). Recent Senate leaders have also exploited parliamentary maneuvers far more aggressively to manage the Senate floor (Davis 2017; Smith 2014). The first session of the 115th Congress established a modern benchmark for the lowest number of amendments considered on the Senate floor (Thorning 2018).

In deciding what issues to bring to the floor, party leaders want to avoid alienating any substantial party bloc. Whenever possible, the goal is to produce a chamber majority from within the House majority party. Former Speaker Dennis Hastert (R-IL) explained, "It was always important to get 218 [a House majority] before we brought a bill to the floor, especially if it was a partisan bill" (Sherman and Cogan 2011). Note that this is a far higher standard than the so-called Hastert Rule, which requires only that legislation garner a majority of the majority party. Instead, Hastert's preferred strategy was to seek legislation that could pass on the strength of majority party votes alone.

Similarly, Boehner was known to admonish Republican members, "When you don't have 218 votes, you have nothing" (Kasperowicz 2014). For her part, House Speaker Nancy Pelosi (D-CA) regularly reminds her colleagues in whip meetings, "If you don't have 218 votes, you're just having a conversation."[17] Contemporary party leaders thus engage in intraparty consultation in advance of bringing significant bills to the floor.

A second key change in the congressional process is that both parties in both chambers meet in caucus much more frequently than they did throughout most of the twentieth century. The House Democratic caucus was dormant for fifty years before 1969 when liberal reformers revived the caucus in their struggle to assert control over conservative committee chairmen (Peters 1990, 152–153). During the 1970s, House Republicans met in conference only about once a month on average; House Democrats met less often. With so little coordination in advance, more internal party divisions played out in public on the chamber floor in the twentieth-century Congress.

The frequency of party caucus meetings began rising in the 1980s for House Republicans and after 1994 for House Democrats (Forgette 2004; Lee 2016, 92–93). Senate Democrats began holding weekly caucus meetings only in 1981. Hill parties now meet weekly while Congress is in session and schedule additional meetings as needed to handle questions that arise in the interim.

These meetings allow leaders to ascertain party support before any possible floor action (Curry 2015; Dynes and Reeves 2017). The increased frequency of party caucus meetings in Congress, of course, endogenously reflects a greater underlying willingness of members to work together as parties in the first place. But it should not be surprising that recent parties in Congress succeed in better maintaining their party's floor voting cohesion, given that they meet much more frequently behind the scenes to coordinate.

As the majority party organizes behind the scenes, issues on which the party cannot develop a consensus position get sidelined to the extent possible. "Must pass" bills (e.g., appropriations and debt limit increases) limit leaders' strategic options, of course. But as fellow partisans consult and organize more as a caucus and leaders opt to pursue issues on which they can avoid party splits, Congress's discretionary agenda is profoundly affected.

The upshot is that parties appear unified on floor votes, because in most cases the measures the majority leadership willingly brings to the floor are those on which the party has found consensus beforehand. When majority party members do not agree on a budget resolution, for example, the majority party will simply decline to schedule a budget for floor consideration. Party leaders do not proceed to bring a budget forward only to put all the party's internal divisions on public display. Congress has passed an annual budget resolution only half the time since 1998 (McCarty 2016). The 115th Congress never passed a budget resolution that was even intended to govern discretionary spending.[18]

This type of censorship shaped the floor agenda of the 115th Congress in numerous ways. Congressional Republicans had little interest in pursuing several top Trump administration priorities, precisely because they lacked internal party agreement. Republicans were not eager to move forward on trade, infrastructure, or immigration. Despite early speculation that President Trump's first legislative priority would be an infrastructure package, Congress took little action on the issue. It passed an FAA reauthorization and a water resources development bill, but these were only routine reauthorizations. Because Republicans did not agree on how or whether infrastructure spending should be offset (Zanona 2017), they did not consider major new commitments on infrastructure policy, despite the president's interest in such a package.

On trade, most Republicans in Congress did not support the new tariffs imposed by the Trump administration. But Republicans in the 115th Congress declined to take up efforts to block the administration's actions and permitted few votes on trade issues. The only notable move on trade was the Senate's passage of a nonbinding resolution to give Congress a role in decisions to impose tariffs for national security reasons.[19] Declining to act on the issue avoided both conflict with the administration and the exposure of rifts within the party (Tankersley and Casselman 2018).

Congressional Republicans likewise wanted to avoid the issue of immigration, given the party's lack of internal consensus. "Virtually nothing can drive Republicans more bitterly apart than immigration policy," observed a 2017 *New York Times* story (Peters 2017). The Trump campaign promise for a southern border wall did not command universal Republican backing.[20] Immigration policy did not come to the floor in the House or the Senate in 2017. In 2018, the issue came up only because Senate Democrats and House Republican dissidents forced the debate. But despite party leaders' best efforts to negotiate consensus legislation, they could not hold their parties together in either chamber.

In the end, Republican leaders were not able to entirely squelch debate on immigration in the 115th Congress, so intraparty divisions on those issues could not be fully suppressed. But considering the prominence of immigration as an issue on the national agenda in 2017–2018, it is striking that Congress only took such a small handful of votes on the issue in either chamber.

If Congress had no choice about the issues on which it took votes, the Republican Party of 2017–2018 would not look so cohesive. Trade, immigration, and infrastructure were all highly salient issues on the national political agenda in the 115th Congress. But these issues rarely appeared on the roll-call agenda, because of the Republican Party's internal divisions. When policy issues that cut across the main line of partisan cleavage are censored from the floor agenda, roll-call votes offer a misleading picture of members' preferences (Snyder 1992, 338–340). There is no doubt that Republicans of the 115th Congress were more disunified on important questions of national policy than their voting cohesion statistics would suggest.

PARTY MESSAGING AS AN OBSTACLE TO GAUGING PARTY UNITY FROM ROLL-CALL VOTES

A second reason the roll-call record affords limited insight into party unity in the contemporary Congress is that many votes have no effect on public policy. On many votes, members know that the measure in question has no prospect of passing, advancing in the other chamber, or being signed by the president. Party leaders deliberately stage messaging votes highlighting differences between the parties to fire up party-base voters, motivate interest groups or donors, or put the opposing party on the wrong side of public opinion (Gelman 2017). Coordinating party messaging has become an important part of a congressional leader's job description in an era when party control of Congress is perceived to be "in play" most election cycles

(Lee 2016). In many cases, votes are scheduled not with the expectation of shifting public policy but with the hope of driving a favorable narrative that will benefit a party politically.

Messaging bills are merely aspirational in policy terms. It was well understood at the outset that bills such as the 2009 Reducing Barack Obama's Unsustainable Deficit Act (H.R. 3140) or the 2013 Big Oil Welfare Repeal Act (H.R. 1426) were not destined for the statute books. Bills designed for partisan messaging purposes do not receive careful attention to legislative detail; they merely need to sound good to external constituencies (Lee 2016, 143–146). Former senator Olympia Snowe (2013, 27) offered a definition: "Much of what occurs in Congress today is what is often called 'political messaging.' Rather than putting forward a plausible, realistic solution to a problem, members on both sides offer legislation that is designed to make a political statement. Specifically, the bill or amendment is drafted to make the opposing side look bad on an issue and is not intended to ever actually pass."

When casting roll-call votes, members weigh different considerations depending upon whether they expect the vote will actually result in the enactment of legislation. A messaging vote is only a political statement. In considering how to vote, all a member needs to ask is whether s/he would like to join in making that statement. A member considering whether to support a messaging bill need not grapple with policy complexity, competing goods, or policy trade-offs, as is required for important legislation. A vote on the enactment of a potential law must be weighed for its real-world effects: Will this work as intended? Will it impose costs on important interests or constituents? Will there be political blowback if it goes into effect?

To put the matter in terms of Kingdon (1981, xi), the "field of forces" surrounding messaging bills is quite different than around legislative proposals that have potential for enactment. Organized interests mobilize their resources accordingly. As one example, consider the Beltway lawyer specializing in financial services who observed: "There is zero chance that the CHOICE Act survives [in the Senate]" (Rappeport 2017). Lobbyists and government affairs directors are aware of the different stakes, depending on the legislative prospects of a proposed bill. Affected interests ramp up their lobbying efforts and capacity for grassroots mobilization when threatened by real legislation. Messaging bills do not spark the same level of interest-group engagement or pressure on members.

The difference between messaging and legislating was on stark display in 2017 when Congress took up legislation aimed at repealing and replacing Obamacare. In the whole period since 2010, no other issue had been subject to nearly as much party messaging activity as Obamacare. Congress had passed dozens of bills to repeal or curb the Affordable Care Act. *Newsweek* identified at least seventy such votes between 2010 and 2017 (Riotta 2017).

In 2015, when it was understood that President Obama would successfully veto the effort, both chambers of Congress easily passed a sweeping Affordable Care Act repeal bill (H.R. 3762). But the politics of the issue were profoundly different after Republicans won unified control of government in the 2016 elections. In 2015, when the legislation was sure to be vetoed, Republican members' town halls were not deluged with protestors, nor were congressional phone lines jammed with calls, as they often were in 2017. In 2015, the AARP did not launch a multimillion-dollar ad campaign against the bill, as it did in 2017. Unlike in 2017, the 2015 bill was not the subject of tearful monologues on *Jimmy Kimmel Live!* Representative Joe Barton (R-TX) explained the difference between the two repeal efforts: "Sometimes you're playing fantasy football, and sometimes you're in the real game" (Alters 2017). Senator John Thune (R-SD) described the 2017 effort as differing from the 2015 repeal in its use of "live ammunition" (Persons 2017).

Being able to hold together on a messaging vehicle that has no chance of becoming law dimly signals, at best, that a party is unified on policy. If one compiled all the Obamacare repeal roll-call votes from 2011 to 2017, Republicans would project total party unity. While Boehner was present for most of those votes, he was under no illusions that Republicans had any genuine consensus: "In the 25 years that I served in the United States Congress, Republicans never, ever, one time agreed on what a health care proposal should look like. Not once" (Tahir 2017).

There is no way to ascertain precisely how much of the roll-call record is messaging votes, but it is likely substantial. Use of roll-call votes for party messaging purposes means that the roll-call record offers an exaggerated picture of the extent of party unity on policy for the simple reason that it is easier for a party to agree on a political statement than it is to enact legislation. In fact, messaging bills are often pursued precisely when Congress is not capable of actually legislating on an issue.

The volume of messaging votes raises questions about potential bias in the measurement of members' preferences using roll-call scaling algorithms. With members subjected to fewer cross-pressures on messaging, the error term should be heterogeneous across messaging votes and substantive policy votes, and the identification of ideal points is sensitive to the distribution of the error term (McCarty 2011).[21] The presence of messaging votes on the agenda likely results in artificially party polarized ideal points, with downwardly biased estimates of within-party deviation.

In early 2018, for example, while Republican leaders expressed pessimism about getting bicameral agreement on a budget resolution, they raised the possibility that they would "pass messaging budgets in their own respective chambers" (Bade and Ferris 2018). When Congress takes such a course of action, a scholar using roll-call votes as a guide to a majority party's budget preferences would see the House and Senate parties each pass messaging budgets on party-line votes. The roll-call record would thus indicate perfect or nearly perfect party cohesion on budget policy, but no actual budget would be enacted, owing to intraparty dissent. By such processes, messaging votes systematically overstate the extent of party unity on policy.

THE INADEQUACY OF ROLL-CALL VOTES AS A MEASURE OF PARTY COHESION ON PUBLIC POLICY

The record of the 115th Congress offers an opportunity for scholars to consider more carefully how we define and measure party unity in Congress. As gauged by roll-call votes, there have been few postwar majority parties more cohesive than the Republicans of 2017–2018. And yet the policy outcomes of the 115th Congress, while highly significant, fell far short of Republican ambitions. Looking beyond roll-call votes to other indicators of Republican Party cohesion—news coverage, leadership instability, primary challenges, and ideological conflict within the party coalition—the post-2010 Republican Party actually appeared less unified than other recent congressional majority parties. In short, there was quite simply a wide gap between our usual measures of party unity based on roll-call votes and the same reality gauged in other ways.

Looking beyond the 115th Congress per se, this chapter explores how and why roll-call-based measures of party cohesion exaggerate intraparty agreement under contemporary conditions. Use of roll-call votes for party messaging, in conjunction with increased party caucus coordination in advance of floor consideration, have rendered roll-call votes a less revealing window into internal party divisions in Congress. When considering serious legislation, party leaders prefer not to hold votes at all, unless the party has found a way to resolve its internal disagreements. But when the party is unable to settle its intramural policy disputes, it can still take votes on messaging bills to trumpet the party's preferred narratives and ideological aspirations.

When assessing a party's capability for collective action on policy, scholars need to consider more than its aggregate cohesion in roll-call voting generally. Roll-call votes are about far more than public policy. Parties regularly use floor votes for purposes of position-taking and narrative-building. A party able to agree on the positions it wants to take may not necessarily be able to agree on the complexities and real-world trade-offs involved in public policy. Likewise, a congressional party may be able to agree to confirm a copartisan president's executive and judicial branch appointments without necessarily agreeing on what precisely these appointees should do in office. In 2019 and 2020, the Republican Party in Congress exhibited remarkable cohesion on collective efforts to protect President Trump from impeachment, but cohesion to sustain their party's president in office does not indicate that the Republican Party in Congress would be able to reach internal consensus on the Trump administration's agenda on trade, infrastructure, or immigration. Given the varied purposes roll-call votes serve, they should not be interpreted as a straightforward measure of members' or parties' policy preferences.

As a result of developments in party messaging and party caucus practices, roll-call voting in Congress now bears a greater resemblance to recorded voting in legislatures elsewhere around the world, where scholars frequently treat the party (not the member) as the unit of analysis and recognize that roll-call votes reveal relatively little about individual members' policy preferences (Aldrich 2011). As in legislatures elsewhere, a great deal of congressional deliberation on policy now occurs in closed-door partisan settings rather than in public on the chamber floor. Issues on which the majority party cannot agree internally are underrepresented on the roll-call record. At the same time, issues on which the majority party would like to engage in partisan position-taking are overrepresented on the roll-call agenda. As with the example of the many votes taken to repeal Obamacare, a party can succeed in portraying itself as highly cohesive via messaging votes, even if it has not resolved thorny problems of public policy. The upshot is that majority parties in Congress can rack up records of extraordinary unity in roll-call voting even while they struggle to make their mark on public policy.[22]

NOTES

1. The "Better Way" agenda included: (1) "revenue neutral" tax reform to lower taxes on corporations, simplify taxes by reducing the number of income tax brackets and deductions, and abolish the alternative minimum tax and the estate tax; (2) repeal and replacement of the Affordable Care Act ("Obamacare"); (3) increased funding for border security and other national security purposes; (4) repeal of the financial regulations adopted in 2010 and (5) repeal of a series of agency rules

adopted under President Obama, along with (6) federal litigation reform; (7) reassertion of the powers of Congress over regulation and government spending; and (8) reform to poverty programs enhancing work requirements for recipients.

2. The series displays the percentage of majority party members that would yield 218 votes.

3. The series displays the percentage of majority party members necessary for fifty or fifty-one votes, depending on whether the vice president shares the Senate majority's party.

4. See the Report of the Task Force on National Security, *A Better Way: Our Vision for a Confident America,* June 9, 2016. The report calls for "putting in place robust, layered defenses to stop unlawful entry" and "gaining operational control and situational awareness along the entire border" (4). The report also calls for enhanced immigration enforcement by "developing the means to track illegal aliens" and "detaining and removing criminal aliens and restoring immigration enforcement within the United States" (4).

5. House roll-call vote 256, May 4, 2017.

6. See Senate roll-call vote 179 on July 28, 2017.

7. The Bipartisan Budget Act (BBA) of 2018 (H.R. 1892) passed the House 240–186 (D 73–119; R 167–67) and the Senate 71–28 (D 36–11; R 34–16). The omnibus appropriations legislation implementing the budget agreement for the balance of FY 2018 (H.R. 1625) passed the House 256–167 (D 111–77; R 145–90) and the Senate 65–32 (D 39–8; R 25–23).

8. House roll-call vote 243, June 7, 2018. All Democrats and nineteen Republicans opposed the rescissions package.

9. Senate roll-call vote 134, June 20, 2018.

10. Senate roll-call vote numbers 33, 35, and 36, February 15, 2018.

11. House roll-call vote 282, June 21, 2018.

12. House roll-call vote 297, June 27, 2018.

13. These measures were: HJ Res 41, HJ Res 38, HJ Res 40, HJ Res 37, HJ Res 44, HJ Res 57, HJ Res 58, HJ Res 42, HJ Res 83, HJ Res 43, HJ Res 67, HJ Res 66, HJ Res 111, and HJ Res 57.

14. The Economic Growth, Regulatory Relief, and Consumer Protection Act passed the Senate 67–31 (R 50–0; D 16–31) and the House 258–159 (R 225–1; D 33–158).

15. Although the timeline in the figure begins with 2005, news coverage of party factionalism in Congress was low for both parties long before 2005.

16. Heritage Action, "'No' on American Health Care Act (H.R. 1628)," March 23, 2017, http://heritageaction.com/key-votes/no-american-health-care-act-h-r-1628/.

17. Veteran Democratic leadership aide, personal communication, January 13, 2018.

18. The only budgets it passed were "shells" intended to facilitate the use of reconciliation for policymaking (Reynolds 2017b).

19. Roll-call vote 151, July 11, 2018.

20. When *USA Today* asked every congressional Republican about whether he or she supported a wall along the US southern border, only 69 of 292 Republicans replied in the affirmative (Singer 2017).

21. I thank Chris Tausanovitch for this important point.

22. This is an extensively revised and updated version of a paper that appeared in *Journal of Politics* 80, no. 4 (2018): 1464–1473.

REFERENCES

Aldrich, John. "Political Parties in and out of Legislatures," in *The Oxford Handbook of Political Science*, ed. Robert E. Goodin. New York: Oxford University Press, 2011.

Alters, Kimberly. "This Republican Congressman Was Shockingly Honest About Why the AHCA Failed." *Week*, March 24, 2017.

Bade, Rachael, and Sarah Ferris. "GOP May Skip Budget, Kneecapping 2018 Ambitions." *Politico*, January 10, 2018.

Boatright, Robert G. "The 2014 Congressional Primaries in Context." Paper presented at a conference cohosted by the Campaign Finance Institute and the Brookings Institution, September 30, 2014.

Brookings Institution. *Vital Statistics on Congress*, https://www.brookings.edu/multi-chapter-report/vital-statistics-on-congress/. September 7, 2017.

Carrubba, Clifford, and Matthew Gabel. "Legislative Voting Behavior, Seen and Unseen: A Theory of Roll-Call Vote Selection." *Legislative Studies Quarterly* 33, no. 4 (2008): 543–572.

Clinton, Joshua D., and John Lapinski. "Laws and Roll Calls in the US Congress, 1891–1994." *Legislative Studies Quarterly* 33 (2008): 511–541.

Cox, Gary W., and Mathew D. McCubbins. *Setting the Agenda: Responsible Party Government in the US House of Representatives.* New York: Cambridge University Press, 2004.

Curry, James M. *Legislating in the Dark: Information and Power in the US House of Representatives.* Chicago: University of Chicago Press, 2015.

Curry, James M., and Frances E. Lee. "Non-Party Government: Bipartisan Lawmaking and Party Power in Congress." *Perspectives on Politics* 17, no. 1 (2019): 47–65.

Davis, Christopher M. "Instances in Which Opportunities for Floor Amendment Were Limited by the Senate Majority Leader or His Designee Filling or Partially Filling the Amendment Tree: 1985–2017." Congressional Research Service Memorandum, June 9, 2017.

Dynes, Adam M., and Andrew Reeves. "Who Benefits from the Party Organization? Evidence from Republican House Members' Attendance at Caucus Meetings." *Legislative Studies Quarterly* 43 (2017): 207–243.

Edwards, George C. "'Closer' or Context? Explaining Donald Trump's Relations with Congress." *Presidential Studies Quarterly* 48 (2018): 456–479.

Egar, William T. "Tarnishing Opponents, Polarizing Congress: The House Minority Party and the Construction of the Roll-Call Record." *Legislative Studies Quarterly* 41 (2016): 935–964.

Forgette, Richard. "Party Caucuses and Coordination: Assessing Caucus Activity and Party Effects." *Legislative Studies Quarterly* 29 (2004): 407–430.

Gelman, Jeremy. "Rewarding Dysfunction: Interest Groups and Intended Legislative Failure." *Legislative Studies Quarterly* 42 (2017): 661–692.

Jenkins, Jeffery A., and Charles Stewart III. "What Happened to John Boehner Hasn't Happened in a Century," Monkey Cage Blog, *Washington Post*, September 30, 2015.

———. *Fighting for the Speakership: The House and the Rise of Party Government.* Princeton, NJ: Princeton University Press, 2012.

Kasperowicz, Pete. "House Passes Clean Debt Hike." *The Hill*. February 12, 2014.

Kingdon, John W. *Congressmen's Voting Decisions.* New York: Harper and Row, 1981.

Lee, Frances E. *Insecure Majorities: Congress and the Perpetual Campaign.* Chicago: University of Chicago Press, 2016.

McCarty, Nolan. "The Decline of Regular Order in Appropriations: Does It Matter?" In *Congress and Policy Making in the 21st Century*, ed. Jeffery A. Jenkins and Eric M. Patashnik, 162–186. New York: Cambridge University Press, 2016.

———. "Measuring Legislative Preferences." In *The Oxford Handbook of the American Congress*, ed. Eric Schickler and Frances E. Lee, 66–94. New York: Oxford University Press, 2011.

McLaughlin, Seth. "Boehner Gets Official Snub by Conservative Activists." *Washington Times*, March 4, 2014, p. A1.

Nelson, Michael. *Trump's First Year.* Charlottesville: University of Virginia Press, 2018.

Pearson, Kathryn. "President Trump and Congressional Republicans: Uncertain Teamwork in the 115th Congress." *Forum* 15, no. 3 (2017): 513–524.

Persons, Sally. "John Thune: Health Care Debacle Makes Republicans Look 'Dysfunctional.'" *Washington Times*, July 18, 2017.

Peters, Jeremy W. "Immigration's Sudden Re-Emergence Scrambles Republican Agenda." *New York Times*, September 14, 2017.

Peters, Ronald M. *The American Speakership: The Office in Historical Perspective.* Baltimore: Johns Hopkins University Press, 1990.

Rappeport, Alan. "Measure to Loosen Dodd-Frank Banking Rules Passes the House." *New York Times*, June 9, 2017, B1.

Reynolds, Molly E. *Exceptions to the Rule: The Politics of Filibuster Limitations in the US Senate.* Washington, DC: Brookings Institution, 2017a.

———. "This Is Why the Congressional Budget Process Is Broken." Monkey Cage, *Washington Post*, October 26, 2017b.

Riotta, Chris. "GOP Aims to Kill Obamacare Yet Again After Failing 70 Times." *Newsweek*, July 29, 2017.

Sherman, Jake, and Marin Cogan. "Right Doesn't Make Might for Boehner." *Politico*, April 15, 2011.

Siegel, Benjamin, and John Parkinson. "House Rejects Republican Compromise Immigration Bill," ABC News. June 21, 2018: https://abcnews.go.com/Politics

/house-rejects-conservative-immigration-bill-delays-vote-measure/story?id=56056627.

Sinclair, Barbara. "Partisan Polarization and Congressional Policymaking." In *Congress and Policymaking in the 21st Century*, ed. Eric M. Patashnik and Jeffery A. Jenkins, 48–72. New York: Cambridge University Press, 2016a.

———. *Unorthodox Lawmaking: New Legislative Processes in the US Congress*, 5th edition. Washington, DC: CQ, 2016b.

Singer, Paul. "Exclusive: Less than 25% of Republicans in Congress Endorse Border Wall Funding in USA Today Survey." *USA Today*, September 20, 2017.

Smith, Steven S. *The Senate Syndrome: The Evolution of Procedural Warfare in the Modern US Senate.* Norman: University of Oklahoma Press, 2014.

Snowe, Olympia. "The Effect of Modern Partisanship on Legislative Effectiveness in the 112th Congress." *Harvard Journal on Legislation* 50, no. 1 (2013): 21–40.

Snyder, James M. Jr. "Artificial Extremism in Interest Group Ratings." *Legislative Studies Quarterly* 17 (1992): 319–345.

Tahir, Darius. "Boehner: Republicans Won't Repeal and Replace Obamacare." *Politico*, February 23, 2017.

Tankersley, Jim, and Ben Casselman. "Opposing Tariffs Puts G.O.P. at Risk." *New York Times*, September 19, 2018, B3.

Thorning, Michael. "Healthy Congress Index: Signs of Progress on Appropriations." Bipartisan Policy Center, July 23, 2018: https://bipartisanpolicy.org/blog/healthy-congress-index-signs-of-progress-on-appropriations/.

Wagner, John. "Trump Pledges to Work with Republicans in 'Busiest Congress . . . Maybe Ever,'" *Washington Post*, January 26, 2017.

Warmbrodt, Zachary. "House Sends Major Bank Bill to Trump, Capping Years of Effort." *Politico*, May 22, 2018.

Weyl, Ben. "Ryan Plans to Steamroll Democrats with Budget Tool." *Politico*, October 6, 2016.

Wong, Scott. "GOP Frets Over Too-High Expectations." *Hill*, February 10, 2017.

CHAPTER 5

Polarization and the Changing American Constitutional System: The Case of Federalism

Nolan McCarty

INTRODUCTION

In 2015, the Federal Communications Commission (FCC) implemented new regulations on internet service providers (ISPs) that would prevent them from discriminating against different content providers. These new rules, implementing so-called net neutrality, prohibited ISPs from blocking any lawful content, throttling specific applications or services, and providing preferential treatment to content providers for pay (Reardon 2015).

Before the FCC's decision, net neutrality, and the regulation of the internet more generally, had been a very contentious issue for more than a decade. Nevertheless, Congress had been unable or unwilling to provide any legislative solutions or guidance on these matters. As a result, the FCC acted under the authority of Title II of the Communication Act of 1934, a provision originally designed to regulate "common carriers" such as radio, broadcast TV, and telephones. This statute, however, was so mismatched to the internet that the FCC had to announce that large parts of the title would not apply to ISP regulation.

The failure to resolve internet access rules through statute also meant that the net neutrality rules would be subject to revision by a future FCC. An opportunity arose after the election of Donald Trump that created a GOP-leaning FCC majority under the leadership of Ajit Pai, a net neutrality opponent. After the FCC proposed a new rule eliminating the net neutrality provisions, there was an intense lobbying campaign to again get Congress to act. But given partisan divisions on the matter, nothing came of those efforts, and the FCC adopted a final rule eliminating the net neutrality provisions on December 17, 2017 (Reardon 2018).

With Congress gridlocked on the matter, the opposition to net neutrality repeal moved to the states. Soon after the repeal, a lawsuit was filed by attorneys general in twenty-two states challenging the basis of the FCC's decision (Kang 2018). Moreover, executives and legislatures in many states moved to promote net neutrality on behalf of their citizens. Several states issued executive orders or passed legislation requiring that all ISPs doing business with state government operate under net neutrality rules. California went one step further in writing a very ambitious law that would apply neutrality rules to all ISPs operating in the state. While the FCC's rule had banned preemptive efforts of the states, ongoing litigation focuses on whether in fact the FCC had the power to do so (Kang 2018). Ultimately, the judicial branch will be pivotal in determining the future of internet policy.

The history of net neutrality reveals a dynamic that has become all too common in American politics. Faced with an important policy problem, Congress is unable to act. As a result, the locus of policymaking moves to the executive branch, the states, and the judiciary. Moreover, the episode demonstrates some of the real costs when Congress is disengaged on policy. For example, policy may be unstable and create uncertainty because rules and executive action lack the durability of statues. Policy also may be kludged around ill-fitting statutory authority. It may be subject to jurisdictional disputes such as those between the national and state governments. And the ultimate resolution of those disputes will be judicial. Thus, legislative failure may not only shift power to other branches but also lead to a deterioration in the quality of policy outputs.

Scholars have identified many sources of legislative weakness in the American constitutional system. Legislative bodies are beset by collective action problems (Moe and Howell 1999). Individual electoral motives trump any incentives for institutional maintenance (Mayhew 1974; Posner and Vermeule 2011). Legislatures cannot move with the urgency required by the problems of a modern society (Posner and Vermeule 2011). They lack the required expertise to make good policy (Epstein and O'Halloran 1999). Legislators are too susceptible to the charms and resources of the special interests (Howell and Moe 2016). There is a great deal of truth to all of these claims, but many blame fairly constant features of legislative politics and are thus less equipped to explain the slow erosion of legislative capacity that we have witnessed over the past few decades.

Consequently, my focus is on the effects of the rise of ideological polarization and partisan conflict to explain changes in legislative capacity. These trends are often heralded as some of the most dramatic developments in American politics of the past forty years (McCarty, Poole, and Rosenthal 2016). The concerns about legislative polarization are so widespread it is difficult to recall that political scientists once lamented the lack of disciplined, distinct congressional parties. Given the centrality of polarization in contemporary congressional politics, a vast literature has developed to explain the rise of polarization and its underlying causes.[1] But there has been considerably less focus on the consequences of partisan polarization for the performance of our constitutional system.

Concerns about the systemic consequences of polarization arise from the belief that the US Congress is not designed to perform well in highly polarized environments. First, bicameralism and other supermajoritarian institutions make the formation of winning coalitions very difficult even in the best of circumstances (Krehbiel 1998; Brady and Volden 2005). Now that polarization has increased the difficulty of building them across party lines, legislating only becomes harder. Second, compounding the problems of legislative partisanship is that each party is heavily factionalized ideologically. Unlike legislative leaders elsewhere who have powers of confidence and dissolution on top of the control of renomination, American party leaders are often unable to manage conflicts within their own ranks (McCarty 2015a; Pildes 2015). These conflicts further narrow the needle's eye that legislation must thread. Finally, as legislative partisanship has increased, legislators of the president's party are often forced to act as advocates of the administration rather than as defenders of the prerogatives of a coequal branch.[2] Thus, executive incursions on legislative prerogatives are likely to remain unchecked.

Some of the negative consequences of polarization have been well-documented. Scholars have documented that as polarization has increased (1) legislative output has declined (Binder 2003; Binder 2015; McCarty, Poole, and Rosenthal 2016), (2) the appropriations process fails to conclude before the beginning of the fiscal year with increasing regularity (Woon and Anderson 2012; Hanson 2014; McCarty 2016), and (3) delays in the confirmation process have increased, leading to growing numbers of vacancies in the executive branch and the judiciary (McCarty and Razaghian 1999; Binder and Maltzman 2002; Joseph O'Connell 2009, 2015).

But the implications of these reductions of legislative capacity performance on the functioning of the American constitutional system have received far less attention. Thus several important questions are unanswered.

How have the other branches of government responded to the decline in legislative capacity occasioned by increased polarization? Have these branches expanded their power, authority, and policy effect at Congress's expense? Or has legislative dysfunction made it more difficult for other actors to carry out their constitutional duties? Moreover, how has political polarization impacted the internal functioning of the executive and judicial branches and the states?

In this chapter, I provide a preliminary discussion and review of some evidence concerning how congressional gridlock and polarization have affected the operation of our federal system and state-level policy activity. The chapter proceeds as follows. In the following section, I provide context for my arguments about polarization by reviewing the historical trends and several arguments about the causes and non-causes of our contemporary partisan divisions. I then review theory and evidence linking polarization to poor legislative performance. Among the many indicators of legislative incapacity, I argue that Congress has produced less legislation, has managed the budget and appropriations process worse, and has been much slower to confirm executive branch appointees as polarization has grown.[3] My chapter then turns to a discussion of how polarization has affected the states. I draw out important distinctions between the impliction of polarization within states and across states. I discuss how polarization and federal gridlock impact federalism and review evidence about changing patterns of state-level policymaking. I conclude with reflections on the potential consequences of polarization on federalism and areas for future study.

TRENDS IN POLARIZATION

To provide some context for my analysis, I begin with a discussion of the trends in legislative polarization. Figure 5.1 presents a measure for the House and Senate based on DW-NOMINATE scores (McCarty, Poole and Rosenthal 1997). Underlying DW-NOMINATE is a statistical model that estimates the left/right positions of legislators based on observed roll-call voting behavior. Larger estimated scores represent more conservative positions. The simplest way to understand the statistical model is that it associates a conservative position for legislators who vote often with conservatives and never with liberals. Liberals are those who vote with other liberals and never with conservatives, and moderates are those who vote with both liberals and conservatives.[4] The DW-NOMINATE scores of individual legislators are aggregated into these measures so that the polarization measure is just the average difference in the scores of Republicans and Democrats.

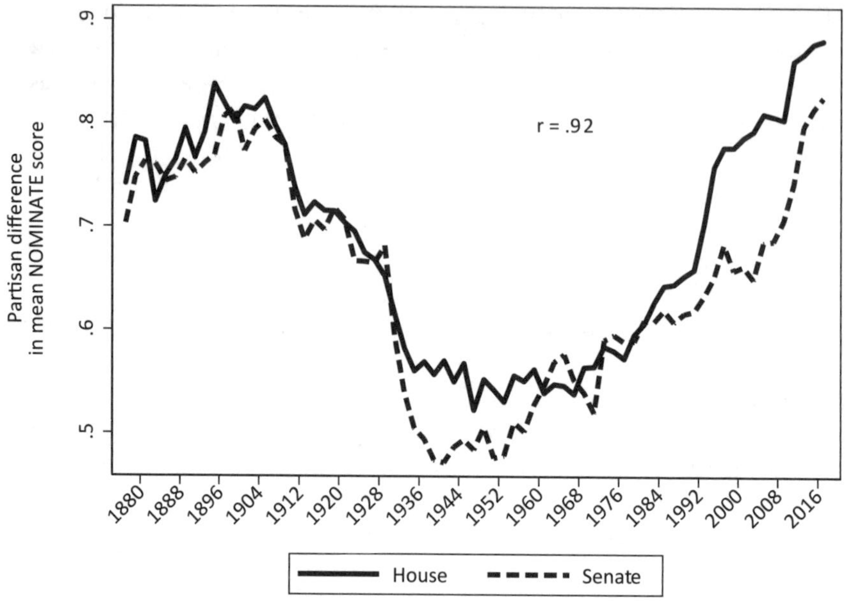

Figure 5.1: Polarization in the US Congress, 1877–2018. Computed from DW-NOMINATE scores. The polarization measure is the difference in the mean score for Republicans and the mean score for Democrats.

Figure 5.1 reveals two important features of congressional polarization. First, the level of polarization in Congress has varied dramatically since Reconstruction. Not surprisingly, congressional polarization was quite high following the Civil War and Reconstruction. But it declined markedly from the 1920s to the 1950s, where the greatest declines appear to be associated with the Great Depression and World War II. Partisan differences in Congress remained low from the 1950s to the 1970s. During this period, both the Democrats and Republicans were divided ideologically between liberal and conservative wings. The current trend toward greater and greater polarization began in the late 1970s and was detectable by academics as early as 1982 (Poole and Rosenthal 1984). Second, the House and the Senate have remarkably similar histories with respect to polarization. The two time series tend to decline together, stabilize together, and increase together. Generally, there is less polarization in the Senate, but there are periods in which the Senate was the more polarized body. Although polarization in the Senate leveled off in the early 2000s, it has increased faster than it has in the House over the past half-dozen years.

Figure 5.2 presents a third important fact about polarization. Rather

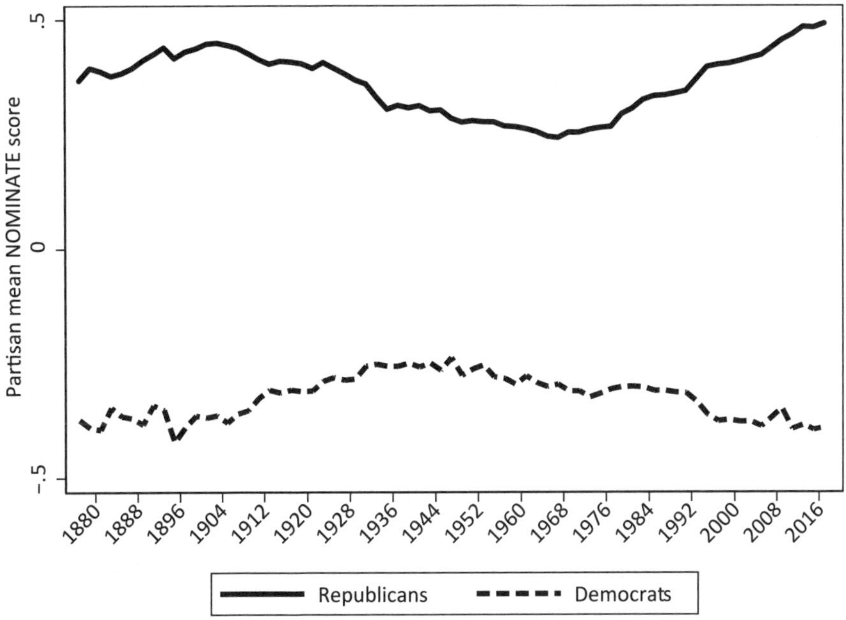

Figure 5.2: Party Positions in the US House, 1877–2018. Figure shows average DW-NOMINATE scores by party.

than both parties moving toward the extremes, polarization over the past forty years has been asymmetric. It is overwhelmingly associated with the increased movement of Republican legislators to the right. Each new Republican cohort has compiled a more conservative record than the returning cohort. Importantly, this has been the case since the 1970s; it is not a reflection of the emergence of the Tea Party movement. The Democratic Party has not followed a similar pattern. While some new cohorts are more liberal than the caucus on average, many are more moderate. The slight movement of the Democratic Party to the left can be accounted for by the increase of African American and Latino legislators in its caucus. Outside of majority-minority districts, the average position of the Democratic Party has changed very little.

Perhaps the most important finding from this section is that our current levels of congressional polarization did not emerge overnight. It has been a forty-year process. These deep roots may explain why political scientists have found very little evidence that electoral reforms would do much to reverse these trends (McCarty 2015b).

POLARIZATION AND LEGISLATIVE CAPACITY

How does polarization affect the capacity of Congress to fulfill its constitutional functions? A variety of theoretical perspectives suggest a set of mechanisms through which polarization reduces the ability of Congress to legislate. At the core of these theories is the reality that Congress is not a majoritarian institution. Constitutional structures such as bicameralism and the separation of powers as well as internal rules such as the Senate's cloture procedures make it difficult for a simple legislative majority to act.

Indeed, if Congress were governed solely by majority rule, legislative outcomes would reflect the preferences of the median legislator.[5] If outcomes were governed by the median legislator, the increasing number of extreme legislators associated with polarization would have no effect on policy outcomes. Moreover, there would be no policy gridlock. If the preferences of the median voter changed, there would be a swift policy response, moving policy to the new median preferred outcome. Indeed, in a more majoritarian setting, the primary policy problem would be policy instability rather than stasis.

If legislative politics were dominated by the majority party as in Westminster parliamentary systems, polarization also would not necessarily imply dysfunction and gridlock. In such a system, the winning party enacts its preferences rather than those of the median voter, leaving no possibility for gridlock. Polarization should simply lead to wider policy swings upon a change in power.

Thus, any connection between polarization and congressional gridlock should be due to the Madisonian Constitution and the non-majoritarian procedures that Congress has adopted. Perhaps the largest deviation from the majoritarian ideal is the institution of cloture in the Senate. Ostensibly to protect its tradition of unfettered and unlimited debate, the Senate requires that three-fifths (i.e., sixty) of its members vote for a cloture resolution before debate can be terminated and votes taken on the measure in question. Because opponents of legislation always have the option to keep talking until cloture is successfully invoked, sixty votes has become the de facto threshold for passing legislation through the Senate.

Cloture rules are very important for legislative responsiveness.[6] Again, assume that the ideal points of senators can be arrayed from left to right. Given the rules for cloture, we can characterize what a successful coalition must look like. Because sixty votes are required for passage, the senator with the sixtieth most liberal ideal point must support cloture. Let's call her Senator 60. Suppose the alternative for consideration is too liberal for Senator 60. Then it is also too liberal for the forty senators with ideal points to her right. These forty senators and Senator 60 would vote against cloture and the bill fails. In a world of liberal-conservative voting Senator 60 is pivotal for policy change. If a policy is too liberal for this senator, it is too liberal for forty more conservative senators and no change will occur. But if the policy appeals to the senator, she can push through the policy by voting with the fifty-nine senators who are more liberal. In this sense, Senator 60 is pivotal. Just knowing the vote of this senator allows us to know if a new policy that is more liberal will pass. Senator 41 (the forty-first most liberal) is similarly pivotal. If the bill is too conservative for him, it will also be for the forty senators to his left and cloture cannot be obtained. For this reason, we refer to Senators 41 and 60 as the filibuster pivots.

Since the support of both pivots is necessary for cloture, the new bill cannot be too liberal for Senator 61 or too conservative for Senator 40. It is easy to see that no bill altering a status quo located between the pivots can be successfully revised. Thus, the ideological distance between Senator 41 and Senator 60's ideal points is a rough gauge of the Senate's propensity to stalemate due to the cloture rule. Because the majority party in the Senate rarely controls sixty seats, the link between polarization and filibuster-induced gridlock is almost immediate.

Internal roadblocks such as bicameralism and the filibuster are not the only impediments to legislative policy change. Bills that survive the legislative process face the presidential veto. Certainly, presidents can from time to time use the bully pulpit to force bills through the barriers posed by partisan agenda control and filibusters. But for the most part, the president's legislative powers are negative (McCarty 1997; Cameron 2000; Cameron and McCarty 2004).

The veto is a tool for blocking change rather than propagating it. A successful bill requires the presidential signature or a two-thirds vote on an override motion. Using logic exactly similar to that for the filibuster, Senator 34 becomes pivotal on the override motion for a leftist president's veto and Senator 66 becomes pivotal on a rightist veto. But because the override motion must carry both chambers, Representatives 148 and 287 are similarly empowered. The more extreme of these two legislators on the president's side of the spectrum is known as the veto pivot. Since adding new pivotal actors can never increase the status quos that can be successfully overturned, the propensity for gridlock expands.

Combining the effects of the filibuster and the veto pivots, we can compute what political scientists call the gridlock interval. This interval is the policy gap between the leftmost pivot and the rightmost pivot. One or the other of these senators could block the change of any status quo in this interval. Therefore, the longer this interval the more likely that policy change can be blocked. Again, the link between the gridlock interval and polarization is quite direct. As the parties' positions diverge, the distance between the pivotal legislative actors will generally move in tandem. Statistics show that a very substantial fraction of the variance in the width of the gridlock interval is due to party polarization.[7]

A second mechanism that might help transform polarization into legislative paralysis is the increased incentives of politicians to engage in strategic disagreement. Strategic disagreement occurs when a president, party, or other political actor refuses to compromise with the other side in an attempt to gain an electoral advantage by transferring blame for the stalemate to the other side (Gilmour 1995; Groseclose and McCarty 2001; Lee 2009). Such electoral grandstanding not only lowers legislative capacity by diverting resources into an unproductive endeavor but also makes both sides less willing to engage in the compromises required by successful legislation (Lee 2016). There are several reasons to believe that polarization may exacerbate these incentives. As the parties have become more extreme relative to voters, making the other side appear to be the more extreme becomes more valuable.

Supermajortarianism and strategic disagreement combined with polarization make it more difficult for Congress to pass important new legislation. David Mayhew's data on landmark legislative enactments have been used to demonstrate polarization's effects on the legislative process (Mayhew 1991). Congress enacted the vast majority of Mayhew's landmark measures during the least polarized period.[8] The ten least polarized congressional terms produced almost sixteen significant enactments per term, whereas the ten most polarized terms produced slightly more than ten.[9]

To control for other factors that might explain these differences, I developed a multivariate model of legislative output.[10] I attempt to isolate the effect of polarization by controlling for unified party control of government, split party control of Congress, the election cycle, changes in party control of the presidency and Congress, and secular trends. This work shows that there are substantively large and statistically significant negative effects of polarization. Based on the estimates, the least polarized congressional term produces 111 percent more legislation than the most polarized.

Congress has not only struggled in passing new legislation. It has also struggled to efficiently exercise its constitutional power of the purse. The 1974 Congressional Budget and Impoundment Control Act calls on Congress to pass a budget resolution. Under "regular" order, both chambers pass resolutions and the differences are reconciled by a conference committee. Congressional performance in this stage of the budget process shows clear deterioration over time. There are four major budgetary milestones: House passage, Senate passage, House passage of the conference report, and Senate passage of the conference report. From 1976 to 1998, Congress successfully cleared all four of these hurdles. Since then, there has been a completed budget resolution in only nine of twenty years. In 2011, neither chamber passed its own budget resolution.

Congress is also expected to pass each of its appropriation bills before the start of the fiscal year (currently October 1). If it fails to do so, Congress and the president must agree to a continuing resolution (CR) or face a government shutdown such as ones that occurred in 1995–1996 and 2013. Generally, CRs continue the funding levels of the previous fiscal year, but many also include some modifications of spending levels. CRs often contain changes to the authorizing statutes, and because they are often "must pass" legislation, unrelated legislation is often attached. Consequently, delays in the passage of appropriation bills and the resulting "governing by CR" has drawn wide concern. Late appropriation bills are said to create budgetary uncertainty for government agencies and private actors, reduce the ability to adjust to new spending priorities, undermine the role of committee expertise, and weaken fiscal governance (White 1988; Devins 1988; Hanson 2013).

To measure the trends in the propensity to begin a fiscal year without completed appropriation bills, I compiled data on each regular appropriation bill for FY1974 to FY2017.[11] To measure delay, I simply compare the date of final passage with the start date of the fiscal year. I consider an appropriation bill to have passed if it is signed by the president as a standalone appropriation bill or as a separate title of an omnibus appropriation bill. My data show that appropriation delays have become the norm. Only about 10 percent of all appropriation bills passed before the beginning of the fiscal year. The modal month of passage is during the third month of the fiscal year (currently December). But a substantial share of bills pass in months four, five, and six. Delays have also become much more common. Very few appropriation bills have been completed on time since 2002, and the frequency of delays exceeding two months has gone up dramatically. In a multivariate analysis of the determinant of appropriation delay, I find that delays correlate directly with polarization and with interbranch and interchamber preference differences, which themselves are functions of partisan polarization (McCarty 2016).

The performance of the Senate in the confirmation process is yet another example of deterioration. While battles over the confirmation of Supreme Court nominees and the overt obstruction of other judicial nominees have received much attention, the scope of the Senate's problems is often unappreciated. Not only have the confirmations of highly salient appointments succumbed to obstruction and delay, but the Senate is much slower on the hundreds of less important nominations that it must approve each term.

In an earlier study, Rose Razaghian and I collected information about the almost five thousand nominations to positions in domestic executive branch agencies from the 49th to the 109th Senates (1885–2004). I have updated these data though the end of 2017 to include another approximately eight hundred confirmations.[12] The main focus of our study was the duration of the confirmation process from the date of the president's official nomination to final action by the Senate.[13]

First, the expected delay in conformations has grown tremendously since the 1960s. In 1961, the average delay was eleven days. In 2017, it had grown to ninety-three days.[14] Second, the variation in the length of confirmations has grown precipitously. It is now quite common for a nominee to languish hundreds of days without Senate action. Interestingly, the 2013 changes to Senate rules that eliminated the filibuster on nominations appear to have had little effect on the speed of confirmation for these appointees.

In our multivariate analysis, Razaghian and I found a strong correlation between the level of polarization and the duration of the confirmation process. Moreover, we found that the association with polarization was strengthened during periods of divided government. So it seems that polarization has not only affected judicial nominations but extends all the way to the lowest levels of Senate-confirmed positions.

POLARIZATION IN THE STATES

As mentioned above, the consequences of congressional gridlock may depend on the extent to which other institutions are themselves directly impacted by polarization. To that end, consider the polarization of state legislatures. Shor and McCarty (2011) measure the polarization of state legislatures using a combination of state legislative journals and online records to acquire the roll-call voting records from every state from the 1990s to the present.[15]

Although the Shor-McCarty measures cover only the past twenty-five years, the trajectory of polarization at the state and national levels has been remarkably consistent over that period. Aggregate trends and patterns of

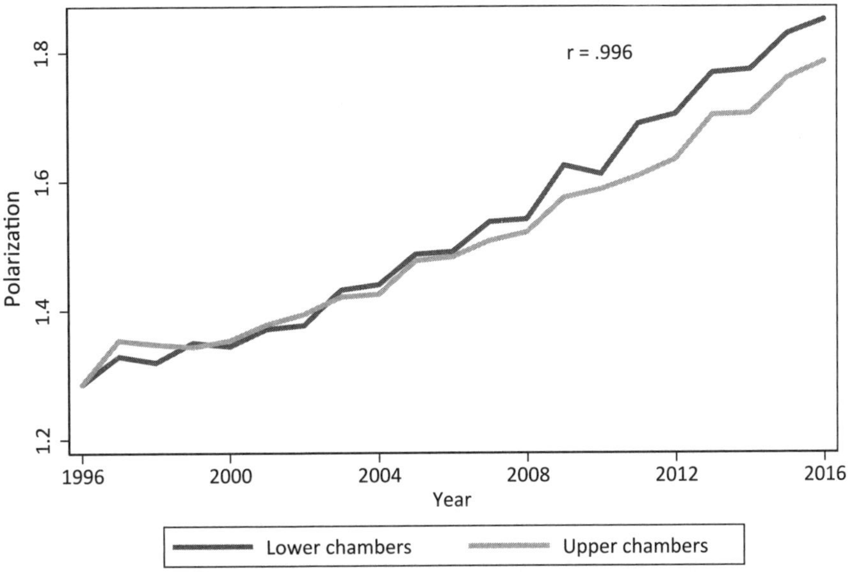

Figure 5.3: Polarization of State Legislators by Party. The polarization measure is the difference in the mean score for Republicans and the mean score for Democrats. *Source*: Author's computations from NPAT common space scores. See Shor and McCarty (2011).

polarization at the state level tend to match those of the US House and Senate. Figure 5.3 shows the average difference between Republican and Democratic state legislators for each each year on the NPAT scale. The first takeaway is that just like members of the US Congress, the partisan differences have been growing steadily. Second, the patterns for members of state lower chambers are essentially identical to those of state senators. That state senators have larger and presumably more heterogeneous constituencies does not seem to lead to a measurable diminution in polarization in those bodies.

But importantly, there is significant variation in the levels and trends in polarization across states and regions. Figure 5.4 plots polarization of lower chamber legislators across the four US census regions for the 1996–2015 period. The figure indicates that polarization tends to be lowest in the South (due to more moderate Democratic parties) and the Northeast (due to more moderate Republican parties). The West and North Central regions have the most polarized parties. Until very recently, the Northeast and the North Central regions have witnessed more modest increases in polarization than those occurring in the South and the West.

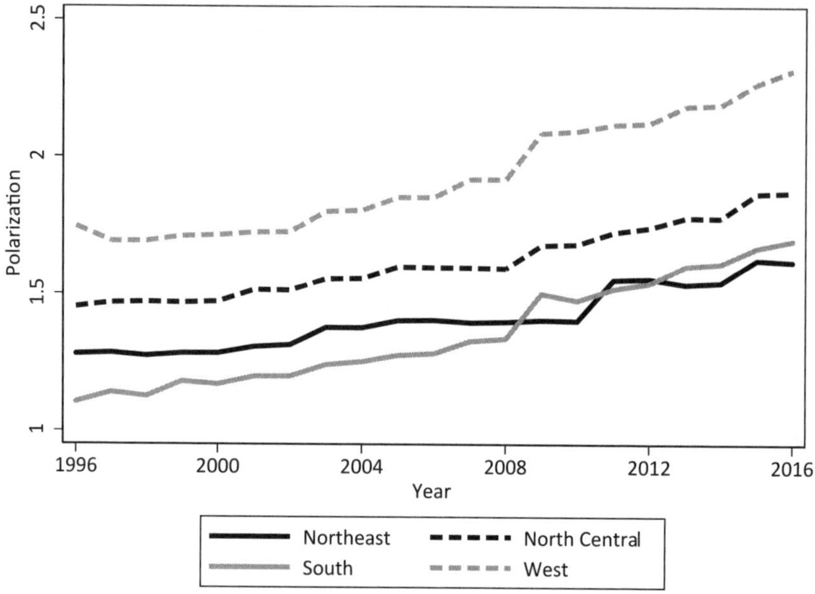

Figure 5.4: Polarization of State Legislators by Region. The polarization measure is the difference in the mean score for Republicans and the mean score for Democrats. *Source*: Computed from NPAT common space scores. See Shor and McCarty (2011).

Given the importance of supermajoritarian institutions and the increasing frequency of divided government, gridlock has been the focus of studies of the effect of polarization on policymaking at the federal level. It is less clear, however, that the states face the same problems. First, it is less common for state legislatures to have supermajority voting or cloture requirements (Scobee 2016). A few states have such requirements on specific legislation such as budgets or tax increases (Hiltz and Martel 2018). But majority rule on other legislation is the norm.

Given the lack of internal supermajoritarian procedures, the main impediments to state legislative action are likely to be split party control of the legislature and divided party government. But split control and divided party government are far less frequent at the state level than at the national level. Moreover, these divisions of party control are declining. Figure 5.5 reveals a sharp downward trend in the frequency by which the partisan control of state legislative chambers is split by parties. In fact, following the 2018 elections, Minnesota was the only state where each party controlled a legislative chamber, representing the lowest frequency of split legislatures

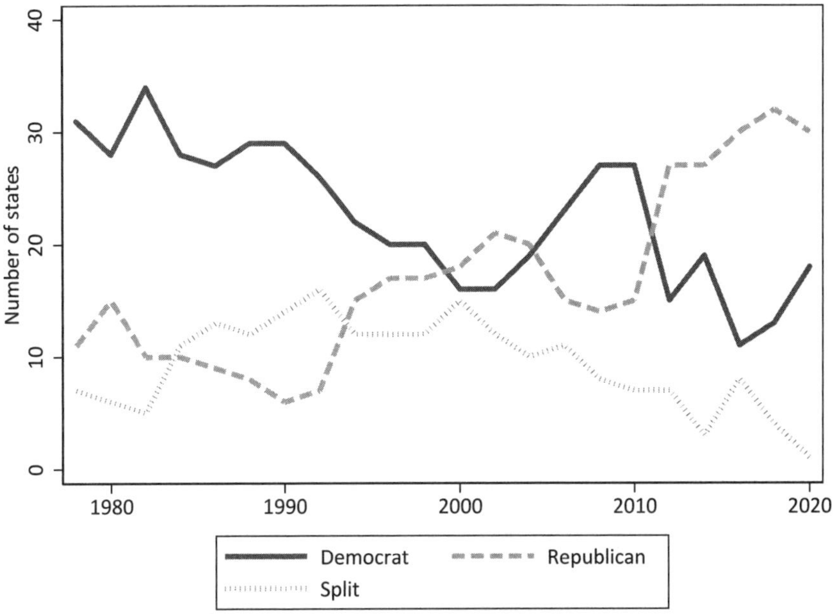

Figure 5.5: Legislative Control. *Source*: From data compiled by the National Conference of State Legislatures.

in more than a century.[16] Not only have the incidences of split legislatures declined, but so have the incidences of divided governments. Whereas power was split between the executive and legislative branches in most states in the 1990s, figure 5.6 shows that the number of divided governments has fallen to the mid-teens. Both types of partisan governments are more common than divided government.

Given the observed increase in single party control, legislative gridlock is less likely to be a problem in the states than at the federal level. Indeed, the combination of polarization and single party control is more likely to produce significant policy divergences across states.

This possibility seems all the more likely given that there has not only been significant partisan polarization within states but also considerable polarization across states. Figure 5.7 shows a large increase in the standard deviation of the median ideal point of state legislatures.

The upshot of figure 5.7 is that the states are much more ideologically divided than they were twenty-five years ago. Thus, it is natural to expect two direct implications. First, we should expect to see policy outcomes increasingly vary across states. Second, we should expect to see greater conflict between states and the federal government as more liberal states will

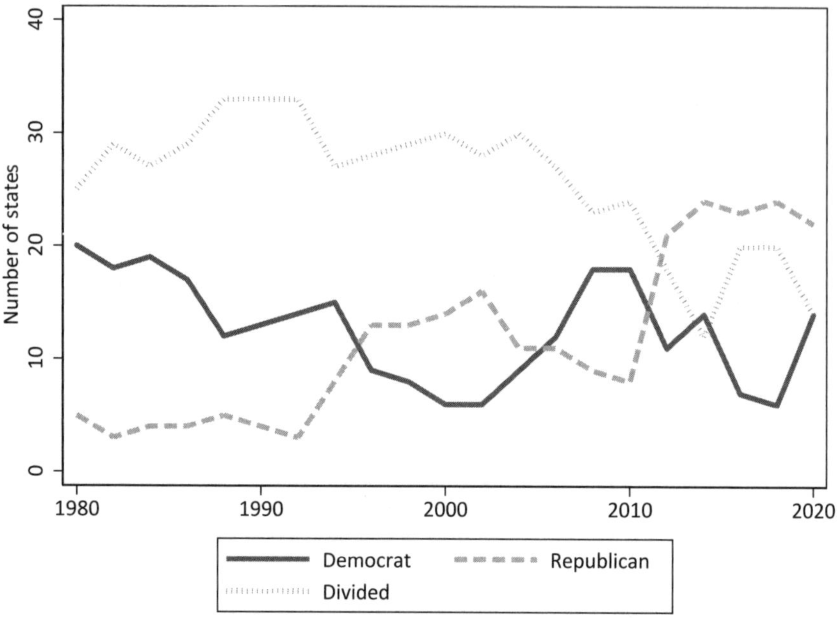

Figure 5.6: Government Control. *Source*: From data compiled by the National Conference of State Legislatures.

oppose conservative national administrations and more conservative state governments will oppose liberal administrations. Both of these implications are explored later in the chapter.

While it is beyond the scope of this chapter to fully explore the sources of this cross-state polarization, a few observations are in order. Perhaps the most obvious hypothesis is that cross-state polarization, as well as the rise in unified party control, is caused by increased state-level sorting of voters on partisanship or ideology. Consistent with such a hypothesis, Hopkins (2017b) notes that presidential contests at the state level have become less competitive over recent years. But other evidence of such sorting is illusive. To illustrate, I use the American National Election Study to evaluate whether the state of residence is increasingly predictive of voting, partisanship, or ideological self-placement. In each case, I regress the individual survey responses against a full set of state indicators. If there were an increase in state-level voter sorting, the predictive power of these state fixed-effect regressions (as measured by 2) should rise over time. In each analysis, I report the 2 for each election study along with a lowess smoothing line to show any trends.[17]

Figure 5.8 illustrates this exercise, conducted on reported vote choice.

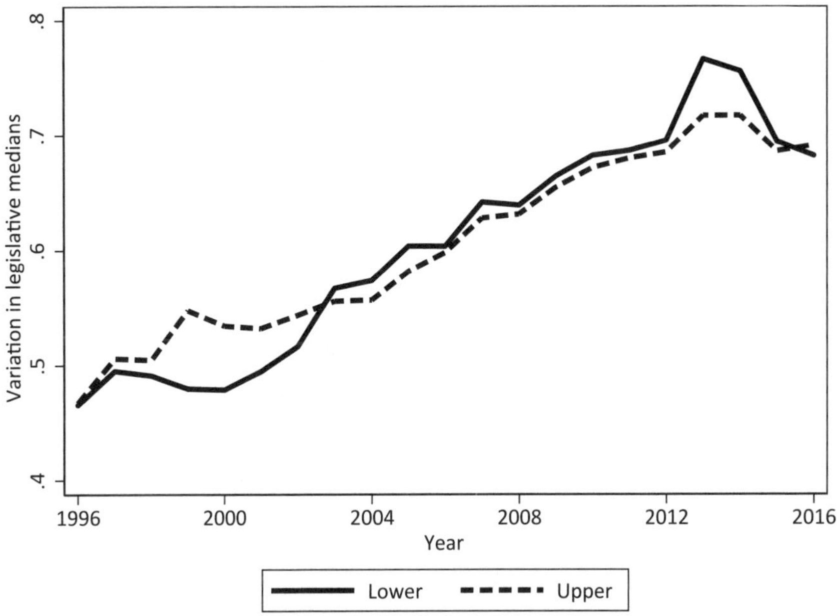

Figure 5.7: Cross-State Polarization. The measure is the cross-state variation in the chamber median ideal point. *Source*: Computed from NPAT common space scores. See Shor and McCarty (2011).

Here, there is modest evidence of increased sorting as the lowess line shows growth from about the year 2000 onward. However, much of the effect is driven by the extreme sorting of the 2012 presidential vote. If the 2012 election is eliminated, the lowess for 2016 is less than 0.01 higher than the value for 2000.

There also seems to be little evidence for sorting on partisanship (figure 5.9) or ideological self-placement (figure 5.10.) There is an uptick in the sorting on partisanship, but it also is largely a consequence of 2012. Sorting on ideology is on a downward trajectory. So it seems unlikely sorting can account for the cross state polarization.

A second, perhaps more promising, hypothesis is that of the nationalization of state and local elections (Rogers 2016; Hopkins 2017a). To the extent that voters now increasingly cast ballots in state elections based on national political issues, we should expect Democratic-leaning states to elect uniformly liberal state governments and Republican-leaning ones to elect conservative ones. Thus, even if sorting is constant, it is possible that nationalization pushes different states in different partisan and ideological direc-

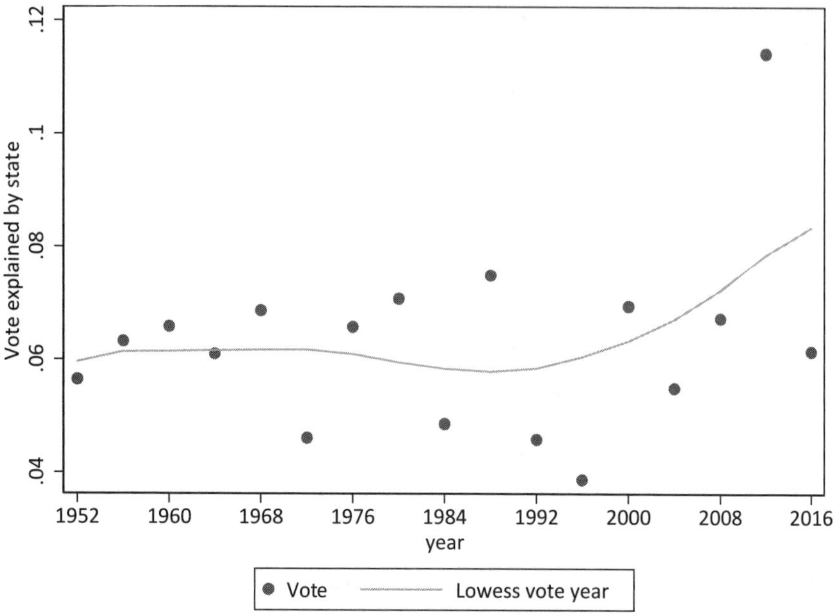

Figure 5.8: Presidential Vote Explained by State. The lowess line represents the smoothed moving average of the R2 over elections. *Source*: Variation in presidential voting explained by state of residence, American National Election Study.

tions. Finally, the patterns of cross-state polarization may relate to increased activity of national-level interest groups at the state level (Hertel-Fernandez 2019; Kroeger 2016).

EFFECTS OF GRIDLOCK ON FEDERALISM

The discussion above suggests several consequences of polarization for state politics and the operation of the federal system. The most direct implication is that federal gridlock may open spaces for states to adopt innovative policies without worries about federal preemption. Consider the liberalization of marijuana laws. Although Congress has not provided statutory authorization for states to legalize medical or recreational marijuana, President Obama's Department of Justice decided not to prosecute certain types of violations of federal marijuana law in those states that have a legal cannabis market (Cole 2013). As discussed in the introduction, net neutrality is another prime example. With federal gridlock increasing in tandem

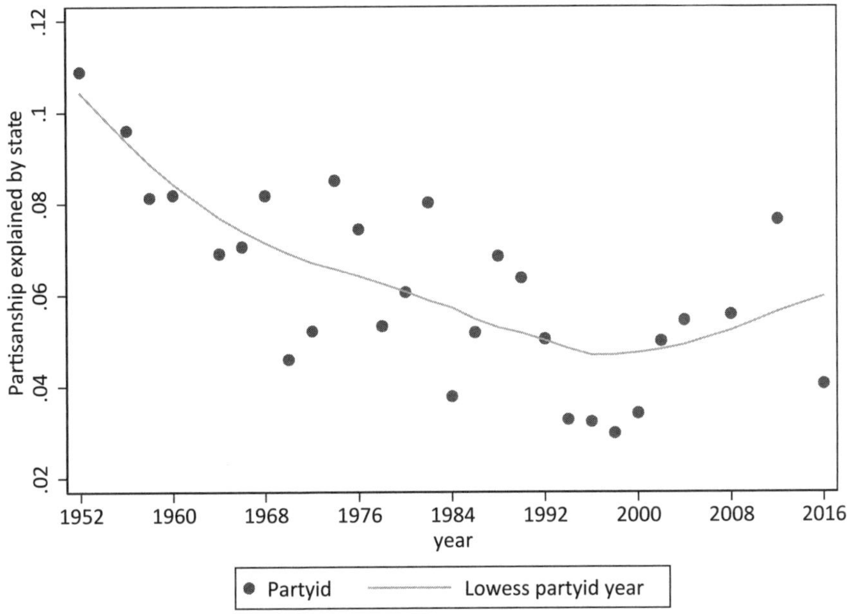

Figure 5.9: Partisanship Explained by State. The lowess line represents the smoothed moving average of the R2 over elections. *Source*: Variation in party identification explained by state of residence, American National Election Study.

with cross-state polarization, we should see not only more policy activity at the state level but also widening differences in policy outcomes between liberal and conservative states.

A second important implication of cross-state polarization is that states will be more likely to be drawn into conflicts with federal policies. States will have enhanced opportunities and incentives to actively resist federal policy. Legal scholars Jessica Bulman-Pozen and Heather Gerken have dubbed this new tendency "uncooperative federalism" (Bulman-Pozen and Gerken 2009). In their account, states are able to use their sovereign powers in a variety of ways that shape and constrain federal policy. They may shape national policy agendas through legislation or litigation or exploit their role as administrators of federal policies to force the federal government to heed state concerns. The power of the states' role in federal agenda setting is attested to by the increased activity of national interest groups such as the American Legislative Exchange Council (ALEC) in promoting model legislation across states as a way of shaping the national policy agenda (Hertel-Fernandez 2019).

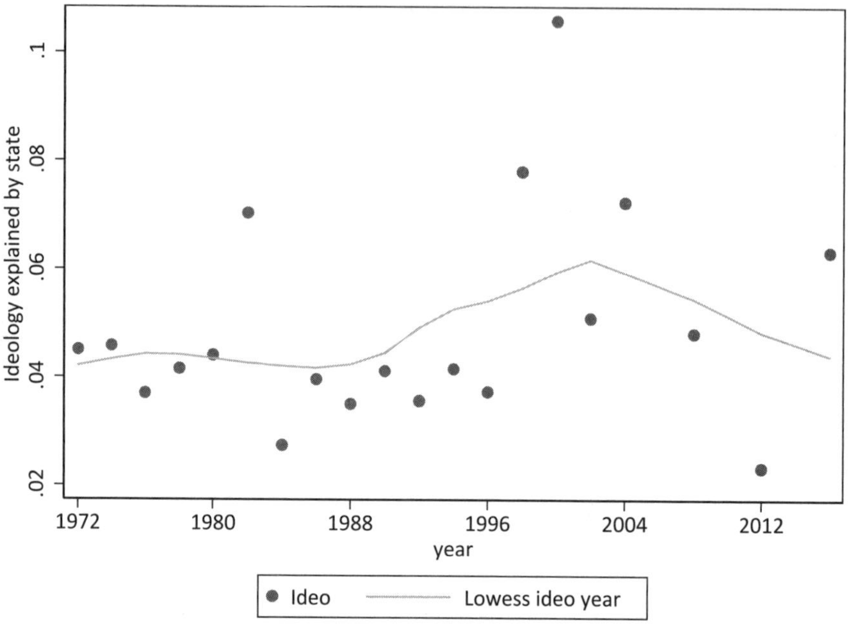

Figure 5.10: Ideological Self-Placement Explained by State. The lowess line represents the smoothed moving average of the R2 over elections. *Source*: Variation in ideological self-placement explained by state of residence, American National Election Study.

Polarization clearly enhances the incentives for state contestation of federal policy (Bulman-Pozen 2014). This is especially true in the case of unified party control at the federal level. In these situations, states controlled by the national out-party become the locus of opposition to federal policy. Just as Republican states resisted and challenged the Affordable Care Act, Democratic states are challenging Trump administration policies on immigration and the environment. Consequently, states become the primary check on federal executive power when Congress has little incentive to play that role. States, through their ability to bring lawsuits, have also had a very important role in shaping policies related to the environment, tobacco, financial regulation, and immigration in the absence of congressional action.

But while polarization and federal gridlock are likely to draw the states into a greater role in national policymaking, polarization may also affect the way the states themselves are governed, especially when combined with the nationalization of state elections. As gubernatorial and state legislative elections become increasingly determined by national-level economic and partisan factors, the payoff to legislative efforts on local issues may decline (Rogers 2016; Hopkins 2017a). Moreover, accountability may be harmed as the nationalization of elections leaves state legislators less constrained by the wishes of their constituents (Rogers 2017).

A major constraint on state-level policymaking on national issues is that the exercise of the states' powers requires the complicity of the federal executive and judicial branches. In January 2018, the Trump administration reversed the DOJ's memorandum on prosecuturial discretion for marijuana cases in states where it is legal.[18] The states' ability to set policy as plaintiffs depends on a sympathetic judiciary. Moreover, congressional gridlock leaves the states in a vulnerable position. States can no longer depend on Congress to check executive encroachments or to override unfavorable statutory interpretations by the courts.

HAS POLARIZATION AFFECTED POLICYMAKING IN THE STATES?

In this section, I review the existing evidence on some of the hypothesized effects of federal gridlock and cross-state polarization. In particular, I explore the idea that the states will have opportunity and incentive to move policies into alignment with the ideological and partisan priorities of the controlling party. Two recent studies provide substantial evidence in favor of this hypothesis.

In the first, Devin Caughey, Yiqing Xu, and Christopher Warshaw use a measure of state policy liberalism to test whether partisan differences in policy outcomes have grown and whether that growth can be attributed to partisan polarization in the states.[19] The authors find that before the 1990s, policy changes associated with changing from a Republican-controlled government to a Democratic-controlled government were small and not statistically significant. But since that time, a switch in party control has led to a statistically significant increase in the liberalism of a state's policies. In support of the idea that polarization can account for this increase, they find that switches in party control lead to bigger policy shifts when either the legislators or the electorate are more polarized. The authors find, however, that the effects of shifts in party control are still relatively small.

But it is worth noting that the study focuses primarily on determining the "causal impact" of a switch in party control. This leads the authors to focus on states that are sufficiently competitive to have transitions in party control. This focus tends to understate the growing correlation between party control and policy choices in the states, as noncompetitive Republi-

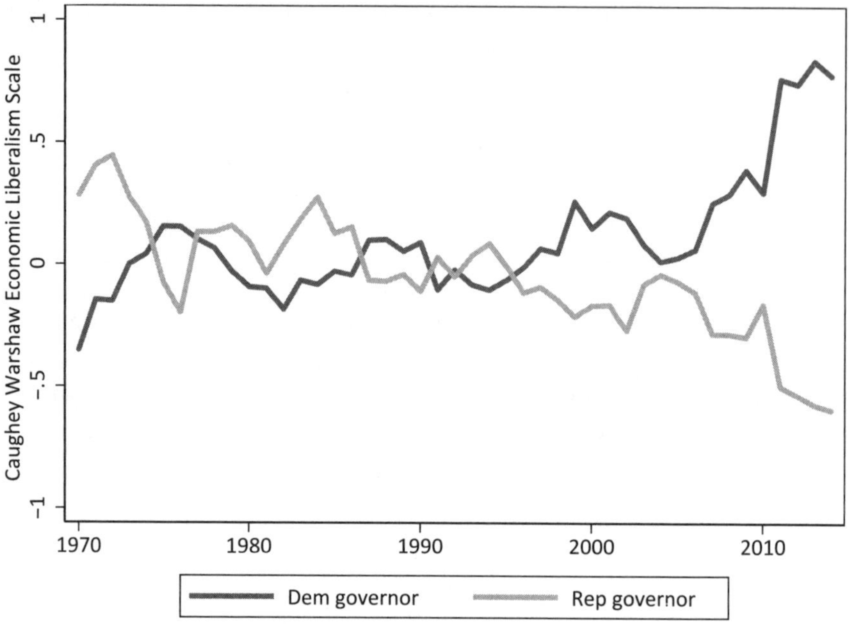

Figure 5.11: Aggregate Party Policy Liberalism Gap. *Source*: Author's computations based on data from Caughey, Xu, and Warshaw (2017).

can states have adopted much more conservative polices, while noncompetitive Democratic states have moved in a liberal direction. To illustrate, figure 5.11 plots the difference in the authors' economic policy scale between states with Democratic and Republican governors. The total difference in policy liberalism between states with Democratic governors and states with Republican governors is much larger than their estimated effect of a party switch.

Jacob Grumbach undertakes a similar study (Grumbach 2018). But rather than focus on a summary measure of state party liberalism, he develops several scales associated with distinct policy domains. He also finds that there was little effect of party control on policy until the 1990s, but that partisan effects have become important over the past fifteen years—a process that he calls "policy polarization." He finds that the extent of policy polarization varies substantially across issues. For some issues, the policy changes associated with a change in party control have become substantial. These include taxes, labor policy, abortion, LGBT issues, the environment, and immigration. But other polices such as criminal justice and education are not correlated with partisan control of state government.[20] Importantly,

Grumbach demonstrates that policy polarization has led to substantial partisan gaps in policy outcomes such as revenue, spending, and health coverage.

CONCLUSION

The arguments and evidence in this chapter raise many normative questions about the performance of federalism in the United States. First, these changes may expand opportunities for federalism to serve some of its primary purposes. The de facto devolution of authority to the states may allow them to adopt policies that better match the preferences of local majorities. In fact, at a time of geographic polarization at the national level, the local customization of policies may help to diffuse the conflicts that have helped generate polarization and gridlock at the national level. These changes may well spark state-level innovation on important policies related to education, health care, and the environment. Of course, given the paucity of evidence of the true geographic sorting of voters, we cannot be entirely confident that the wider array of policies that we observe do indeed reflect voter desires. Thus future research will have to develop better longitudinal measures of state-level voter preferences to assess whether the policies are indeed a better match or reflect the ideological commitments of elites and interest groups.

Second, even if it were true that state policies were becoming better matches for local majorities, we must remain concerned that this trend may come at the expense of local political minorities. This becomes a more pressing problem depending on the extent to which the increasing predominance of single-party control cements itself into local political monopolies.[21] Such monopolies have the incentive and opportunity to manipulate electoral and legislative rules to maintain power and insulate themselves from citizen demands.

To the extent to which the nationalization of state politics is a driver of these trends, we also have to be concerned about the loss of attention to local issues and the implications for accountability of governors and state legislators.

Finally, it is important to remember that enhanced policymaking by the states can never be a perfect substitute for national-level legislative solutions. Spillovers, races-to-the-bottom, and other collective action problems remain a major obstacle to decentralized policymaking. Some issues are intrinsically national or global and require action on those levels.

NOTES

1. See Barber and McCarty (2013) for a recent review.

2. For a general argument, see Levinson and Pildes (2006). In support of this claim, Kriner and Schickler (2016) find evidence that the effect of divided government on House investigatory activity of the executive has been magnified by polarization, but they find no similar effect for the Senate.

3. While I focus primarily on Congress's legislative role, there is also evidence of similar problems related to its oversight functions, for example, Kriner and Schickler (2016).

4. See McCarty, Poole, and Rosenthal (2016) for a more extensive discussion of the measurement.

5. See Black (1948) on the median voter theorem. Technically, the median voter theorem requires that preferences be aligned on a single dimension. Unidimensionality is a reasonably good approximation of the contemporary Congress. See McCarty, Poole, and Rosenthal (2016), figure 2.2.

6. For a detailed explication of the underlying theory, see Krehbiel (1998) and Brady and Volden (2005).

7. See McCarty, Poole, and Rosenthal (2016), table 6.1.

8. See also Binder (2003) and Binder (2015).

9. The gap would be even bigger except for the enormous legislative output following the September 11 terrorist attacks during the polarized 2000s.

10. It is an updated version of that from McCarty (2007).

11. See McCarty (2016) for details.

12. McCarty and Razaghian (1999). To avoid complications related to senatorial courtesy, we did not collect data on nominees to head regional offices such as US attorneys or custom officials. Finally, to limit our focus to domestic politics, we did not collect data on the Departments of State or Defense.

13. Thus, we ignore the delay between an announced vacancy and the president's nomination. Clearly, the Senate's performance might also affect the duration of the prenomination selection and vetting process.

14. This estimate is subject to substantial censoring, as more than forty of Donald Trump's 2017 nominations to these positions were returned to the president unconfirmed at the end of session. This happened to only a couple of Kennedy's nominations in 1961.

15. To make cross-state comparisons, they use the National Political Awareness Test (NPAT), a survey of state and federal legislative candidates administered by Project Vote Smart, a nonpartisan organization. The questions asked by Project Vote Smart cover a wide range of policy matters, including foreign policy, national security, international affairs, social issues, fiscal policy, environmentalism, criminal justice, and many more. While the NPAT survey could have been used to estimate the ideal points of all respondents, the response rate of the survey is fairly low and thus provides ideal points for a fraction of state legislators. Consequently, they com-

bine the NPAT data with roll-call voting data. Under the assumption that each legislator's survey response and roll-call voting reflect the same underlying political preferences, they are able to estimate a common ideological scale for almost all state legislators serving since the 1990s. Since members of Congress also answer the NPAT, their scores can also be compared with those of federal legislators.

16. As the Republican majority in the Minnesota senate is only two seats, split control came perilously close to extinction.

17. A lowess line represents an approximation of the relation between variables where the expected value of y given the value of x is based primarily on observations close to x.

18. Department of Justice, "Justice Department Issues Memo on Marijuana Enforcement," January 4, 2018, https://www.justice.gov/opa/pr/justice-department-issues-memo-marijuana-enforcement.

19. See Caughey, Xu, and Warshaw (2017). See Caughey and Warshaw (2016) for the details of their measure.

20. Thus, the small average effect found in Caughey, Xu, and Warshaw (2017) may be the result of their policy liberalism averaging issues with some large partisan effects with those without such effects.

21. While Fraga and Hersh (2018) show that most Americans still experience competitive elections, party control of state government is becoming more persistent within states.

REFERENCES

Barber, Michael, and Nolan McCarty. "The Causes and Consequences of Polarization." In *Negotiating Agreement in Politics,* ed. Cathie Jo Martin and Jane Mansbridge. Washington, DC: American Political Science Association, 2013.

Binder, Sarah A. "The Dysfunctional Congress." *Annual Review of Political Science* 18 (2015): 85–101.

———. *Stalemate: Causes and Consequences of Legislative Gridlock.* Washington, DC: Brookings Institution, 2003.

Binder, Sarah A., and Forrest Maltzman. "Senatorial Delay in Confirming Federal Judges, 1947–1998." *American Journal of Political Science* (2002): 190–199.

Black, Duncan. "The Decisions of a Committee using a Special Majority." *Econometrica* 16, no. 3 (1948): 245–261.

Brady, David W., and Craig Volden. *Revolving Gridlock: Politics and Policy from Jimmy Carter to George W. Bush.* Boulder, CO: Westview, 2005.

Bulman-Pozen, Jessica. "Partisan Federalism." *Harvard Law Review* 127, no. 4 (2014): 1077–1146.

Bulman-Pozen, Jessica, and Heather K. Gerken. "Uncooperative Federalism." *Yale Law Journal* 118 (2009): 1256–1310.

Cameron, Charles M. *Veto Bargaining: Presidents and the Politics of Negative Power.* Cambridge: Cambridge University Press, 2000.

Cameron, Charles M., and Nolan McCarty. "Models of Vetoes and Veto Bargaining." *Annual Review of Political Science* 7 (2004): 409–435.

Caughey, Devin, and Christopher Warshaw. "The Dynamics of State Policy Liberalism, 1936–2014." *American Journal of Political Science* 60, no. 4 (2016): 899–913.

Caughey, Devin, Yiqing Xu, and Christopher Warshaw. "Incremental Democracy: The Policy Effects of Partisan Control of State Government." *Journal of Politics* 79, no. 4 (2017): 1342–1358.

Cole, James M. US Department of Justice Memorandum, August 29, 2013. https://www.justice.gov/iso/opa/resources/3052013829132756857467.pdf.

Devins, Neal E. "Appropriations Redux: A Critical Look at the Fiscal Year 1988 Continuing Resolution." *Duke Law Journal* 1988, no. 2 (1988): 389–421.

Epstein, David, and Sharyn O'Halloran. *Delegating Powers: A Transaction Cost Politics Approach to Policy Making under Separate Powers.* New York: Cambridge University Press, 1999.

Fraga, Bernard L., and Eitan D. Hersh. "Are Americans Stuck in Uncompetitive Enclaves? An Appraisal of US Electoral Competition." *Quarterly Journal of Political Science* 13, no. 3 (2018): 291–311.

Gilmour, John B. *Strategic Disagreement: Stalemate in American Politics.* Pittsburgh: University of Pittsburgh Press, 1995.

Groseclose, Tim, and Nolan McCarty. "The Politics of Blame: Bargaining Before an Audience." *American Journal of Political Science* 45, no. 1 (2001): 100–119.

Grumbach, Jacob M. "From Backwaters to Major Policymakers: Policy Polarization in the States, 1970–2014." *Perspectives on Politics* 16, no. 2 (2018): 416–435.

Hanson, Peter. *Too Weak to Govern: Majority Party Power and Appropriations in the US Senate.* New York: Cambridge University Press, 2014.

———. "Abandoning the Regular Order: Majority Party Influence on Appropriations in the United States Senate." Typescript: University of Denver, 2013.

Hertel-Fernandez, Alexander. *State Capture: How Conservative Activists, Big Businesses, and Wealthy Donors Reshaped the American States—and the Nation.* New York: Oxford University Press, 2019.

Hiltz, Allison, and Luke Martel. "Supermajority Vote Requirements to Pass the Budget." *NCSL Blog,* November 9, 2018. http://www.ncsl.org/research/fiscal-policy/supermajority-vote-requirements-to-pass-the-budget635542510.aspx.

Hopkins, Daniel J. *The Increasingly United States: How and Why American Political Behavior Nationalized.* Chicago: University of Chicago Press, 2017a.

Hopkins, David A. *Red Fighting Blue: How Geography and Electoral Rules Polarize American Politics.* New York: Cambridge University Press, 2017b.

Howell, William G., and Terry M. Moe. *Relic: How Our Constitution Undermines Effective Government–and Why We Need a More Powerful Presidency.* New York: Basic, 2016.

Joseph O'Connell, Anne. "Shortening Agency and Judicial Vacancies through Filibuster Reform? An Examination of Confirmation Rates and Delays from 1981 to 2014." *Duke Law Journal* 64 (2015): 1645–1715.

———. "Vacant Offices: Delays in Staffing Top Agency Positions." *Southern California Law Review* 82 (2009): 913.

Kang, Cecilia. "States Push Back after Net Neutrality Repeal." *New York Times*, January 11, 2018. https://www.nytimes.com/2018/01/11/technology/net-neutrality-states.html.

Krehbiel, Keith. *Pivotal Politics: A Theory of US Lawmaking*. Chicago: University of Chicago Press, 1998.

Kriner, Douglas L., and Eric Schickler. *Investigating the President: Congressional Checks on Presidential Power*. Princeton, NJ: Princeton University Press, 2016.

Kroeger, Mary A. "Plagiarizing policy: Model Legislation in State Legislatures." Paper presented at 15th Annual State Politics and Policy Conference, Sacramento, California, 2016.

Lee, Frances E. *Insecure Majorities: Congress and the Perpetual Campaign*. Chicago: University of Chicago Press, 2016.

———. *Beyond Ideology: Politics, Principles, and Partisanship in the US Senate*. Chicago: University of Chicago Press, 2009.

Levinson, Daryl J., and Richard H. Pildes. "Separation of Parties, Not Powers." *Harvard Law Review* 119 (2006): 2311–2386.

Mayhew, David R. *Divided We Govern*. New Haven, CT: Yale University Press, 1991.

———. *Congress: The Electoral Connection*. New Haven, CT: Yale University Press, 1974.

McCarty, Nolan. "The Decline of Regular Order in Appropriations—Does It Matter?" In *Congress and Policy Making in the 21st Century*, ed. Jeffrey Jenkins and Eric Patashnik, 162. New York: Cambridge University Press, 2016.

———. "Reducing Polarization by Making Parties Stronger." In *Solutions to Political Polarization in America*, ed. Nathaniel Persily. New York: Cambridge University Press, 2015a.

———. "Reducing Polarization: Some Facts for Reformers." *University of Chicago Legal Forum* (2015b): 243–278.

———. "The Policy Effects of Political Polarization." In *Transformations of American Politics*, ed. Paul Pierson and Theda Skocpol. Princeton, NJ: Princeton University Press, 2007.

———. "Presidential Reputation and the Veto." *Economics & Politics* 9, no. 1 (1997): 1–26.

McCarty, Nolan, Keith T. Poole, and Howard Rosenthal. *Polarized America: The Dance of Ideology and Unequal Riches*. Cambridge, MA: MIT Press, 2016.

———. *Income Redistribution and the Realignment of American Politics*. Washington, DC: AEI, 1997.

McCarty, Nolan, and Rose Razaghian. "Advice and Consent: Senate Responses to Executive Branch Nominations 1885–1996." *American Journal of Political Science* 44, no. 4 (1999): 1122–1143.

Moe, Terry M., and William G. Howell. "The Presidential Power of Unilateral Action." *Journal of Law, Economics, and Organization* 15, no. 1 (1999): 132–179.

Pildes, Richard H. "Focus on Fragmentation, Not Polarization: Re-Empower Party Leadership." In *Solutions to Political Polarization in America,* ed. Nathaniel Persily. New York: Cambridge University Press, 2015.

Poole, Keith T., and Howard Rosenthal. "The Polarization of American Politics." *Journal of Politics* 46, no. 4 (1984): 1061–1079.

Posner, Eric A., and Adrian Vermeule. *The Executive Unbound: After the Madisonian Republic.* New York: Oxford University Press, 2011.

Reardon, Margerite. "What You Need to Know about the FCC's 2015 Net Neutrality Repeal." *CNet,* December 14, 2018. https://www.cnet.com/news/fcc-net-neutrality-repeal -ajit-pai-what-you-need-to-know/.

———. "What You Need to Know about the FCC's 2015 Net Neutrality Regulation." *CNet,* March 14, 2015. https://www.cnet.com/news/13-things-you-need-to -know-about-the-fccs-net-neutrality-regulation/.

Rogers, Steven. "Electoral Accountability for State Legislative Roll Calls and Ideological Representation." *American Political Science Review* 111, no. 3 (2017): 555–571.

———. "National Forces in State Legislative Elections." *Annals of the American Academy of Political and Social Science* 667, no. 1 (2016): 207–225.

Scobee, Paige. "Ahoy! The Future of the Filibuster." *NCSL Blog,* June 29, 2016. http://www.ncsl.org/blog/2016/06/29/ahoy-the-future-of-the-filibuster.aspx.

Shor, Boris, and Nolan McCarty. "The Ideological Mapping of American Legislatures." *American Political Science Review* 105, no. 3 (2011): 530–551.

White, Joe. "The Continuing Resolution: A Crazy Way to Govern?" *Brookings Review* 6, no. 3 (1988): 28–35.

Woon, Jonathan, and Sarah Anderson. "Political Bargaining and the Timing of Congressional Appropriations." *Legislative Studies Quarterly* 37, no. 4 (2012): 409–436.

PART THREE

Public Opinion and Political Behavior in a Polarized Era

CHAPTER 6

She's Not My Governor: Negative Partisanship and Trust in Government in the American States

Kristin Kanthak

Political scientists used to think of American voters as people who put their political party first, using their affiliation with a party as a "perceptual screen" through which they understood the issues of the day (Campbell et al. 1960). Rather than figuring out what they personally thought about each issue, voters could just support their party's own views and figure that was close enough. But for many American voters, their own political party no longer operates as a lens through which to understand politics. Rather, voters go to the polls to select the party they dislike the least (Abramowitz and Webster 2016a, 2016b). This phenomenon—called "negative partisanship"—has had a profound impact on how politics operates in the United States, leading to decreased trust among citizens (Hetherington 2006), a historically polarized Congress (Bafumi and Herron 2010; McCarty, Poole, and Rosenthal 2016), and subsequent gridlock. Outside of the United States, scholars have linked negative partisanship to vote choice (Medeiros and Noël 2014), turnout (Mayer 2017), and other political activities (McGregor, Caruana, and Stephenson 2015). Negative partisanship can even lead to decreased satisfaction with democracy itself (Spoon and Kanthak 2019). This chapter addresses the question of how negative partisanship affects attitudes toward government within the United States and tries to understand how political institutions might moderate the effects of negative partisanship.

The evidence presented here indicates that negative partisanship can affect a voter's perception of the quality of democracy, but the political institutions that define the governor and the legislature within a state can mitigate or exacerbate that effect. Furthermore, these effects are different based on what kind of negative partisan the respondent is: Negative partisans who dislike their opposing party are vastly different from those who dislike *both* parties. Specifically, the results here indicate that how much negative partisans dislike the opposing party moderates the effect for negative partisans of political institutions on trust in government. Gubernatorial power has little effect on trust, but negative partisans who feel warmly toward their own party (here called "intense negative partisans") experience less trust in government as the power of the legislature increases, an effect that does not exist for negative partisans who dislike both parties (here called "indifferent negative partisans").

The United States is an example of a majoritarian political system—the candidate with the most votes is the sole winner of the election—as opposed to other types of political systems, such as proportional representation, where representation is divided among several candidates, in proportion to their vote share. Linz (1990) shows that majoritarian systems tend to be less stable—meaning they are more likely to fail—than proportional systems because majoritarian elections create clear winners and losers, and losers are relegated to the sidelines. The majoritarian nature of American election means that nearly half (and sometimes more than half, in the cases of the US presidential elections of 2000 and 2016) of all citizens are consigned to the position of outsider in their own governments.

Indeed, Linz argues that the relative stability in the United States is the exception that proves his "majoritarian systems are unstable" rule. He claims that the United States has avoided the inherent instability of presidential democracies partially due to what he calls "the uniquely diffuse character of American political parties" (Linz 1990, 53). American parties in the mass public were, at the time of Linz's writing, ideologically undisciplined (Fiorina, Abrams, and Pope 2010), and evidence indicates that they remain so today (Kinder and Kalmoe 2017). Yet, the rise of negative partisanship could represent a change to that dynamic.

And clearly, negative partisanship can affect how voters think about their government, particularly when their least preferred party is in power. Hetherington (2006) found that a voter's trust in government to do the right thing can decrease for Americans when their less preferred party is in power, a phenomenon that goes back many years. And although the relationship between not liking the party in power and not trusting government has long been in evidence in the United States, Hetherington and

Rudolph (2015) show the relationship is becoming more dramatic as time goes on. Indeed, they find that the Obama presidency is correlated with a steep decline in trust for Republicans but not for Democrats. Furthermore, Towler and Parker (2018) find that among African American voters in the 2016 election, those who strongly disapproved of Trump were as politically engaged as African Americans in the historic election of 2008, when the election of the first black president prompted record-breaking African American turnout. In other words, having a candidate who a voter finds to be historically bad is as motivating as having a candidate who a voter finds to be historically good.

And while there is little research on the effect of US state political institutions on support for democracy itself, the same cannot be said for political efficacy. Indeed, there is a good deal of controversy in the political science literature on the question of how state characteristics might be related to citizens' political efficacy, with some finding correlations with efficacy and political culture (Hanson 1980), ballot initiatives (Bowler and Donovan 2002), and referenda (Mendelsohn and Cutler 2000) and others showing little correlation (Dyck and Lascher 2009; Kelleher and Wolak 2007). More recently, furthermore, Wolak (2018) finds that states with political structures that make voters feel their voices are heard also make voters feel more efficacious.

Certainly, part of the reason that questions of attitudes toward government have not reached the state level in the United States is that researchers in American politics tend to pay little attention to these questions as they may relate to stability of government, perhaps believing the relatively high levels of stability in the United States render the question moot. Yet the rise of negative partisanship in the United States may present a strong test of Linz's claim that weak parties insulate the United States from the inherent instability of majoritarian systems. More important, ignoring the role of the effect of institutions on feelings about government in the US context may mask an important threat to the health of the American democratic system. But researchers with less ingrained faith in the stability of democracy in the countries they study have produced an easy-to-follow trail as to how one might assess how much of a threat democratic stability in the United States could face from rising negative partisanship (Anderson and Guillory 1997; Norris 1999, 2004; Wagner, Schneider, and Halla 2009; Lijphart 2012). Drawing on this extensive research, then, we now turn to a theoretical model of satisfaction with democracy in the US states.

THEORETICAL MOTIVATION

Spoon and Kanthak (2019) posit in part that as the ability of the prime minister in a parliamentary system to change policy increases, dissatisfaction with democracy among voters who dislike the party of the prime minister will also increase. In a parliamentary system, the major check on the power of the prime minister's party is the number of parties in the prime minister's coalition. Of course, there is no similar check in a majoritarian winner-takes-all system like in the United States. Rather, the main check on the power of the governor is the institutional authority that is part of the job of the governor.

And indeed, the power of the governor differs widely from state to state. For example, the governor of North Carolina, perhaps the weakest governor in all of the states, shares power with a Council of State, a nine-member elected body that vastly curtails the ability of the governor to act independently (Morrill 2018). By contrast, the governor of Kentucky has wide latitude to control the state's government, with a line-item veto, the ability to call the legislature into session, the ability to make unilateral appointments, and other powers (Blanchard 1992).

A negative partisan in the context of a state is a person who dislikes the party of the governor. Similar to the case in a parliamentary system in which a disliked prime minister must share power with other parties, I argue here that when a disliked governor is weak, this decreases the effect of negative partisanship on a citizen's assessment of the quality of democracy. In other words, I expect those negative partisans whose governors are more powerful to be less pleased with government than those negative partisans whose governor is weaker.

But not all negative partisans are the same, and so we should not expect that institutional differences would affect all negative partisans similarly. Negative partisans are partisan identifiers who think negatively about the opposing party, but negative partisanship makes no claims about feelings about one's own party. A negative partisan could dislike *both* parties, in which case changes in institutional power will make little difference because his dissatisfaction with government is not based on being represented by one party when he would strongly prefer being represented by the other. On the other hand, partisans who would much prefer one party to the other are likely to be more sensitive to differences in institutional structure.

This thinking is laid out in hypothesis one: *As the power of the governor increases, trust in government decreases for intense negative partisans but not for indifferent negative partisans.*

States vary not only in how powerful the governor is but also in how powerful the legislature is. I would therefore expect a similar logic to apply for legislatures as well, as laid out in hypothesis two: *As the power of the legislature increases, trust in government decreases for intense negative partisans but not for indifferent negative partisans.*

The next section describes the data used to test these hypotheses.

DATA

Data for this analysis come from the American National Election Study (ANES) Time Series Panel between 2000 and 2016. Subjects were asked their opinion on several issues of interest, and those answers were linked to information about the respondent's state of residence. The unit of analysis, then, is the individual respondent (i.e., a voter) nested in the year and state of residence. I therefore use a multilevel mixed-effects linear regression, following Steenbergen and Jones (2002).

The dependent variable "Trust" is an index of answers to questions relating to the level of trust the respondent has in government in general, ranging from 100, corresponding to the least trusting, to 0, corresponding to the most trusting. The state of residence for each respondent is coded, allowing for the analysis of differences in trust across states. Differences in average levels of trust by state are depicted in figure 6.1.

The key independent variables of interest are *NegPartisan*, *Intensity*, *GovPower*, and *LegPower*, each described below. First, *NegPartisan* is a variable coded 0 if the respondent shares a political party with the institution of interest (either governor, lower chamber, or upper chamber), and a value from 0 to 100, where 100 is the most disliked and 0 is the least disliked Subjects are asked how much they like a party on a scale of 0 to 100, and so this measure of "dislike" is that answer "flipped," so that high numbers mean a great deal of "dislike." In other words, a Democrat living in a state with a Democratic governor would receive a 0, and a Democrat who dislikes the Republican Party as much as possible (coded as 100) living in a state with a Republican governor would receive a 100. This implies that each respondent has a separate value for *NegPartisan Gov*, *NegPartisan Lower*, and *NegPartisan Upper*, but some of those values will be the same. For example, a Democrat who registers a 75 on the Republican dislike scale and has a Republican governor, a Democratic lower chamber, and a Republican upper chamber would be coded as 75 for *NegPartisan Gov*, 0 for *NegPartisan Lower*, and 75 for *NegPartisan Upper*.

Intensity is a measure of the difference between the respondent's feeling

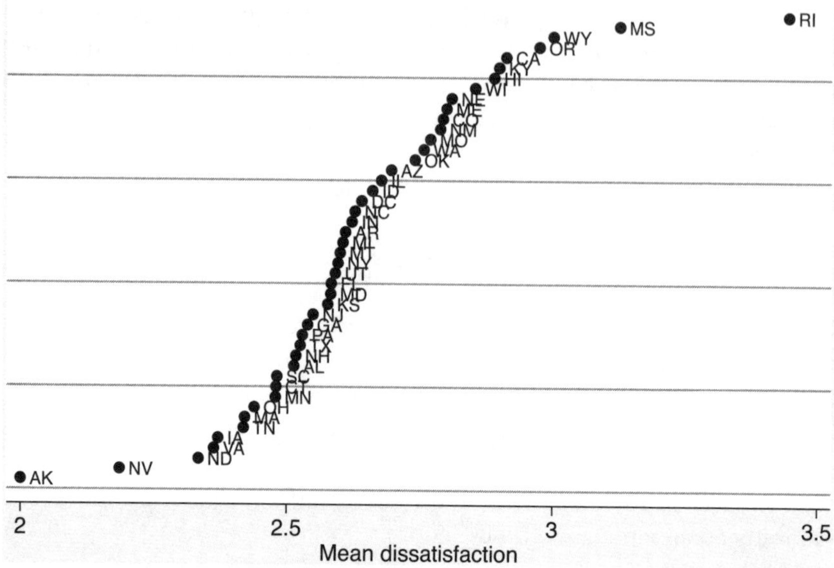

Figure 6.1: Mean Level of Trust by State. *Source*: Author's computations.

thermometer score for each of the two parties. In other words, if a respondent either greatly likes or greatly dislikes *both* parties, he will have a low score for *Intensity*, with a score of 0 when the respondent feels exactly equally warm toward both parties. Values of *Intensity* increase as the difference between the feeling thermometers of the two parties increase. In this sense, we can think of respondents as roughly divided into four groups: intense negative partisans, indifferent negative partisans, intense positive partisans, and indifferent positive partisans. An intense negative partisan is a respondent whose preferred party is not in power and who sees a big difference between the two parties. An indifferent negative partisan is a respondent whose preferred party is not in power but sees little difference between the two parties. An intense positive partisan is someone whose preferred party is in power (and therefore receives a value of 0 on *NegPartisan*) and sees a big difference between the two parties, and an indifferent positive partisan is a respondent whose preferred party is in power but sees little difference between the parties.

GovPower is a five-point scale that measures the institutional power of the governor. The measure is culled from Ferguson (2018, 252) and is a summary of the institutional powers of the governor of each state. Larger values of *GovPower* are associated with greater institutional power of the governor.

Similarly, *LegPower* is a measure of the institutional power of the legislature. Specifically, it is an updated Squire power index (Squire 2017). Because the hypotheses imply interactive terms, interacted variables are also included in the analysis.

The estimation includes two sets of controls, one measuring differences among individuals and one measuring differences among states. The individual-level variables include a dichotomous (taking on the value of either 0 or 1) gender measure, a self-reported ideology measure that comprises a seven-point scale ranging from very liberal (coded 1) to very conservative (coded 7), a measure of ideological extremity that is coded 1 if self-reported ideology is either 1 or 7 and zero otherwise, a dichotomous party variable coded 1 if the respondent is a Democrat and zero otherwise, a dichotomous education variable coded 1 if the respondent has attended college and zero otherwise, and an age range variable. State-level variables include polarization measures for both the upper and lower chambers of the legislature made up of the difference between the party medians of Shor-McCarty ideology scores for state legislators (Shor and McCarty 2011), a measure of how tight the last presidential election was that is constructed from the absolute difference between the Democratic and Republican candidates in the last presidential election, the Gini coefficient for the state, the state's poverty rate, the number of women in the state legislature, the percent of the state that is urban, and a dichotomous variable indicating whether or not the state has a closed primary.

I now turn to the analysis.

ANALYSIS

Table 6.1 presents the results of the multilevel mixed-effects linear regression. Because of the large number of control variables, I report only the coefficients on the variables of interest here. The results presented here represent three separate regressions for each of the dependent variables of interest. A regression with all three estimated at the same time yields substantially similar results to those reported here. The number of observations is different for each regression due to data missing because states without either a partisan governor, a partisan lower house, or a partisan upper house are dropped.

Intensity of feelings about one party (liking one party more than the other) is negatively and significantly correlated with lower levels of trust in government. Furthermore, the interaction between intensity and being represented by a powerful governor is statistically significant in the positive di-

Table 6.1: Trust in the US States

	Governor	Upper House	Lower House
NegPartisan Gov	0.301		
	(1.29)		
NegPartisan Gov × GovPower	-0.0684		
	(-0.93)		
NegPartisan Gov × Intensity	-0.00223		
	(-0.82)		
GovPower × Intensity	0.0587*		
	(2.19)		
NegPartisan Gov × GovPower × Intensity	0.000373		
	(0.44)		
NegPartisan Upper		0.0529	
		(0.89)	
NegPartisan Upper × LegPower		0.130	
		(0.74)	
NegPartisan Upper × Intensity		-0.000391	
		(-0.56)	
NegPartisan Upper × LegPower × Intensity		-0.00235	
		(-1.14)	
LegPower × Intensity		-0.0895	-0.115*
		(-1.56)	(-2.03)
NegPartisan Lower			0.0307
			(0.52)
NegPartisan Lower × LegPower			0.208
			(1.19)
NegPartisan Lower × Intensity			-0.000306
			(-0.45)
NegPartisan Lower × LegPower × Intensity			-0.00258
			(-1.25)
GovPower	-1.959	0.601	0.443
	(-1.04)	(0.53)	(0.40)
LegPower	-4.587	1.544	1.476
	(-1.42)	(0.32)	(0.32)
Intensity	-0.249*	-0.0432*	-0.0374
	(-2.91)	(-2.04)	(-1.80)
Observations	6140	6037	6166

Note: t statistics in parentheses

* $p < 0.05$

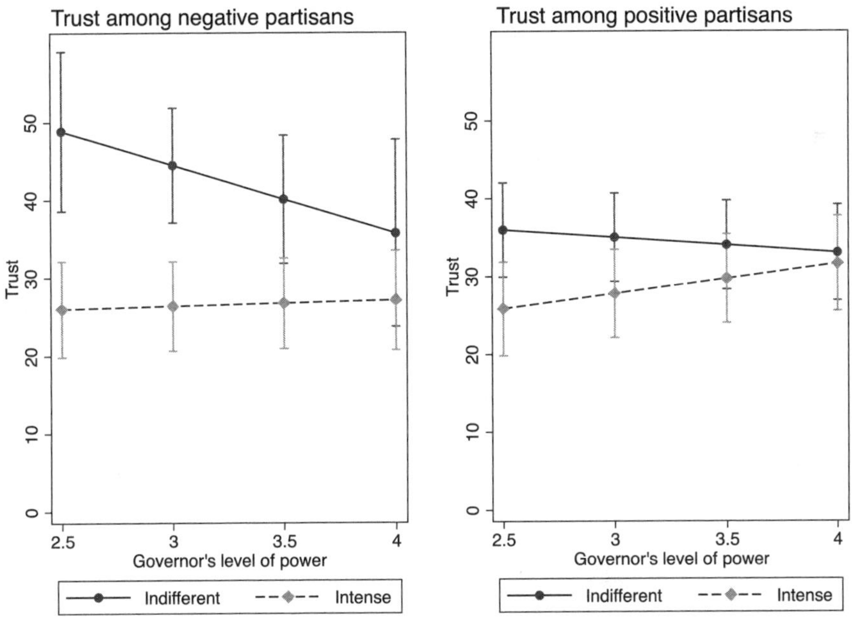

Figure 6.2: Effect of Governor's Power on Levels of Trust (90 percent CI). *Source*: Author's computations.

rection, whereas the interaction between intensity and being represented by a powerful legislature is negative, and in the case of the lower house statistically significant. But interactions—particularly triple interactions like the ones presented here—are notoriously difficult to interpret from a table. For that reason, I present a set of simulations based on the regression below.

The simulations are constructed by holding the *Intensity* variable to extremes and labeling the low extreme "Indifferent" for respondents who do not see much difference between the parties and "Intense" for respondents who see the opposing party as much worse than their own party. Furthermore, I hold the *NegPartisan* variables to extremes as well. "Negative partisans" are those who are represented by the opposing party and dislike that party a great deal. "Positive partisans" are coded as zero because they are represented by someone of their own party. I allow governor's level of power or legislature's level of power to vary in an effort to highlight differences in trust for different values of power.

Figure 6.2 depicts the effect of the power of the governor on levels of trust. Notably, those who see little difference between the parties are the most trusting, a result that is significantly different among negative partisans

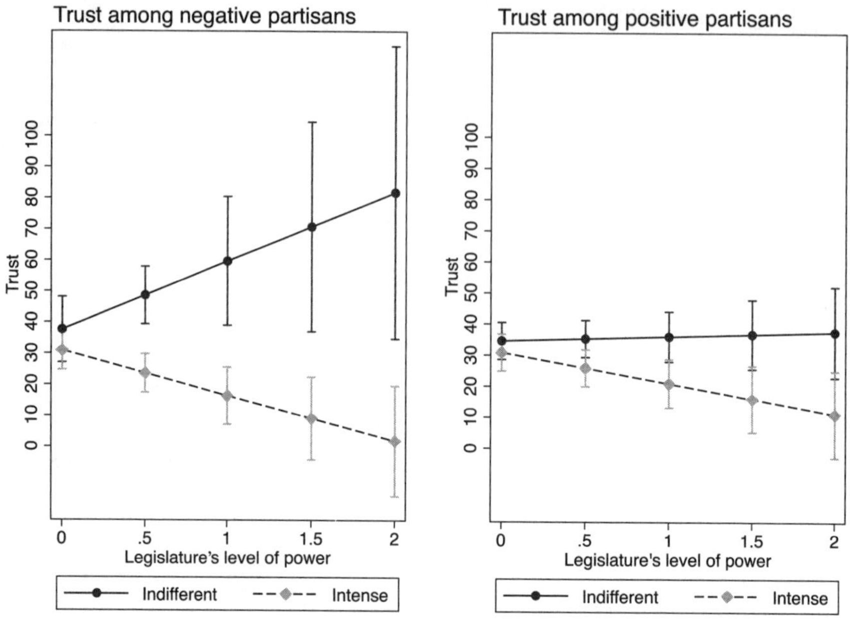

Figure 6.3: Effect of Lower Chamber's Power on Levels of Trust (90 percent CI). *Source*: Author's computations.

at all but the highest levels of gubernatorial power, as is clear on the left-hand side of the graph. In other words, at most levels of gubernatorial power, respondents who dislike both parties are more trusting in government than respondents who dislike only the party of the governor. For intense positive partisans (shown on the right-hand side of the graph), increases in the power of the governor lead to increases in trust, but the result is not significant. And indeed, there are no statistically significant differences between intense negative partisans and intense positive partisans. At no time, furthermore, does a change in the governor's level of power result in a statistically significant change in levels of trust for any type of respondent. Gubernatorial power, then, seems to have little effect on trust in government.

Figure 6.3, however, tells a somewhat different story with respect to the power of the lower chamber of the legislature, as measured using the Squire index of legislative professionalism. Indeed, intense negative partisans—those who dislike the majority party of the lower chamber but do like the out party—experience a statistically significant decrease in trust as legislatures move from most to least powerful. In other words, active negative partisans are significantly less trusting when legislatures are powerful than

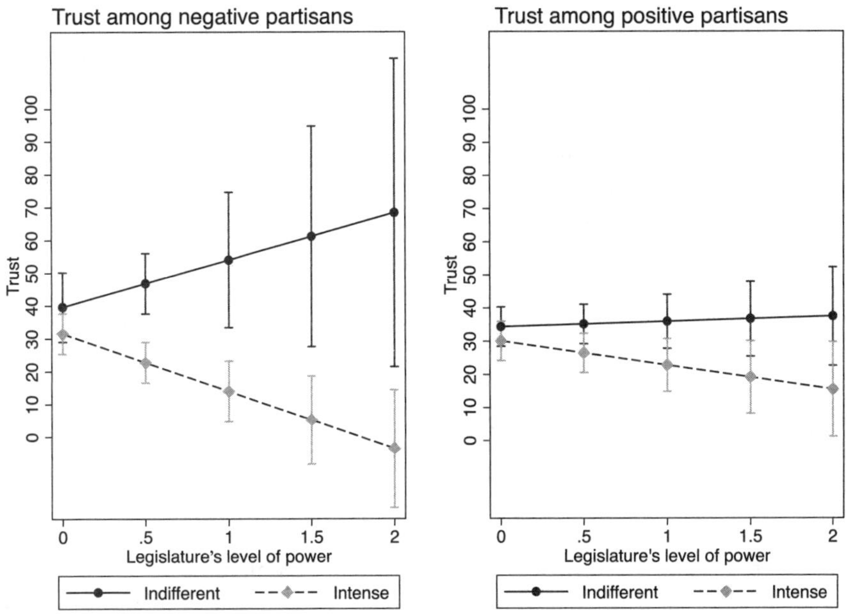

Figure 6.4: Effect of Upper Chamber's Power on Levels of Trust (90 percent CI).
Source: Author's computations.

when they are not. Notably, there is no significant difference in trust for respondents who dislike both parties but associate themselves with the out party (indifferent negative partisans).

Similarly, there is no real effect of legislative power on positive partisans, who are either those who like only the in-party or those who consider themselves members of the in-party but see little difference between the two parties. Notably, the direction of the change for active positive partisans is the same as that for active negative partisans, but the difference is not statistically significant for active positive partisans. In other words, for those who see differences between the two parties, increasing the power of the legislature decreases trust for negative partisans, but there is no concomitant increase in trust for positive partisans.

Figure 6.4 depicts a nearly identical story for the effect of the power of the upper chamber on trust. Intense negative partisans see a significant decline in trust as legislatures become more powerful, but no other type shows evidence of a change because of changes in the power of the legislature. Again, no one sees a significant increase in trust from an increase in legislative power, and only active negative partisans see a decrease in trust.

It is noteworthy as well that in every graph, those who see the least difference between the parties also have the most trust in government. The pattern is true everywhere but is not always statistically significant. These results seem to indicate, then, that there is an important difference among negative partisans. It is polarization, not negativity, that decreases trust. One can dislike (or like) both parties equally and still trust the government. The real harm in trust comes from active negative partisans—those who dislike the party in power a good deal more than they like the party out of power. It is the difference between the parties, then, not just the negativity, that matters.

CONCLUDING THOUGHTS

Those who study contemporary American politics—either as scholars or as amateur observers—rarely consider questions of democratic stability, likely assuming that if the nation has endured for nearly 250 years, its continued endurance is a good bet. But as the work of Linz (1990) and others show, the United States is exceptional as a majoritarian system that has managed to endure. Most majoritarian political systems, the research shows, end up falling prey to the large number of "losers" they create, when candidates who achieve near-majorities (or in some cases, actual majorities) end up outside the rooms where political decisions are made.

And researchers argue that it is the unusual historical role of American political parties as "perceptual screens" (Campbell et al. 1960)—what Linz (1990) calls their "uniquely diffuse character"—that may prevent the ills of majoritarianism from taking hold. When John F. Kennedy won the presidential election in 1960, more than half of voters had selected another candidate, rendering them "losers" under the winner-takes-all political system. But Kennedy went on to become one of the most popular presidents since public opinion polling began. Indeed, many of those voters who opted not to support him in 1960 simply seemed to forget their loser status quite literally: by 1963, nearly 60 percent of respondents in a Gallup survey claimed to have voted for him in 1960 (Brinkley 2013).

But the evidence presented here paints a picture of today's political parties as being quite different from those of Kennedy's time. As expected, negative partisanship is tied to trust in government, and the extent of this relationship is based at least in part on political institutions. Furthermore, the evidence shows that active negative partisans—those who like the party out of power but not the party in power—experience the most dramatic decreases in political trust.

Researchers in American politics ought to carefully consider the effect of negative partisanship on attitudes toward government, and particularly on how political institutions can exacerbate or mitigate that effect. Given the changes in political parties over the last several years, we may want to consider changes to our political institutions that might help mitigate the effects of being a majoritarian "loser" in the American political system. More important, all of us ought to consider the potential effect of negative partisanship on the health of American democracy.

NOTES

An earlier version of this chapter was presented at the Dynamics of American Democracy: Partisan Polarization, Political Competition, and Government Performance conference at Brown University, Providence, RI, November 14–15, 2018. Thanks to Shane Redman, Jae-Jae Spoon, and Dave Peterson for helpful conversations. Errors remain my own.

REFERENCES

Abramowitz, Alan I., and Steven Webster. "The Rise of Negative Partisanship and the Nationalization of U.S. Elections in the 21st Century." *Electoral Studies* 41 (2016a): 12–22.

———. "Negative Partisanship: Why Americans Dislike Parties But Behave Like Rabid Partisans." *Political Psychology* 39 (2016b): 119–135.

Anderson, Christopher J., and Christine A. Guillory. "Political Institutions and Satisfaction with Democracy: A Cross-National Analysis of Consensus and Majoritarian Systems." *American Political Science Review* 91, no. 1 (1997): 66–81.

Bafumi, Joseph, and Michael C. Herron. "Leapfrog Representation and Extremism: A Study of American Voters and Their Members in Congress." *American Political Science Review* 104, no. 3 (2010): 519–542.

Blanchard, Paul. "Office of Governor." In *The Kentucky Encyclopedia*, ed. John E. Kleber, Lowell Hayes Harrison, and Thomas Dionysius Clark, 380–381. Lexington: University of Kentucky Press, 1992.

Bowler, Shaun, and Todd Donovan. "Democracy, Institutions and Attitudes About Citizen Influence on Government." *British Journal of Political Science* 32, no. 2 (2002): 371–390.

Brinkley, Alan. "The Legacy of John F. Kennedy" *Atlantic*, 2013. https://www.theatlantic.com/magazine/archive/2013/08/the-legacy-of-john-f-kennedy/309499/. Accessed February 18, 2020.

Campbell, Angus, Philip E. Converse, Warren E. Miller, and Donald E. Stokes. *The American Voter*. Chicago: University of Chicago Press, 1960.

Dyck, Joshua J., and Edward L. Lascher. "Direct Democracy and Political Efficacy Reconsidered." *Political Behavior* 31, no. 3 (2009): 401–427.

Farnsworth, Stephen J. "Federal Frustration, State Satisfaction? Voters and Decentralized Governmental Power." *Publius* 29, no. 3 (1999): 75–88.

Ferguson, Margaret. "Governors and the Executive Branch." In *Politics in the American States: A Comparative Analysis,* ed. Virginia Gray, Russell L. Hanson, Thad Kousser, 235–274. Washington, DC: CQ, 2018.

Fiorina, Morris P., Samuel J. Abrams, and Jeremy C. Pope. *Culture War? The Myth of a Polarized America,* 3rd ed. New York: Longman, 2010.

Hanson, Russell. "Political Culture, Interparty Competition and Political Efficacy in the American States." *Publius* 10, no. 2 (1980): 17–36.

Healy, Andrew J., Neil Malhotra, and Cecilia Hyunjung Mo. "Irrelevant Events Affect Voters' Evaluations of Government Performance." *Proceedings of the National Academy of Sciences* 107, no. 29 (2010): 12804–12809.

Hetherington, Marc J. *Why Trust Matters: Declining Political Trust and the Demise of American Liberalism.* Princeton, NJ: Princeton University Press, 2006.

Hetherington, Marc J., and Thomas J. Rudolph. *Why Washington Won't Work: Polarization, Political Trust, and the Governing Crisis.* Chicago: University of Chicago Press, 2015.

Kelleher, Christine A., and Jennifer Wolak. "Explaining Public Confidence in the Branches of State Government." *Political Research Quarterly* 60, no. 4 (2007): 707–721.

Kinder, Donald P, and Nathan P. Kalmoe. *Neither Liberal nor Conservative: Ideological Innocence in the American Public.* Chicago: University of Chicago Press, 2017.

Lijphart, Arend. *Patterns of Democracy: Government and Performance in Thirty-Six Countries. 2nd Edition.* New Haven, CT: Yale University Press, 2012.

Linz, Juan J. "The Perils of Presidentialism." *Journal of Democracy* 1, no. 1 (1990): 51–69.

Mayer, Sabrina Jasmin. "How Negative Partisanship Affects Voting Behavior in Europe: Evidence from an Analysis of 17 European Multi-Party Systems with Proportional Voting." *Research & Politics* 4, no. 1 (2017): https://doi.org/10.1177/2053168016686636.

McCarty, Nolan, Keith T. Poole, and Howard Rosenthal. *Polarized America: The Dance of Ideology and Unequal Riches.* Cambridge, MA: MIT Press, 2016.

McGregor, R. Michael, Nicholas J. Caruana, and Laura B. Stephenson. "Negative Partisanship in a Multi-Party System: The Case of Canada." *Journal of Elections, Public Opinion and Parties* 25, no. 3 (2015): 300–316.

Medeiros, Mike, and Alain Noël. "The Forgotten Side of Partisanship: Negative Party Identification in Four Anglo-American Democracies." *Comparative Political Studies* 47, no. 7 (2014): 1022–1046.

Mendelsohn, Matthew, and Fred Cutler. "The Effect of Referendums on Democratic Citizens: Information, Politicization, Efficacy and Tolerance." *British Journal of Political Science* 30, no. 4 (2000): 685–698.

Morrill, Jim. "NC Governor Doesn't Have Much Power and Could Get Weaker: 'He'd Be a Nice Figurehead.'" *Charlotte Observer,* 2018. https://www.charlotteobserver.com/latest-news/article213995539.html.

Norris, Pippa. *Electoral Engineering: Voting Rules and Political Behavior.* Cambridge: Cambridge University Press, 2004.

———. "Institutional Explanations for Political Support." In *R Critical Citizens: Global Support for Democratic Governance,* ed. Pippa Norris. Oxford: Oxford University Press, 1999.

Shor, Boris, and Nolan McCarty. "The Ideological Mapping of American Legislatures." *American Political Science Review* 105, no. 3 (2011): 530–551.

Spoon, Jae-Jae, and Kristin Kanthak. "He's Not My Prime Minister: Negative Partisanship and Satisfaction with Democracy." *Journal of Elections, Public Opinion, and Parties* 29, no. 4 (2019): 511–532.

Squire, Peverill. "A Squire Index Update." *State Politics & Policy Quarterly* 17, no. 4 (2017): 361–371.

Steenbergen, Marco R., and Bradford S. Jones. "Modeling Multilevel Data Structures." *American Journal of Political Science* 46, no. 1 (2002): 218–237.

Towler, Christopher C., and Christopher S. Parker. "Between Anger and Engagement: Donald Trump and Black America." *Journal of Race, Ethnicity, and Politics* 3 (2018): 219–253.

Wagner, Alexander F., Friedrich Schneider, and Martin Halla. "The Quality of Institutions and Satisfaction with Democracy in Western Europe: A Panel Analysis." *European Journal of Political Economy* 25, no. 1 (2009): 30–14.

Wolak, Jennifer. "Feelings of Political Efficacy in the Fifty States." *Political Behavior* 40, no. 3 (2018): 763–784.

CHAPTER 7

Gender Attitudes and American Public Opinion in the Trump Era

John Sides, Michael Tesler, and Lynn Vavreck

The day after Donald Trump was inaugurated as the forty-fifth president of the United States, an estimated 3–5 million Americans protested as part of the Women's March, making it almost certainly the largest single-day protest in the country's history (Chenoweth and Pressman 2017). The march was a direct response to gendered issues in the 2016 presidential campaign—a campaign that pitted the first major-party female presidential candidate against a male candidate with a long history of sexist statements and alleged misconduct against women. According to the Women's March's mission statement, "The rhetoric of the past election cycle has insulted, demonized, and threatened many of us . . . and our communities are hurting and scared. We are confronted with the question of how to move forward in the face of national and international concern and fear" (Women's March 2017). This outpouring of activism foreshadowed the salience of gender issues during Trump's presidency.

In this chapter, we document the growing importance of gender attitudes to American public opinion under Trump. We focus on Americans' beliefs about the experiences of women, especially how much discrimination and harassment women face. After first recounting the role of gender attitudes in the 2016 presidential election, we show that gender attitudes were even more strongly related to support for President Trump in 2018 than for candidate Trump in 2016. We then show that gender attitudes were an unusually strong predictor of support for Brett Kavanaugh's 2018 nomination to the Supreme Court. This gendering of public opinion about Trump and Kavanaugh helped make gender attitudes more strongly associated with voting in the 2018 midterm election than in earlier elections. Finally, we show that gender attitudes, which were already divided along party lines, are now even more so.

These findings confirm that Americans are much more divided by gender attitudes than by gender (Huddy and Willmann 2017; Stimson 2004). Indeed, gender attitudes actually create divisions *within* genders, such that men who believe that women face a great deal of discrimination have different political attitudes than men who do not. The same is true among women, even though political commentators often treat women as a homogeneous group.

These divides based on gender attitudes also signal another dimension of partisan polarization in American politics. Many analyses have shown that partisanship is increasingly correlated with attitudes about race, ethnicity, and religion—including how Americans feel about African Americans, immigrants, and Muslims (Enders and Scott 2019; Sides, Tesler, and Vavreck 2018; Tesler 2016b). We show that gender attitudes have become yet another way in which fundamental questions about identity fragment the country.

GENDER ATTITUDES AND THE 2016 ELECTION

Before the 2016 presidential campaign, many speculated that Hillary Clinton's historic bid to become the first female president would mobilize unprecedented support from women. One headline published the week before the election read, "How Women Could Vote Hillary Clinton into the White House" (Siddiqui and Gambino 2016). Clinton herself reported hearing this idea. As she wrote after the election, "even before I ran, political commentators wondered whether I'd inspire an unbeatable wave of women to come out and vote for me, in the same way President Obama inspired record-breaking black turnout." But she always had doubts, noting, "Gender hasn't proven to be the motivating force for women that some hope it might be" (Clinton 2017, 128).

Clinton's doubts were based on personal experience. Her 2008 run for the Democratic presidential nomination did not mobilize women and Democrats with liberal gender attitudes in the same way that Barack Obama's campaign galvanized African Americans and white Americans with more liberal racial attitudes (Kinder and Dale-Riddle 2012; Tesler and Sears 2010). In fact, it was the opposite: those with traditional attitudes about gender were actually more likely to support Clinton because those attitudes are correlated with less favorable views of African Americans.

But a lot changed after 2008. Clinton occupied the historically male-dominated position of secretary of state and saw her public image reach new heights. Many strategists believed that she could now embrace her gender because she had shown that she was "tough enough" for the job during her time as secretary of state (Chozick and Martin 2015). Clinton did exactly this. For example, in the October 2015 primary debate, she said, "Finally, fathers will be able to say to their daughters, 'You too can grow up to be president.'" She answered a question about being an insider by saying, "I can't think of anything more of an outsider than electing the first woman president" and "being the first woman president would be quite a change from the presidents we've had." Republicans regularly attacked her for playing the gender card, but she typically responded, "Well, if calling for equal pay and paid leave and women's health is playing the gender card, then deal me in." After Trump said in April 2016 that "the only thing she has going for her is the woman card," the Clinton campaign issued donors a hot pink "woman card" with the phrase "deal me in" at the bottom.

Did this strategy work? Some evidence suggested that it may have. In states that conducted Democratic primary exit polls in both 2008 and 2016, Clinton increased her vote share by 9 points among women (53 percent to 62 percent) compared to 5 points among men (45 percent to 50 percent), although that difference may not have derived from gender per se. Clinton's argument about daughters may also have mattered: in YouGov/*Economist* polls, Clinton performed about 8 points better among parents of daughters than among similarly situated parents of only sons (Tesler 2016a), a result consistent with other studies showing that having daughters makes parents more supportive of feminist positions (Glynn and Sen 2015; Sharrow et al. 2018; Warner and Steel 1999; Washington 2008).

At the same time, however, there was little evidence that women were attracted to Hillary Clinton in the primary because of their own gender or feminist consciousness. Women who were more concerned about discrimination and harassment were not particularly likely to support Hillary Clinton in the 2016 primaries (Sides, Tesler, and Vavreck 2018), and neither were women who said that gender was a very important part of their identity. Similarly, women who described themselves as feminists—35 percent of female voters in the Democratic primaries—were no more likely to support Clinton than women who did not identify as feminists (Tesler 2016c).

The weak effects of gender consciousness were not all that surprising. Compared to racial consciousness among African Americans, gender consciousness among women has not been as strong a force in American political behavior. As the political scientists Nancy Burns and Donald R. Kinder

(2012, 159) have written, "The social organization of gender emphasizes intimacy between men and women; the social organization of race emphasizes separation between whites and blacks. Separation fosters solidarity among African Americans. Integration impairs solidarity among women."

But many people thought that the general election would be different. There, the salience of gender was magnified by Trump's history of sexist comments, campaign controversies involving his remarks about Megyn Kelly, Alicia Machado, and others, and the accusations of sexual misconduct leveled against him—behavior that he explicitly acknowledged in the *Access Hollywood* tape. In fact, Trump predicted back in 1998 that his record with "the women" would be controversial if he ever ran for president (NBC News 2016).

Certainly Trump's opponents, including Clinton, tried to ensure that these controversies would cost him. During the primaries, the anti-Trump group Our Principles PAC produced an ad in which women read insulting quotes from Trump to show how the candidate "talks about our mothers, our sisters, our daughters." This ad, which concluded with Trump's saying, "Women, you have to treat them like shit," was one of the most effective anti-Trump ads in 2016. Women who were randomly assigned to watch the ad rated Trump 19 points less favorably than those who did not watch it (Vavreck 2016). In the final month of the campaign, Hillary Clinton aired a similar attack ad in which adolescent girls looked into the mirror while Trump objectifying statements played in the background. The ad concluded with Trump saying in an interview that he does not treat women with respect.

Most Americans were well aware of Trump's controversies involving women. In a Monmouth University survey conducted shortly after the *Access Hollywood* tape surfaced, 63 percent of Americans said that they were paying close attention to "the recent news about allegations that Donald Trump made unwanted advances on different women," compared to just 5 percent who were unaware of the news. Among those paying attention to the allegations, two-thirds thought that they were probably or definitely true. Thus, it was not surprising that in four different late October surveys, many Americans thought that Trump was a sexist and did not respect women.[1] Nor was it surprising that far more respondents in the American National Election Study's (ANES) post-election survey said Trump treated women poorly (54 percent) than said he treated them well (21 percent).

Donald Trump appeared to face an extraordinary deficit with female voters heading into November. In an October 17 article titled "Men Are Treating 2016 as a 'Normal' Election; Women Aren't," *FiveThirtyEight*'s

Harry Enten (2016) showed that Trump's standing among men was typical of Republican presidential candidates, but he was way behind among women—"a historically overwhelming share" of whom supported Clinton. At that point, Clinton had a 20-point lead among women while Trump was winning men by 7 points. It appeared, then, that the 2016 election would see a record gender gap driven by female voters' unusually strong aversion to Trump.

That did not happen. The exit polls showed Clinton winning women by 12 percentage points, which was similar to Obama's 13- and 11-point margins of victory among women in 2012 and 2016, respectively. Instead, it was men whose voting behavior changed. Trump won men by 12 points in 2016. By comparison, John McCain won men by only 1 point in 2008, and Mitt Romney won them by 7 points in 2012. In fact, Trump did better among men than any presidential candidate since George H. W. Bush in 1988.

Why did Clinton fail to perform better among female voters? One reason was relatively weak gender solidarity among women—a pattern consistent with earlier research (Gurin 1985). For example, in the September 2016 wave of RAND's Presidential Election Panel Study, only about one-third of women said that being a woman was "extremely important" to their identity. By comparison, a much larger percentage of black Americans (61 percent) said their race was extremely important to their identity. This relative lack of gender solidarity was politically consequential. Hillary Clinton was significantly less popular than Obama was among the majority of women who did not see gender as extremely important to their identities (Tesler 2016c). Thus, Clinton's performance among women in both the Democratic primary and the general election confirmed past research showing that race and partisanship are more important than gender to how people vote (Burns and Kinder 2012; Kinder and Dale-Riddle 2012). The salience of race and partisanship helped explain why Clinton lost white women by 9 points—a deficit larger than Barack Obama's in 2008 and Al Gore's in 2000.

If Clinton did not benefit from gender solidarity, was she penalized because of sexism? There is reason to believe she was. To show this, we rely on a measure of sexism known as "modern sexism" in the scholarly literature (Swim et al. 1995; Swim and Cohen 1997). It is intended capture subtle biases against women, such as the belief that there is no real discrimination against women and that women get undeserved special favors. The measure asks people to agree or disagree with statements like, "Women who complain about harassment cause more problems than they solve." This measure of sexism was already related to views of the presidential candidates in the 2012 election (McThomas and Tesler 2016).

But in 2016, modern sexism had a stronger relationship with white Americans' presidential vote choice—even after accounting for other factors, including party identification, self-reported ideology on the liberal-conservative spectrum, and a measure of attitudes toward African Americans called "racial resentment" (Kinder and Sanders 1996).[2] This conclusion is based on evidence from two surveys: the ANES, which included two questions derived from the modern sexism measure in its 2012 and 2016 surveys, and the VOTER Survey, which included five such questions in its 2016 survey (although none in 2012). The VOTER Survey is a long-running panel of Americans that began in December 2011 and has continued through 2020. It therefore allows us to track changes within the same Americans. After the 2016 election, the survey reinterviewed eight thousand respondents who had previously been interviewed in 2012. (For more details about all analyses in this chapter, see the appendix.)

Among white women, it is not clear whether Clinton gained additional support from those who scored lower in modern sexism: the results in the ANES show that she did, but the results in the VOTER Survey show that she did not (left-hand panels of figure 7.1). The results from both surveys, however, suggest that Clinton's candidacy generated greater opposition from white women with higher modern sexism scores. These findings are consistent with Clinton's post-election contention that many of the women who voted against her "were quite sexist, too" (Clinton 2017, 128).[3]

The results do show that Clinton's candidacy generated unusually strong opposition from men with more sexist attitudes (right-hand panels of figure 7.1). In both surveys, Clinton was less popular than Obama was among white men with moderate to high levels of modern sexism—and this was half or more of men, as the distribution of modern sexism in the VOTER Survey suggests.[4] Clinton did somewhat better than Obama among white men with lower levels of modern sexism, but this was a smaller number of men overall. The role of sexism is likely one reason that Clinton lost white men to Trump by a whopping 31 points—a wider margin than any candidate since Walter Mondale's landslide loss to Ronald Reagan in 1984.

Clinton's inability to activate support from women ensured that gender did not define the election in the same way that social identities like race, ethnicity, and party did. But gender *attitudes* appear to have been activated by the issue's heightened salience in a campaign between the potential first female president and Donald Trump. Our analyses and several other studies all show that gender attitudes predicted vote choice more powerfully in

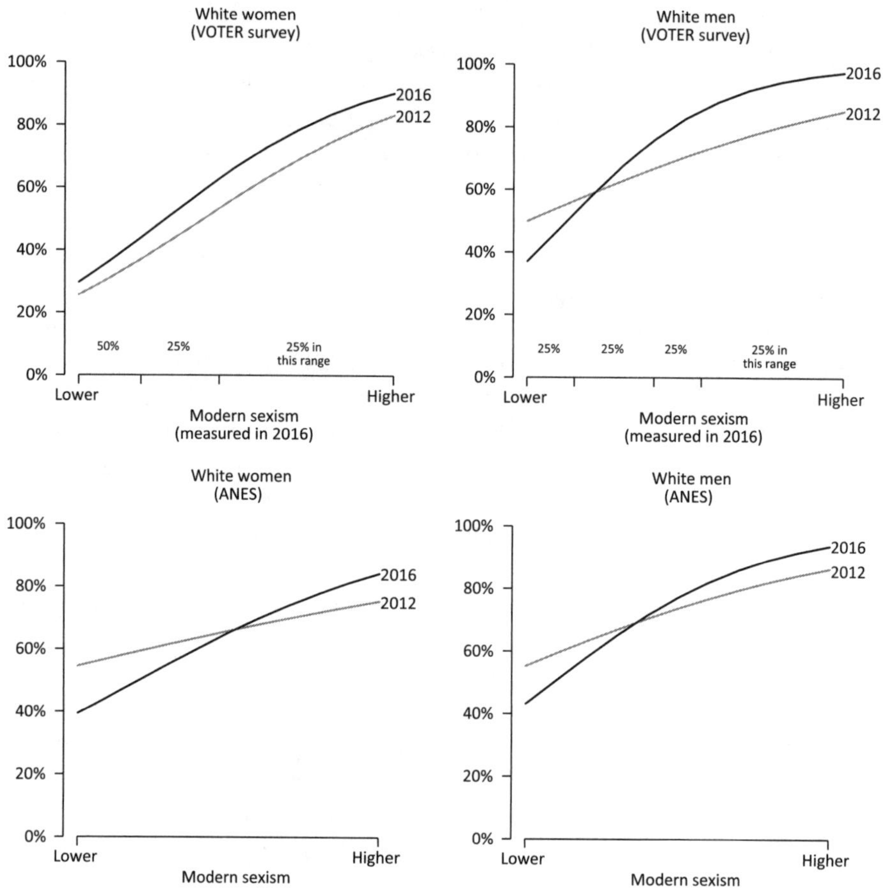

Figure 7.1: Gender Attitudes and White Americans' Likelihood of Voting for the Republican Presidential Candidate in 2012 and 2016. The lines represent predicted probabilities from statistical models that also include party identification, self-reported ideology, and racial resentment. For the VOTER Survey, the distribution of modern sexism is presented above the horizontal axis.
Sources: 2012–2016 VOTER Survey; 2012–2016 ANES.

the 2016 presidential election than they had in prior elections (Cassese and Barnes 2019; Schaffner, MacWilliams, and Nteta 2018; Valentino, Wayne, and Oceno 2018).

One important caveat to these studies, however, is that sexism was measured in surveys conducted during and after the 2016 campaign. Some people may have changed their answers to questions about sexual harassment and discrimination against women based on their views of Trump and his accusers. If so, gender attitudes may be both a cause and a consequence of how people voted. Either way, the stronger correlation between gender attitudes and vote choice in 2016 set the stage for partisan politics to become increasingly polarized by gender politics during Trump's presidency.

#METOO, GENDER ATTITUDES, AND THE TRUMP PRESIDENCY

It did not take long for gender to emerge as a salient issue in Trump's presidency. The Women's March was soon followed by another movement that revealed the extent of the discrimination that women continue to face. The #MeToo movement, which was established in 2006, became prominent in October 2017 after several women accused movie producer Harvey Weinstein of sexual harassment and assault. More women then came forward to share their own stories of being harassed and assaulted, including by powerful men in the media, entertainment, and politics. The accused political figures included Minnesota senator Al Franken, Alabama Senate nominee Roy Moore, Supreme Court nominee Brett Kavanuagh, and of course Trump himself.

While Democrats successfully pressured Franken to resign, Republicans in general, and Trump in particular, closed ranks around fellow Republicans accused of sexual harassment and assault. Trump defended not only himself but also other powerful men accused of sexual misconduct, including Moore, Kavanaugh, and Roger Ailes and Bill O'Reilly of Fox News. He also mocked the #MeToo movement and expressed sympathy for young men. In October 2018, he said, "It's a very scary time for young men in America, when you can be guilty of something that you may not be guilty of" (Morin 2018). When asked for his message to young women, he said, "Women are doing great."

Given the president's rhetoric, it is not surprising that there was an enormous partisan divide over #MeToo. According to an October 2018 YouGov/*Economist* poll, 82 percent of Clinton voters had a favorable opinion of the #MeToo movement, but only 18 percent of Trump voters did. Far more Trump voters than Clinton voters said the movement had gone too far (75 percent vs. 8 percent) and were very or somewhat worried that young men would be falsely accused of sexual assault (90 percent versus 28 percent).

The #MeToo movement and the president's response helped make attitudes about gender increasingly linked to attitudes about Trump—more so even than in 2016. This finding emerges clearly among VOTER Survey pan-

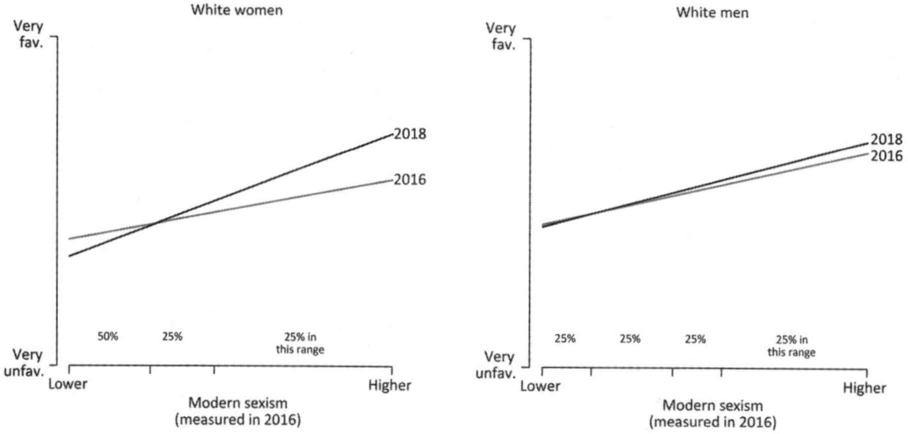

Figure 7.2: Gender Attitudes and White Americans' Views of Donald Trump, 2016 and 2018. The lines represent predicted values from statistical models that also include party identification, self-reported ideology, and racial resentment. The distribution of modern sexism is presented above the horizontal axis. *Source*: VOTER Surveys conducted November 29–December 29, 2016, and November 17, 2018–January 7, 2019.

elists who were interviewed after both the 2016 and the 2018 elections: modern sexism was more strongly associated with white people's opinions of Trump in late 2018 than it was in late 2016 (figure 7.2). This was especially true among white women (left panel). If we imagine views of Trump on a 100-point scale, a shift from the lowest to highest modern sexism score was associated with an 18-point increase in how favorably white women viewed Trump in 2016 but a 37-point increase in 2018. By contrast, the relationship of Trump's favorability among white women to racial resentment, ideology, and partisanship was stable or smaller in 2018 compared to 2016. Among white men, the relationship between gender attitudes and Trump favorability increased more modestly between 2016 and 2018. Still, men who scored higher on modern sexism did become more supportive of Trump.[5]

Modern sexism thus became a more potent ingredient in white Americans' opinions of Trump during the first two years of his presidency. Factors such as racial resentment did not show an increasing correlation with opinions of Trump, although they were certainly powerfully correlated with Trump support. And Trump appeared distinctive compared to other Republican leaders as well: Luks and Schaffner (2019) find that President

Trump was much more popular than then–House Speaker Paul Ryan or Senate Majority Leader Mitch McConnell among Americans who score higher on a sexism scale. Thus, gender attitudes, which seemed less important than attitudes about race, immigration, and Islam in the 2016 election, grew in their significance under President Trump.

GENDER ATTITUDES AND THE KAVANAUGH CONFIRMATION

The salience of gender reached a new apex during the confirmation of Brett Kavanaugh to the Supreme Court. Near the end of the confirmation process, Kavanaugh was accused by Dr. Christine Blasey Ford of sexual assault when the two were high school students in 1982. In response, the Senate postponed Kavanaugh's confirmation vote so that Ford could testify before the Senate Judiciary Committee. On September 27, 2018, Ford said that Kavanaugh had pinned her down and tried to take her clothes off. Kavanaugh then defended himself in response to Ford's accusations and questions from Democrats on the committee.

Reactions to the testimony were sharply polarized by partisanship among both senators and the American public. Only one Democratic senator (West Virginia's Joe Manchin) voted to confirm Kavanaugh and only one Republican senator (Alaska's Lisa Murkowski) voted against. According to an NPR/Marist Poll conducted shortly after the hearings, 76 percent of Democrats said that they believed Ford and only 5 percent said that they believed Kavanaugh. Among Republicans, it was the opposite: 76 percent believed Kavanaugh and 8 percent believed Ford. Democrats and Republicans were similarly polarized about Kavanaugh's confirmation—more so than about any other Supreme Court nominee on record (Jones 2018; Valencia and Mehta 2018). In YouGov/*Economist* polls conducted right before the confirmation vote, Republicans were 70 points more likely than Democrats to support Kavanaugh's confirmation (77 percent versus 7 percent). By contrast, Republicans were 60 points more likely to support Neil Gorsuch's confirmation in April 2017 (68 percent versus 8 percent).

The partisan divide on Kavanaugh's confirmation was also larger than when the nominee's treatment of women had last affected a Supreme Court nomination battle. In 1991, Anita Hill accused nominee Clarence Thomas of sexual harassment when she worked for him at the Equal Employment Opportunity Commission. Even still, eleven Democratic senators voted to confirm Thomas and rank-and-file Democrats were far less opposed to him than they were to Kavanaugh. In an October 1991 NBC/*Wall Street Journal* poll of registered voters, 56 percent of Democrats and 79 per-

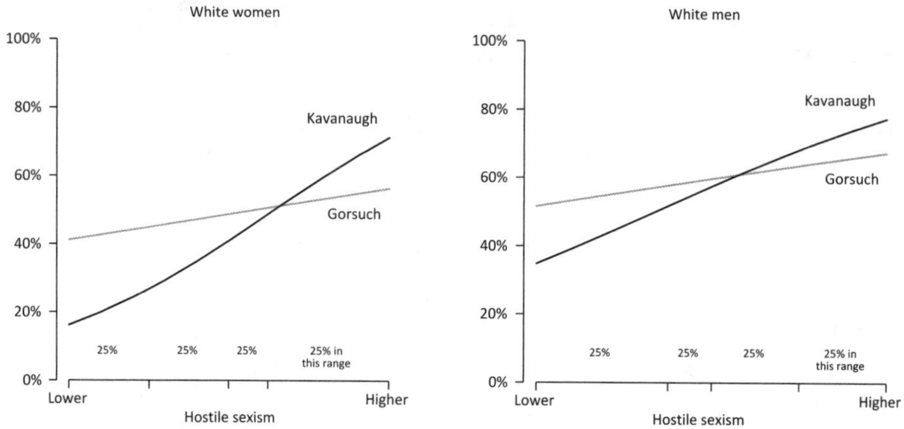

Figure 7.3: Gender Attitudes and White Americans' Likelihood of Supporting Neil Gorsuch and Brett Kavanaugh. The lines represent predicted probabilities from statistical models that also include party identification, self-reported ideology, and racial resentment. The distribution of modern sexism is presented above the horizontal axis. *Source*: 2018 Cooperative Congressional Election Study.

cent of Republicans supported Thomas's confirmation. Democrats' differing reactions to the Thomas and Kavanaugh hearings show just how the politics of gender have changed.

But public opinion about Kavanaugh's confirmation was not just a function of partisanship. Gender attitudes were also more strongly related to support for Kavanaugh than Gorsuch (figure 7.3). This finding is based on the 2018 Cooperative Congressional Election Study (CCES), which was fielded from September 27 to November 5, 2018—meaning that all of its fifty thousand respondents were interviewed during or after the Kavanaugh confirmation. Respondents were asked whether they supported the confirmations of Kavanaugh and Gorsuch and also whether they agreed or disagreed with two statements that tap a concept called "hostile sexism" in the scholarly literature (Glick and Fiske 1996): "Feminists are making entirely reasonable demands of men" and "When women lose to men in a fair competition, they typically complain about being discriminated against."

Gender attitudes were relatively weakly related to both white men's and white women's support for Gorsuch. Among white women and men, a shift from the lowest to highest scores on the hostile sexism measure was associated with about a 15-point increase in support for Gorsuch, after accounting for party identification, ideology, and racial resentment. That same shift was associated with a 43-point increase in support for Kavanaugh among white men and a 55-point increase among white women. Thus, opposition to Kavanaugh was not just about being a Democrat: it was also related to people's views of feminism and women's claims of discrimination.[6]

GENDER ATTITUDES AND THE 2018 MIDTERM ELECTION

Only weeks after the Kavanaugh confirmation came the 2018 midterm election. Political science research has long shown that political campaigns and media coverage can affect voter decision-making by activating or "priming" such factors as partisanship, racial attitudes, and moral values (Iyengar and Kinder 1987; Lenz 2012; Stoker 1993; Tesler 2015). In 2018, there were several reasons to expect that gender attitudes would become more central to voting.

One was the Kavanaugh confirmation itself. Americans with more sexist attitudes rated Republicans in Congress significantly more favorably after the Kavanaugh hearings than they did before (Luks and Schaffner 2019). This could have carried through until Election Day.

Another reason was the broader gendering of public opinion about Trump. The president's image always looms large in midterm elections, making presidential approval ratings a strong predictor of voting in down-ballot elections for Congress, governor, and the state legislature (Tufte 1978; Carsey and Wright 1998; Rogers 2016). Consequently, voting in Trump-era congressional elections may have become more linked to gender attitudes, just as voting in Obama-era congressional elections was more linked to racial attitudes (Luttig 2017; Tesler 2016b).

Third, the background of the 2018 congressional candidates arguably magnified the gender dynamics of the election. Democrats nominated a record 183 women in US House races—a surge often attributed to the backlash against Trump (Dittmar 2018). Republicans, by contrast, nominated only fifty-three women in US House races. Although female candidates for the House do not necessarily face a "gender penalty" (Hayes and Lawless 2016), gender attitudes are most strongly correlated with views of prominent female Democrats (McThomas and Tesler 2016).

The VOTER Survey again allows a test of whether gender attitudes became activated—in particular, by examining the 3,400 respondents who reported voting in both the 2012 and the 2018 congressional elections. (The survey did not include any interviews in 2014 and did not ask about congressional vote choice in 2016.)

As expected, modern sexism was more strongly related to white Ameri-

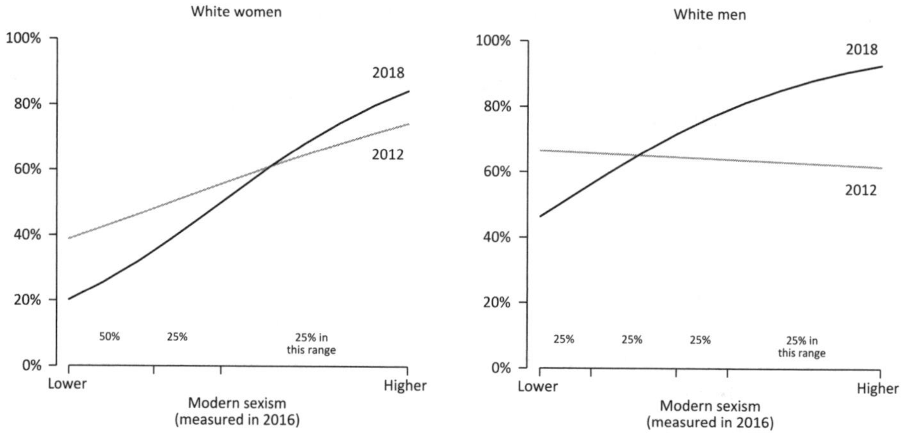

Figure 7.4: Gender Attitudes and White Americans' Likelihood of Voting for a Republican US House Candidate in 2012 and 2018. The lines represent predicted probabilities from statistical models that also include party identification, self-reported ideology, and racial resentment. The distribution of modern sexism is presented above the horizontal axis. *Source:* VOTER Survey.

cans' vote preference in their US House race in 2018 than in 2012, even after accounting for party, ideology, and racial resentment (figure 7.4). This was true among both white women and white men. Among white women voting in 2012, a shift from lowest to highest values of the modern sexism scale was associated with a 35-point increase in the likelihood of voting for the Republican House candidate. In 2016, the comparable number was 70 points. A strong pattern of activation is visible among white men as well.[7] Other analyses have also found that sexism was correlated more strongly with vote preferences in 2018 than in 2016 (Schaffner 2018) and with turnout in 2018 than in the previous midterm in 2014 (Kam and Archer 2019).

These results are somewhat complicated by the fact that modern sexism is measured in the 2016 wave and may have changed in response to Trump's candidacy. But the activation of modern sexism in public opinion about Trump from 2016 to 2018 (see figure 7.2) increases our confidence that gender attitudes became more important to congressional voting during Trump's presidency.

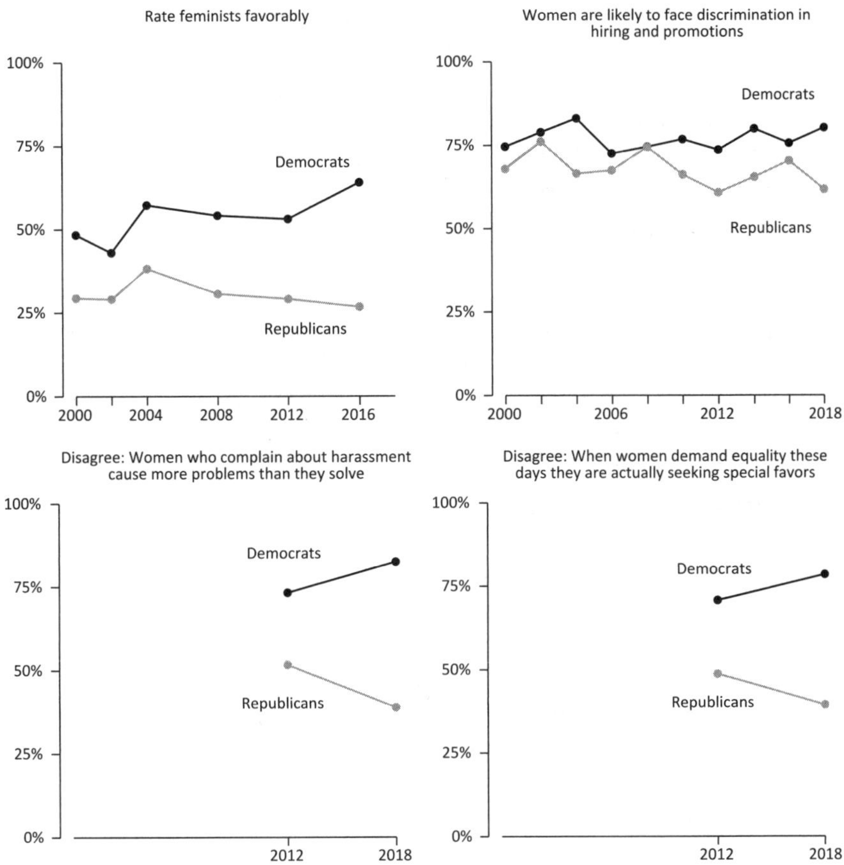

Figure 7.5: Party Identification and Gender Attitudes, 2000–2018. Independents who lean toward a party are included as partisans. *Sources*: ANES Cumulative File; GSS Cumulative File; 2012 & 2018 CCES Team Modules.

PARTY IDENTIFICATION AND GENDER ATTITUDES

The salience of gender attitudes for views of Trump and Kavanaugh as well as for congressional voting has been accompanied by a broader shift in the political landscape: the increasing alignment between gender attitudes and party identification itself. Democrats and Republicans are now further apart on a number of questions related to gender equality and the experiences of women, and at least some of this polarization appears unique to the Trump era.

For example, Democrats and Republicans are now further apart in how favorably they rate feminists (figure 7.5, upper left panel). In the ANES, Democrats were about 10 percentage points more likely to rate feminists favorably in 2016 than they were in 2008 and 2012. Meanwhile, fewer Republicans rated feminists favorably after the 2016 election than they had in any prior ANES survey. Similarly, in the General Social Survey (GSS), Democrats and Republicans have diverged on the question of how much workplace discrimination women face (figure 7.5, upper right panel).

There has been even greater polarization on the modern sexism questions, according to the 2012 and 2018 CCES surveys (figure 7.5, lower panels). Democrats became about 10 percentage points more likely to disagree with statements like "Women who complain about harassment cause more problems than they solve" and "When women demand equality these days, they're actually seeking special favors." Republicans moved about 10 points in the opposite direction. This polarization may stem in part from the timing of the 2018 CCES, which was conducted shortly after the Kavanaugh hearings.

Of course, these data cannot determine whether people are updating their partisanship to match their views about gender or whether partisans are changing their gender attitudes. But the latter appears more likely than the former. Other research shows that recent partisan polarization on racial issues derives more from partisans' changing their racial attitudes (Engelhardt 2020), and it seems logical that a similar process would underpin polarization on gender attitudes. But whatever the process, the outcome is the same: gender attitudes and party identification have become increasingly entangled.

Notably, the growing partisan divide over gender attitudes in the Trump era does not extend to old-fashioned sexist sentiments. In recent decades, more Democrats and Republicans have rejected the idea that it is better for men to work outside the home and for women to take care of the home and family. That trend has continued, with Republican support for traditional gender roles declining especially sharply in the 2018 GSS.

The politics of gender has therefore moved away from twentieth-century questions of whether women should work. Now the issue is much more how women are treated at work—how much sexual harassment and discrimination they face and how far and how fast women and their male allies should push for gender equality. Those questions have become a major dividing line between Democrats and Republicans.

CONCLUSION

We have documented a growing alignment between gender attitudes and political attitudes in the era of Donald Trump. This reveals an American public that is divided not so much by gender itself but by how they feel about issues that affect women, including sexual harassment and assault.

It is tempting to attribute this divide to Trump himself, as his personal history and behavior have likely helped make gender attitudes salient to ordinary Americans when they think about politics. We may therefore see that gender attitudes are central to both the 2020 Democratic presidential primary and the 2020 general election—even if the Democratic presidential nominee is not a woman.

But this alignment between Americans' gender attitudes and their other political views may persist even after Trump. Our findings suggest that gender attitudes are central not only to how people think about Trump but also to their broader partisanship. Democrats and Republicans increasingly differ on questions about feminism, sexual harassment, and gender discrimination, and those differences may not go away or even decrease after Trump leaves the White House. If so, then gender attitudes will become another issue that both is inflected by social identities and increasingly divides the two parties. That process is already well underway for many other social identities and for attitudes about racial, ethnic, and religious groups (Mason 2018; Sides, Tesler, and Vavreck 2018).

A durable partisan divide on these gender issues will also challenge the ability of movements like #MeToo to combat discrimination against women. Of course, no one—Democrat or Republican—thinks that women should face discrimination, harassment, or assault. But Democrats and Republicans do appear to disagree on how serious those problems are, what are the appropriate remedies, and whether movements like #MeToo are having a positive impact. The same pattern—agreement that discrimination is wrong, disagreement on how to combat it—has characterized battles for civil rights for other groups, including African Americans (see, e.g., Kinder and Sanders 1996). Once an issue such as gender discrimination becomes bound up with the increasingly competitive two-party politics in the United States, it becomes more difficult to achieve a consensus broad enough to address the problem effectively.

Thus, the country faces the very real prospect that party politics will become more and more about which identities are respected and recognized in American society. We have called this growing partisan divide the "American identity crisis." If gender attitudes continue to be yet another manifestation of this divide, we can only expect the identity crisis to intensify.

APPENDIX

This appendix contains details about the analyses that underlie each of the figures in the chapter.

Figure 1: Gender Attitudes and Whites' Likelihood of Voting for the Republican Presidential Candidate

This analysis is based on two surveys, the VOTER Survey and the American National Election Study. The VOTER Survey is a panel survey, and we rely on waves of interviewing in December 2011, November 2012, and December 2016 (total N = 8,000). We also rely on the cross-sectional ANES time-series studies in the fall of 2012 and the fall of 2016.

In the VOTER Survey, the measure of gender attitudes ("modern sexism") is based on five items that asked respondents how much they agreed or disagreed with these statements:

"Women should return to their traditional roles in society."

"When women demand equality these days, they are actually seeking special favors."

"Women often miss out on good jobs because of discrimination."

"Women who complain about harassment often cause more problems than they solve."

"Sexual harassment against women in the workplace is no longer a problem in the United States."

This measure was included in the December 2016 wave and has a scale reliability among white respondents of 0.78. In the ANES, only two of these items were included ("special favors" and "complain about harassment"). The scale reliability among white respondents is 0.62 in the 2012 ANES and 0.77 in the 2016 ANES.

In addition, the statistical models include racial resentment, party identification, and ideology. Racial resentment is based on the traditional four items, with which respondents could agree or disagree:

"Over the past few years, blacks have gotten less than they deserve."

"Irish, Italian, Jewish, and many other minorities overcame prejudice and worked their way up. Blacks should do the same without any special favors."

"It's really a matter of some people not trying hard enough. If blacks would only try harder they could be just as well off as whites."

"Generations of slavery and discrimination have created conditions that make it difficult for blacks to work their way out of the lower class."

In the VOTER Survey, we use December 2016 measures of these other variables to ensure comparability with the modern sexism measure.

In these models and all models that follow, all variables are scaled to the 0–1 interval and all models are estimated using survey weights. The figures in the main text present predicted probabilities or values from these models, with other variables set to their means.

Table 7.1 presents the results from the VOTER Survey. The dependent variable is self-reported vote choice for a major-party candidate in the 2016 presidential election (1 = Trump, 0 = Clinton). In addition to separate models for 2012 and 2016, the column "2012 vs. 2016" reports two-tailed *p*-values from statistical tests of the differences between the coefficients in 2012 and 2016.

Table 7.2 presents the same models for the ANES. These results also suggest larger effects of modern sexism in 2016 than in 2012—with coefficients roughly twice as large in 2016. However, the differences in the coefficients are less precisely estimated.

Figure 2: Gender Attitudes and Whites' Views of Donald Trump

This analysis relies on respondents interviewed in both the December 2016 and December 2018 waves of the VOTER Survey. The dependent variable is a four-category measure of favorability toward Donald Trump, with higher values indicating more favorable views. Altogether, almost five thousand white voters expressed a view of Trump in both survey waves, and these constitute the baseline sample for this analysis. The results are presented in table 7.3 and show that the coefficient for modern sexism was larger for both white men and white women in 2018 compared to 2016, although the difference was larger and more precisely estimated for white women.

Figure 3: Gender Attitudes and Whites' Support for Neil Gorsuch and Brett Kavanaugh

This analysis is based on the 2018 Cooperative Congressional Election Study (CCES). The CCES asked respondents, "Over the past two years, Congress voted on many issues. If you were in Congress would you have voted for or against each of the following?" Then respondents were shown a list that included "Appoint Neil Gorsuch to the Supreme Court of the United States" and "Appoint Brett Kavanaugh to the Supreme Court of the United

Table 7.1: The Relationship between White Americans' Gender Attitudes and Vote for President (VOTER Survey)

	White Women			White Men		
	2012	2016	2012 vs. 2016	2012	2016	2012 vs. 2016
Modern sexism	2.67*	3.09*	$p = 0.685$	1.76*	4.20*	$p = 0.005$
	(0.42)	(0.48)		(0.49)	(0.65)	
Racial resentment	2.32*	3.59*	$p = 0.166$	2.56*	4.61*	$p = 0.001$
	(0.35)	(0.41)		(0.42)	(0.54)	
Party identification	4.32*	4.72*	$p = 0.491$	5.17*	5.84*	$p = 0.237$
	(0.30)	(0.34)		(0.35)	(0.43)	
Ideology	1.89*	3.36*	$p = 0.289$	6.10*	8.44*	$p = 0.046$
	(0.50)	(0.60)		(0.62)	(0.82)	
Constant	-5.61*	-7.15*		-7.91*	-11.44*	
	(0.32)	(0.41)		(0.43)	(0.72)	
Unweighted N	2,438	2,438		2,540	2,540	

Source: VOTER Survey.

Note: Cell entries are logit coefficients with standard errors in parentheses. The dependent variable is coded 1 = Trump and 0 = Clinton. Party identification and ideology are coded such that higher values equal stronger Republican and conservative identification, respectively. Racial resentment is coded such that higher values equal more emphasis on black people's perceived lack of effort. Modern sexism is coded such that higher values equal higher levels of sexism.

*$p < 0.05$.

Table 7.2: The Relationship between White Americans' Gender Attitudes and Vote for President (ANES)

	White Women			White Men		
	2012	2016	2012 vs. 2016	2012	2016	2012 vs. 2016
Modern sexism	0.93	2.10*	$p = 0.292$	1.64*	2.99*	$p = 0.272$
	(0.58)	(0.60)		(0.57)	(0.70)	
Racial resentment	2.81*	5.23*	$p = 0.008$	3.27*	4.41*	$p = 0.251$
	(0.45)	(0.58)		(0.53)	(0.61)	
Party identification	5.06*	4.82*	$p = 0.742$	5.98*	5.05*	$p = 0.268$
	(0.36)	(0.43)		(0.43)	(0.51)	
Ideology	5.01*	2.81*	$p = 0.047$	4.18*	3.59*	$p = 0.661$
	(0.64)	(0.77)		(0.67)	(0.91)	
Constant	-7.08*	-7.19*		-7.64*	-7.63*	
	(0.49)	(0.57)		(0.54)	(0.64)	
Unweighted N	1,151	1,036		1,094	932	

Source: 2012–2016 American National Election Studies.

Note: Cell entries are logit coefficients with standard errors in parentheses. The dependent variable is coded 1 = Trump and 0 = Clinton. Party identification and ideology are coded such that higher values equal stronger Republican and conservative identification, respectively. Racial resentment is coded such that higher values equal more emphasis on black people's perceived lack of effort. Modern sexism is coded such that higher values equal higher levels of sexism.

*$p < 0.05$.

Table 7.3: The Relationship between White Americans' Gender Attitudes and Views of Donald Trump

	White Women			White Men		
	2012	2016	2012 vs. 2016	2012	2016	2012 vs. 2016
Modern sexism	0.18*	0.37*	$p < 0.001$	0.22*	0.26*	$p = 0.119$
	(0.04)	(0.03)		(0.03)	(0.03)	
Racial resentment	0.25*	0.20*	$p = 0.005$	0.38*	0.34*	$p = 0.095$
	(0.03)	(0.03)		(0.03)	(0.03)	
Party identification	0.53*	0.51*	$p = 0.159$	0.47*	0.50*	$p = 0.066$
	(0.03)	(0.02)		(0.03)	(0.03)	
Ideology	0.22*	0.24*	$p = 0.297$	0.17*	0.22*	$p = 0.046$
	(0.04)	(0.03)		(0.03)	(0.03)	
Constant	−0.15*	−0.17*		−0.17*	−0.20*	
	(0.02)	(0.01)		(0.02)	(0.02)	
Unweighted N	2,340	2,350		2,349	2,349	

Source: VOTER Survey.

Note: Cell entries are least squares coefficients with standard errors in parentheses. The dependent variable ranges from 0 = very unfavorable view of Trump to 1 = very favorable view. Party identification and ideology are coded such that higher values equal stronger Republican and conservative identification, respectively. Racial resentment is coded such that higher values equal more emphasis on black people's perceived lack of effort. Modern sexism is coded such that higher values equal higher levels of sexism.

$^*p < 0.05$.

Table 7.4: The Relationship between White Americans' Gender Attitudes and Support for Neil Gorsuch and Brett Kavanaugh

	White Women			White Men		
	Gorsuch	Kavanaugh	Gorsuch vs. Kavanaugh	Gorsuch	Kavanaugh	Gorsuch vs. Kavanaugh
Hostile sexism	0.61*	2.56*	$p < 0.001$	0.66*	1.86*	$p < 0.001$
	(0.08)	(0.12)		(0.09)	(0.13)	
Racial resentment	0.50*	2.69*	$p < 0.001$	0.80*	3.33*	$p < 0.001$
	(0.07)	(0.11)		(0.09)	(0.12)	
Party identification	0.77*	3.08*	$p < 0.001$	1.22*	3.69*	$p < 0.001$
	(0.07)	(0.09)		(0.07)	(0.10)	
Ideology	1.44*	2.75*	$p < 0.001$	1.72*	2.85*	$p < 0.001$
	(0.09)	(0.13)		(0.09)	(0.14)	
Constant	-1.79*	-6.1*		-2.10*	-6.36*	
	(0.01)	(0.01)		(0.05)	(0.11)	
Unweighted N	21,020	21,045		17,738	17,748	

Source: 2018 CCES.

Note: Cell entries are logit coefficients with standard errors in parentheses. The dependent variable is coded 1 = support Kavanaugh/Gorsuch to 0 = oppose Kavanaugh/Gorsuch. Party identification and ideology are coded such that higher values equal stronger Republican and conservative identification, respectively. Racial resentment is coded such that higher values equal more emphasis on black people's perceived lack of effort. Hostile sexism is coded such that higher values equal higher levels of sexism.

*$p < 0.05$.

Table 7.5: The Relationship between White Americans' Gender Attitudes and Vote for US House (VOTER Survey)

	White Women			White Men		
	2012	2016	2012 vs. 2016	2012	2016	2012 vs. 2016
Modern sexism	1.51*	3.05*	$p = 0.054$	−0.21	2.70*	$p = 0.007$
	(0.47)	(0.63)		(0.51)	(0.61)	
Racial resentment	1.12*	3.67*	$p = 0.003$	2.73*	2.81*	$p = 0.926$
	(0.37)	(0.56)		(0.44)	(0.52)	
Party identification	4.10*	5.93*	$p = 0.004$	3.99*	5.32*	$p = 0.045$
	(0.33)	(0.48)		(0.35)	(0.44)	
Ideology	3.16*	5.08*	$p = 0.070$	4.73*	4.66*	$p = 0.946$
	(0.52)	(0.80)		(0.56)	(0.68)	
Constant	−4.81*	−9.21*		−6.16*	−7.76*	
	(0.29)	(0.63)		(0.36)	(0.50)	
Unweighted N	1,833	1,833		1,967	1,967	

Source: VOTER Survey.

Note: Cell entries are logit coefficients with standard errors in parentheses. The dependent variable is coded 1 = Republican candidate and 0 = Democratic candidate. Party identification and ideology are coded such that higher values equal stronger Republican and conservative identification, respectively. Racial resentment is coded such that higher values equal more emphasis on black people's perceived lack of effort. Modern sexism is coded such that higher values equal higher levels of sexism.

*$p < 0.05$.

States." We code responses as 1 = support appointment and 0 = oppose appointment.

The independent variables are similar except for the measure of gender attitudes. It is based on respondents' agreement or disagreement with two statements:

"When women lose to men in a fair competition, they typically complain about being discriminated against."

"Feminists are making entirely reasonable demands of men."

Among white respondents, the reliability of an index based on these two items is 0.64.

The models in table 7.4 show that this measure of gender attitudes is more strongly related to views of Kavanaugh than of Gorsuch, as are the other factors in the model.

Figure 4: Gender Attitudes and Whites' Likelihood of Voting for a Republican US House Candidate in 2012 and 2018

This analysis is based on VOTER Survey respondents who were interviewed after both the 2012 and the 2018 elections. All independent variables were measured in the December 2016 wave.

NOTES

1. In an ABC News/ *Washington Post* poll conducted October 29–November 1, 55 percent said Trump was biased against women, compared to 40 percent who said not biased. In an Associated Press poll conducted October 20–24, 46 percent said that "sexist" describes Trump "very well," 13 percent said "somewhat well," 18 percent said "slightly well," and 21 percent said "not well at all." In a CBS News/*New York Times* poll conducted October 28–November 1, 20 percent said that Trump respects women "a lot," 25 percent said "some," 15 percent said "not much," and 38 percent said "not at all." In a Pew Research Center poll conducted October 20–25, 14 percent said that Trump respects women "a great deal," 24 percent said "a fair amount," 24 percent said "not too much," and 36 percent said "not at all." These results were accessed from the Roper Center's iPoll Archive.

2. We focus our analyses on whites only because attitudes about gender were not significantly related to the vote choices of nonwhites in the 2016 election (Frasure-Yokley 2018; Bracic, Israel-Trummel, and Shortle 2019). Racial resentment captures whether white Americans tend to attribute racial inequality to structural forces, like slavery and discrimination, or to black Americans' individual choices and especially their perceived lack of effort (Kam and Burge 2018). More "resentment" on this measure indicates a stronger belief that racial inequality stems from black people's choices.

3. The relationship between modern sexism and vote choice among white women is not statistically significantly different in 2016 than it is in 2012 in both the VOTER Survey ($p = 0.68$) and the ANES ($p = 0.29$). Thus, we cannot definitively say that modern sexism was more strongly correlated with the presidential vote among white women in 2016 than in 2012.

4. In the VOTER Survey, the relationship between modern sexism and vote choice among white men is statistically significantly larger in 2016 than in 2012 ($p = 0.005$), although the evidence in the ANES is less conclusive ($p = 0.27$).

5. Among white women, the relationship between modern sexism and views of Trump was statistically significantly larger in 2016 than in 2012 ($p < 0.001$). Among men, the difference in the relationship was less precisely estimated ($p = 0.11$).

6. Among both white women and white men, the relationship between modern sexism and support for Kavanaugh is statistically significantly larger ($p < 0.001$) than the relationship between modern sexism and support for Gorsuch. To be sure, other factors—including party identification, self-reported ideology, and racial resentment—were also more strongly associated with support for Kavanaugh than with support for Gorsuch. This suggests that the contentious battle over Kavanaugh's confirmation created greater polarization along several dimensions (see the appendix). But gender attitudes do appear to have been one such dimension.

7. The 2012–2018 change in the relationship between modern sexism and congressional voting was statistically significant among white women ($p = 0.05$) and white men ($p = 0.007$).

REFERENCES

Bracic, Ana, Mackenzie Israel-Trummel, and Allyson F. Shortle. "Is Sexism for White People? Gender Stereotypes, Race, and the 2016 Presidential Election." *Political Behavior* 41, no. 2 (June 2019): 281–307.

Burns, Nancy, and Donald R. Kinder. "Categorical Politics: Gender, Race and Public Opinion." In *New Directions in Public Opinion,* ed. Adam Berinsky, 139–167. New York: Routledge, 2012.

Carsey, Thomas M., and Gerald C. Wright. "State and National Factors in Gubernatorial and Senatorial Elections." *American Journal of Political Science* 42, no. 3 (July 1998): 994–1002.

Cassese, Erin C., and Tiffany D. Barnes. 2019. "Reconciling Sexism and Women's Support for Republican Candidates: A Look at Gender, Class, and Whiteness in the 2012 and 2016 Presidential Races." *Political Behavior* 41, no. 3 (September 2019): 677–700.

Chenoweth, Erica, and Jeremy Pressman. "This Is What We Learned by Counting the Women's Marches." Monkey Cage, *Washington Post,* February 7, 2017.

Chozick, Amy, and Jonathan Martin. "Clinton '16 Would Give Gender More of a Role Than Clinton '08 Did." *New York Times,* February 24, 2015.

Clinton, Hillary Rodham. *What Happened.* New York: Simon & Schuster, 2017.

Dittmar, Kelley. "By the Numbers: Women Congressional Candidates in 2018." Center for American Women and Politics, Rutgers University, 2018.

Enders, Adam M., and Jamil Scott. "The Increasing Racialization of American Electoral Politics, 1988–2016." *American Political Science Research* 47, no. 2 (March 2019): 275–303.

Engelhardt, Andrew. "Racial Attitudes through a Partisan Lens." *British Journal of Political Science,* 2020.

Enten, Harry. "Men Are Treating 2016 as a 'Normal' Election; Women Aren't." *FiveThirtyEight,* October 17, 2016.

Frasure-Yokley, Lorrie. "Choosing the Velvet Glove: Women Voters, Ambivalent Sexism, and Vote Choice in 2016." *Journal of Race, Ethnicity and Politics* 3, no. 1 (March 2018): 3–25.

Glick, Peter, and Susan T. Fiske. "The Ambivalent Sexism Inventory: Differentiating Hostile and Benevolent Sexism." *Journal of Personality and Social Psychology* 70, no. 3 (March 1996): 491–512.

Glynn, Adam N., and Maya Sen. "Identifying Judicial Empathy: Does Having Daughters Cause Judges to Rule for Women's Issues?" *American Journal of Political Science* 59, no. 1 (March 2015): 37–54.

Gurin, Patricia. "Women's Gender Consciousness." *Public Opinion Quarterly* 49, no. 2 (Summer 1985): 143–163.

Hayes, Danny, and Jennifer L. Lawless. *Women on the Run: Gender, Media, and Political Campaigns in a Polarized Era.* New York: Cambridge University Press, 2016.

Huddy, Leonie, and Johanna Willmann. "Partisan Sorting and the Feminist Gap in American Politics." Unpublished manuscript, Stony Brook University, 2017.

Iyengar, Shanto, and Donald Kinder. *News That Matters: Television and American Opinion.* Chicago: University of Chicago Press, 1987.

Jones, Jeffrey. "Opposition to Kavanaugh Had Been Rising before the Accusation." *Gallup,* September 16, 2018.

Kam, Cindy D., and Allison M. N. Archer. "Modern Sexism and Turnout in the 2018 Midterm." Unpublished manuscript, Vanderbilt University, 2019.

Kam, Cindy D., and Camille D. Burge. "Uncovering Reactions to the Racial Resentment Scale across the Racial Divide." *Journal of Politics* 80, no. 1 (March 2018): 314–320.

Kinder, Donald R., and Allison Dale-Riddle. *The End of Race?: Obama, 2008, and Racial Politics in America.* New Haven, CT: Yale University Press, 2012.

Kinder, Donald R., and Lynn M. Sanders. *Divided by Color.* Chicago: University of Chicago Press, 1996.

Lenz, Gabriel S. *Follow the Leader?: How Voters Respond to Politicians' Policies and Performance.* Chicago: Chicago University Press, 2012.

Luks, Samantha, and Brian Schaffner. "Sexism, Efficacy, and the Kavanaugh Confirmation." Paper presented at the Annual Meeting of the Midwest Political Science Association, 2019.

Luttig, Matthew D. "Obama, Race, and the Republican landslide in 2010." *Politics, Groups, and Identities* 5, no. 2 (June 2017): 197–219.

Mason, Lilliana. *Uncivil Agreement: How Politics Became Our Identity.* Chicago: University of Chicago Press, 2018.

McThomas, Mary, and Michael Tesler. "The Growing Influence of Gender Attitudes on Public Support for Hillary Clinton, 2008–2012." *Politics & Gender* 12, no. 1 (March 2016): 28–49.

Morin, Rebecca. "Trump on Sexual Assault Claims: 'It's a Very Scary Time for Young Men in America.'" *Politico,* October 2, 2018.

NBC News. "Decades Old Video Shows Trump Predict His Campaign Problems with Women." October 10, 2016.

Rogers, Steven. "National Forces in State Legislative Elections." *ANNALS of the American Academy of Political and Social Science* 667, no. 1 (September 2016): 207–225.

Schaffner, Brian. "Republicans Are Being Punished for Trump's Sexism." *Data for Progress,* November 8, 2018.

Schaffner, Brian F., Matthew MacWilliams, and Tatishe Nteta. "Understanding White Polarization in the 2016 Vote for President: The Sobering Role of Racism and Sexism." *Political Science Quarterly* 133, no. 1 (March 2018): 9–34.

Sharrow, Elizabeth A., Jesse H. Rhodes, Tatishe M. Nteta, and Jill S. Greenlee. "The First-Daughter Effect: The Impact of Fathering Daughters on Men's Preferences for Gender-Equality Policies." *Public Opinion Quarterly* 82, no. 3 (Fall 2018): 493–523.

Siddiqui, Sabrina, and Lauren Gambino. "How Women Could Vote Hillary Clinton into the White House." *Guardian,* November 3, 2016.

Sides, John, Michael Tesler, and Lynn Vavreck. *Identity Crisis: The 2016 Presidential Campaign and the Battle for the Meaning of America.* Princeton, NJ: Princeton University Press, 2018.

Stimson, James A. *Tides of Consent: How Public Opinion Shapes American Politics.* New York: Cambridge University Press, 2004.

Stoker, Laura. "Judging Presidential Character: The Demise of Gary Hart." *Political Behavior* 15, no. 2 (June 1993): 193–223.

Swim, Janet. K., Kathryn J. Aikin, Wayne S. Hall, and Barbara A. Hunter. "Sexism and Racism: Old-Fashioned and Modem Prejudices." *Journal of Personality and Social Psychology* 68, no. 2 (June 1995): 199–214.

Swim, Janet K., and Laurie Cohen. "Overt, Covert, and Subtle Sexism: A Comparison between the Attitude Toward Women and Modern Sexism Scales." *Psychology of Women Quarterly* 21, no. 1 (March 1997): 103–118.

Tesler, Michael. "Parents of Daughters Support Hillary Clinton More than Parents of Sons." Monkey Cage, *Washington Post,* January 5, 2016a.

———. *Post-Racial or Most Racial? Race and Politics in the Obama Era.* Chicago: University of Chicago Press, 2016b.

———. "Why the Gender Gap Doomed Hillary Clinton." Monkey Cage, *Washington Post,* November 9, 2016c.

———. “Priming Predispositions and Changing Policy Positions: An Account of When Mass Opinion Is Primed or Changed.” *American Journal of Political Science* 59, no. 4 (October 2015): 806–824.

Tesler, Michael, and David O. Sears. *Obama’s Race: The 2008 Election and the Dream of a Post-Racial America.* Chicago: University of Chicago Press, 2010.

Tufte, Edward R. *Political Control of the Economy.* Princeton, NJ: Princeton University Press, 1978.

Valencia, Jamie, and Dhrumil Mehta. “A Final Look at Where Voters Stand on Kavanaugh Before They Vote.” *FiveThirtyEight,* October 5, 2018.

Valentino, Nicholas A., Carly Wayne, and Marzia Oceno. “Mobilizing Sexism: The Interaction of Emotion and Gender Attitudes in the 2016 US Presidential Election.” *Public Opinion Quarterly* 82, no. S1 (April 2018): 799–821.

Vavreck, Lynn. “Insults and Ads: How Gender Hurts Trump but Doesn’t Lift Clinton.” *New York Times,* April 30, 2016.

Warner, Rebecca L., and Brent S. Steel. “Child Rearing as a Mechanism for Social Change: The Relationship of Child Gender to Parents’ Commitment to Gender Equity.” *Gender & Society* 13, no. 4 (August 1999): 503–517.

Washington, Ebonya. “Female Socialization: How Daughters Affect Their Legislator Fathers’ Voting on Women’s Issues.” *American Economic Review* 98, no. 1 (March 2008): 311–332.

Women’s March. “Mission and Vison.” 2017. https://web.archive.org/web/20170125034852/https://www.womensmarch.com/mission/.

CHAPTER 8

Curating the News: How Social Media Facilitates Selective Exposure

Samara Klar and Yotam Shmargad

THE RIGGED AND CORRUPT MEDIA IS THE ENEMY OF THE PEOPLE!

—President Donald Trump, Twitter, February 17, 2019
(formatted as per original)

President Donald Trump makes no secret of his concern for agenda-setting, though he might not use the term "agenda-setting" to explain his discontent. "While the mass media may have little influence on the direction or intensity of attitudes," wrote McCombs and Shaw (1972, 177), "it is hypothesized that the mass media *set the agenda* . . . influencing the salience of attitudes toward the political issues" (emphasis added). In sum, media may not tell viewers what to think, but they do tell them what to think about (Iyengar and Kinder 1987). President Trump thus, in his own unique way, appears to share the same curiosity that many social scientists do regarding the power of media to influence listeners, readers, and viewers of the news.

In the early to mid-twentieth century, when war propaganda provided the bulk of evidence on media effects, scholars viewed media as having an enormous influence over public attitudes. Messages were seen as "magic bullets"—once a passive viewer was hit, her attitudes were altered (Lasswell 1927). It was during this era of communications studies that Walter Lippmann famously wrote, "The press is like the beam of a searchlight that moves restlessly about, bringing one episode and then another out of the darkness into vision" (1922). Media were viewed, at this time, as a paramount influence over the political information people received and the political attitudes they subsequently formed.

In the postwar era, however, scholars began to take a dramatic shift in how they conceived of media influence. Lazarsfeld and his colleagues (1952) questioned the degree to which media might actually change minds and found that attitudes rather appeared stable throughout the course of a campaign, as measured in surveys and interviews over time. They introduced the influential notion of the "two-step flow," arguing that information flows from media to opinion leaders and then on to the mass public. This critical second phase (the opinion leaders) filters information; indeed, it is from one's friends and associates, and not from media directly, that people receive the most influential political information. Not only do opinion leaders act as conduits of information, but, as Katz wrote in a follow-up to the initial description of the two-step flow, "interpersonal relations are also sources of pressure to conform to the group's way of thinking and acting, as well as sources of social support" (1957, 77).

Yet, empirically, evidence of media influence persisted. McCombs and Shaw (1972) found, for example, that the political problems voters thought to be most important also happened to be the same problems to which the media gave the greatest amount of attention. A decade later, with experimental tools at their disposal, social scientists set out to demonstrate the causal relationship between media and public opinion. For example, Iyengar and Kinder (1987) experimentally manipulated the salience of political issues in otherwise identical news broadcasts and then measured the importance that viewers placed on each issue and the influence that the issue had on overall presidential evaluations. The scholars found that news media do indeed hold large persuasive powers when it comes to setting the agenda. Television news in particular, they argued, "shapes the American public's conception of political life in pervasive ways."

The introduction of online news and social media provides scholars with another completely new media environment to understand. Boydstun (2013) suggests that reading newspapers online constrains the range of perspectives to which readers are exposed (relative to print editions). More recently, Dunaway and colleagues (2018) compared media exposure on various Internet devices (computers, phones, and tablets), finding that the device itself has implications for news consumption. Specifically, people who read political news on tablets and phones pay less attention to what they see than those reading their news on a computer. Tablets, in particular, reduce the amount of time spent on, and attention paid to, news. As Prior argued more than a decade before, "political science tends to treat ordinary people's political behavior as if it can be explained without reference to the media environment in which they live . . . yet as the environment changes, so might the behavior" (Prior 2007, 3–4).

In December 2018, the Pew Research Center reported that more Americans claimed to read their news from social media than from newspapers. By social media, we refer not to online news websites (e.g., www.nytimes.com) but to social media platforms, such as Facebook, Twitter, or Instagram. Specifically, 16 percent of Americans told Pew that they read their news using print newspapers and 20 percent said they read their news on social media. Television usage had dropped by nearly 10 percentage points in just two years. Social media, by contrast, had become a more popular news source over the same period. It is perhaps no surprise that the youngest cohorts of news viewers rely on social media most of all. According to Pew, those aged eighteen to twenty-nine years old are four times as likely to receive their news on social media than are those aged sixty-five years and older.

Our collective scholarly understanding of how social media environments affect exposure to political news and attitudes toward American politics more generally are still in their infancy. In this chapter, we review evidence for how this new media landscape might influence political attitudes and behaviors, and we present a new study that experimentally manipulates one of the key features of social media platforms—the news feed—to help illustrate how consuming news on social media might change how we think about politics. We find that the news feed has potentially profound effects on how social media users see news by ordering news items to prioritize the most ideologically congruent items at the top of the feed. By favoring political like-minded content over items that might challenge a user's preexisting views, social media can contribute to polarizing views of politics. Contrary to President Trump's troubling tweet, the American media are neither rigged nor corrupt, but media do play an important role in determining how consumers consume and evaluate the news.

THE INFLUENCE OF SOCIAL MEDIA ON POLITICAL ATTITUDES: WHAT DO WE KNOW SO FAR?

A great deal of work on the political implications of social media focuses on the network of users that develops and, in particular, the tendency to connect with like-minded individuals. Examining Twitter, Barbera (2014) finds that political discussions tend to occur primarily among like-minded users. Conover et al. (2011) find a similar pattern in the messages that people share: by connecting users who "retweet" (or share) each other's messages and estimating their ideology by using content analysis, they find that Democrat-leaning and Republican-leaning individuals tend to cluster in ideologically homogeneous spaces. However, when connecting users based on who they "mention" in tweets, the researchers find potential for cross-cutting exposure. Gruzd and Roy (2014) also find that Twitter offers both "pockets of polarization" and opportunities for cross-party dialogue.

The network component of social media has also been exploited by researchers to study contagion of political engagement, such as turnout. Bond et al. (2012) randomly assigned all Facebook users over the age of eighteen to one of three experimental conditions on Election Day in 2010. A random selection of users who logged into Facebook that day saw an "informational message," including a button to click if the user had voted and a running tally of self-identified voters on Facebook. Another randomly selected group saw a "social message," which included the same "I voted" button but also photos of up to six of their friends who had already clicked the button. As users' friends clicked the button, those in the "social message" condition saw that more of their friends had voted. A final randomly selected group of Facebook users saw no changes—they were in the control group, unbeknownst to them. The researchers then used validated voter files to determine the percent within each group who voted. They found that the "social message" significantly increased the rate of voter turnout among those who saw it as compared to those who saw the informational message or none at all. Mobilizing messages are a promising benefit of media that can leverage such social signals.

Turning to less normatively desirable implications, Settle (2018) argues that Facebook's newsfeed (the scrolling list of posts that appears when users login to their account) is uniquely designed to heighten negative attitudes about those with whom we disagree, contributing to what Settle refers to as "psychological polarization." Settle explains that users who generate political content on Facebook tend to be more ideologically extreme and partisan than the average American, yet users who see this content assume that the individual who posted it is an average representation of his or her partisan group. Encountering these types of messages thus "biases upwards the amount of perceived difference between the parties and the amount of support for one's own political views" (Settle 2018, 79).

One particular element of social media platforms that has great consequence for how users engage with political news is the algorithm by which posts are sorted in the news feed. On Facebook, the default setting is called "Top Stories." While the specific algorithm that curates this default feed is proprietary, and thus not publicly divulged, researchers estimate that it is based upon several features, including the strength of the relationship between the poster and the user, the user's expressed interests, the user's implicit preferences, and the content of the post (DeVito 2017). Although users can manually change their setting to instead show posts in order of recency, Facebook automatically returns the setting to Top Stories at periodic intervals (though there are third-party browser plug-ins that prevent this, such as www.socialfixer.com). As a result of this default setting, the vast majority of Facebook users do not see the news feed in chronological order but rather according to a ranking based on the preferences of their friends. Twitter similarly curates each user's feed according to the extent that posts align with the user's preexisting preferences, leading to a similarly popularity-based scoring system that determines the order in which users see the posts—be they photos, messages, or news articles—that appear in their feed.[1]

We argue that this presents a dramatic shift in the news consumption experience from what is offered by traditional media. Whereas print media and television media curate news items before the readers and viewers consume them, social media rearranges news according to what is popular in one's network. Moreover, they do this in real time, throughout the day, so as to make the items that are most in line with the user's preferences most accessible. In this chapter, we engage with the possibility that newsfeed algorithms can indeed have important consequences for how news consumers evaluate political information they see on social media and, subsequently, how they evaluate politics generally.

THE ROLE OF THE NEWS FEED IN SHAPING POLITICAL ATTITUDES

Existing work clearly demonstrates that the order in which people see the news has tremendous impact for how they evaluate it. The placement of news items tells readers what is important and what is not: front-page articles (Althaus and Tewksbury 2002), above-the-fold articles (Clayman and Reisner 1998), headline size (Carlson 2007), and lead television stories (Iyengar and Kinder 1987) are viewed as more important. Furthermore, these prominently displayed news items tend to have a greater influence over subsequent evaluations of which news items are important and which are not (Iyengar and Kinder 1987). Feezell (2018) carried out an experiment on Facebook in which she randomly assigned people to various "Facebook Groups," which exposed them to different assortments of political content. She found that exposure to political information on Facebook, even incidental (i.e., by simply scrolling though the site), increases the salience of the issues to which people were exposed. Social media platforms can thus hold the same agenda-setting powers that Iyengar and Kinder (1987) first noted with respect to television news. We expect that the algorithms that curate the social media "news feed" can effectively determine which items are seen and with what effect.

The location of news items within Facebook's news feed, specifically, appears to exert important influence over a viewer's behavior. Bakshy, Messing, and Adamic (2015) examined user data from Facebook and compared the rate at which users click on posts that are first (i.e., higher) or later (i.e., lower) in their news feeds. They found that individuals are significantly more likely to click on posts that are higher up in their news feed, even when they contain political content that conflicts with their preexisting views (Bakshy, Messing, and Adamic 2015, 21, supplemental material). This suggests that location is a tremendous determinant of engagement with a particular news item and can even outweigh the tendency, known as selective exposure, to engage only with news that affirms our preexisting views (Stroud 2008). Their finding suggests that the social media news feed might even encourage exposure to a wider range of ideological viewpoints, given that the placement of the story appears in their observational data to be less associated with user engagement than the ideological congruence of the content.

One limitation to Bakshy, Messing, and Adamics (2015) observational dataset is that, by virtue of its observational nature, the placement of the story might be confounded with its content. Popularity-based algorithms, such as those employed by social media platforms like Facebook and Twitter, prioritize agreeable content. This can elevate like-minded articles to higher positions on the news feed. Most social media users appear to be connected to like-minded networks (Eady et al. 2019), increasing the odds that popularity-based algorithms will increase the accessibility of articles with which the user already agrees. By examining the rate at which users click on articles at the top of the news feed without randomizing the content in the articles, it is difficult to know whether ordering truly does outweigh partisan-motivated selective exposure.

To determine the relative importance of the placement of an article in the news feed versus the ideological congruence of the article itself, we conducted a randomized trial. We now turn to discussing this study and the outcomes it allowed us to observe.

A RANDOMIZED CONTROLLED STUDY OF A SOCIAL MEDIA ALGORITHM

Most Americans view political news on social media, and most social media sites curate these news items according to how well they will align with the user's preexisting views. To test the effects of these popularity-based algorithms, we randomly assigned a large sample of adults to view a news feed in which we randomly ordered a selection of articles.[2] To determine the ideological congruency of the participants, we asked them to tell us their party identification. To determine the ideological leaning of each news article, we turned to the website www.AllSides.com. This website uses a multilayered ranking approach to score the ideological leaning of articles in the daily news. Based on reader feedback, editorial decisions, and surveys, Allsides ranks each article on a scale from 1 (most liberal) to 5 (most conservative), with 3 serving as a neutral "moderate" score. We chose eight "liberal" articles and eight "conservative" articles with which to populate a simulated news feed.

We created the news feed using the Qualtrics survey software. A sample of 445 adult Americans (recruited by Survey Strategy International) participated in this study. Each participant completed the Qualtrics survey from their computer or mobile device, just as one would access their own social media accounts. The survey directed them to a news feed–like arrangement of sixteen news articles, each with a "like" button underneath. Participants were instructed to scroll through the feed and to "like" as many or as few articles as they chose. The articles were randomized for each respondent—no two respondents were exposed to the same order of articles, though the same sixteen articles were presented to each participant.

Once the participants viewed the articles and clicked "like" on as many as they wished, we simply tallied up the number of likes to help us understand how participants engage with political news based on the order in which the different articles are presented. Since we also collected information about participants' party identification, we could identify whether each article was cross-cutting (i.e., from the opposing side of the political spectrum) or self-aligned (i.e., from the same side of the political spectrum). All self-identifying independents (i.e., those who responded 4 on the 7-item partisanship scale) were dropped from the analysis, since articles were neither cross-cutting nor self-aligned for this set of participants.

In figure 8.1, we display the proportion of "likes" that each position in the news feed received, based on the participant's party identification and whether the article presented was cross-cutting or self-aligned. Even though

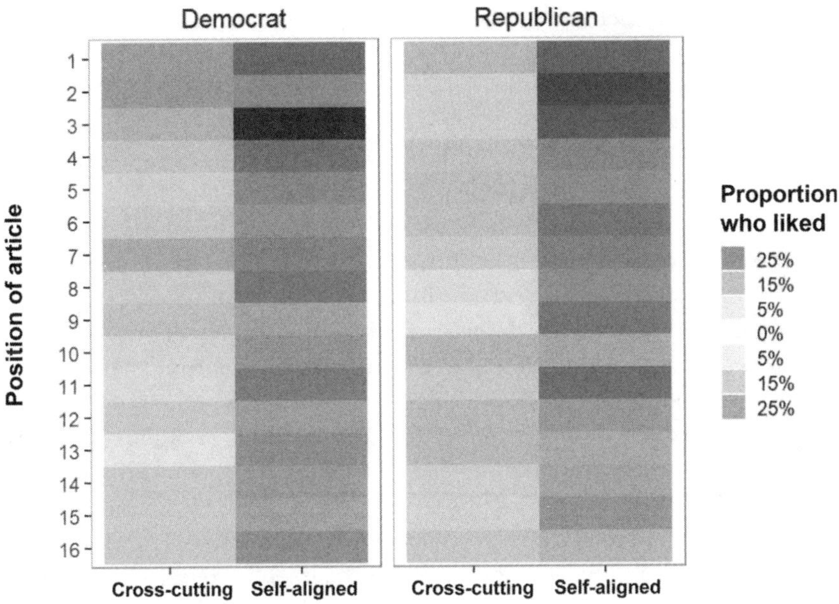

Figure 8.1: Proportion of "Likes" by Position, Party Identification, and Self-Alignment. *Source*: Authors' computations.

the articles in the top positions changed with each participant, we still see that articles receive a boost in attention simply by being near the top. This complements the observational work of Bakshy and his colleagues at Facebook. Just as they observed in their study, we find that stories appearing higher up in the news feed are more likely to draw attention than articles featured further down in the news feed.

Just as the position of the article was influential for amassing "likes," figure 8.1 makes it clear that the ideological leaning of the article was also important. In particular, both Democrats and Republicans tended to "like" articles that were aligned with their own ideological viewpoint more than they liked articles from the opposing side. Indeed, contrary to Bakshy, Messing, and Adamic (2015), self-alignment appears to be a more important characteristic of an article than its position, at least when it comes to liking behavior. To make a more formal comparison of self-alignment and article position, we next describe the statistical models that we use to assess which articles participants in our study liked.

Since article "likes" are binary outcomes, we use a logit specification in estimating how article position and political alignment correspond to liking behavior. In addition to using an ordinary logit, we also estimate models that include article and subject (i.e., participant) fixed effects. This ensures that our estimates of article position and alignment are not confounded with specific articles that are liked more or particular research subjects that like many or few articles. Finally, we capture the position of an article in the news feed in three different ways: (1) as a continuous variable from 1 to 16, (2) as fifteen variables, each capturing the individual effect of positions 2 through 16 (compared to being in the top position), and (3) as a partially discretized variable capturing whether the article was in the bottom half of the news feed (i.e., positions 9 through 16). In table 8.1, we present the estimates of our different models.

The results reported in table 8.1 represent odds ratios from a logit specification. The left-most column (Model A) shows results of a model without fixed effects for article and subject, while the remaining columns (Models B–D) show results including these fixed effects. Model A shows that people are more than twice as likely to like an article that aligns with their political views than they are to like one that is crosscutting. Moreover, moving an article's position down by one slot decreases the likelihood of liking the article by only about 3 percent. These data suggest that the content of the news item (and, specifically, whether or not it aligns with the reader's views) appears to hold a greater influence on the tendency to engage with it than the position of the article in an individual's news feed. As shown in Model A, an article has to move from the very top slot (position 1) to the very bottom (position 16) to match the effect of changing the article's content from politically agreeable to politically disagreeable.

Model A suffers from a couple of problems that we address in the remaining models. First, it assumes that the effect of lowering an article's position by one slot is the same regardless of where it falls in the news feed. That is, moving an article from position 1 (i.e., the very top of the news feed) to position 2 is assumed to be the same as moving it from position 15 to position 16. A second issue is that Model A does not take into account that some news articles may generate more likes than others, or that some research subjects may be under- or over-represented, respectively, simply by liking fewer or more news articles. We address the first issue by discretizing the position variable into the sixteen different slots. We address the second issue by including article and subject fixed effects in our models.

Models B–D include fewer observations than Model A, since subjects who either "liked" all of the articles (2 percent of participants) or none of them (38 percent) are dropped in the fixed effects specification. The constant term is also dropped under a fixed effects specification. Estimates from Models B–D show that self-aligned articles were nearly three and half

Table 8.1: Logit Models of Article Liking

	Model A Ordinary Logit		Model B Logit wih Fixed Effects		Model C Position Fully Discretized		Model D Position Partly Discretized	
	OR	SE	OR	SE	OR	SE	OR	SE
Constant	.230**	.016						
Self-aligned	2.21**	.135	3.40**	.267	3.44**	.271	3.40**	.266
Position (1–16)	.968**	.006	.952**	.008				
Position > 8							.669**	.050
Position 2					.893	.179		
Position 3					.960	.194		
Position 4					.669	.138		
Position 5					.562**	.116		
Position 6					.596*	.123		
Position 7					.736	.150		
Position 8					.528**	.110		
Position 9					.473**	.010		
Position 10					.468**	.098		
Position 11					.574**	.120		
Position 12					.517**	.107		
Position 13					.460**	.097		
Position 14					.445**	.094		
Position 15					.469**	.099		
Position 16					.496**	.104		

(continued on the next page)

Table 8.1: *Continued*

	Model A Ordinary Logit	Model B Logit wih Fixed Effects	Model C Position Fully Discretized	Model D Position Partly Discretized
Article fixed effects	Not Included	Included	Included	Included
Subject fixed effects	Not Included	Included	Included	Included
LR χ^2	200.47	303.74	317.77	295.33
Observations	6,912	4,176	4,176	4,176

Note: OR = Odds Ratio; SE = Standard Errors; LR = Likelihood Ratio.
$*p < 0.05$; $**p < 0.01$

times as likely to be "liked," compared to cross-cutting articles. This suggests that the effects reported in Model A were deflated by including participants who did not like any of the articles. Among those that liked between one and fifteen articles, the ideological alignment of an article seems to play a large role in determining people's liking behavior, even after controlling for article- and subject-specific characteristics.

We now turn to the effects of position under Models B–D. Estimates from Model B show that moving an article down by one slot increases from Model A, from 3 percent to 5 percent. However, as mentioned earlier, this estimate assumes that position changes do not vary by location in the news feed. Fully discretizing the position variable in Model C allows us to make a more precise estimate of moving an article from the top of the news feed (position 1) to the bottom (position 16). The estimates from Model C show that such a move decreases the probability of "liking" by half. These estimates also show that position moves do not have a consistent effect until articles are "under-the-fold" (i.e., about position 8). We thus partly discretized the position variable to distinguish between articles that were above-the-fold (i.e., positions 1–8) and under-the-fold (i.e., positions 9–16). Estimates from Model D show that moving an article from above- to under-the-fold decreases liking tendency by about one-third.

DISCUSSION

Do social media facilitate exposure to a wider range of news items? Bakshy, Messing, and Adamic's (2015) analysis of observational Facebook data suggest that the news feed might indeed encourage engagement with ideologically incongruent information by presenting stories in a vertical timeline, which encourages engagement with more prominent stories regardless of their content. Yet Facebook (and many other social media platforms, including Twitter) prioritizes content that aligns with a user's views. This means that higher-ranked items *also* align with a user's ideological views. Observational data thus do not allow us to isolate the influence of content separately from the influence of the article's position in the news feed. Our experiment provides a unique opportunity to do so.

We find that selective exposure is indeed alive and well. While the news feed itself encourages engagement with items that appear earlier, ideological congruence is still the strongest predictor of engaging with the news. Given that popularity-based algorithms determine the ordering of news presented in a news feed, *higher items on the news feed also tend to be ideologically congruent with the user*. Our unique experiment demonstrates that users are more likely to engage with ideologically congruent articles and also exhibit weaker preferences toward items placed toward the top of the feed. This suggests that popularity-based algorithms, which raise agreeable posts to the top of the feed, likely exacerbate selective exposure.

We find that an article's ideological alignment has an even stronger effect than position on its tendency to be liked. Participants in our study were three and a half times more likely to "like" articles that aligned with their partisanship than those that were cross-cutting. In other words, consuming news on social media may facilitate exposure to news items that support users' preexisting beliefs and, conversely, suppress exposure to new and potentially disagreeable information.

We contrast our finding to those of Bakshy, Messing, and Adamic (2015), which suggest that position may have a stronger effect than ideological alignment. We argue that the observational nature of their study makes it difficult to compare an article's position and its ideological alignment directly. By randomizing the order of the articles presented in our study, we are able to investigate the causal effect of article position. While the effect of an article's position was not negligible, it was dwarfed by the effect of ideological alignment.

Our study is not without limitations. First, while we attempted to design the feel of the news feed in our survey to match what we observe online, there are certainly differences between real social platforms and our virtual lab. By administering the survey online, made accessible via computer and mobile phones (rather than a physical lab), we are also more likely to match the physical and mental environment that participants occupy when accessing social media. However, features such as social endorsements and comment threading play an important role in how people use and think about social media platforms. Our study does not provide a rich enough experience to investigate these other features.

Another limitation of our study is that the sixteen articles we chose to show participants do not allow us to investigate the self-aligning and cross-cutting nature of articles at a granular level. While the new stories we selected included stories from both sides of the political aisle, as determined by the AllSides.com ranking system, the set of articles is a negligible set of the articles to which social media users are exposed on a daily basis. Any biases that are present in the articles we selected could no doubt constrain the generalizability of our findings. We encourage researchers to build experimental setups that allow us to continue to investigate how the content and design choices of these companies shape political learning, sharing behaviors, and opinions.

In addition to informing our views on agenda-setting within the realm of social media, this study also helps to inform a broader audience about techniques that allow us to study interactive media environments at a relatively low cost. We conclude this chapter with some remarks about methodological strategies for understanding how social media might affect political attitudes and evaluations. If we are to heed Prior's (2007) wisdom and update our understanding of political behavior as our media environments change, we must also update our tools for carrying out these analyses.

Indeed, there are only a few scholars who are able to work with social media companies to carry out studies and experiments using the platforms themselves. Bond et al. (2012), as we previously discussed, manipulated what Facebook users see on their real news feeds to see how social pressure mobilizes voter turnout throughout a network. Kramer, Guillory, and Hancock (2014) also worked with Facebook researchers to test whether emotions are contagious—they manipulated the posts that Facebook users saw on their news feeds according to whether the posts conveyed positive or negative emotions. Bakshy et al. (2012) randomly filtered out information from Facebook's news feed to investigate how information propagation varied across weak and strong ties.

The vast majority of scholars, however, do not have the personal or professional connections necessary to work within the structure of a social media organization. Others have expressed concern about the lack of informed consent that occurs when real social media users are, unbeknownst to them, participants in a large-scale experiment (Flick 2015). The costs and technical skills required to create an entirely new social network platform are, to be sure, beyond the scope of what many researchers have the resources for. Instead, we offer a template for a relatively low-cost and user-friendly approach to studying the influence of social media on political outcomes. Using a straightforward survey software (like Qualtrics, which is the software we employ), researchers can design appearances that resemble key aspects of social media environments. Our design even included the number of "likes" that the articles received from a separate sample during a pretest. The "like" button, which the participants can click, is a graphic embedded into the response scale.

According to the Pew Research Center, more Americans rely on social media (20 percent) to receive their political news than they do on print newspapers (15 percent). This gap is sure to widen in the very near future. Our motivation in pursuing this project is to understand the implication of digital political information on subsequent political attitudes and behaviors. One important first step is to identify the causal relationship between the way the news is presented by social media and people's engagement with the news. Our randomized experiment indicates that users seek ideological congruence and engage with agreeable articles even when they appear lower in a news feed. Rather than exposing users to an especially diverse menu of political news, our work suggests that social media might, in fact, do the opposite. By elevating agreeable information (via popularity-based algorithms), social media companies run the risk of further exacerbating selective exposure.

NOTES

1. See Nicolas Koumchatzky and Anton Andryeyev, "Using Deep Learning at Scale in Twitter's Timelines," May 9, 2017, https://blog.twitter.com/engineering/en_us/topics/insights/2017/using-deep-learning-at-scale-in-twitters-timelines .html.

2. The data and study we described here are part of a larger project we describe in more detail elsewhere (Shmargad and Klar 2020), but the analyses we present in this chapter are conducted exclusively for this chapter and we present them only here.

REFERENCES

Althaus, Scott L., and David Tewksbury. "Agenda Setting and the 'New' News: Patterns of Issue Importance among Readers of the Paper and Online Versions of the New York Times." *Communication Research* 29, no. 2 (2002): 180–207.

Bakshy, Eytan, Solomon Messing, and Lada A. Adamic. "Exposure to Ideologically Diverse News and Opinion on Facebook." *Science* 348, no. 6239 (2015): 1130–1132.

Bakshy, Eytan, Itamar Rosenn, Cameron Marlow, and Lada Adamic. "The Role of Social Networks in Information Diffusion." In *Proceedings of the 21st International Conference on World Wide Web*, 519–528. New York: ACM, 2012.

Barbera, Pablo. "How Social Media Reduces Mass Political Polarization: Evidence from Germany, Spain, and the US." Presented at the annual meeting of the 2014 American Political Science Association. Washington, DC, 2014.

Bond, Robert M., Christopher J. Fariss, Jason J. Jones, Adam D. I. Kramer, Cameron Marlow, Jaime E. Settle, and James H. Fowler. "A 61-Million-Person Experiment in Social Influence and Political Mobilization." *Nature* 489, no. 7415 (2012): 295–298.

Boydstun, Amber. *Making the News: Politics, the Media, and Agenda Setting*. Chicago: University of Chicago Press, 2013.

Carlson, Matt. "Order versus Access: News Search Engines and the Challenge to Traditional Journalistic Roles." *Media Culture Society* 29, no. 6 (2007): 1014–1030.

Clayman, Steven E., and Ann Reisner. "Gatekeeping in Action: Editorial Conferences and Assessments of Newsworthiness." *American Sociological Review* 63, no. 2 (1998): 178–199.

Conover, Michael D., Jacob Ratkiewicz, Matthew Francisco, Bruno Goncalves, Filippo Menczer, and Alessandro Flammini. "Political Polarization on Twitter." In *Proceedings of the Fifth International AAAI Conference on Weblogs and Social Media*, 2011.

DeVito, Michael A. "From Editors to Algorithms: A Values-Based Approach to Understanding Story Selection in the Facebook News Feed." *Digital Journalism* 5, no. 6 (2017): 753–773.

Dunaway, Johanna, Kathleen Searles, Mingxiao Sui, and Newly Paul. "News Attention in a Mobile Era." *Journal of Computer-Mediated Communication* 23, no. 2 (2018): 107–124.

Eady, Gregory, Jonathan Nagler, Andy Guess, Jan Zilinksy, and Joshua A. Tucker. "How Many People Live in Political Bubbles on Social Media? Evidence from Linked Survey and Twitter Data." *SAGE Open* 9, no. 1 (2019): 1–21.

Feezell, Jessica T. "Agenda-Setting through Social Media: The Importance of Incidental News Exposure and Social Filtering in the Digital Era." *Political Research Quarterly* 71, no. 2 (2018): 482–494.

Flick, Catherine. "Informed Consent and the Facebook Emotional Manipulation Study." *Research Ethics* 12, no. 1 (2015): 14–28.

Gruzd, Anatoliy, and Jeffrey Roy. "Investigating Political Polarization on Twitter: A Canadian Perspective." *Policy & Internet* 6, no. 1 (2014): 28–45.

Iyengar, Shanto, and Donald R. Kinder. *News That Matters: Television and American Opinion*. Chicago: University of Chicago Press, 1987.

Katz, Elihu. "The Two-Step Flow of Communication: An Up-To-Date Report on an Hypothesis." *Public Opinion Quarterly* 21, no. 1 (1957): 61–78.

Kramer, Adam D. I., Jamie E. Guillory, and Jeffrey T. Hancock. "Experimental Evidence of Mass-Scale Emotional Contagion through Social Networks." *Proceedings of the National Academy of Sciences of the United States (PNAS)* 111, no. 24 (2014): 8788–8790.

Lasswell, Harold D. *Propaganda Technique in the World War.* Eastford, CT: Martino Fine, 1927.

Lazarsfeld, Paul, Bernard Berelson, and Hazel Gaudet. *The People's Choice: How the Voter Makes Up His Mind in a Presidential Campaign.* New York: Columbia University Press, 1952.

Lippmann, Walter. *Public Opinion.* New York: Harcourt, Brace, 1922.

McCombs, Maxwell E., and Donald L. Shaw. "The Agenda-Setting Function of Mass Media." *Public Opinion Quarterly* 36, no. 2 (1972): 176–187.

Prior, Markus. *Post-Broadcast Democracy: How Media Choice Increases Inequality in Political Involvement and Polarizes Elections.* New York: Cambridge University Press, 2007.

Settle, Jaime. *Frenemies: How Social Media Polarizes America.* New York: Cambridge University Press, 2018.

Shmargad, Yotam, and Samara Klar. "Sorting the News: How Ranking by Popularity Polarizes Our Politics." *Political Communication* 37 (2020): 423–446.

Stroud, Natalie J. "Media Use and Political Predispositions: Revisiting the Concept of Selective Exposure." *Political Behavior* 30 (2008): 341–366.

CHAPTER 9

Charge and Retreat: Asymmetric Patterns of Political Engagement among Liberals and Conservatives

Deborah J. Schildkraut, Jeffrey M. Berry, and James M. Glaser

In July 2018, noted lawyer and professor Alan Dershowitz earned national media attention when he wrote an op-ed describing how he has been shunned by liberals from summer dinner parties on Martha's Vineyard owing to arguments he had made against the impeachment of Donald Trump (Dershowitz 2018). Although many on social media mocked his complaint, his argument struck a nerve with political observers because it tapped into a phenomenon that many people feel to be true: Americans are less willing to talk about politics with people who disagree with them than they used to be and prefer to inhabit so-called ideological bubbles. In particular, the concern is that *liberals* shun political discussion with the other side. Upon clarification, Dershowitz noted that he was not complaining but rather "reveling" in the controversy (Chokshi 2018) because he enjoys being provocative. While Dershowitz calls himself a liberal Democrat, this stance of preferring provocation is one that is closely tied in current politics to conservative media, where saying things to anger liberals has become a tried-and-true business model. Our aim in this study is to examine whether these two modes of political engagement—conservatives charging toward conflict and liberals retreating—characterize the behavior of the American public.

This is a particularly contentious moment in American political history. Binder and Spindel (2017) argue that the parties in government are more divided now than at any point in the past century. Clearly, there is also an ideological and partisan divide in the electorate that is unusual by historical standards (Levendusky 2009). Here we analyze increasing polarization in the context of our broader project on how liberals and conservatives engage politics in the contemporary era. We argue here that liberals and conservatives both contribute—albeit differently—to the division that defines the present moment.

Conservatives, we contend, are more likely to approve of political division, to be less troubled by its harshness and consequences, and to participate in it more readily. For one thing, conservatives tend to consume a more combative political media, what Berry and Sobieraj (2014) call "outrage" media. There is, of course, liberal outrage media, but it is milder than what conservatives produce, and there is less of it available. The larger market for conservative outrage could be a by-product of a general conservative combativeness or a cause of it. At any rate, the media environment and patterns of consumption offer some sense that conservatives thrust themselves into political conflict more vigorously than liberals do.

We also note that the Republican Party in Washington has become ever more combative, a reflection not just of the ideas of its base voters, but their militancy. As Mann and Ornstein write, "The Republican Party has become a radical insurgency—ideologically extreme, scornful of facts and compromise, and dismissive of the legitimacy of its political opposition" (2013, 15). They argue that the base of the party is driving its agenda and the behavior of its representatives into a more aggressive style of politics.

But our argument does not end there. We also show that liberals are more likely than conservatives to withdraw from political conflict when it gets unpleasant. As we will show, liberals are more likely to retreat, to take offense, to desire harmonious conversations, and to avoid arguing online. It is not that some on the left are unwilling to shake a fist or to protest, but liberals say they are less likely than conservatives to want to engage the other side. This liberal impulse of avoidance also contributes to our divided political environment. Furthermore, we will also show than when it comes to actual political discourse online, liberals are not necessarily more civil than conservatives.

We make this argument through a series of public opinion studies as well as analyses of social media. This approach allows us to test whether self-reported behaviors in public opinion surveys align with actual behavior on social media. Our argument is reminiscent of a theory of behavior posited almost a half century ago by Albert Hirschman (1972). Hirschman's essential idea was that people have different alternatives when responding to something they do not like. They can either go along, express their concerns, or detach—"loyalty," "voice," and "exit," so to speak. Hirschman does not speculate that liberals and conservatives are more prone to one response or the other, but we do: conservatives prefer voice (charge) while liberals prefer exit (retreat).

In the next section, we review self-reported behavior of political discussion among liberals and conservatives, where we find a consistent pattern of charge and retreat across available years. We then describe our attempt to verify whether this pattern appears when we examine actual behavior on social media. There are many difficult methodological choices scholars need to make when compiling and analyzing a data set of social media behavior; we describe the choices we made and then report the results. Some findings confirm our expectations. For example, among elite political actors, liberals tend to be followed on social media by both liberals and conservatives whereas conservatives tend to be followed mainly by other conservatives. Other findings do not confirm our expectations. For example, we find no difference in the level of toxicity in political tweets that come from liberals and conservatives. We do, however, find that liberals and conservatives tend to be toxic on different issues and that the level of toxicity may depend on whether the presidency is held by a Democrat or by a Republican. We conclude by noting that conservatives are more likely to savor or enjoy political conflict with the other side and liberals more likely to want to avoid that unpleasantness. This pattern has important implications for our politics going forward.

HETEROGENEOUS NETWORKS AND "GOOD" CITIZENSHIP

At the core of this inquiry are widely held normative assumptions about the characteristics of a democratic society and of the good citizens who propel it forward. In this theorizing, good citizens are ones who *deliberate.* That is, they talk to others, listen to both like-minded and contrary views, and truly think about the issue at hand. They are engaged and, at least at a minimal level, active through some forms of participation. As Peter Levine writes, "If more Americans were involved in constructive and empowered ways, we could make progress on [our most important] problems. Put more positively, as active citizens, we could help to build a better commonwealth" (2013, 162).

Talking is key to this participation because talking is key to deliberation. Although we can become more informed through solitary activity, reading a newspaper, for example, we don't deliberate without others to deliberate with. Deliberation at work, through voluntary organizations and through networks of friends and family, leads one toward a possible next step, which is collective action. Deliberation entails exposure to various viewpoints, and talk back and forth requires reflection on what is heard. Exposure to those who are not like-minded might lead to a better understanding of our own arguments as we are pushed to consider why we believe what we believe. At the same time, exposure may lead to a greater understanding of arguments that are different from our own. Another possible consequence is that broader exposure leads to increased general tolerance toward others in the political system (Mutz 2006).

Despite the many virtues of deliberation, it easily collides with human nature. Most of us desire harmony in our lives, and exposure to crosscutting political views can be uncomfortable. A perverse consequence of crosscutting exposure is that it can disincentivize subsequent political participation (Mutz 2006). Being confronted with contrary views at work or at a meeting may lead individuals, consciously or not, to avoid putting themselves in the same situation again. It is often easier to say nothing and go on with our day. And, of course, there are larger societal dynamics that teach us to be silent or apathetic (Eliasoph 1998).

One of the challenges of thinking about civic engagement in the online world is to understand how it differs from face-to-face interaction. We can criticize, even insult, those in our online networks or feeds in ways we would not consider in a face-to-face context. Given the nature of Facebook, Twitter, and other online platforms, considerable interaction is with those with whom we have "weak ties" (Granovetter 1973). Both exit and voice seem easier with those who are peripheral members of our own network. One distinguishing feature of the online world is the low barriers to entry. On Twitter, for example, it is usually the case that anyone can follow anyone else. Still, not all tweets are created equal. As online participants, we most value those that come from somebody we regard as trustworthy (Morris et al. 2012). This is to say that we expect that the asymmetric patterns of interactions outside the bubble between liberals and conservatives will generally be similar whether they pertain to online or off-line interactions.

These broad theories do not, by themselves, tell us why liberals and conservatives may favor charge or retreat. Since our initial exploration of this behavior, described in the next section, shows that conservatives are less likely to retreat in the face of crosscutting missives, can we conclude that conservatives are more tolerant of contrary information? Some might assume the opposite in terms of conservatives' relative level of tolerance. Perhaps President Trump is emblematic of conservatives with his constant taunting of those he disagrees with. The flip side of this is the common complaint that liberals direct toward their own side: they mistakenly refrain from fighting because they regard that behavior with contempt. Recall Michelle Obama proudly telling her fellow liberals at the 2016 Democratic Convention that "when they go low, we go high" (Flegenheimer 2018). But this is an empirical question: Do liberals really go "high" when they respond to conservatives?

BEFRIENDING AND UNFRIENDING

We begin by asking whether liberals, more than conservatives, have a stronger preference for being with people who share their political views, looking at various public opinion surveys from recent years, both before and after the 2016 election. We examine a variety of questions to come at our research from different angles and at different moments in time. The consistency of the responses, even in answer to different questions, offers some confidence in the phenomena we are studying. Going all the way back to Berelson, Lazersfeld, and McPhee (1954), we know that the social circles that most individuals form are populated by people like themselves. Our question is whether this is more the case for those on the left than for those on the right, and ultimately we conclude that it is. In this sense, our primary goal is descriptive: to establish that this asymmetrical pattern of political engagement exists in both self-reported behavior and actual social media behavior. We document that difference in the paragraphs to come and will attempt to explain it in subsequent work.

We start at the most general level, studying responses to survey questions about social circles and whether they are politically heterogeneous. A Pew Survey from 2016 asked, "Do most of the people you know have similar political beliefs, different political beliefs, or a mix of various political beliefs?"[1] Liberals are slightly more likely than conservatives (34 percent to 31 percent) to report that most of the people they know have similar beliefs. It is moderates who stand out as different, with only 23 percent reporting that most of the people they know have similar political beliefs. In 2014, Pew asked a similar question, this time focusing on friendship circles instead of the wider set of "people I know." On this question, respondents were asked whether "most/some of my close friends share my views on government and politics," with the alternative being "I don't really know what most of my close friends think about government and politics." Here, we find that conservative friendship networks are more homogenous than liberal circles, though not by much. Just short of 43 percent of conservatives and 38 percent of liberals report that most of their friends share their political views, compared to roughly one-quarter of moderates.[2] Given that moderates are less likely to have strong political views, and perhaps less likely to care about what their friends think, this is unsurprising.

A different construction of the question, again from Pew, asked partisans about the partisanship of their friends and offers a slightly different picture. In 2017, Pew asked, "How many of your close friends are of your own party?" This is a question that requires looking at partisans rather than ideologues to make sense of it. Here, a modest gap emerges, with 67 percent of Democrats and 57 percent of Republicans saying that "a lot" of their friends share a partisan affiliation. Democrats are also less likely to have "a lot" of Republicans in their social circle than vice versa, 9 percent versus 14 percent, respectively (Pew Research Center 2017).

There is nothing in these questions that gets at intentionality, however. The questions simply get at whether one's friends or "people I know" are politically similar or dissimilar. There are many things about others that might make them attractive as friends, and if political viewpoint is important, then it is in the mix with other personal qualities and attitudes. We are therefore also interested in the intentional behavior to engage with politically similar others, or befriend them, and to avoid or shun politically dissimilar others. In the social media world, we even have the convenient and particularly modern phenomenon of "defriending," that is, explicitly and officially removing someone from one's circle. We are interested in two things here: first, whether liberals are less likely to purposefully place conservatives in their social circle than conservatives are for liberals, and second, whether they are more likely to politically disengage across ideological lines, with friends or others.

Looking at purposeful attempts to disengage with politically dissimilar others, we find a strong pattern. To illustrate, the 2014 Pew survey asked respondents if they had "ever stopped talking to or being friends with someone because of something they said about government and politics?" Ending a friendship over politics is not the usual thing, but it is more usual for liberals (17 percent agreeing) than conservatives (9 percent) and moderates (9 percent). Family members cannot be dropped as easily as friends, but they can be avoided. Here, again, there is a yawning gap between liberals, on the one hand, and conservatives and moderates, on the other. In a December 2016 poll from the Public Religion Research Institute, 17 percent of liberals, but only 3 percent and 5 percent of conservatives and moderates, respectively, said yes when asked in "this holiday season, have you decided to spend less time with certain family members because of their political views?"[3]

Purposeful disengagement is also measurable by looking at online behavior, and here, again, we see that liberals are considerably more likely than conservatives to pull out of a social media relationship if they are offended by something that someone has posted on Facebook or some other social media site. In the 2014 Pew Survey, 33 percent of liberals respond that they have "hidden, blocked, defriended, or stopped following someone on a social networking site because [they] did not agree with something that they posted about government and politics." Just 22 percent of conservatives did the same. The 2016 presidential election heightened this difference even further, with 41 percent of liberals in the Pew survey and only 26 percent of conservatives "changing their settings to see fewer posts from someone in [their] feed" because of something related to politics, and 41 percent of liberals versus 26 percent of conservatives "block[ing] or [unfriending] someone because of politics."

One might think that these differences are attributable to the fact that liberals lost the election, making them sorer and more sensitive to commentary from the other side. Yet data from 2012 suggest that even when Obama was in office, liberals were also more likely than conservatives to unfriend someone because of their political views (Bode 2016). We therefore do not believe that this pattern is unique to the Trump era.

TOLERANCE OF CONFLICT

One of the reasons for disengagement is certainly distaste for those with other views, but disengagement could also reflect a generalized discomfort with political conflict. It is probably a mix of both. Social scientists have shown that there is a natural predilection to prefer agreement when talking about politics (Mutz and Reeves 2005; Mutz 2006). It is less usual, but some are willing to debate and openly disagree with others they interact with. The unpleasantness of conflict is profound for many, and we argue that this is more the case for those left of center than for those to the right. Put another way, we expect conservatives to favor and engage in political conflict more readily than liberals. This is based on studies of personality characteristics of ideologues (McClosky 1958; Carney et al. 2008) as well as studies that show a difference in the political cultures of the left and the right, such as Berry and Sobieraj (2014) and Mann and Ornstein (2013).

We begin with survey questions that get at an embrace of political debate and tolerance of political conflict. Here we see the obverse of what we found for blocking and unfriending. Conservatives appear to be more comfortable in conflict, whereas liberals and especially moderates are less so.

When asked in 2016 by Pew whether political disagreements on social media are "interesting and informative" or "stressful and frustrating," conservatives are more likely to find disagreement about politics informative (34 percent to 28 percent) and less likely to find it stressful (59 percent to 66 percent). Moderates are least likely to find political disagreement stressful (54 percent), though, perhaps, that is due to the fact that disagreement is less intense in their circles. The fact that such a large percentage of people of any ideological persuasion find political disagreement unpleasant is a reminder that, for most people, political agreement is preferred.

We also see a difference in attitudes toward political discussion in questions about "political correctness." A 2016 American National Election Studies preelection survey item that was intended to capture attitudes about restrictions on offending political sensibilities was framed as such: "Some people think that the way people talk needs to change with the times to be more sensitive to people from different backgrounds. Others think that this has already gone too far and many people are just too easily offended."[4] This question reveals huge differences between liberals and conservatives. Three times as many liberals as conservatives believe that "a lot" more sensitivity is required (30 percent to 9 percent) and a 43-percentage-point gap exists when we add "a little" to "a lot" (66 percent versus 23 percent). Conversely, 45 percent of conservatives but only 11 percent of liberals think people are "much too easily offended." We would fold attitudes about political correctness into our argument about attitudes toward political dialogue and conflict. Conservatives do seem to favor and savor a political environment that is more aggressive and wherein fewer rules prevail and political opponents can be goaded into frustrated outrage.

While there is still much we do not know about political engagement, such as whether liberals and conservatives experience different emotional reactions to political disagreement, past surveys have demonstrated that liberals and conservatives have contributed to the division in our polity though in different and distinctive ways, with liberals more likely to avoid deliberation and conservatives more likely to be comfortable with conflict. With these findings in mind, we now turn to an analysis of social media behavior to see if what people do is aligned with what people say they do.

MEASURING CHARGE AND RETREAT ON TWITTER

The differential pattern between liberals and conservatives on charge and retreat of self-reported behavior led us to try to broaden our understanding by considering individuals' online activity. Does actual behavior affirm the asymmetric pattern that emerges from examinations of self-reported behaviors? One of the attractions of social media is that individuals can shape their feeds and followers. We approach this phenomenon by looking at real-time interaction. In a nutshell, who do liberals and conservatives read, follow, and respond to online? And when they respond, to what extent do they use aggressive and uncivil language?

There is no single agreed-upon way to take such measurements online, but our approach is to utilize Twitter as a database for this part of our research (Conover et al. 2011; Jones et al. 2018; Romero, Meeder, and Kleinberg 2011; Tumasjan et al. 2011). Twitter is widely used in research on social media, and "no other platform has attracted as much attention from academics" (Ahmed 2017). The reasons for its popularity with political scientists are both substantive and pragmatic. The online world continues to expand its presence in everyday life, and fully two-thirds of Americans get a significant portion of their news from online sources. Twitter is not as ubiquitous as Facebook, but it has a higher penetration of users who consume news on the site. Seventy-four percent of Twitter users get news from it as compared to 68 percent from Facebook. Moreover, news usage at Twitter is up 15 percent in just the last year, compared to 2 percent at Facebook (Shearer and Gottfried 2017). As Bode and Dalrymple (2016) note, Twitter users are unusually engaged in politics: "Twitter contains a unique audience for political elites to target. Political Twitter users are in many ways the ideal subpopulation with which elites might choose to communicate. They are extremely interested in politics, very likely to turn out at the polls, and wealthy enough to contribute to campaigns. Moreover, political Twitter use makes it even more likely for these super-interested political junkies to participate in politics in other ways" (325–326). Twitter users may thus be unrepresentative of the broader population in terms of their level of political interest and engagement, but that is also the quality that makes them a valuable population to investigate. Additionally, it will be instructive to determine whether self-reported behaviors of social media users in nationally representative public opinion surveys align with measurable behaviors of social media activity.

Without elaborating here, Facebook is also a more difficult medium for political scientists to work with, both in terms of access to data and of analyzing exchanges of opinion. Twitter, though, has advantages beyond its comparative accessibility. Twitter is, ultimately, a medium of words, and of not many words in each missive, just 280 characters (up from 140 characters before November 2017). Although photos and graphs can be appended to a tweet, ultimately it is the written message that is the medium.

For the writer, the skill involved is to craft those words in a way that grabs attention in the flow of tweets rapidly floating by in the feeds of the writer's network of followers. Even more challenging is enticing other potential readers that Twitter algorithms will also include in those exposed to any individual tweet.

Twitter seems unusually well suited to political debate in the online world. Readers can respond even if they are not in the writer's network. Response is often immediate, and debate can ensue, and a circle of respondents can grow as new people tweet a response and draw their own network into the debate. The online conversation can be civil or uncivil or somewhere in between. Twitter is also widely used by political leaders to get the message out; it is a way to go public without having to answer questions from the press. President Trump, of course, has made Twitter the center of his communications strategy. And ordinary users can choose to follow any political leader they want; they can follow political actors from across the ideological spectrum, or they can create their own Twitter bubble.

Lines of Inquiry

We draw on these data to explore three lines of inquiry. The first centers on the heterogeneity of networks. This is a logical beginning point, as tweeters have control over the accounts they choose to follow. Additionally, Twitter algorithms extend exposure to those who appear to be like existing followers in any user's network. What this means is that the universe of tweets that a person sees will reflect the ideological makeup of the accounts that they choose to follow. These dynamics of Twitter and the survey research we described earlier lead us to expect that liberal and conservative networks will be distinctive. More specifically, *conservatives' Twitter networks are hypothesized to be more heterogeneous in their ideological makeup.* We will test this hypothesis by analyzing the followers of elite actors. In particular, we expect that the followers of conservative elites will themselves be conservative, whereas the followers of liberal elites will come from a broader range of the ideological spectrum. Put another way, ordinary Twitter users who are conservative will follow both liberal and conservative elites, while ordinary Twitter users who are liberal will inhabit more of a bubble, following liberal elites but not conservative elites (Eady et al. 2019).

Our second line of inquiry focuses on civility. Civility is broadly accepted as a core norm of democratic deliberation, but, of course, incivility is part and parcel of a free society. For social scientists, the concern is that incivility can degrade the democratic processes and change the way that citizens regard government (Mutz and Reeves 2005; Rohlinger 2007). With the rise of social media, such concern has intensified as millions of Americans have become direct participants in back and forth uncivil behavior and as their own representatives have done the same (Gervais and Morris 2018). Beneath this broader trend of increasing interaction, we suspect that there is differential behavior by conservatives and liberals. In addition to the survey findings we have cited, language cues from cable, talk radio, and blogs are much harsher on the conservative side, and conservatives are more prone to watch shows that are uncivil (Berry and Sobieraj 2014; Mutz 2015). *We therefore expect that in comparison to liberals, conservatives' responses are more likely to be uncivil.* The higher level of incivility, we argue, would be indicative of a "charge" mentality.

Third, we take civility to one of its confrontational ends, name-calling. It is one thing to read tweets that are uncivil on a topic of interest and quite another to be attacked either individually or as part of a group. "Name-calling" may seem to be overly vague, but we follow a content analysis template that defines it as "words and context that make the subject look foolish, inept, hypocritical, deceitful, or dangerous" (Berry and Sobieraj 2014, 246). Our expectation is that conservatives more frequently utilize such language in taunting opponents.

Methods

For our first line of inquiry, we randomly selected a minimum of two thousand followers of twenty-six elite actors (thirteen liberal, thirteen conservative) who are prominent in either electoral politics or political commentary.[5] We then used an ideology estimator developed by scholars at New York University, which is available as a package on GitHub.[6] The tool has pre-estimated ideologies for more than one thousand elite political accounts and media outlets, and it can estimate any user's ideology by looking at the composition of elite accounts that they follow. User ideologies that earn a negative score are considered "likely liberal," while ideologies that earn a positive score are considered "likely conservative." Our final sample for this portion of the analysis includes 202,613 Twitter users.[7]

For our other two lines of inquiry, we used a web scraping tool to randomly select tweets that met certain date and keyword criteria. First, we selected tweets in English that were posted in March 2013, 2014, 2017, and 2018 from accounts based in the United States. These periods were selected to create comparable political contexts. The periods occur during the first two years of President Barack Obama's second term and President

Donald Trump's term, a time when postelection momentum fueled the presidents' agendas. We selected March for its frequency of high-profile political events, which occurred in that month across all years. We randomly selected times within each day of each selected month and then randomly selected tweets that related to seven topics we identified as particularly relevant during the period, using keywords associated with the following categories: discrimination, environment, fiscal issues, government, gun violence, health care, and immigration.[8] We then dropped any user who was included in that list of more than one thousand elites in the ideology estimator tool to increase the likelihood that our sample consisted mainly of "ordinary Americans." Once duplicate tweets and elite accounts were dropped from our sample, we had a database of 11,156 tweets.[9]

This data set allows us to sample political discussion on Twitter that is initiated by everyday users. We can also examine whether the behaviors of liberals and conservatives persist across the topics and time periods being discussed. If so, then it is plausible that these behaviors are intrinsic qualities of their political ideology.

To estimate a user's ideology, we use the same ideology estimator tool described above. To estimate the level of incivility, or toxicity, of a tweet, we use Perspective API, a tool developed by Jigsaw and Google's Counter Abuse Technology team. Perspective uses machine learning to detect toxic posts, which it defines as "a rude, disrespectful, or unreasonable comment that is likely to make you leave a discussion."[10] Perspective assigns a continuous score between 0 and 1, ranging from highly unlikely to be toxic to highly likely to be toxic. Finally, to assess the degree of name-calling in our sample, we searched the tweets in our database for a set of keywords associated with political insults.[11]

PATTERNS OF CHARGE AND RETREAT ON TWITTER

Network Ideology

Our database of followers of elite accounts allows us to test whether conservative elite actors have a more ideologically homogeneous set of followers than do liberal elite actors. As the results in table 9.1 illustrate, that is indeed what we find. Recall that with the ideology estimator, positive scores are considered conservative and negative scores are considered liberal. The scale ranges from −2.36 to +2.36. Table 9.1 shows that the mean score for followers of conservative elites is 1.185, while the mean score for followers of liberal elites is −0.362. These results indicate that followers of conserva-

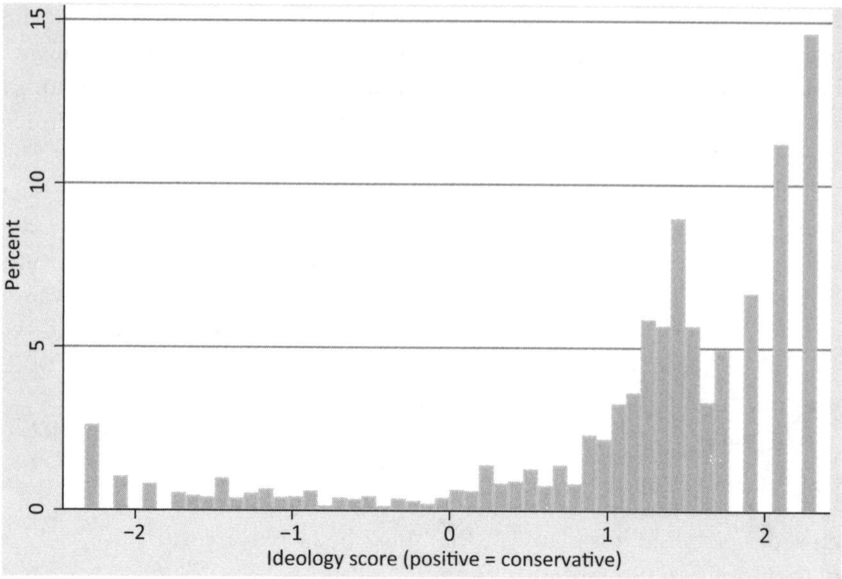

Figure 9.1a: Ideology Scores of Followers of Conservative Elites. *Source*: Authors' computations.

tive accounts are concentrated on the conservative side of the spectrum, while followers of liberal accounts are closer to the midpoint. Put another way, liberal elites have followers who are both liberal and conservative while conservative elites have followers that tend to be conservative. The larger standard deviation for liberal elites is further indication that their followers are more likely to span the ideological spectrum than followers of conservative accounts.

Figures 9.1a and 9.1b provide another illustration of this finding. Figure 9.1a shows the distribution of ideology scores for followers of conservative elites. It clearly demonstrates that followers are concentrated on the positive (conservative) side of the x-axis. Figure 9.1b, on the other hand, shows the distribution of ideology scores for followers of liberal elites. Although a majority of followers are clearly on the liberal end of the scale, there is also a cluster of followers on the conservative side.

Table 9.1 also breaks down the elite accounts by profession, separating politicians, such as Donald Trump and Hillary Clinton, from commentators, such as Sean Hannity and Rachel Maddow. We find that the overall pattern holds: the means for conservative politicians and pundits are further from zero than the means for liberal politicians and pundits. Addition-

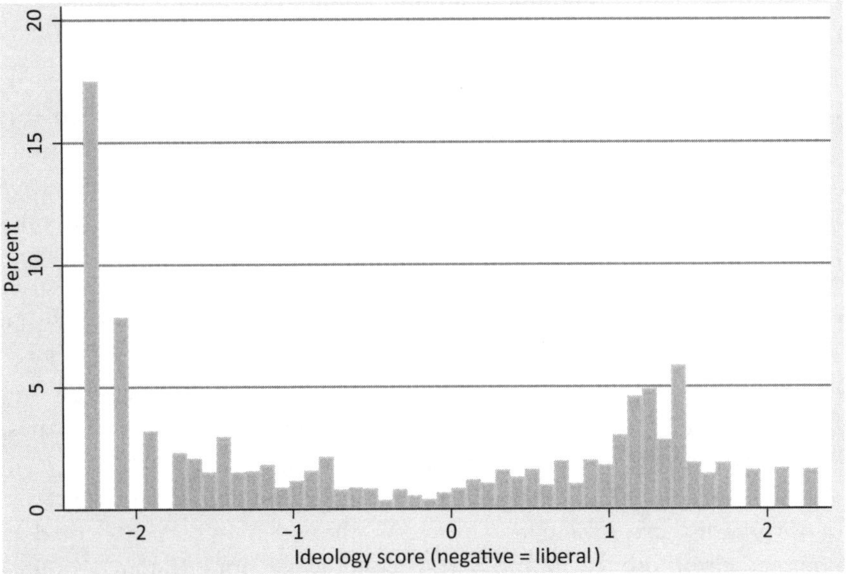

Figure 9.1b: Ideology Scores of Followers of Liberal Elites. *Source*: Authors' computations.

ally, the standard deviation for conservative politicians and pundits is smaller than the standard deviation for their liberal counterparts.

Overall, our analysis of followers of elite accounts leads us to conclude that actual behavior on Twitter corresponds to self-reported behavior in public opinion surveys: liberals are more likely than conservatives to seal themselves off from exposure to people with whom they disagree. Recent scholarship by Eady and colleagues (Eady et al. 2019) using alternative methods to analyze Twitter users reaches a similar conclusion.

Table 9.1: Ideology Scores for Followers of Elite Accounts

Account type	Mean	Median	Std. Dev.
All Conservatives	1.185	1.476	1.152
Conservatives (Politicians)	1.054	1.341	1.135
Conservatives (Commentators)	1.414	1.751	1.146
All Liberals	-0.362	-0.553	1.543
Liberals (Politicians)	-0.078	0.385	1.543
Liberals (Commentators)	-0.844	-1.341	1.419

Toxicity and Ideology on Twitter

Next, we turn to our examination of the substance of the Twitter behavior of ordinary Americans. Recall that the toxicity estimator ranges from 0 to 1, with a higher score indicating a greater likelihood that the tone of the tweet lacks civility. Our hypothesis was that, in contrast to liberals, conservatives would be more likely to relish aggressive engagement with political opponents and would therefore be more likely to post tweets that lack civility. Across all issues and all time periods in our database, the mean toxicity score for all Twitter users was 0.265. This number did not vary with the ideology of the user. There are two points to take away from this result. First, the overall toxicity score is rather low, an encouraging sign for those who may be worried about the tone of political discourse in the United States. We suspect one reason the average toxicity score is low is that when we skim through the content of the tweets in our data set, we see that many consist of tweets that share links to news articles, a phenomenon that has been documented elsewhere (Leetaru 2019). Second, we do not find that conservatives are more likely to post toxic tweets than liberals are.

Deeper analysis of our data reveals, however, that there are important variations to consider. First, levels of toxicity vary by topic and by the ideology of the user. As figure 9.2 shows, tweets associated with discrimination,

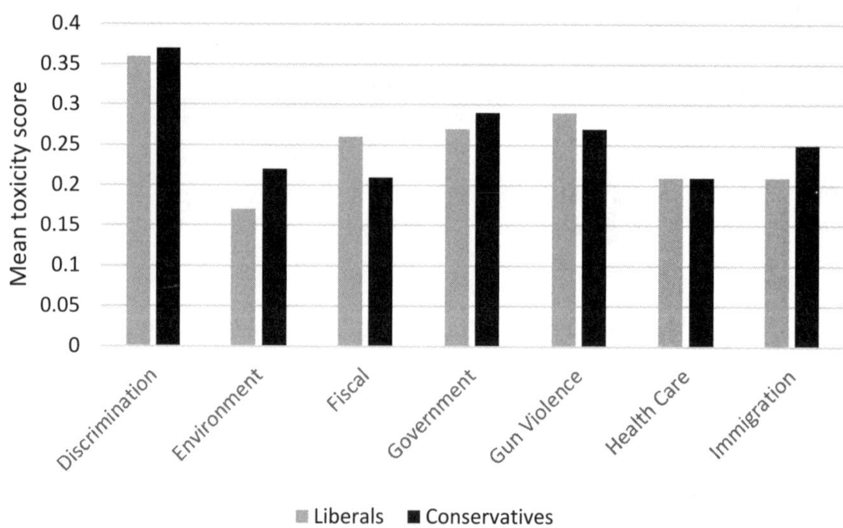

Figure 9.2: Mean Toxicity by Keyword and Ideology. *Source*: Authors' computations.

Table 9.2: Participation in Each Topic by Ideology

Topic	Conservatives (%)	Liberals (%)
Discrimination	6	14
Environment	6	9
Fiscal	11	14
Government	48	43
Gun Violence	7	8
Health Care	22	10
Immigration	1	2
Total	100	100

or what is pejoratively considered "identity politics," are far more likely to be toxic than tweets associated with the other topics. Figure 9.2 also shows that the level of toxicity is similar for liberals and conservatives for some topics, such as health care, but quite different for others, such as immigration, fiscal issues, and the environment. Overall, then, when disaggregated by issue, ideology is not linked to "charge." Instead we find that both sides of the spectrum have issues that incite more emotional and abrasive responses than those from the other side.

As table 9.2 shows, there was also asymmetry in which issues drew attention on Twitter from liberals and conservatives. Liberals were far more likely to tweet about discrimination than conservatives, while conservatives were far more likely to tweet about health care than liberals. Powerfully, the numbers in table 9.2 affirm more everyday observations of real-world politics. In the debate over the Affordable Care Act, conservatives have been more vocal and more emotional over the government's role in health insurance. It also makes sense that liberals are more concerned about discrimination, as it has a more direct effect on demographic groups positioned on the left side of the ideological spectrum.

To establish the validity of both the toxicity and ideology estimators, we think it is instructive to review some of the tweets in our data set and their corresponding ideology and toxicity scores. Table 9.3 lists tweets for each topic at both high and low levels of toxicity. We believe that a quick skim of the tweets in the second column establish the face validity of the estimators used in this study.[12]

What about toxicity over time? Does the toxicity level remain constant for liberals and conservatives over time, or does the toxicity level vary with the party in power? We do not find variation in tone over time for the full sample, but as figure 9.3 illustrates, we do find that conservatives became more

Table 9.3: Tweet, Toxicity, and Ideology Examples

Topic	Tweet	Toxicity	Ideology
Discrimination	Targeting immigrants, imposing tariffs, harming our environment, racism, killing wildlife, KEEP AMERICA GREAT, MY ASS!	0.953	−2.326
Discrimination	I have one question. . . . Where do you draw the line for who can marry who or "what" in marriage equality?	0.091	2.054
Environment	One just said global warming isn't real because it's so cold. What even? I can't, you're so stupid, I hate you.	0.966	−1.405
Environment	Man can do as much about Earth's Climate Change as Jupiter's . . . but don't tell a liberal they will pass a Trillion $ Jupiter Aid package!	0.159	2.326
Fiscal	but, she is collecting unemployment benefits, so technically, isn't she paid by the gov't to be a bitchy, stupid troll?	0.933	2.326
Fiscal	It seems to me the only issue is our debt. We can't afford to pay for Medicare Medicaid & social security & yet Rs & Ds refuse to address!	0.106	2.326
Government	Obama is the worst President in the history of the United States of America and 51% of you idiots elected him twice. wake up America!	0.952	2.054
Government	I hear so often: "nothing's gonna change no need to vote." Let GOP have both House & Senate there will be change—none can live with.	0.074	−2.326
Gun violence	Are all Americans Stupid or just the fucking Republicans? Yes I said it! How can the Surgeon General's nomination turn into a NRA issue? WTF.	0.953	−2.326
Gun violence	Do republicans know that when the 2nd amendment was written there were only muskets? Someone should tell them! I did.	0.129	−1.341
Health care	#DearMrPresident, trumpcare is disgusting, $600 blln gift to rich, higher costs to older n poorest, kill Medicaid, u r worst pres in history	0.872	0.806

Health care	Why no mention of the more than 5 million of us who've lost our insurance and can't afford #Obamacare?	0.116	2.326
Immigration	All these #republican pricks talking Shit about "illegal" immigrants are the 1st ones to take advantage of the cheap labor immigrants provide	0.764	-2.326
Immigration	Why is that Dreamers get access to Congressmen and Congresswoman and their Staff and the Voter does not? RT Please	0.071	1.476

Source: Authors' computations.

toxic just after Trump took office and then became less toxic the following year. Liberals, on the other hand, saw a boost to their toxicity level in 2018.

In sum, we do not find clear evidence that conservatives are more likely than liberals to charge at their opponents with aggressive and toxic tweets. Rather, the level of toxicity used by liberals and conservatives appears to vary with the topic under discussion and perhaps with the party of the president. Additionally, our examination of individual tweets provides confidence that the ideology and toxicity estimators are valuable tools for scholars interested in this line of inquiry.

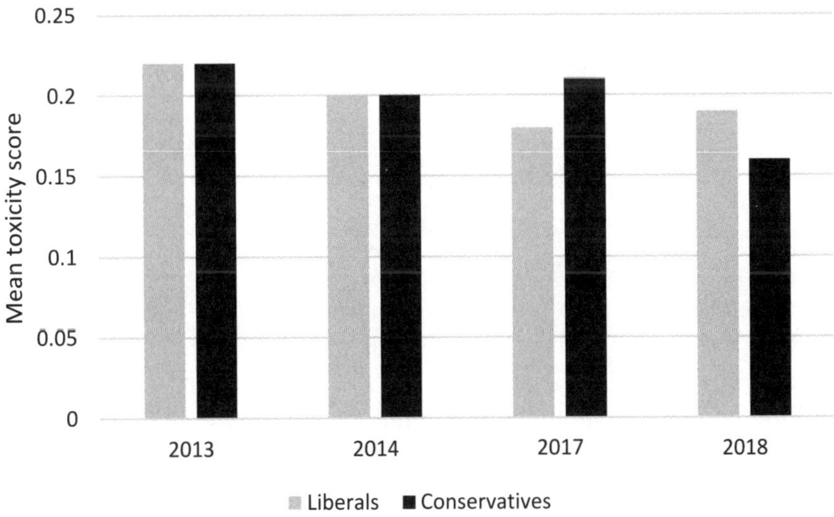

Figure 9.3: Mean Toxicity Score by Year and Ideology. *Source*: Authors' computations.

Name-Calling

Finally, we turn our attention to name-calling. Our search yielded 277 tweets (2.5 percent of total tweets) that involved name-calling.[13] As with our mean toxicity score, it is perhaps encouraging that the percentage of tweets that used name-calling was not higher. Not surprisingly, the overall toxicity of tweets involving name-calling is high, with a mean of 0.75, a finding that provides further validation of this tool. Our main expectation, however, was that conservatives would be more likely to use name-calling than liberals. This expectation was not borne out: 2.7 percent of liberal users in our database posted a tweet that involved name-calling versus 2.4 percent of conservative users.

And as before, there is noteworthy variation by topic. Most of the name-calling tweets about discrimination came from liberals (71.4 percent), while most of the name-calling tweets about gun violence and health care came from conservatives (72 percent for each topic).

We focused on name calling because it seems to be the perfect Twitter tool for both attracting attention and goading the other side. In the limited character space of tweets, "jerk" is only four characters and "idiot" just five. Perhaps its playground quality works against name-calling, and more subtle insults may better suit aggressive but politically sophisticated tweeters. Overall, these results affirm what we found in our test of hypothesis two, enhancing our confidence that these findings are not artifactual. The commonality of tweets linked to articles also moves commentary toward content and away from simple declarations of how stupid or evil the other side is (Leetaru 2019). At the same time, it is clear that certain topics elicit vitriol from liberals while other topics do so for conservatives.

DISCUSSION

National concern continues to mount about significantly rising levels of polarization. Polarization in the United States is usually measured in terms of mass opinion or partisan voting patterns. Despite what we see in aggregate measures of opinion and partisan division, though, most Americans still refrain from sharp political debate in face-to-face contexts or in online interactions. As we have pointed out, most of us prefer agreement and would rather avoid situations where political disagreement might arise. Here we have taken a deeper dive into polarization by looking at a subset of highly politically engaged participants on social media to assess the degree to which their behavior corresponds to self-reported behavior on public opinion surveys. How does online behavior fit into this broader tableau of what seems to be an increasingly acrimonious town square?

Our findings are nuanced but revealing. After documenting a pattern in a set of surveys showing that liberals are much more likely than conservatives to retreat from politically divisive interaction on social media, we turned to our original data collection on Twitter users. In our analysis we began by asking about the heterogeneity of social networks. Our data demonstrate that liberal elites have much more ideologically broad sets of followers, indicating that rank-and-file conservatives hear a wider variety of voices on Twitter.

Our finding that conservatives are more engaged with the other side may seem to fly in the face of the widespread belief that conservatives are more closed off in their consumption of news and opinion than are liberals. Conservatives are frequently described as living in a Fox News bubble. The most recent survey of media trust and utilization by Pew (2020) concluded that Americans live in "two nearly inverse news media environments." Pew calls this the "Fox News phenomenon," emphasizing the level of trust that conservatives have in Fox and the lack of diversity in news sources used by conservatives.

This idea that conservatives live in a media bubble doesn't always hold up to deeper analysis. We looked at another of our data sets to judge whether conservatives are bound by a Fox News bubble. In a module that we ran on the 2018 Congressional Cooperative Election Study, we included a wide-ranging set of questions about media usage, trust, and accuracy for eleven major news outlets. We have been using our CCES module to analyze the differences between liberals and conservatives across a range of behaviors (Berry, Glaser, and Schildkraut, 2019; Schildkraut, Berry, and Glaser, forthcoming). Our media data show that 70 percent of respondents who watch Fox also used one or more mainstream media outlets during the previous month (mainstream sites were the ABC, NBC, and CBS network news, CNN, the *New York Times,* the *Washington Post,* and NPR). Viewers of MSNBC used mainstream sites at an even higher level, 97 percent, so there is a difference in usage between the liberals and conservatives who are the dominant viewers of each network. Nevertheless, the 70 percent level of mainstream consumption by Fox viewers is *not* bubble behavior, and it's all the more impressive as the mainstream media is held to be the enemy by conservative sources like Fox and talk radio. What we found in our Twitter analysis is thus in line with this broader pattern of media usage that does show engagement with the other side.

Although this makeup of networks confirmed our expectations of charge vs. retreat, our second hypothesis was disconfirmed. Conservative and liberal tweeters are equally likely to use toxic language. The same tests reveal that the overall toxicity of all tweeters in our samples was relatively low. We refined these tests further by looking at just one particular type of toxic verbiage, name-calling. Again, there was not much difference between conservatives and liberals on this score.

Why were expectations on the toxicity of tweets not borne out by these data? One explanation is that these patterns are an artifact of delimiting those who are active in following, tweeting, and retweeting. As the surveys show, there is a stronger inclination among liberals to retreat from verbal combat by their own self-policing of their networks. Thus, we have a distillation, essentially a selection bias, that left us with those liberals who are more likely to tweet in an abrasive fashion. In turn, this led to subsamples with equal propensity among all ideologues toward toxicity. Although liberals are more likely than conservatives to avoid directly following the other side, liberals are just as likely as conservatives to use uncivil language when expressing their views online.

We have utilized a complex and sophisticated approach to studying Twitter networks. The academic study of social networks is burgeoning, and there is no one methodology that is widely followed and different measurement choices may yield different results. Our research is built on tools that others have developed but that were modified to address the specific questions we asked. Notably, one of our key findings—that liberals are less likely to follow accounts on the other side—is corroborated by other emerging research (Eady et al. 2019).

Despite our own concerns about the polarization of American politics, we come away from this research enterprise a bit more optimistic than when we began. After whatever distillation our methodology yielded, the fact remains that the toxicity scores of tweeters are relatively low. Thus, even among those highly active in the political Twitterverse, much of the discussion is restrained and civil. Our stereotype of political discussion by the most highly active on social media may be much too harsh.

At the same time, the fact remains that deliberation across the ideological divide is an essential feature of democratic politics. Although the tone of discourse may not be as harsh as we anticipated and the harshness is not as concentrated among conservatives as we anticipated, we have also provided ample evidence that liberals are less willing to engage with the other side than conservatives. As scholars have only recently begun to document this trend, it is vital that we continue to do so. Additionally, we need to consider the reasons why this asymmetry exists and examine its political effects.[14]

NOTES

1. Wave 19 of the American Trends Panel survey, conducted July 12–August 8, 2016, available here: http://www.people-press.org/dataset/american-trends-panel-wave-19/.

2. The 2014 and 2016 Pew surveys are part of the American Trends Panel. Data sets are available for download here: http://www.pewresearch.org/american-trends-panel-datasets/.

3. The data set for this survey is available for download here: https://www.prri.org/research/poll-post-election-holiday-war-christmas/.

4. American National Election Study surveys are available at https://electionstudies.org/.

5. The actors are: Donald Trump, Mike Pence, Paul Ryan, Mitch McConnell, Ted Cruz, Susan Collins, Lindsey Graham, John McCain, Barack Obama, Joe Biden, Hillary Clinton, Nancy Pelosi, Chuck Schumer, Bernie Sanders, Joe Manchin, Kirsten Gillibrand, Bill O'Reilly, Sean Hannity, Laura Ingraham, Ben Shapiro, Hugh Hewitt, Rachel Maddow, Bill Maher, Van Jones, Chris Hayes, and Lawrence O'Donnell.

6. The tool is available here: https://github.com/pablobarbera/twitter_ideology?fbclid=IwAR3BdRPALjLfF5jtm3h3T8kdFoUBMYG50f3-rrmkdiECPAPgzRKeYdNxjrA.

7. Users whose ideology could not be estimated because they do not follow at least two of the more than one thousand elite accounts were dropped from our sample.

8. The specific search terms are the following: *Health care*: Obamacare, Affordable Care Act, American Health Care Act, Trumpcare, Ryancare, repeal and replace; *Gun violence*: school shooting, Sandy Hook, Parkland, Marjory Stoneman Douglas, gun rights, gun control, NRA, Second Amendment, 2nd Amendment; *Environment*: the environment, climate change, global warming, carbon emissions, sustainability, fossil fuels; *Fiscal*: government deficit, national debt, budget deficit, entitlements, welfare, social security, Medicare, minimum wage, unemployment, tax reform, tax plan, Tax Cuts and Jobs Act, economic inequality, income inequality; *Immigration*: DACA, Deferred Action for Childhood Arrivals, DREAMers, Muslim ban, illegal immigrants, illegal immigration, border security, southern border, border wall; *Discrimination*: marriage equality, same-sex marriage, homophobia, black lives matter, police brutality, racism, discrimination, sexism, feminism; *Government*: Congress, SCOTUS, Supreme Court, House of Representatives, Senate, Executive Branch, Presidency, POTUS, President of the United States, Trump, Obama, State of the Union, SOTU.

9. We ran our web scraping tool for more than twelve hours. With a longer time frame, this research could be replicated with a larger sample size.

10. This tool is available at https://www.perspectiveapi.com/#/.

11. List of name-calling search terms: SJW, social justice warrior, snowflake,

bigot, hack, troll, idiot, moron, loon, elitist, extremist, shill, radical, fool, stupid, ignorant, ideologue, nut, lunatic, zealot, hippie, ass, dumbass, and bitch.

12. Personal Twitter handles tagged in these tweets have been deleted.

13. Our search originally yielded a higher number of name-calling tweets, but many were false positives that were manually discarded. For example, tweets that had "ass" in some form, such as in the word "embarrassed," were designated false positives.

14. We wish to thank our research assistants, Alexis Tatore, Andrew Savage, and Cole Koester.

REFERENCES

Ahmed, Wasim. "Using Twitter as a Data Source: An Overview of Social Media Research Tools (Updated for 2017)." LSE Impact Blog. 2017. http://blogs.lse.ac.uk/impactofsocialsciences/2017/05/08/using-twitter-as-a-data-source-an-overview-of-social-media-research-tools-updated-for-2017/.

Berelson, Bernard, Paul Lazarsfeld, and William McPhee. *Voting: A Study of Opinion Formation in a Presidential Election.* Chicago: University of Chicago Press, 1954.

Berry, Jeffrey M., James M. Glaser, and Deborah J. Schildkraut. "Ideology, Racial Resentment, and the Mass Media." Paper delivered at the annual meeting of the American Political Science Association, Washington, DC, 2019.

Berry, Jeffrey M., and Sarah Sobieraj. *The Outrage Industry: Political Opinion Media and the New Incivility.* New York: Oxford University Press, 2014. https://books.google.com/books?id=-co8BAAAQBAJ.

Binder, Sarah, and Mark Spindel. "This Is Why Trump's Legislative Agenda Is Stuck in Neutral." *Washington Post,* 2017. https://www.washingtonpost.com/news/monkey-cage/wp/2017/04/26/this-is-why-trumps-legislative-agenda-is-stuck-in-neutral/?noredirect=on&utm_term=.67522f826d04.

Bode, Leticia. "Pruning the News Feed: Unfriending and Unfollowing Political Content on Social Media." *Research & Politics* 3, no. 3 (2016): 205316801666187. https://doi.org/10.1177/2053168016661873.

Bode, Leticia, and Kajsa E. Dalrymple. "Politics in 140 Characters or Less: Campaign Communication, Network Interaction, and Political Participation on Twitter." *Journal of Political Marketing* 15, no. 4 (2016): 311–332. https://doi.org/10.1080/15377857.2014.959686.

Carney, Dana R., John T. Jost, Samuel D. Gosling, and Jeff Potter. "The Secret Lives of Liberals and Conservatives: Personality Profiles, Interaction Styles, and the Things They Leave Behind." *Political Psychology* 29, no. 6 (2008): 807–840. https://doi.org/10.1111/j.1467-9221.2008.00668.x.

Chokshi, Niraj. "Alan Dershowitz Says Martha's Vineyard Is 'Shunning' Him over Trump." *New York Times,* July 3, 2018. https://www.nytimes.com/2018/07/03/us/alan-dershowitz-marthas-vineyard.html.

Conover, Michael, Jacob Ratkiewicz, Matthew R. Francisco, Bruno Gonçalves, Filippo Menczer, and Alessandro Flammini. "Political Polarization on Twitter." *ICWSM* 133 (2011): 89–96. https://www.semanticscholar.org/paper/Political-Polarization-on-Twitter-ConoverRatkiewicz/0c46b067779d7132c5fd097baadc261348afb261.

Dershowitz, Alan. "Maxine Waters Does Not Speak for Democrats or Liberals." *The Hill*, 2018. https://thehill.com/opinion/civil-rights/394346-maxine-waters-does-not-speak-for-democrats-or-liberals.

Eady, Gregory, Jonathan Nagler, Andy Guess, Jan Zilinsky, and Joshua A. Tucker. "How Many People Live in Political Bubbles on Social Media? Evidence From Linked Survey and Twitter Data." *SAGE Open* 9, no. 1 (2019): 215824401983270. https://doi.org/10.1177/2158244019832705.

Eliasoph, Nina. *Avoiding Politics: How Americans Produce Apathy in Everyday Life.* New York: Cambridge University Press, 1998.

Flegenheimer, Matt. "Michelle Obama Wanted Democrats to 'Go High.' Now They Aren't So Sure." *New York Times*, October 12, 2018. https://www.nytime.com/2018/10/12/us/politics/trump-democrats-insults.html.

Gervais, Bryan T., and Irwin L. Morris. *Reactionary Republicanism: How the Tea Party in the House Paved the Way for Trump's Victory.* New York: Oxford University Press, 2018.

Granovetter, Mark S. "The Strength of Weak Ties." *American Journal of Sociology* 78, no. 6 (1973): 1360–1380. https://doi.org/10.1086/225469.

Hischman, Albert O. *Exit, Voice, and Loyalty: Responses to Decline in Firms, Organizations, and States.* Cambridge, MA: Harvard University Press, 1972.

Jones, Kevin L., Sharareh Noorbaloochi, John T. Jost, Richard Bonneau, Jonathan Nagler, and Joshua A. Tucker. "Liberal and Conservative Values: What We Can Learn From Congressional Tweets." *Political Psychology* 39, no. 2 (2018): 423–443. https://doi.org/10.1111/pops.12415.

Leetaru, Kalev. "Twitter Users Mostly Retweet Politicians and Celebrities. That's a Big Change." *Washington Post*, March 8, 2019. https://www.washingtonpost.com/politics/2019/03/08/twitter-users-mostly-retweet-politicians-celebrities-thats-big-change/?utm_term=.5affoboeac05.

Levendusky, Matthew. *The Partisan Sort: How Liberals Became Democrats and Conservatives Became Republicans.* Chicago: University of Chicago Press, 2009.

Levine, Peter. *We Are the Ones We Have Been Waiting For.* New York: Oxford University Press, 2013.

Mann, Thomas E., and Norman J. Ornstein. "Finding the Common Good in an Era of Dysfunctional Governance." *Daedalus* (Spring 2013): 15–24.

McClosky, Herbert. "Conservatism and Personality." *American Political Science Review* 52, no. 1 (1958): 27–45.

Morris, Meredith Ringel, Scott Counts, Asta Roseway, Aaron Hoff, and Julia Schwarz. "Tweeting Is Believing? Understanding Microblog Credibility Perceptions." In *Proceedings of the ACM 2012 Conference on Computer Supported Cooperative Work—CSCW '12*, 441. New York: ACM, 2012. https://doi.org/10.1145/2145204.2145274.

Mutz, Diana C. *In-Your-Face Politics: The Consequences of Uncivil Media.* Princeton, NJ: Princeton University Press, 2015.

———. *Hearing the Other Side: Deliberative versus Participatory Democracy.* New York: Cambridge University Press, 2006.

Mutz, Diana C., and Byron Reeves. "The New Videomalaise: Effects of Televised Incivility on Political Trust." *American Political Science Review* 99, no. 1 (2005): 1–15. https://doi.org/10.1017/S0003055405051452.

Pew Research Center. "Most Democrats, Republicans Have 'Just a Few' or No Friends in Opposing Party." 2017. http://www.people-press.org/2017/10/05/8-partisan-animosity-personal-politics-views-of-trump/8_02/.

Pew Research Center. "US Media Polarization and the 2020 Election: A Nation Divided." 2020: https://www.journalism.org/2020/01/24/u-s-media-polarization-and-the-2020-election-a-nation-divided/.

Rohlinger, Deana A. "American Media and Deliberative Democratic Processes." *Sociological Theory* 25, no. 2 (2007): 122–148. https://doi.org/10.1111/j.1467-9558.2007.00301.x.

Romero, Daniel M., Brendan Meeder, and Jon Kleinberg. "Differences in the Mechanics of Information Diffusion across Topics." In *Proceedings of the 20th International Conference on World Wide Web—WWW '11*, 695. New York: ACM, 2011. https://doi.org/10.1145/1963405.1963503.

Schildkraut, Deborah J., Jeffrey M. Berry, and James M. Glaser. "Ideological Bubbles and Two Types of Conservatives." *Public Opinion Quarterly*, forthcoming.

Shearer, Elisa, and Jeffrey Gottfried. "News Use Across Social Media Platforms 2017." Pew Research Center. 2017. http://www.journalism.org/2017/09/07/news-use-across-social-media-platforms-2017/.

Tumasjan, Andranik, Timm O. Sprenger, Philipp G. Sandner, and Isabell M. Welpe. "Election Forecasts With Twitter." *Social Science Computer Review* 29, no. 4 (2011): 402–418. https://doi.org/10.1177/0894439310386557.

PART FOUR

Ideas for Reform

CHAPTER 10

Politics Industry Theory

Katherine M. Gehl and Michael E. Porter

America's political system has become the major barrier to solving the important challenges facing our nation. About this there is little disagreement. However, there is far less agreement about the reasons why this is the case and what to do about it. In this chapter, we apply the lens of imperfect competition thinking and industry analysis to shed new light on these questions.

We are far from the first to draw the comparison between political and economic competition. This tradition dates back to Joseph Schumpeter, who characterized democracy as a political market in which "competitive leadership" was the goal, relating parties to firms, voters to customers, votes to currency, and policies to products (Schumpeter 1942). Since then, scholars from the so-called Public Choice School and others have applied economic concepts and tools to explain political outcomes.[1]

Too often, however, this approach has been stymied by the complexity of how political competition works in practice, and the rich, granular, and changing institutional structure it involves. The simplicity of the models employed (Green and Shapiro 1994) has led to inaccurate conclusions, prominent among them being the Downsian prediction of competitive convergence by the parties (Downs 1957).[2]

To understand the nature of competition in the politics industry, we must apply the imperfect competition concepts that have emerged and been used for decades to understand competition in other industries. The use of these concepts is part of a systemic approach reflecting both the complex nature of our political system and its interconnected actors and the role of the rules and institutional practices that have arisen over the decades, especially since the 1960s. These concepts shed new light on the causes of the dysfunctional competition in politics that has emerged and the set of reforms necessary to improve the performance of our democracy, which are overlooked in other models.

The politics industry is centered on private, gain-seeking actors, that is, our two political parties, who with their industry allies comprise what we call the "political industrial complex." They behave as a "duopoly," an industry with two dominant competitors, and have jointly optimized the industry structure to serve their own interests. The end result is unhealthy competition. In industries with unhealthy competition, customers are not well served. The politics industry thus fails to serve the public interest.

The ultimate purpose of our analysis is not to address the wide range of questions examined in the political science literature or to fit within the existing political science literature (although we have benefited greatly from the field's research and data), and we are not political scientists. Instead, we approach the topic from a different perspective, with different tools and a clear, singular purpose: action for change (e.g., how can we change the system of politics industry competition powerfully enough to change the outcomes the system reliably delivers?). We use Politics Industry Theory to produce a cohesive strategy for the political innovations needed to restructure the politics industry, positively alter incentives, and reinvigorate American democracy.[3]

POLITICAL SYSTEM OUTCOMES IN THE PUBLIC INTEREST

Today's political competition diverges sharply from the public interest and fails to deliver the outcomes citizens want and need. To address the reasons why, we need clarity on what these desired outcomes look like. In business competition, certain key desired outcomes are clear: profitability and growth. But what are the essential outcomes we citizens should expect from our elected officials?

Despite the fundamental importance of this question, there is surprisingly little discussion of outcomes in politics, much less consensus on the outcomes we want the system to deliver. This has created a vacuum that has allowed political actors to define success in ways that fit their own purposes, not the needs of citizens.

Instead, much literature in the field focuses on individual practices of politics, and not on results.[4] This has led to a rich and endless commentary on the practice of politics rather than on the actual outcomes political systems achieve.[5] Clarity on desired outcomes also allows us to link the nature of political competition to the outcomes of this competition.

Our work proposes five key outcomes that a healthy political system should deliver.

Practical and Effective Solutions to Solve Our Nation's Important Problems and Create Opportunities

Solutions are policies that address important problems, expand opportunities for citizens, and make things better in practice. Practical and sustainable solutions are not unidimensional but nuanced. They integrate the range of relevant and important considerations involved in virtually every good public policy. While the importance of solutions seems obvious, solutions are almost nonexistent in America's political system today.

Action

Legislation and executive action that matters must actually be enacted and implemented. Our system today often delivers gridlock, not action. The vast majority of promises made by candidates and political leaders in today's system never get acted upon. Unrealistic promises and talk without action are worthless. They benefit only political actors, not citizens.

Reasonably Broad-Based Buy-In by the Citizenry over Time

Good solutions should be able to gain—over time—reasonably broad-based acceptance and consensus by citizens. While there will never be 100 percent support for any policy, true solutions (which most often involve bipartisanship) can be accepted over time, by a range of constituents across the political spectrum.

This can occur when the political dialogue helps citizens understand the facts and realities of policy options and the rational compromises needed for a solution to work. This is not to say that elected officials should respond only to public opinion. Political leadership is required and must, at times, be ahead of popular opinion in order to move the country forward or to do "the right thing" (that's why it's called leadership). At its best, political competition educates, unites, and inspires citizens, which is certainly not the case today.

A Balance of Near- and Long-Term Needs

Good outcomes involve policies that are designed and enacted in a way that balances the needs and interests of both current and future citizens. This makes solutions sustainable, rather than subject to radical shifts over time that penalize citizens who had little say in the original policies. Instead of sustainability, our political leaders today regularly enact short-term measures that even they admit just "kick the can down the road."

Respect the Constitution and the Rights of All Citizens

This final outcome is essentially "table stakes" for our democracy—it would not be acceptable to deliver the first four outcomes while trampling on the Constitution and individual rights. While an important principle of democracy is majority rule, our Constitution is designed to also protect individual and minority rights and to avoid a "tyranny of the majority."

What kind of political system is necessary to deliver these outcomes? How can political competition drive good outcomes? These are questions we turn to next.

STRUCTURE OF THE POLITICS INDUSTRY AND ITS IMPLICATIONS

The nature of competition in any industry—and the degree to which it is healthy or unhealthy competition—depends on its underlying structure.[6]

Industry structure starts with *rivals*, or the competitors themselves. Rivals are affected by four additional competitive forces: the power of buyers (customers, channels),[7] the power of suppliers, the threat of new entrants, and the existence of substitutes. An industry's structure is the overall configuration of these five competitive forces and defines the power relationships between rivals and each of the other forces. This web of dynamic relationships determines how an industry competes, the value it delivers to its customers, and who has the power to capture that value. Industry structure, for example, explains how rivals and other actors can thrive even while customers are dissatisfied—as is the case in the politics industry.

The five competitive forces in the politics industry are shown in figure 10.1, and we will examine each of them and their implications.

Before we begin, we note two interesting aspects of the politics industry competition that distinguish it from other industries. First, competition in politics occurs on two levels: contesting elections and governing. These occur together and reinforce each other. Second, the politics industry competition operates with two currencies: votes and money.

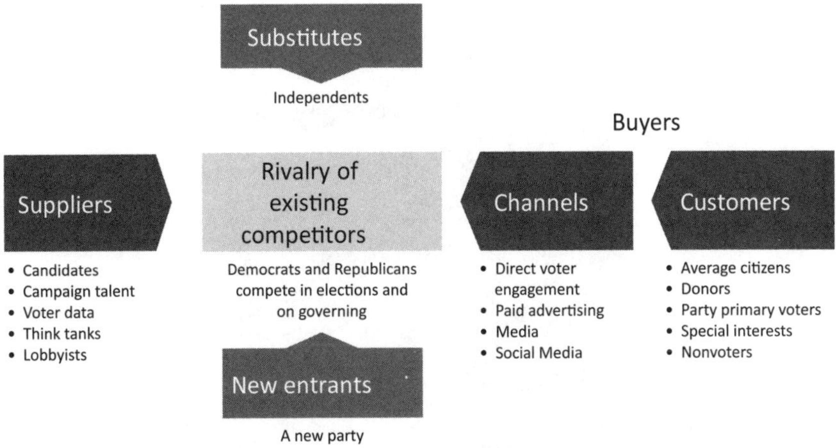

Figure 10.1: The Structure of the Politics Industry. *Source*: Author analysis. The Five Forces framework is attributed to Michael Porter, "The Five Competitive Forces That Shape Strategy," *Harvard Business Review* 86, no. 1 (2008): 78–93.

Customer Power Is Skewed against the Average Citizen

The nature of competition is manifested in the target customers that rivals choose to serve and who, thus, have the most power to shape outcomes in their favor. A political system is supposed to serve the public interest, so its customers should be all citizens. But, just as savvy businesses often choose to prioritize their most profitable customers, the political duopoly chooses to prioritize the customers that most advance its interests.

Customers in the politics industry can be divided into five major segments based on how they engage with the industry and their bargaining power: partisan primary voters, special interests, donors, average voters, and nonvoters. The most important customers for the political industrial complex are those who reliably deliver votes, or money, or both. Three powerful customer groups shape today's political competition: partisan primary voters, donors, and special interests. They are often overlapping, as shown in figure 10.2. The weakest customers are average voters and nonvoters.

Partisan primary voters: The first of the three powerful customer groups, partisan primary voters, are the "guardians" at the gate—any candidate must pass by them to get elected despite their representing only a small percentage of the total electorate.

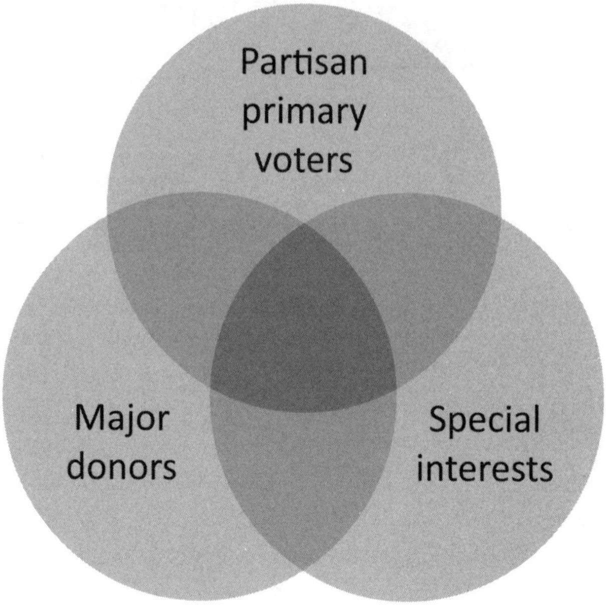

Figure 10.2: Customer Power in Politics. *Source*: Authors.

Special interests: A second powerful customer group is special interests. These are organized groups—either policy-related or industry-related—that are heavily focused on influencing political outcomes on particular issues in their favor.

Note that some special interests deliver both kinds of currency: votes (by turning out their "members" or supporters in both primaries and the general election) and money. Funding from special interests can include both spending on elections and spending on lobbying.

Donors: The third customer group—donors—is powerful because parties seek to maximize the dollars raised. Donors were traditionally wealthy individuals who made direct contributions to candidate campaigns. Since the Supreme Court rulings on campaign finance in *Citizens United v. Federal Election Commission* and *McCutcheon v. Federal Election Commission,* however, the distinction between donors and special interests has blurred, as individuals and special interest groups (including corporations) can make unlimited donations not only to super PACs but also to social welfare organizations, unions, and trade associations (Open Secrets 2017). All of these groups can use these funds for the purpose of influencing elections and public policies.

Average voters: The fourth customer group is average voters. Average voters represent a substantial proportion of voters who don't vote in primaries and are not regular donors. The parties, as we will see, do not have to compete for average voters by delivering outcomes for their benefit.

Nonvoters: The final, least powerful customer group is nonvoters. Almost 40 percent of eligible Americans did not vote in the 2016 general election.[8] Those who don't vote have no influence and, thus, have ceded their customer power to the duopoly and its allies. These individuals, perhaps not surprisingly, tend to be more moderate and more independent.[9]

Recent research supports these conclusions about where customer power actually lies. In 2014, researchers at Princeton and Northwestern examined congressional action on 1,779 policy issues. Their sad finding: "When the preferences of economic elites and the stands of organized interest groups are controlled for, the preferences of the average American appear to have only a minuscule, near-zero, statistically non-significant impact upon public policy" (Gilens and Page 2014).

This perverse influence of customer power on the nature of rivalry has become self-perpetuating. The more voters who drop out in disgust and don't vote, the more power is ceded to the parties, partisan voters, special interests, and big money. Yet, a major reason that so many citizens do not vote is a direct result of the nature of the competition the parties have created. Many nonvoters are turned off by Washington, DC. They believe their vote will make little difference.[10]

Finally, many candidates, and the attendant policy solutions that could have appealed to less ideological citizens, are driven out by today's political competition. Thus, more and more average voters drop out. Or—and this may be worse—voters acquiesce and play the game that the duopoly has created by focusing their participation on advancing their special interests and making donations. Outcomes only get worse.

Overall, then, most of the customers our political system should be designed to serve—citizens—have the least power to influence its results. Until this changes, bad outcomes will persist.

Channels Have Been Co-Opted by the Duopoly

Channels are the means by which rivals in an industry reach customers. In healthy competition, channels help customers better understand and access the products and services that meet their needs. Independent channels often play a significant role in objectively informing and influencing customer choices, which improves the vitality of competition. In healthy markets, when existing channels poorly serve customers, new channels often emerge and can be a disruptive force in shaking up the competition and pressuring rivals to better meet customer needs.

Channels in the politics industry are the means by which parties, elected officials, and candidates reach customers with information and persuasion. There are four major channels: paid advertising, traditional independent media, social media, and direct voter contact. The problem is that many channels are not independent, and even those that are—both new and old—benefit financially by aligning with the duopoly and embracing the partisan competition it has created.

Suppliers Are Controlled by the Duopoly

Suppliers provide the key inputs that enable industry competition. In most industries, suppliers make competitors better at serving customer needs. They help improve products and stimulate greater industry efficiency while often encouraging and supporting new competitors, thereby reducing the clout of incumbent rivals. This is not the case in the politics industry.

In the political industrial complex, there are five supplier groups that provide the key inputs needed to run a modern campaign and govern: candidates, specialized talent, voter data suppliers, idea suppliers, and lobbyists. Overall, these suppliers are now tightly connected to, and often controlled by, the duopoly. Suppliers, then, have limited power to shape competition, and they face strong pressures to align with one side of the duopoly. In fact, as elections and governing become more complex and partisan, suppliers prosper and their revenues grow. Rather than supporting solutions and finding common ground, then, suppliers have a stake in and amplify partisan competition.

High and Rising Barriers to Entry

Industries that fail to serve their customers are ripe for new entrants that better serve and improve value for customers and shake up the market. Barriers to entry determine the extent to which new competitors pose a threat. High barriers to entry make it hard for new competitors to gain a foothold. Low barriers to entry have the opposite effect.

In the politics industry, the barriers to entry are extremely high, and they

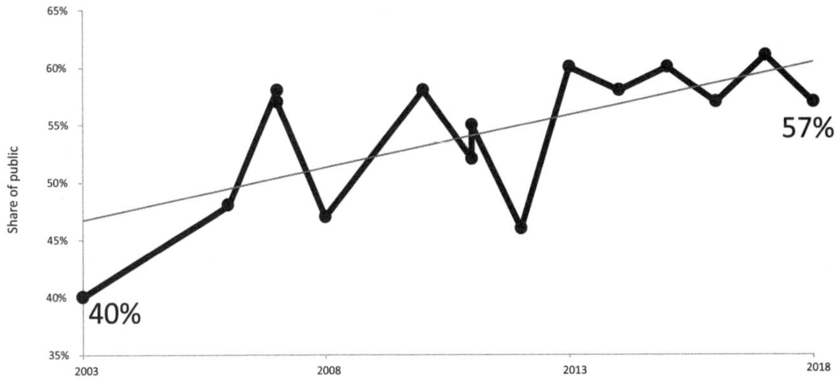

Figure 10.3: Increasing Desire for a Third Major Party. Circles correspond to date of survey. The first poll in which Gallup asked whether a third party is needed was October 10–12, 2003. *Source*: Chart data from Gallup, "Majority in US Still Say a Third Party Is Needed," https://news.gallup.com/poll/244094/majority-say-third-party-needed.aspx, July 2019.

affect not only conventional new entrants but also many potential substitutes (which we will discuss next) as well. A sure sign of this is the fact that no major new party has emerged since the founding of the Republican Party in 1854. The Progressive Party (1912) and the Reform Party (1992), both serious efforts, elected only a small number of candidates and disbanded within a decade. Despite widespread and growing public dissatisfaction with the existing parties (see figure 10.3), contemporary third parties and independent candidates continue to fare poorly.[11]

Today's entrenched duopoly owes its dominance, in large part, to the high barriers to entry that confront any new competition, many of which are artificial and have been created by the duopoly itself. The key entry barriers are the following:

Plurality voting: Plurality voting disadvantages new competitors. In the United States, elections can be won with only a plurality of the vote. The winner has the most votes but not necessarily a true majority. For example, a candidate can win with 34 percent in a three-way race, meaning that 66 percent of the voters preferred someone else. Plurality voting is an enormous barrier to new competition for two reasons:

First: The "spoiler argument": Sometimes, voters don't vote for the candidates they really want out of fear that vote will inadvertently help elect the candidate they like the least. For example, a citizen can't vote for Jill Stein because that would take votes away from Hillary Clinton ("spoil the election for her") and help elect Donald Trump. A citizen cannot vote for Gary Johnson because that would take votes away from Trump ("spoil the election for him") and help elect Hillary.

Second: The "wasted vote" argument. Whenever a citizen wants to vote for someone not considered likely to have a strong chance of winning, it is said that they are wasting their vote.

Both the "spoiler" argument and the "wasted vote" argument are wielded against all potential competition to the duopoly: don't run because you'll just ruin the race for so-and-so (i.e., the major party candidate to whom the potential new competitor is considered most similar). This structural impediment to the emergence of new competition, which persists even in the face of majority dissatisfaction with the two major parties, is one of the most serious obstacles to healthy competition—results and accountability—in the politics industry.

Party primaries: Voters in partisan primaries are generally more ideological and partisan than voters in the general electorate (Kamarck and Podkul 2018). This causes candidates to need to go further to the extremes to get elected. The most deleterious effect of party primaries is the disincentive they create for passing bipartisan, compromise legislation in Washington, DC. Effectively, party primaries create an "eye of the needle" problem, which makes it almost impossible for legislators (or new entrants) to keep their eye on the public interest instead of the ideological far wing of the party. New competitors wanting to stake out new positions (e.g., new or different "value to the consumer") cannot get to the general election ballot through the low-turnout primaries.

Other election machinery rules and practices: Gerrymandering, onerous general election ballot access rules for non-major-party candidates, presidential debate access rules (which artificially exclude candidates outside the duopoly), and other rules like sore loser laws, create major disadvantages for third-party candidates, independents, and even moderates within the major parties.

Partisan legislative machinery: Numerous rules give parties substantial control over the governing process, adding to barriers to entry for third parties and independent candidates, because voters hesitate to support them, fearing (sometimes legitimately) that such candidates will be marginalized in governing.[12]

Economies of scale: The national scope of the two major parties allows them to spread the large fixed investments needed in infrastructure, data, specialized skills, and other functions across elections nationally. This leaves independents and emerging parties contesting one or a few races at a severe disadvantage.

Incumbency advantages in brand recognition, relationships, expertise, and infrastructure: The major parties have universal brand recognition, credibility, experience, talent, resources, infrastructure, and long-term voter relationships.

Access to key suppliers and channels: The duopoly now controls much of what is needed to run a modern campaign and govern and has preferential access to or control of the channels.[13]

Access to funding: Raising the major funding needed for a new party, or even for an independent candidate, is challenging because the new competitors have limited donor lists and fundraising infrastructure relative to those of the parties. They face enormous skepticism that competitors outside the duopoly are viable. Campaign financing rules are also stacked against independent candidates. For example, the duopoly created fundraising rules that allow an individual donor to contribute $855,000 annually to both the Democratic Party or the Republican Party, but only $5,600 per two-year election cycle to an independent candidate committee.[14]

All these barriers to entry are made even more formidable by the winner-takes-all nature of competition in elections. In politics, capturing a non-plurality share of votes leads to a lost election, not to influence or to a position on which to build. Thus, new competitors must surmount the entry barriers and win, not just make a good showing.

While some of the barriers to entry facing new competition in politics reflect the inherent nature and cost of modern campaigns and governing, many are purely artificial. They have been created by the political industrial complex through the strategic adoption and refinement of a wide array of competitive choices, rules, and practices that preferentially benefit the duopoly.

With little threat of new competition, better aligning political competition with the public interest is an uphill battle at best.

Few Practical Substitutes

A final potential force for shifting industry competition is substitutes, which offer very differentiated or entirely different ways of competing than those of incumbent competitors. In an industry with entrenched rivals, real competition must often come from substitutes. In many industries where customer needs are poorly met, substitutes emerge and can shake up even dominant competitors. What are substitutes to the current two-party system?

Independents unaffiliated with a party: Independents could be a major force for shifting competition, but they face similar barriers to entry as new parties do. At the federal level, Ross Perot was the last major independent presidential candidate in 1992, and he failed to win a single state.

Organizations that overlay the existing major-party model: Consider, for example, No Labels, a bipartisan organization whose goal has been to bring incumbent elected officials together to find common ground and solve problems. While this is a laudable effort that has attracted significant support, delivering solutions through this approach is challenging given the strong partisan incentives in the current industry structure. A call for bipartisanship—no matter how inspiring—is usually less powerful (when crunch time, or reelection, or difficult votes come up) than the clout of the parties and the strong competitive incentives to appeal to partisan primary votes and special interests.

Self-funded candidates running through the parties: A form of substitute is heavily self-funded candidates who will have greater independence. However, party support remains indispensable in running and governing.

Coalitions of independent candidates with similar views: A group of like-minded legislators could become a swing coalition and have the power to influence the process of governing. This is particularly true if their numbers are sufficient to deny either major party a majority on its own. The coalition could then negotiate with the existing parties to shape legislation by offering, in return, the votes needed to pass legislation.

Why haven't more effective substitutes emerged in politics despite the poor outcomes? The most important reason is that any substitute faces virtually all the same entry barriers as forming or growing a significant new party.

In addition, politics is different from other industries, where substantially new ways of competing are possible. Disrupting or radically reshaping political competition is highly constrained by the fact that there is only one government structure. A new competitor in politics can't simply choose to create an alternative government structure and different rules. (The largely symbolic independence movements in a few US states are futile efforts to do just that.)

WHY POLITICAL RIVALRY FAILS TO SERVE THE PUBLIC INTEREST

All the elements of industry structure we have discussed come together to shape the intensity of industry rivalry and the dimensions on which rivals compete. In healthy political competition, industry actors would be competing to deliver the desired outcomes, but the politics industry is delivering outcomes that benefit the political industrial complex and fail to serve the public interest.

Why the disconnect? Our political outcomes today are not an accident but the logical result of the industry structure the duopoly has created through deliberate choices made by both sides.

The Nature of a Duopoly

The root causes of our poor political outcomes start with the fundamental nature of a duopoly—an industry with two dominant competitors. The existence of a duopoly, in politics or any industry, is not inherently good or bad. However, where competitors in any industry have market power, we know that competition can diverge from customer interests. In a duopoly, this divergence can be substantial. The extent of the divergence depends on the configuration of the competitive forces. Given the structure of the politics industry today, the divergence is extreme.

Typically in a duopoly, the rivalry appears intense, and that is certainly the case in US politics. But what looks like intense competition to the casual observer is not at all what it appears to be. What's really going on is that today's political duopoly seeks to enhance differentiation and industry attractiveness.

The Duopoly Seeks to Enhance Differentiation

Rivalry in a duopoly is almost always constrained, because the two rivals recognize that head-to-head competition is mutually destructive. Instead, the two rivals seek to compete in ways that reinforce their differentiation and separation from each other, pursuing three key competitive practices.

Choosing which customers to serve: The fateful and fundamental strategy choice made by the duopoly has been the types of customers they have chosen to prioritize and serve. As we discussed earlier, not all customers in the politics industry are created equal, and the most important customers are not average voters. Instead, the duopoly has prioritized those attractive customer groups who best serve their interests—partisan primary voters, special interests, and donors.

The parties do not compete for the middle. They avoid competing head-to-head for the same customers, which is a competition that is hard to win and would make the parties more accountable. Instead, the parties have divided voters into two partisan camps, each aligned with their party's ideology.

Competing on ideology and advancing partisan interests, not on solutions or action: Parties compete to create and reinforce partisan divisions rather than to deliver the solutions that are the most important outcome we need our political system to achieve. The duopoly appeals to its partisan supporters based on ideology, not on policies that work. Ideology offers simplistic and polarized approaches to addressing issues. It is no surprise, then, that today's political competition favors talk over action and relies on making unrealistic promises that are rarely, if ever, fulfilled.

Avoiding compromise: Most real solutions require finding common ground, compromising, and taking steps to move policy agendas forward over time rather than achieving everything at once. The ability to compromise is even more important in America, because our governmental system is not designed for simplistic majority rule.

Today's political competition treats compromise as failure. Industry structure dictates that bipartisanship, finding common ground, and compromise—fundamental principles of good political outcomes—are now anathema to the duopoly. Even in areas where the sides agree, they fail to pass legislation that would represent progress and instead hold out to deny the other side any victory.

The Duopoly Cooperates to Enhance Industry Attractiveness

In a duopoly, rivals also understand that while they compete, they will both benefit from an "attractive" industry as defined from their perspective—

one that strengthens and reinforces their way of competing, limits the power of suppliers and customers, and is protected by high barriers to entry. In a duopoly, rivals work together to sustain and improve industry attractiveness for the two of them by pursuing three additional key competitive practices.

Set industry rules and practices that reinforce partisan division: Most citizens mistakenly think the rules of our political system are set in the Constitution. It turns out that most of the rules and practices for elections and governing are set by the political industrial complex and for their benefit.

A series of election rules and practices—what we call the "elections machinery"—have enhanced and expanded partisan division and resulted in more and more extreme candidates and elected officials. Partisan primaries push candidates to the left or the right. This is reinforced and amplified by gerrymandered districts that virtually guarantee that one party will always win. Ballot access rules and fundraising biases invariably disadvantage independents, third-party candidates, and often moderates as well. As a result, pragmatic moderates in both parties are becoming an endangered species in Congress.

Governing rules and practices—what we call the "legislative machinery"—have also evolved to amplify partisanship and work against compromise solutions. Party leaders have created powerful levers to reward "loyal soldiers" and to discipline those who stray from ideological purity. Party leaders decide committee assignments and choose committee chairs (positions formerly based on seniority). Legislators who are considered insufficiently loyal can be kept off important committees, limiting their influence (Kosar and Chan 2016). Bipartisan-minded legislators can be marginalized and threatened with a primary challenge in their next election.

Meanwhile, the duopoly has also embraced practices such as the Hastert Rule that put partisan interests ahead of the national interest (Binder 2013). Now, the Speaker of the House will almost never allow a floor vote unless a majority of the majority party supports the bill—even if the majority of the entire House would vote to pass it. Party leaders have also suppressed reconciliation, the process by which bipartisan conference committees reconcile House and Senate legislation. Parties hold separate discussions, often restricted to party leadership. This leads to more partisanship and gridlock and less compromise and solutions.

Raise barriers to new competition: The very existence of the entrenched duopoly in US politics reflects the very high barriers to entry facing new competition, as we described in detail earlier. The parties have taken major steps to increase and widen the barriers to entry. The election and governing rules and practices we just discussed substantially increase barriers to entry facing new parties and independents. The tight connections forged between parties and the key suppliers needed to contest elections and govern also raise barriers to new competition. So does the growing party alignment with the media and party control of other key channels.

Avoid independent regulation. What's unique about the politics industry as compared to almost every other industry is that there is no independent regulation. The actors in the industry are the ones who themselves make the rules of the game. For example, the Federal Election Commission and the Commission on Presidential Debates are controlled by the two parties. The industry's freedom to set its own rules and competitive practices has tightened its stranglehold over the competition.

SYSTEMIC IMPLICATIONS

Beyond this failure to deliver good outcomes, the structure of the politics industry has resulted in three other devastating implications for the citizens.

An Incentive Not to Solve Problems

In today's partisan political competition, there is actually an incentive not to solve problems. Keeping a problem or controversy alive and festering is a way to attract and motivate partisan voters, special interests, and committed donors to each side. Once an issue is "solved," voters focused on that particular issue may become less motivated to affiliate with and support the party.

No Accountability for Results

Most amazing is that the duopoly is not held accountable for results. There's no accountability for two reasons. First, with government so often divided, voters don't know who to blame for the bad outcomes. The duopoly has exploited this feature of the system, taking extreme ideological positions that even they know could never be enacted into policy (Lee 2018). Second, the customer has only two choices. The only thing each party must do to win is convince enough voters to choose them as the lesser of two evils or to choose them because at least they say they're for what those voters believe. What neither party has to do, in this duopoly with high barriers to entry, is produce results, because no matter how disappointed a voter is, that voter still likely prefers what "her side" says it's for over what the only other side says it's for.

That's not to say that parties never lose power in the short term. When a party overreaches in pursuing its partisan agenda, it is often punished at the ballot box (Fiorina 2017). Yet it is never in danger of losing its entrenched position in the industry. The party is merely stuck in the minority until the other party overreaches, and it retakes control. The cycle just continues. All the while, the escalating partisan competition excites partisan voters, donors, and special interests, drawing more and more dollars into the system.

No Countervailing Forces to Restore Healthy Competition

The current dysfunction is not a phase or a cycle that will correct itself. The failure of politics has persisted because the normal checks and balances of healthy competition are intentionally neutralized. In other industries, countervailing forces that make up industry structure would keep competition aligned with the needs of customers. Customers who were poorly served (i.e., the majority of customers in politics) would rebel and look for new kinds of competitors. Powerful channels or suppliers would apply pressure on rivals to serve customers better. And new competitors or substitutes would emerge that met customer needs better.

In the politics industry, however, these forces have been co-opted or eliminated. The duopoly can sustain this incredible divergence from the public interest because of the high barriers they have created.

As a result of the anticompetitive industry structure—and the partisan-corrupted rules, norms, and practices of both elections and legislating (what we call, respectively, the elections machinery and the legislative machinery)—our political system operates under an incentive structure guaranteed to fail to solve problems: currently, there is virtually no intersection between an elected official acting in the public interest (i.e., delivering the five desired outcomes we described earlier) and the likelihood of getting reelected (see figure 10.4).

This must change. The question is how? And the answer is found by again using the tools of competition thinking and industry structure to redesign the most critical pieces of the elections and legislative machineries.

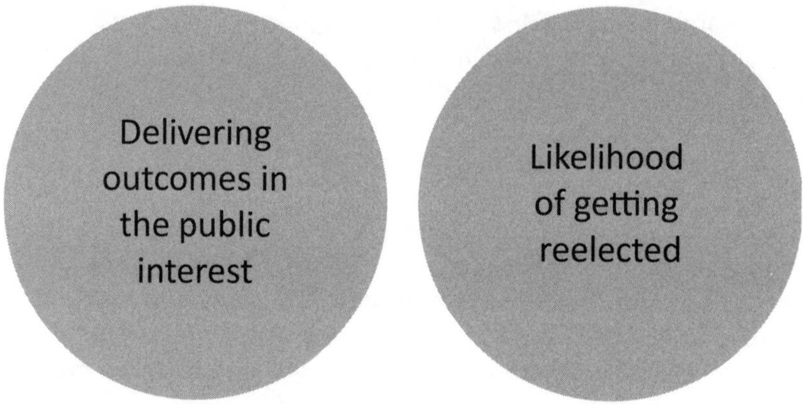

Figure 10.4: Current Unhealthy Competition in the Politics Industry. *Source*: Authors.

A WAY FORWARD

The structure of the politics industry and the nature of the competition that has been created consistently fail to serve the public interest and deliver the outcomes most citizens want and need. This is not an accident. It is the direct result of the competitive choices the parties have made and the industry structure that the duopoly has created. It follows, then, that this unhealthy competition is also not inevitable. We propose a comprehensive strategy—derived from this analysis of politics industry competition—to address the root causes of the unhealthy competition and fix the system.[15] Changing key rules of both the elections and legislative machinery will fundamentally alter the incentives in the system to deliver healthy competition on dimensions that matter to the public interest.

These innovations will free officials to do their jobs without the fear of getting primaried or blocked by partisan-serving red tape. This will also clear the way for innovative new competitors if the current duopoly fails to deliver the outcomes we need.

Reengineering Electoral Machinery: The Final Five Voting System

Two specific dimensions of our election machinery structures have a greater effect on the unhealthy competition to win elections and make laws: *partisan primaries* and *plurality voting*. To revive our democracy, we must start here.

We propose "Final Five Voting": Composed of two constituent parts—Top Five open, single-ballot, nonpartisan primaries (top five) and ranked-choice voting general elections (RCV)—Final Five Voting eliminates the negative effects of both partisan primaries and plurality voting. Final Five Voting constitutes a powerful-and-achievable transformation of the election rules that loom over every decision our legislators make. A Final Five Voting system requires two changes—one in primary elections, and one in general elections. It's critical to do them both together for maximum impact.

Top Five Primaries: Partisan primaries have dramatically distorted healthy competition in our elections, empowering partisan gatekeepers at the expense of most voters and shaping the behavior of our elected officials with perverse incentives while in office. We propose their elimination and the substitution of open, single-ballot, top-five, nonpartisan primaries.

Voters will no longer vote in a Democrat primary or a Republican primary. Instead there will be a single primary ballot. Every candidate from any party and independents appear on that single ballot. All voters are eligible to vote in the primary. The top five finishers advance to the general election, again regardless of their partisan affiliation.

Candidates would still be able to run with a partisan affiliation next to their name on the ballot. The parties can choose which candidate(s) they want to support and allow them to use their partisan label, rather than being forced to accept as their nominee whoever makes it through the partisan primary. Meanwhile, voters have more choice, no longer beholden to choosing between the lesser-of-two-evils. That's good for democracy.

Most importantly, Top Five alters the calculus for legislators: they know they won't automatically lose their seat if they vote on a bipartisan landmark bill. The "eye of the needle" through which no problem-solving politician can pass is eliminated.

Ranked-Choice Voting General Election: As discussed, plurality voting—and the resulting spoiler and wasted vote arguments—is a tremendous barrier to new competition in the politics industry, not to mention the incentives it creates for negative campaigning and dividing voters and the fact that plurality winners win with a majority of voters preferring someone else. We propose eliminating plurality voting in general elections and substituting it with ranked-choice voting (RCV).

In general elections, we will institute RCV. The concept is simple. Whereas plurality voting elects candidates without majority support, RCV

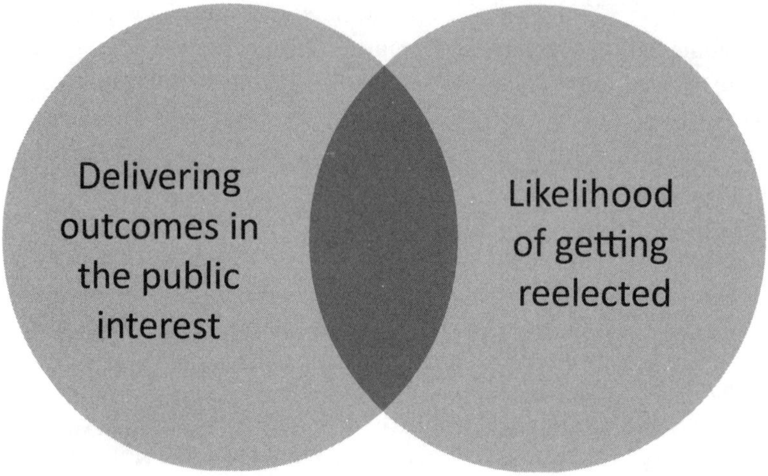

Figure 10.5: Healthy Competition in Politics: After Elections Machinery Innovation. *Source*: Authors.

does the opposite: for candidates to win, they must pass the 50 percent threshold.

Here's how RCV works in practice. When a voter arrives at the polling station on Election Day, they receive a ballot with the names of the five primary winners. As always, they pick their favorite candidate. But then, if desired, they may also indicate the candidate they like the second, third, fourth, and fifth best.

After the polls close, the first-place votes are counted. If one candidate receives more than 50 percent of the first-place votes (a true majority), the election is over and that candidate wins. If no candidate gets a true majority (50 percent plus one), the candidate in last place is eliminated. Votes cast for that candidate aren't "wasted," though, because voters who had selected that candidate—who's now out of the running—as their first choice have their ballots automatically transferred to their second choice. This process of elimination and reallocation continues until a single candidate passes the 50 percent mark. Whereas, under plurality voting, a candidate might have won by securing the turnout of a strong base (for example, perhaps only 35 percent of votes cast), RCV always results in the election of the candidate with the broadest appeal to the highest number of voters.

Far and away, the most important benefit of RCV is its elimination of the greatest structural barriers to entry for new competition (e.g., the spoiler and wasted vote arguments). RCV general elections, combined with the elimination of the "eye of the needle" party primary—what together we call

"Final Five Voting"—realigns the incentives in the politics industry to support results and create accountability for those results. The change is evident in the Venn diagram, post-innovation (see figure 10.5).

Reengineering Legislative Machinery: Innovation Commission

It won't be enough to reengineer our elections machinery via Final Five Voting. The legislative machinery has been carefully constructed over time for the duopoly's benefit. It is designed to serve partisans, not to solve problems.

The Constitution doesn't prescribe the inner workings of Congress. Instead, it directs each chamber to "determine the rules of its proceedings." It is interesting how constrained the usual debate is around legislative practices. The normal discussions are about tinkering around the edges—changing the filibuster or altering some aspect of committee structure—and the fact that these changes seem big is indicative of the sclerotic acceptance of the dysfunctional processes.

Our prescription is to use a proven management practice to reimagine the legislative machinery from scratch: *zero-based design.* Put aside the Rules of the House of Representatives, the Standing Rules of the Senate, the Authority and Rules of Senate Committees, the Rules Adopted by the Committees of the House of Representative, and the Rules of the Committee on Rules—the volume of rules upon rules optimized and weaponized over the decades. Put aside the informal rules, too—practices such as the Hastert Rule. Put aside customs that create separate podiums, separate cloakrooms, and separate dining rooms for Democrats and Republicans and seating the chamber according to party. Put it all aside. And then, reimagine from a clear white space.

Analyze the needs and goals of the legislature—principally, to deliver the outcomes we proposed earlier—and design rules and practices engineered from the ground up, though free to reincorporate past elements if they are beneficial, to support that endeavor.

THE POWER OF HEALTHY COMPETITION IN THE POLITICS INDUSTRY

Competition in the politics industry is failing America. By understanding the structure and rules of the industry that create the incentives driving behavior, it is possible to determine the most powerful leverage points for changing that behavior. Final Five Voting (i.e., reengineered elections machinery) combined with a model, modern legislative machinery will powerfully alter the incentives in the industry. Healthy competition will both deliver *results* to the most important customers in the industry, the voters, and create *accountability* for those results by dramatically lowering the barriers to entry for new competition. That's the power of political innovation and healthy competition in the politics industry.

NOTES

1. The Public Choice literature is too extensive to cite in detail. For an example of this approach, see *The Calculus of Consent: Logical Foundations of Constitutional Democracy* (Buchanan and Tullock 1965).

2. These inaccurate predictions not only muddy our understanding of how our political system works, but, more importantly, they also inform and shape the design of that system, with serious negative consequences. For example, the Public Choice School's opposition to the delegation of public functions to "unelected civil servants" was used as intellectual cover by our political parties to infiltrate executive agencies and independent regulatory agencies by increasing the number of political appointees. This has led to the erosion of checks and balances so central to our governmental structure and further undermined democratic outcomes. See "Agencies, Polarization, and the States," by Gillian Metzger (2015), and *The Politics of Presidential Appointments: Political Control and Bureaucratic Performance*, by David E. Lewis (2008).

3. This article is adapted from the report "Why Competition in the Politics Industry Is Failing America: A Strategy for Reinvigorating Our Democracy," by Katherine M. Gehl and Michael E. Porter (2017).

4. There are, however, notable exceptions. For example, see *How Democratic Is the American Constitution?* (Dahl 2002).

5. These types of procedures are routinely used in indexes that measure democratic performance across countries. The Economist Intelligence Unit's (EIU) Democracy Index ranks democracies worldwide, classifying them into four regime types: full democracy, flawed democracy, hybrid regime, and authoritarian regime. The EIU attempts to capture a thick conception of democracy by focusing on five categories: (1) electoral process and pluralism, (2) functioning of government, (3) political participation, (4) political culture, and (5) civil liberties. See the *Democracy Index 2017: Free Speech Under Attack* (Economist Intelligence Unit 2018). While the terms "democracy" and "freedom" are not synonymous, they are often used interchangeably, and therefore the Freedom House "Freedom in the World" Rankings are relevant to assessing democratic performance. Freedom House ranks countries on a scale of 1 to 7 based on two broad categories: political rights and civil liberties. The political rights measurements are grouped into three subcategories: (1) electoral process, (2) political pluralism and participation, and (3) functioning of government. The civil liberties measurements are grouped into four subcategories: (1)

freedom of expression and belief, (2) associational and organizational rights, (3) rule of law, and (4) personal autonomy and individual rights. See the *Freedom in the World 2018: Methodology* (Freedom House 2018). Additionally, the Polity IV Index, according to Steiner (2016), is "presumably the most widely used non-dichotomous measure of democracy in empirical research." Published by the Center for Systemic Peace (CSP), Polity covers all independent countries of population 500,000+ and provides data since 1800 (Steiner 2016, 337). For Polity's methodology, see *Polity IV Project: Political Regime Characteristics and Transitions, 1800–2016: Dataset Users' Manual* (Marshall, Gurr, and Jaggers 2017).

6. The five forces framework used in this section was originally developed by Michael Porter. For a more detailed explanation of the concept of industry structure, including "Porter's Five Forces," see two works by Michael E. Porter, *Competitive Strategy: Techniques for Analyzing Industries and Competitors* (1980) and "The Five Competitive Forces That Shape Strategy" (2008).

7. There can be multiple levels of buyers. In this industry, there are two levels: end customers (citizens) and channels.

8. Midterm-year general election turnout (based on voting-eligible population) figures since 1980 have been around 40 percent. Presidential-year general election turnout figures have more variance, usually between 50 percent and 60 percent. Data from *United States Election Project* (McDonald 2017).

9. For ideological comparisons of voters and nonvoters, see the chapter on the representativeness of voters in *Who Votes Now?* (Leighley and Nagler 2013, 154–181) and "The Electoral Origins of Polarized Politics: Evidence from the 2010 Cooperative Congressional Election Study" (Jacobson 2012, 1612–1630). For partisanship comparisons, see *Beyond the Core and Periphery: A New Look at Voter Participation across Elections* (Ansolabehere and Schaffner 2015).

10. According to a 2006 Pew Research Center survey, of the 22 percent of age-eligible Americans who were not registered to vote, 33 percent believed that "voting doesn't change things," 43 percent were "bored by what goes on in DC," and 22 percent were "angry with government." For the 23 percent of Americans who were registered but rarely voted, the corresponding figures were 30 percent, 42 percent, and 14 percent, respectively. According to a 2014 Census Bureau survey, the top reasons registered voters did not vote in the midterm election were: "too busy" (28 percent), "not interested" (16 percent), "illness/disability" (11 percent), "out of town" (10 percent), "forgot to vote" (8 percent), and "disliked candidates/issues" (8 percent). See the Pew Research Center's report, "Who Votes, Who Doesn't, and Why" (2006), and "Why Don't Americans Vote? We're 'too Busy,'" by Scott Clement (2015).

11. The most significant new party since 1860, the Progressive Party (also known as the Bull Moose Party) dates back to the period from 1912 to 1916. It was founded by Teddy Roosevelt so that he could run for president after he lost the 1912 Republican nomination. The party successfully elected thirteen representatives, but it disintegrated when most of its members rejoined the Republican Party. The Reform Party, the most recent party that achieved any electoral success, grew out of Ross

Perot's 1992 presidential candidacy in which he won 19 percent of the popular vote. The Reform Party lasted from 1992 to 2000, with its major success being the election of Jesse Ventura as governor of Minnesota in 1998.

Today's most significant third parties, the Libertarians and the Greens, each run numerous candidates every year, but they have yet to win a single congressional or gubernatorial campaign. See "Bull Moose Party," in the *Encyclopædia Britannic* (2015). "Progressive (Bull Moose) Party (1912)," in *Guide to US Elections* (2010); the Reform Party National Committee website page "About"; and "Third Party Results," from CQ Press Electronic Library (2017).

12. For overviews of the evolution of the legislative machinery, see: Kenneth Shepsle, "The Changing Textbook Congress" (1989); David W. Rohde, *Party Leaders and the Postreform House* (1991); Sam Rosenfeld, chapter 1 in *The Polarizers: Postwar Architects of Our Polarized Era* (2018); Jeffrey Jenkins, "The Evolution of Party Leadership," *The Oxford Handbook of the American Congress* (2011); Barbara Sinclair, *Unorthodox Lawmaking*, 5th ed. (2016): chapter 6; Steven S. Smith, *Party Influence in Congress* (2012); Steven S. Smith and Gerald Gamm, "The Dynamics of Party Government in Congress," in *Congress Reconsidered*, 10th ed., ed. Bruce Oppenheimer and Lawrence Dodd (2013); Barbara Sinclair, "The Dream Fulfilled? Party Development in Congress, 1950–2000," in *Responsible Partisanship? The Evolution of American Political Parties Since 1950*, ed. John C. Green and Paul S. Hernson (2002); John Aldrich and David Rohde, "Congressional Committees in a Partisan Era," in *Congress Reconsidered*, 8th ed., ed. Lawrence Dodd and Bruce Oppenheimer (2005); Nathan Monroe, Jason Roberts and David Rhode, *Why Not Parties? Party Effects in the United States Senate* (2008); Sean M. Theriault, part 3, in *Party Polarization in Congress* (2008); Barbara Sinclair, *Party Wars* (Norman: University of Oklahoma Press, 2006); Lawrence Dodd and Bruce Oppenheimer, "The House in a Time of Crisis," in *Congress Reconsidered*, 10th ed., ed. Lawrence Dodd and Bruce Oppenheimer (2013). Some, however, argue that the party's power in Congress has not changed dramatically over time. This view is associated with the "Cartel Theory" detailed in Gary Cox and Matthew McCubbins, *Legislative Leviathan: Party Government in the House*, 2nd ed. (2007).

13. David Dodson, a former CEO, experienced the duopoly's power over suppliers firsthand when he challenged Senator John Barroso in the Republican Senate primary in Wyoming in 2018. "When I tried to hire the law firm to which I'd directed millions of dollars in business while I was a chief executive, it turned me away, explaining that it could work only for Democrats. When I contacted a law firm known to serve Republicans, that firm told me it couldn't work for a candidate running against an incumbent because it would put its entire practice at risk. As I tried to build an organization to run a credible primary challenge, this story repeated itself, whether I was recruiting campaign staff or a marketing firm." See "Why Do We Let Political Parties Act Like Monopolies?" by David Dodson (2019).

14. Author calculations based on Federal Elections Committee individual contribution limits. The $855,000 annually is composed of 1) $10,000 to each of fifty

state party committees' federal accounts, 2) $35,500 to the party federal committee, and 3) $106,500 to each of the party convention, building, and legal accounts. See Federal Elections Committee, "Contribution Limits," https://www.fec.gov/help-candidates-and-committees/candidate-taking-receipts/contribution-limits/.

15. The full strategy is outlined in *Why Competition in the Politics Industry Is Failing America: A Strategy for Reinvigorating Our Democracy* by Katherine M. Gehl and Michael E. Porter (2017).

REFERENCES

Aldrich, John H., and David W. Rohde. "Congressional Committees in a Partisan Era." In *Congress Reconsidered*, 8th ed., ed. Lawrence C. Dodd and Bruce I. Oppenheimer. Washington, DC: CQ, 2005.

Ansolabehere, Stephen, and Brian Schaffner. "Beyond the Core and Periphery: A New Look at Voter Participation Across Elections." Working Paper, November 30, 2015, accessed August 2017: https://cces.gov.harvard.edu/files/cces/files/ansolabehere_schaffner_core_periphery.pdf.

Bernstein, Sharon. "More Californians Dreaming of a Country without Trump: Poll." Posted on *Reuters*. January 2017. https://www.reuters.com/article/us-usa-trump-california-secession/more-californians-dreaming-of-a-country-without-trump-poll-idUSKBN1572KB.

Binder, Sarah A. "Oh 113th Congress Hastert Rule, We Hardly Knew Ye!" Posted on *Brookings*. January 2013. https://www.brookings.edu/blog/up-front/2013/01/17/oh-113th-congress-hastert-rule-we-hardly-knew-ye/.

Buchanan, James M., and Gordon Tullock. *The Calculus of Consent: Logical Foundations of Constitutional Democracy*. Ann Arbor: University of Michigan Press, 1965.

Clement, Scott. "Why Don't Americans Vote? We're 'Too Busy.'" Posted on *Washington Post*. March 2015. https://www.washingtonpost.com/news/the-fix/wp/2015/07/17/why-dont-americans-vote-were-too-busy.

Cox, Gary W., and Mathew D. McCubbins. *Legislative Leviathan: Party Government in the House*, 2nd ed. Cambridge: Cambridge University Press, 2007.

Dahl, Robert. *How Democratic Is the American Constitution?* New Haven, CT: Yale University Press, 2002.

Economist Intelligence Unit. 2017. Democracy Index 2017: Free Speech Under Attack. https://www.eiu.com/public/topical_report.aspx?campaignid=DemocracyIndex2017.

Dodd, Lawrence, and Bruce Oppenheimer. "The House in a Time of Crisis." In *Congress Reconsidered*, 10th ed., ed. Bruce Oppenheimer and Lawrence Dodd. Washington, DC: CQ, 2012.

Dodson, David. "Why Do We Let Political Parties Act Like Monopolies?" Posted on *New York Times*. May 2019. https://www.nytimes.com/2019/05/20/opinion/primary-challengers.html.

Downs, Anthony. *An Economic Theory of Democracy*. New York: Harper and Row, 1957.

Fiorina, Morris P. *Unstable Majorities: Polarization, Party Sorting, and Political Stalemate.* Chicago: Hoover Institution, 2017.

Freedom House. Freedom in the World 2018: Methodology. https://freedom-house.org/report/methodology-freedom-world-2018.

Gehl, Katherine M., and Michael E. Porter. "Why Competition in the Politics Industry Is Failing America." Harvard Business School Report. September 2017. https://www.hbs.edu/competitiveness/research/Pages/research-details.aspx?rid=84.

Gilens, Martin, and Benjamin I. Page. "Testing Theories of American Politics: Elites, Interest Groups, and Average Citizens." *Perspectives on Politics* 12, no. 3 (2014): 564–581.

Green, Donald, and Ian Shapiro. *Pathologies of Rational Choice Theory: A Critique of Applications in Political Science.* New Haven, CT: Yale University Press, 1994.

Green, Jeffrey E. *The Eyes of the People: Democracy in an Age of Spectatorship.* Oxford: Oxford University Press, 2010.

Green, John C., and Paul S. Herrnson, eds. *Responsible Partisanship? The Evolution of American Parties Since 1950.* Lawrence: University Press of Kansas, 2002.

Jacobson, Gary C. "The Electoral Origins of Polarized Politics: Evidence from the 2010 Cooperative Congressional Election Study." *American Behavioral Scientist* 56, no. 12 (2012): 1612–1630.

Jenkins, Jeffrey A. "The Evolution of Party Leadership." In *The Oxford Handbook of the American Congress,* ed. Eric Schickler and Frances E. Lee. Oxford: Oxford University Press, 2011.

Kamarck, Elaine, and Alexander R. Podkul. "The 2018 Primaries Project: The Ideology of Primary Voters." Brookings Institution, 2018. https://www.brookings.edu/research/the-2018-primaries-project-the-ideology-of-primary-voters/.

Kosar, Kevin R., and Adam Chan. "A Case for Stronger Congressional Committees." *R Street Policy Study No. 66.* August 2016. https://www.rstreet.org/wp-content/uploads/2016/08/66.pdf.

Lee, Frances E. "The 115th Congress and Questions of Party Unity in a Polarized Era." *Journal of Politics* 80, no. 4 (October 2018): 1464–1473.

Leighley, Jan E., and Jonathan Nagler. *Who Votes Now?* Princeton, NJ: Princeton University Press, 2013.

Lewis, David E. *The Politics of Presidential Appointments: Political Control and Bureaucratic Performance.* Princeton, NJ: Princeton University Press, 2008.

Marshall, Monty G., Ted R. Gurr, and Keith Jaggers. Polity IV Project: Political Regime Characteristics and Transitions, 1800–2016: Dataset Users' Manual, 2017. http://www.systemicpeace.org/inscr/p4manualv2016.pdf.

McDonald, Michael. National General Election VEP Turnout Rates, 1789–Present Data from United States Elections Project. March 2017. http://www.electproject.org/national-1789-present.

Metzger, Gillian. "Agencies, Polarization, and the States." *Columbia Law Review* 115, no. 7 (2015): 1739–1788.

Monroe, Nathan W., Jason M. Roberts, and David W. Rohde, eds. *Why Not Parties? Party Effects in the United States Senate.* Chicago: University of Chicago Press, 2008.

Open Secrets. "Center for Responsive article on Dark Money Basics." August 2017. https://www.opensecrets.org/dark-money/basics.

Pew Research Group. "Who Votes, Who Doesn't, and Why." March 2017. http://www.peoplepress.org/2006/10/18/who-votes-who-doesnt-and-why/.

Porter, Michael E. "The Five Competitive Forces That Shape Strategy," *Harvard Business Review* 86, no. 1 (2008): 78–93.

———. *Competitive Strategy: Techniques for Analyzing Industries and Competitors.* New York: Free Press, 1980.

Rohde, David W. *Parties and Leaders in the Postreform House.* Chicago: University of Chicago Press, 1991.

Rosenfeld, Sam. *The Polarizers: Postwar Architects of Our Partisan Era.* Chicago: University of Chicago Press, 2018.

Schumpeter, Joseph. *Capitalism, Socialism, and Democracy.* New York: Harper and Brothers, 1942.

Shapiro, Ian. *The State of Democratic Theory.* Princeton, NJ: Princeton University Press, 2003.

Shepsle, Kenneth. "The Changing Textbook Congress." In *Can the Government Govern?*, ed. John E. Chubb and Paul E. Peterson. Washington, DC: Brookings Institution, 1989.

Sinclair, Barbara. *Unorthodox Lawmaking: New Legislative Processes in the US Congress, 5th Edition.* Washington, DC: CQ, 2016.

———. *Party Wars.* Norman: University of Oklahoma Press, 2006.

———. "The Dream Fulfilled? Party Development in Congress, 1950–2000." In *Responsible Partisanship: The Evolution of American Political Parties,* ed. John C. Green and Paul S. Herrnson. Lawrence: University of Kansas Press, 2002.

Smith, Steven S., and Gerald Gamm. "The Dynamics of Party Government in Congress." In *Congress Reconsidered,* 10th ed., ed. Bruce Oppenheimer and Lawrence Dodd. Washington, DC: CQ, 2012.

Steiner, Nils D. "Comparing Freedom House Democracy Scores to Alternative Indices and Testing for Political Bias: Are US Allies Rated as More Democratic by Freedom House?" *Journal of Comparative Policy Analysis: Research and Practice* 18, no. 4 (2016): 337.

Theriault, Sean M. *Party Polarization in Congress.* Cambridge: Cambridge University Press, 2008.

Timsit, Annabelle. "5 US Independence Movements Inspired by Brexit." *Politico.* July 2016. https://www.politico.com/magazine/story/2016/07/5-us-independence-movements-inspired-by-brexit-214010.

YesCalifornia. "The 2019 #Calexit Independence Referendum." March 2017. http://www.yescalifornia.org.

CHAPTER 11

Spoiler Alert: Why Americans' Desires for a Third Party Are Unlikely to Come True

Lee Drutman, William A. Galston, and Tod Lindberg

INTRODUCTION

Third parties are a perpetual fascination of American politics. Each presidential election cycle brings its own new wave of punditry wondering whether this will be the year in which a third party *finally* breaks through, upending a system in which the two parties have existed in lockstep competition for 170 years—longer than most of the world's democracies.

Our report offers two reasons to be skeptical that a new third party is imminent, at least without major electoral reform. First, while support for a hypothetical third party is high, consensus collapses on the specifics of what, exactly, that third party should stand for. About one-third of those who are supportive of a third party want a party of the center, but about one-fifth want a party that is *more conservative* than the Republicans and about one-fifth want a party that is *more liberal* than the Democrats.[1] No single third party emerges as a focal point of change. It would take at least five parties to adequately represent the ideological yearnings of the American people, possibly six.

Second, partisans are reasonably well contented with their parties and particularly motivated by a dislike of the *other* party. In a single-round plurality election system, taking a chance on a third party is a costly gamble when you believe that there are real differences between the two parties. Even voters who have some qualms about their own party view the opposing party as far worse. In a single-round plurality system, voting for a third party requires widespread feelings of indifference between the two major parties. The overwhelming majority of voters, including self-identified Independents, *do* see a difference.

Certainly, there are many signs of discontent with the current party system. But currently, that discontent doesn't add up to support for an alternative that could topple the two leading choices given the existing electoral system.

But could the existing system change to allow for more parties? It's possible. But it would take major structural reforms. Our analysis suggests that voters are largely unaware of possible reforms to open up the party system to a third party (as well as to fourth and fifth parties). And they don't connect those reforms to changing the party system. If Americans are to fulfill their stated desire for a third party, it will take considerable work by reformers to make the connection between electoral laws and electoral choices.

And finally, *should* the system change in this manner? We conclude our analysis with a separate normative response from each author.

SUPPORT FOR A THIRD PARTY IS HIGH

Almost seven in ten Americans (68 percent) say a third party is needed in American politics, higher than any other poll to date.[2] Below, we put this finding in historical context, reconstructing data from Pew and Gallup going back to the mid-1990s to construct a fuller time series (figure 11.1).[3]

The time series shows that support for a third party was close to 60 percent in the mid-1990s, then declined for about a decade until 2003, when majorities reported being satisfied with the two parties. By the mid-2000s, support for a third party was again the majority view, and it has been edging up since 2012. Only time will tell whether this 68 percent finding represents a temporary peak or a harbinger of more dissatisfaction.

The trend in support for a third party appears related to feelings toward the major parties. Since 1964, the American National Election Studies (ANES) Time Series has asked respondents to place both parties on a feeling thermometer ranging from 0 to 100. The share of respondents who gave either (or both) of the two major parties a rating of at least 70, suggesting real warmth toward one of the two parties, has ebbed and flowed in a mirror-image fashion to support for a third party.

As with previous polling around this issue, those who identify as Independent are more likely to want a third party (85 percent) than those who identify as Democrats (64 percent) or Republicans (58 percent). At no

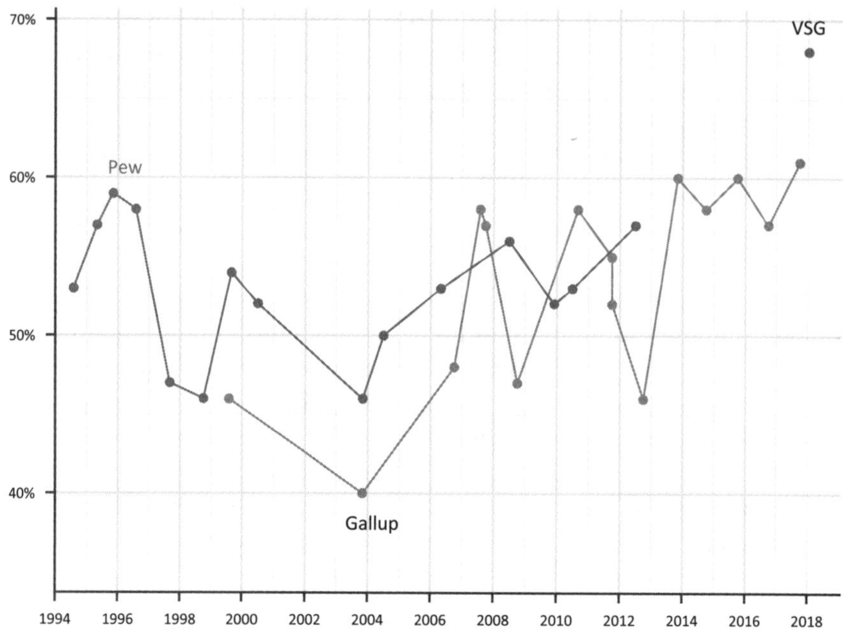

Figure 11.1: Support for a Third Party Is at a Twenty-Year High. *Source*: 1994–2017, Pew and Gallup; 2018 Voter Study Group.

point in Gallup's time series have both a majority of Democrats *and* a majority of Republicans simultaneously supported a third party.

Support for a third party was higher in the 1990s, when around 60 percent of ANES respondents viewed either of the two parties warmly. But it fell as favorable feelings toward a major party increased and peaked in 2004, when 65 percent viewed at least one party very favorably. Since then, this percentage has declined, hitting a low of 50 percent in 2016—just as support for a third party has increased.

Broken down by the strength of their identification with either party, Independents, "leaners,"[4] and "not very strong" party supporters are more likely to favor a third party than are "strong" supporters of the existing parties, but majorities even of those who strongly identify with one party or the other would like to see a third party.

There is also some asymmetry. Strong Democrats are 8 percentage points more likely to say a third party is needed than are Strong Republicans (59 percent to 51 percent), and those who "Lean Democrat" are nine points more likely to call for a third party than are those who "Lean Republican" (85 percent to 76 percent).

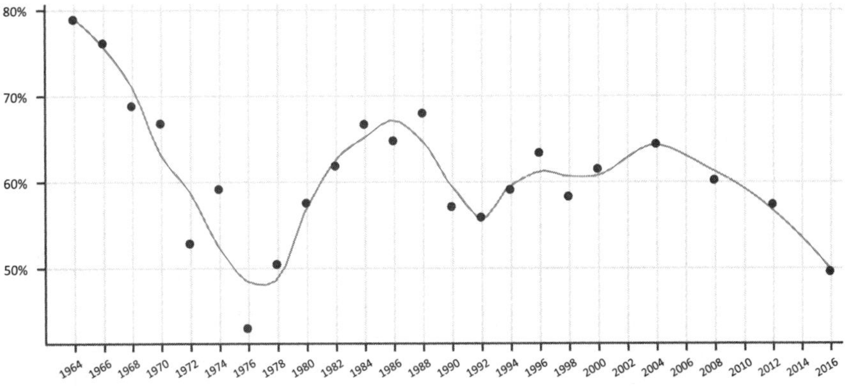

Figure 11.2: Percentage of Respondents with "Very Warm" Feelings About at Least One Party Is Declining. "Very Warm" is defined as greater than or equal to 70 on the feeling thermometer scale. *Source*: American National Election Studies Time Series.

A similar pattern emerges with ideology, with an even more pronounced asymmetry between those who are "very liberal" (73 percent want a third party) and those who are "very conservative" (57 percent want a third party). But self-described moderates are also very dissatisfied with the two

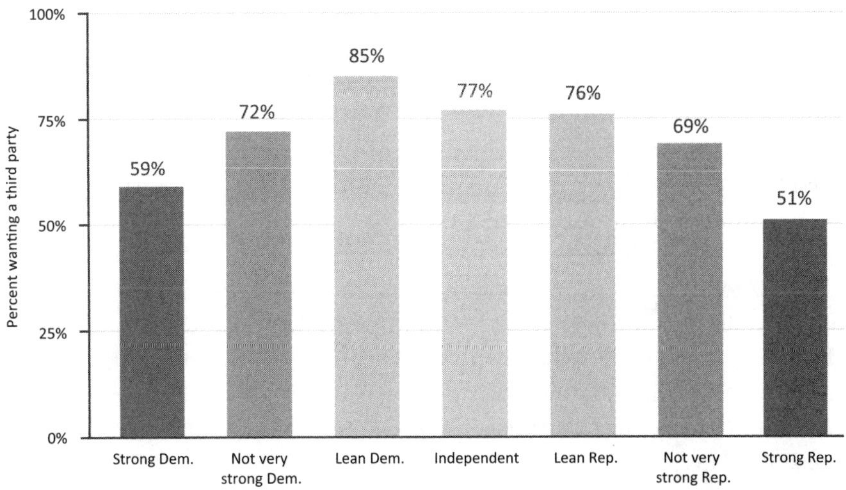

Figure 11.3: Support for a Third Party (by Partisan Affiliation). *Source*: Authors' computations.

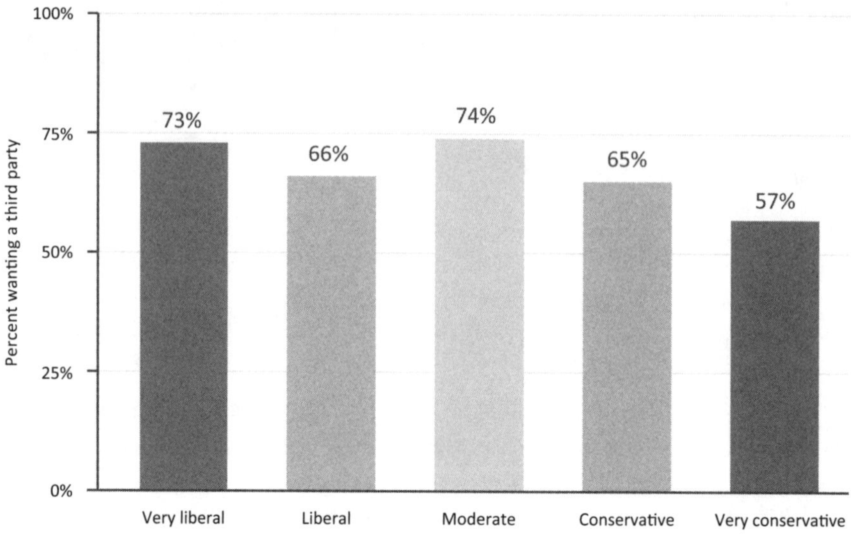

Figure 11.4: Support for a Third Party (by Ideology). *Source*: Authors' computations.

parties (74 percent want a third party). A more detailed analysis of the relationship between partisanship, ideology, and desire for a third party is in appendix A.

Segmenting the population by 2016 primary vote, the highest support for a third party comes from those who supported Bernie Sanders in the 2016 primary (83 percent desire a third party). As the 2017 Voter Study Group report *Political Divisions in 2016 and Beyond: Tensions Between and Within the Two Parties* showed, Sanders voters tended to be distinguished from Clinton voters by their distrust of and antipathy toward the political establishment. It is not surprising they would call for a third party.

The next highest desire for a third party comes from those who supported Kasich in the Republican primary (74 percent want a third party). These voters tend to be independent and moderate, which both correlate with the desire for a third party. It is notable that even though Trump is president, 69 percent of those who supported him in a primary want a third party. Among primary supporters of the two most conventionally conservative candidates, Cruz and Rubio, perceived need for a third party is lower but still stands at 65 percent.

In summary, desire for a third party is widespread across the ideological and partisan spectrum, though it is highest among those who identify as Independent, moderate, and very liberal, and those who supported Bernie

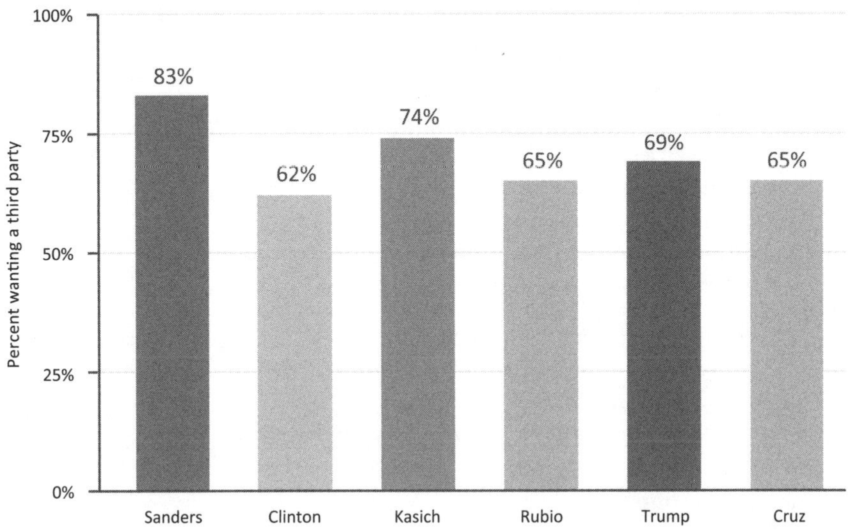

Figure 11.5: Support for a Third Party (by 2016 Primary Vote). *Source*: Authors' computations.

Sanders and John Kasich. But in every single category, majorities agree that the two parties do an inadequate job and a third party is needed.

DISAGREEMENT ON WHAT A THIRD PARTY SHOULD BE

While majorities agree that a third party is needed, consensus breaks down quickly when we probe further. What should that party look like? Here, there is no agreement.

We also asked respondents where they would locate a third party, should such a party exist, in relation to the existing parties on questions of social welfare and immigration, the two most salient issues in American politics right now.[5]

Here are the top-line results, among all voters:

Below, we show the results along both dimensions for those who affirmatively want a third party. Shading represents frequency. The more populated the cell, the darker the color.

This shows clearly why a third party does not form. There is no agreement on what that third party should be. There is demand for a party that is more liberal, a party that is more centrist, and a party more conservative than the current two parties. In short, to represent the diversity of views, American democracy needs not three parties but at least five parties.

Table 11.1: Where Should a Third Party Locate? (Among All Respondents)

	Economics	Immigration
More liberal than the Democratic Party	16%	13%
About where the Democratic Party is now	13%	21%
In between the Democratic Party and the Republican Party	39%	30%
About where the Republican Party is now	9%	13%
More conservative than the Republican Party	22%	23%

Among those who support a third party (again, 68 percent):

Almost one in five (18 percent) want a party that is *more liberal* than the Democrats on one or both dimensions, and 11 percent want a party that is more liberal than the Democrats on *both* dimensions.

Almost one in four (37 percent) want a party that is *more centrist* than either of the two parties on one or both dimensions (while not also being more liberal/conservative than a major party on another dimension), and 22 percent want a party that is more centrist on both dimensions.

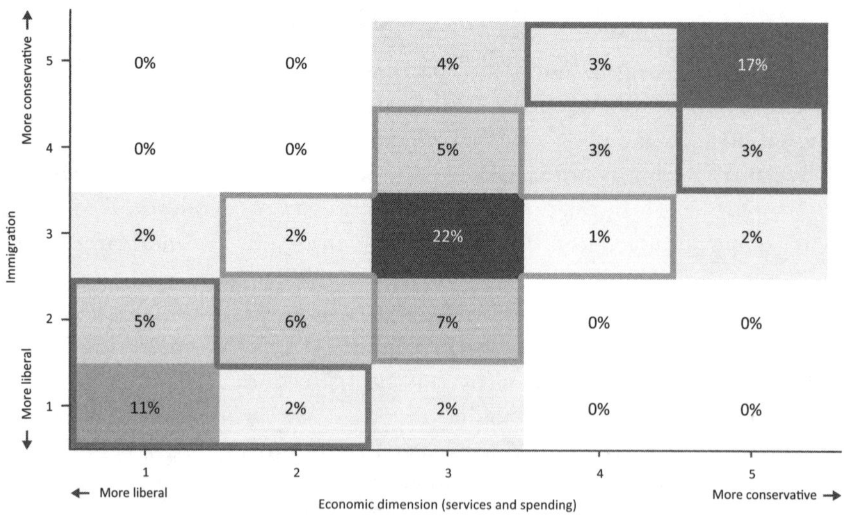

Figure 11.6: Where Should a Third Party Locate (among Respondents Who Want a Third Party). *Source*: Authors' computations.

Slightly more than one in five (23 percent) want a party that is *more conservative* than Republicans on one or both dimensions, and 17 percent want a party that is more conservative than Republicans on *both* dimensions.

We also note that there is no support for a Michael Bloomberg–style party that would be more liberal on immigration and centrist on economics. This is consistent with the *Political Divisions in 2016 and Beyond* report, which found only 4 percent of voters who held economically conservative but culturally liberal views.

To be sure, there are two important caveats here.

First, these data suggest little support for a "populist" candidate who promises to spend more on social welfare while tightening the borders, which seems to contradict both the rise of *candidate* Donald Trump and the *Political Divisions in 2016 and Beyond* report, which showed that almost three in ten voters held left-of-center views on economic issues and right-of-center views on cultural and social issues. This may reflect the framing of the question, which asked respondents whether they wanted a party that was more *liberal* than the Democratic Party on how much the government spends and how many services it provides. Political science literature has long shown that while many self-described conservatives want government to spend more on *specific* programs, they also want to spend less on government *in general* (Grossmann and Hopkins 2016; Ellis and Stimson 2012; Free and Cantril 1967). Trump exploited this contradiction in the 2016 primaries. If there is support for a populist third party that these data do not capture, it only bolsters the broader takeaway: a third party does not emerge because those who want a third party can't agree on what third party they want.

Second, substantial political science evidence suggests that ideology is not particularly stable and may be more a reflection of identity (partisan and otherwise) than a reflection of deeply held beliefs (Kinder and Kalmoe 2017; Converse 1964). If so, support for a possible third party could depend on the emergence of a particularly compelling candidate. After all, despite stated preferences among Republican voters for a "conservative" candidate, they voted for Donald Trump, who, as a candidate, broke with conservative orthodoxy in many policy areas.

But there is a caveat to the caveat: given the nature of plurality-winner elections, even those who might prefer a charismatic third-party candidate should still vote strategically for one of the major two parties, unless they see no difference between the two parties. It turns out they do see a difference. We now turn to that question.

PARTY DIFFERENCES AND PARTISAN REPRESENTATION

A second complicating factor working against the emergence of a third party is that even if they'd like a third party in *theory*, few partisans seem likely to abandon their own party *in practice*. This is both because partisans feel well-represented by their parties and because they feel very poorly represented by the other party.

In our survey, we asked voters how well represented they felt by each of the two parties.

Below, we report the results of how well represented each group feels by both parties. Independents here are self-identified Independents, including leaners.

Two points should jump out from this analysis.

First, partisans generally feel well-represented by their parties. Four in five Democrats (81 percent) feel somewhat or very well-represented by their party, while three in four Republicans (75 percent) feel somewhat or very well-represented by their party.

Second, partisans feel *very poorly represented* by the other party. About seven in ten Democrats and seven in ten Republicans feel very poorly represented by the opposite party.

In other words, few partisans seem likely to abandon their own parties for a third party, assuming they calculate that doing so would mean a victory for the *other* major party. While the majority of partisans describe themselves as being "somewhat well-represented" by their parties (54 percent of Democrats and 55 percent of Republicans), as compared to "very well-represented" (27 percent of Democrats, and just 20 percent of Republicans), "somewhat well-represented" is a reasonable standard in a country with big-tent parties and a long history of anti-party sentiment.

In our sample, 36 percent identify as Democrats and 26 percent identify as Republicans, which adds up to only 62 percent of the electorate identify-

Table 11.2: How Well-Represented Do You Personally Feel by *the Democratic Party*?

	Democrats	Independents	Republicans
Very well-represented	27%	3%	2%
Somewhat well-represented	54%	27%	8%
Somewhat poorly represented	13%	23%	16%
Very poorly represented	4%	45%	71%

Table 11.3: How Well-Represented Do You Personally Feel by *the Republican Party*?

	Democrats	Independents	Republicans
Very well-represented	3%	2%	20%
Somewhat well-represented	11%	24%	55%
Somewhat poorly represented	16%	26%	18%
Very poorly represented	68%	45%	6%

ing as partisan. Gallup's polling finds that over the past year, the share of the population identifying as Republican has hovered around 25 percent, the share identifying as Democrat has hovered around 29 percent, and the share identifying as Independent has hovered around 43 percent (Gallup). Our sample has 30 percent identifying as Independents, with another 8 percent refusing to state.

The focus below is on self-identified Independents, to see whether they are uniquely unrepresented by the parties.

Two points are key here.

First, two-thirds of Independents feel more represented by one of the parties. The share of self-identified independents who are truly equivocal between the two parties is equal to the sum of the squares from the bottom left to the upper

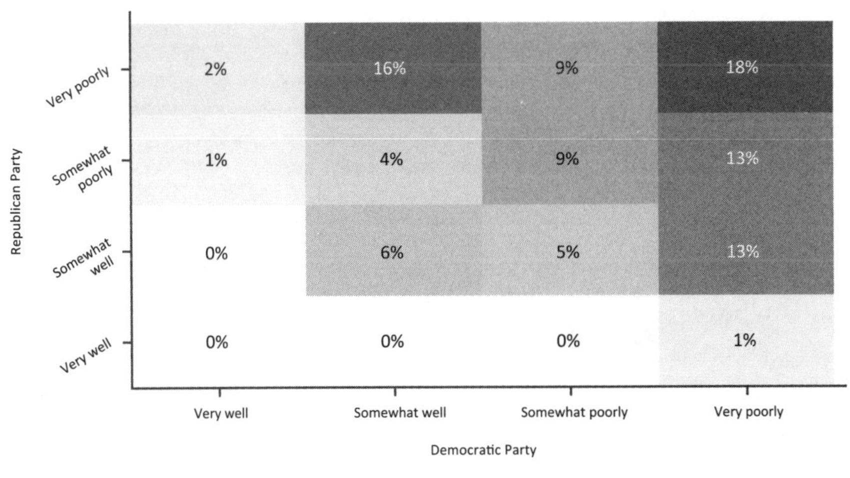

Figure 11.7: How Well Do the Two Parties Represent You? (Independents). *Source*: Authors' computations.

right. In total, 33 percent of Independents see both parties as representing them equally well (just 6 percent) or equally poorly (27 percent). This is consistent with much political science literature on independents, which shows that independents do have a preference and tend to vote like closet partisans (Sides 2014; Klar and Krupnikov 2016). Assuming Independents constitute 40 percent of the overall electorate, that would give us only 12 percent of the electorate that is both self-identified Independent and equivocal between the two parties.

Second, a slight majority of Independents feel poorly represented by both parties. At the same time, adding the four cells in the upper-right quadrant shows that more than half (51 percent) of Independents feel somewhat or very poorly represented by both parties, and 18 percent feel *very* poorly represented by both parties. While this might suggest more support for a third party, Independents are like the broader population in one important respect. Even if they want a third party, they can't agree on what it should stand for. (For a breakdown of third-party positioning by partisanship and by 2016 primary support, see appendix B.)

Among all respondents, 23 percent are equivocal between the two parties, which is hardly the basis for a strong third party. Put another way, 77 percent of Americans feel more represented by one party or the other. About 29 percent of the electorate feels somewhat or poorly represented by

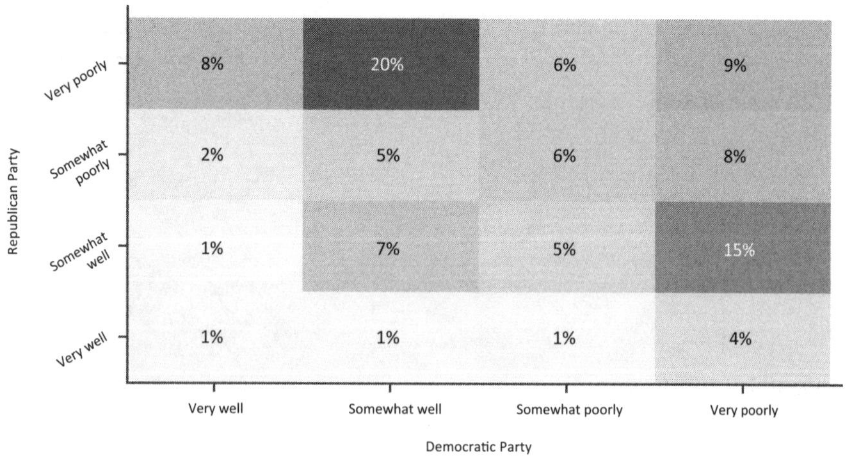

Figure 11.8: How Well Do You Feel Represented by the Parties (All Respondents). *Source*: Authors' computations.

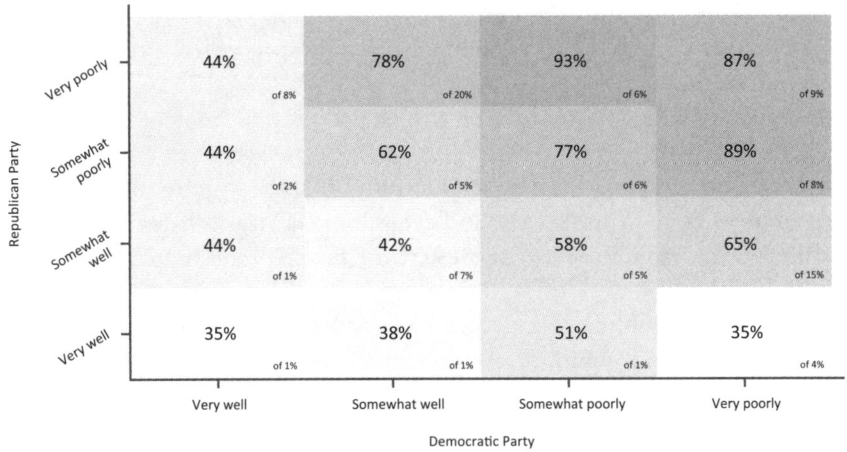

Figure 11.9: Support for a Third Party (by Respondents' Feelings of Representation by the Parties). *Source*: Authors' computations.

both of the two major parties. This is also not enough for a viable third party that's not a spoiler, though it's getting closer—but only if there were agreement on what that third party should stand for.

Feeling unrepresented by the parties does contribute to supporting a third party. Below, we present the same matrix but report the percentage of respondents in each cell who say a third party is needed, and we shade accordingly.

Not surprisingly, the strongest support for a third party comes from those in the upper right-hand quadrant, namely, those who don't feel well-represented by either party.

In terms of support for a third party, there is a difference between feeling very and somewhat well-represented, especially among partisans who feel very unrepresented by the *other* party. Among Democrats who feel very well-represented by their party, and very poorly represented by Republicans (the upper left single cell, 8 percent of respondents), only 44 percent want a third party. But among the 20 percent who feel *somewhat* well-represented by the Democratic Party and very poorly represented by the Republican Party, 78 percent support a third party.

A similar pattern holds among Republicans. The weakest support for a third party is in the lower right-hand corner—the 4 percent of voters who feel *very* well-represented by Republicans and *very* poorly represented by Democrats. Only 35 percent want a third party. But among the 15 percent who feel *somewhat* well-represented by the Republicans but very poorly represented by the Democratic Party, 65 percent support a third party. Thus, there is a difference between feeling very well-represented and somewhat well-represented.

Of course, telling a pollster that a third party is needed is not equivalent to being likely to vote for a third party. Most Americans see a clear difference between the two parties, self-identified partisans generally feel well-represented by their own party, and even the majority of Independents see a difference between the two parties. These facts will not help a third party become truly viable.

Even more forbidding for a third party is the lack of agreement on what a third party should stand for. Americans don't want a third party so much as they want third, fourth, and fifth parties. The emergence of a third party may therefore require electoral reforms that make it easier for third parties to develop without being viewed as "spoilers."

PUBLIC SUPPORT FOR REFORM

The structural reason the United States has two parties is its electoral institutions, specifically the "first-past-the-post" system of single-winner plurality electoral districts, which renders third parties as spoilers, thus discouraging support for and investment in them. Nationalized and presidentialized politics also play an important role in focusing attention on two major parties, and primaries open to all aspirants provide a path for dissenting voices to try to take over a major party rather than form their own. Encouraging third parties would thus require major changes to electoral rules.

One approach is ranked-choice voting, which was just approved by Maine voters for a second time and is used in several cities across the country. In a ranked-choice voting system, voters rank candidates on the ballot in order of preference: first choice, second choice, third choice, and so on. The votes are then tallied as follows: If one candidate has more than 50 percent of the first-place votes, that candidate is the winner. If not, the last-place finisher is eliminated, and those who picked that candidate as first choice get their second-choice selection tabulated. This continues until a single candidate achieves a 50 percent majority. In close elections with many candidates, it can take several rounds. Ranked-choice voting can encourage third parties because it takes away the "spoiler" aspect of third parties. Voters can support a third party sincerely and vote for a major party as a second choice strategically.

As applied to single-winner elections, however, ranked-choice voting would still leave many House seats in very liberal or very conservative districts, so the expansion of third parties would be limited. Opening space for more parties would necessitate combining ranked-choice voting with multimember districts (Farrell and McAllister 2005; Gallagher and Mitchell 2005). This system is known as single transferable vote (STV) and is used in Ireland and to elect the Australian Senate. It also was used in twenty-four American cities up to the middle of the twentieth century, as part of a series of city-government reforms (Santucci 2016). In both Ireland and Australia, two dominant parties consistently garner about 75 percent of the vote, with a handful of smaller parties coming and going (Bowler and Grofman 2000; Amy 2002).[6]

Under STV, candidates are elected in multimember districts. On election day, voters rank the candidates in their preferred order. Like the single-winner ranked-choice voting system, candidates get eliminated from the bottom up, and their supporters have their votes transferred to their second-favorite candidate. The difference is that there are multiple winners, creating some proportionality (Farrell and Katz 2014).[7] Instead of votes being aggregated up until a single candidate gets a majority, all the votes are aggregated up. In a five-member district, the top five finishers (after all votes were redistributed) would go to Congress.

Creating multimember districts with ranked-choice voting would require an act of Congress. Increasing the size of the House would make this politically easier, because individual members would be more likely to retain their seats even as multimember districts are created, and smaller states would get enough representatives to create multimember districts.[8]

The purest version of proportional representation is a party list system such as the Netherlands employs, in which parties choose candidates, and voters choose parties in one nationwide election. Parties get seats in the legislature in direct proportion to how many votes they gather, with very low thresholds.

The VOTER Survey asked about support for multi-member districts, increasing the house size, ranked-choice voting, and the party list system. It also asked about replacing the electoral college with a national popular vote, a reform that has enjoyed much more public discussion.

The questions about multimember districts were framed two ways. One emphasized the benefit of increased competition, while the other emphasized the benefit of better translation of votes-to-seats. While "Don't Know" was the most common response, those who answered the question preferred reform to the status quo.

The questions on ranked-choice voting and party list proportional representation did not emphasize benefits and instead simply described the systems. Support for them was weaker.

Table 11.4: Support for Potential Electoral Reforms by 2018 VOTER Survey Respondents

	Status Quo	Reform	Don't Know
Multimember question 1: *Status quo*: All congressional districts have a single representative, but it is possible for a party to control a majority of seats in the US House while winning less than half of the national votes cast for the US House. *Reform*: Congressional districts are larger and have multiple representatives instead of a single representative, but the percent of US House seats won by each party is closer to its percentage of the national votes cast for the US House.	25%	32%	43%
Multimember question 2: *Status quo*: All congressional districts have a single representative, but most US House elections are not competitive because districts tend to be dominated by voters from one party. *Reform*: Congressional districts are larger and have multiple representatives instead of a single representative, but almost all US House elections are competitive.	23%	38%	39%
House size question: Since 1910, the US House has had 435 members even though the US population has more than tripled since then. Which comes closer to your view? *Status quo*: The House should continue to have 435 members or else it will become too large and hard to manage. *Reform*: The House should increase the number of members so that the ratio of House members to the US population comes closer to what it was before 1910.	42%	32%	26%
Ranked-choice voting question: Here are two ways to elect candidates to office such as the US House of Representatives. Which one do you prefer? *Status quo*: Voters select the single candidate they most prefer. Then the winner is the candidate with the most votes.	60%	23%	18%

Reform: Voters rank candidates on the ballot in their order of preference; the winner is the most popular candidate overall, taking into account voters' second, third, and other choices.			
Party-list/proportional representation question:	52%	17%	31%
Status quo: People elect representatives by voting for individuals rather than for parties. Each party gets the number of seats in the legislature that its individual candidates win, regardless of the percentage of votes cast for that party's candidates overall.			
Reform: People elect representatives by voting for a party rather than for a single individual. Each party receives a percentage of seats in the legislature that is roughly equal to the percentage of the vote that this party received.			
National popular vote question:	33%	51%	16%
Under the Electoral College system used in US presidential elections, two of the last five presidential elections have been won by the candidate who did not receive the most votes nationally. Would you support changing the system to guarantee that the presidential candidate who wins the national popular vote would also win a majority of electoral votes?			
Status quo: Oppose			
Reform: Support			

One question is whether respondents actually understand the implications of these reforms. Are supporters of third parties more likely to support reforms that would allow third parties to flourish? The evidence here suggests that few make the connection.

For one, even respondents who do follow politics closely are not more likely to connect any desire for a third party to support for these reforms. The differences between those who do and do not favor a third party are similar no matter whether respondents reported a higher or lower level of attention to politics.

By contrast, there are much larger differences between Democrats and Republicans, especially among those with higher political interest, suggesting that respondents are seeing these questions more in partisan terms than in reformist terms. Democrats are more willing to change the status quo—

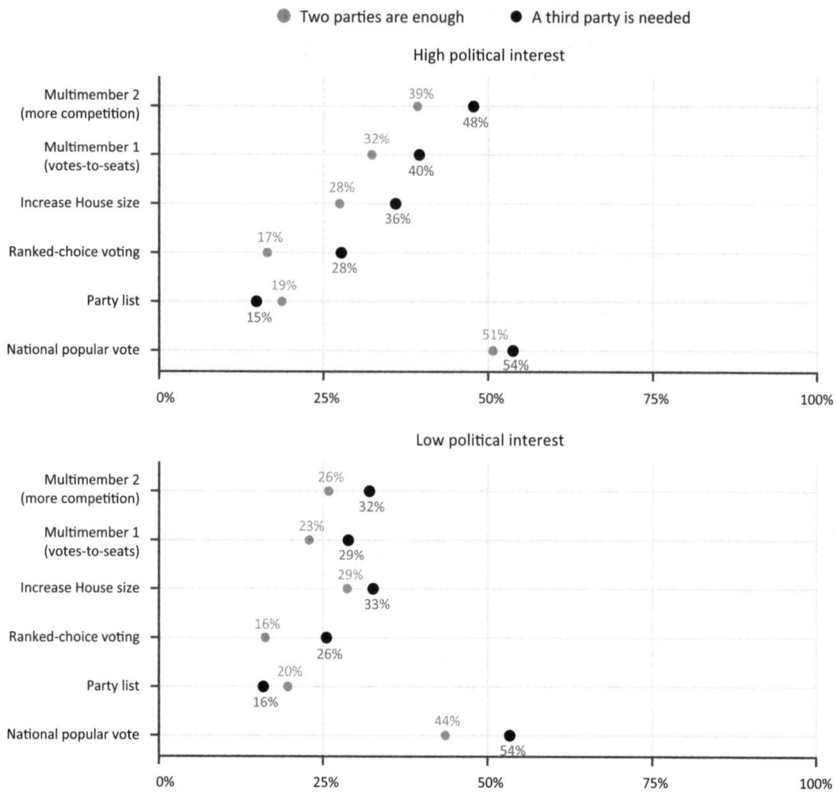

Figure 11.10: Support for Reforms (by Desire for a Third Party). *Source*: Authors' computations.

perhaps because the status quo appears to benefit Republicans, or perhaps because Democrats tend to be more willing to undertake reforms generally.[9]

We suspect that had the reforms been framed in terms of making it easier for third parties to compete, they would have been more popular, and other recent polling suggests that this is indeed the case. When respondents are given more extensive pro-con arguments for both reforms and when pro arguments involve making space for third parties, they became more supportive of these reforms (Voice of the People and University of Maryland's Program for Public Consultation, 2018). Overall, 55 percent of respondents (and 64 percent of Democrats) supported ranked-choice voting after hearing a case for it that explained how it can prevent spoilers and encourage third-party candidates. Similarly, 55 percent of respondents (and 66 percent of Democrats) supported multi-member districts after

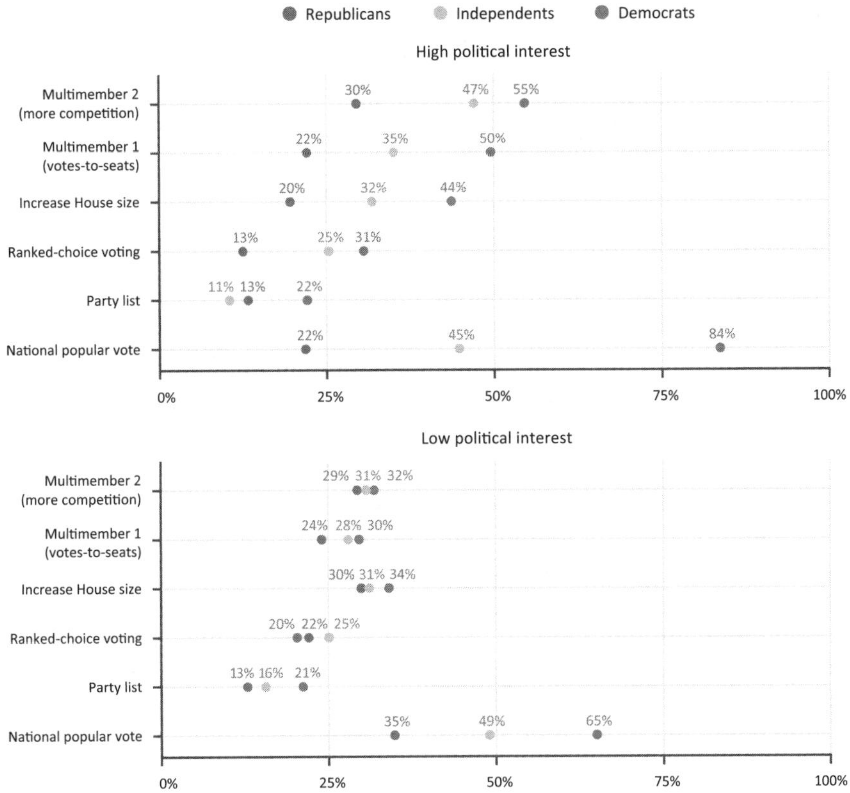

Figure 11.11: Support for Reforms (by Political Interest and Partisan Affiliation). *Source*: Authors' computations.

reading a more detailed explanation of how a single-transferable-vote system could work in multi-member districts (Voice of the People and University of Maryland's Program for Public Consultation 2018).

But absent a polling question that makes the connection, few respondents make the connection themselves. These results suggest that reformers have considerable work to do if they are to convert widespread support for a third party into support for a reform that would make it easier for third parties to gain traction.

IMPLICATIONS FOR FUTURE ELECTIONS

The quadrennial excitement about the possibility of a breakthrough third party candidate is likely to continue in future election cycles. After all, as decades of polling data show, majorities of Americans would like there to be a third party. But as decades of experience show, it's almost impossible for a single third party to break through in American politics.

The VOTER Survey data have something for the boosters but much more for the skeptics. The 68 percent of Americans who want a third party is suggestive of a widespread desire to transcend the current binary competition. And there is also *some* dissatisfaction with representation by the existing two parties, though this is nothing new.

But the weight of the data is on the side of the skeptics. Desire for a third party does not translate into support for a single third party but rather for multiple parties. No hypothetical party would be more popular than either the Democrats or the Republicans in its policy positions. Likewise, partisans mostly feel well-represented by their parties and see clear differences between the two parties.

For a third party to gain traction in the existing electoral system, a plurality of voters would have to feel *equally* unrepresented by both parties and have similar enough political preferences to unite behind a third party. This is currently not the case.

This doesn't mean things will always be this way, however. The historical record suggests at least two ways in which a third party could emerge.

The first would be a new issue that cuts across the existing parties, splitting them in ways that cause their downfall. This is how the Republican Party emerged in the 1850s. As westward expansion forced the slavery issue to center stage, the Whig Party couldn't hold together its Northern and Southern wings. The Republicans united Northern Whigs, some Northern Democrats, and a few smaller parties into a new party and won the 1860 election with 39 percent of the popular vote when Democrats also split, nominating separate Northern and Southern candidates. It would take a similar scenario for a third party to break through at the national presidential level.

The second possibility is for a popular movement for electoral reform to catch on and for elected politicians to support electoral reforms like ranked-choice voting or single transferable vote. Perhaps the introduction of ranked-choice voting in Maine will spark more movement in this direction. While history is full of examples of democracies that *have* changed their electoral systems—New Zealand, Israel, Italy, and Japan have recently done so—it takes a rare combination of popular discontent with the electoral system and political entrepreneurs who see reform as in their own interest to make change happen.

The VOTER Survey provides no basis for concluding that either of these scenarios is imminent.

OUR INDIVIDUAL VIEWS ON THE MERITS OF A MULTIPARTY SYSTEM

Although the evidence we have presented and analyzed sheds new light on Americans' views about third parties and the reforms that would be needed to facilitate their emergence, it leaves the core normative question unanswered: Should we move away from our long-standing two-party duopoly toward some kind of multiparty system?

As it happens, the authors of this study do not entirely agree about the answer or even about the best way of approaching it. Rather than presenting a bland statement of our lowest common denominator, we decided to conclude with three summary statements of our individual views on these matters.

Lee Drutman

The descriptive data presented here raise several normative and interpretative questions: If broad majorities of Americans say they want more than two parties, does that mean that Americans would be happier and better represented in a multiparty democracy? Or is this just idle frustration with the status quo? After all, Americans are not voting for third parties and do not show wide support for structural reforms that would make it easier for more parties to thrive. How should we reconcile these contrasting and somewhat contradictory impulses? Should American democracy have *more parties?*

Historically, few serious third-party candidates have run in the first place, and the media mostly treats third-party candidates as curiosities and spoilers rather than as serious contenders. The vast majority of resources and ambitious politicians go into the two major parties. The only "serious" third-party candidate in modern American politics was H. Ross Perot, who won 19 percent of the popular vote in 1992, though not a single state. Perot was treated as a serious candidate largely because he was able to self-fund, buying himself enough attention.

Perot's relative success in 1992, however, also depended on another condition: Americans were simultaneously growing distrustful of the two major parties *and* didn't see much of a difference between the two parties. In 1992, almost half of voters (49 percent) saw no difference between the two major parties in their ability to solve pressing problems. And 40 percent did not see *any policy differences* between the two major parties (Gold 1995).

In other words, in 1992, many Americans didn't care whether a Democrat or a Republican was in the White House; they thought both parties were equally rotten. Casting a vote for Perot, then, not only required that Perot was seen as a serious candidate but also that the voter did not care whether George H. W. Bush or Bill Clinton became president. Since 2000, as the two parties have become much more distinct and separate political coalitions, voters have developed much clearer preferences on which party they want in power. Even if they are not always enthusiastic about the party for which they vote, they are deeply fearful of the *other* party winning (Abramowitz 2018). Indeed, our data bear this out: more than three-quarters of Americans feel better represented by one party or the other.

Political distrust in America has been scraping rock-bottom now for a decade, returning to the nadir it also hit in the 1990s. But unlike in the 1990s, Americans now see a sharp difference between the two parties. Voters understand the stakes of elections, and even if they say they want more parties, they are not willing to risk spoiling an election to get them. Ambitious politicians understand this and so seek major-party nominations.

And yet, there *is* a third party in America that has outperformed Republicans and Democrats in every election for more than a century. It is the party of nonvoters. Consistently, between 40 and 50 percent of eligible adults have stayed home, while only between one-quarter and one-third of voters have supported Democrats or Republicans.

By global standards, Americans are uniquely disengaged in the democratic process, with American voter turnout consistently at the bottom of advanced industrial democracies (DeSilver 2018). As a general rule, countries with more parties have higher turnout, both because more parties competing for votes means more parties recruiting voters to the polls and because of a greater likelihood that voters will find a party that they feel represents them well enough to justify voting (Cancela and Geys 2016; Geys 2006). Additionally, countries with more parties tend to have proportional representation, which makes every vote equally important. The American winner-takes-all system generates a preponderance of lopsided safe seats, where votes don't matter, further discouraging voters.

If Americans wanted *more* parties, the obvious solution, then, would be to support proportional representation with multimember districts. Such electoral systems are common in advanced democracies. By faithfully translating vote shares into seat shares in larger districts, they remove the wasted-vote "spoiler effect" of winner-takes-all elections, making it possible for more parties to compete. Surely, if Americans truly wanted more parties, they should support proportional representation! Yet, this link is arcane to most Americans.

Which brings us to the final question: are Americans truly serious in their desire for more parties? Two-thirds support is historically high. The historic trend lines match with other measures of disaffection and rising disaffiliation with major political parties. Whatever these numbers reflect, they correspond to a frustration with the status quo and a sense that the two-party system is indeed broken.

Americans are right to be frustrated and to demand more parties. The comparative record shows that multiparty democracies are more stable (Colomer 2012). They represent diverse interests better (Canon 1999). Policy corresponds more closely to the median voter (Powell 2000; Kim and Fording 2010). Economic inequality is lower. Parties are stronger. Voter turnout is higher (Selb 2009). Compromise is more valued. Citizens who live in them are happier and more satisfied with the state of democracy (Altman, Flavin, and Radcliff 2017).

At the very least, when two-thirds of citizens say they want more choices, we should listen. The current level of disaffection and distrust with the status quo are fundamentally destabilizing. Structural reforms are needed.

Tod Lindberg

When we started looking into the question of potential support for a third party, my baseline presumption was that because other polls had already shown rising levels of public support for the idea, its time might be coming.

The anecdotal context giving rise to this presumption was the perceived deep polarization in American politics, with social media-driven partisan rancor running at very high levels and President Trump as polarizer-in-chief. With the two major parties increasingly inclined to cater to the most fervid ideological portion of their base, yet with each such fervid base representing a rather small share of the electorate—8 percent of the electorate on the "progressive activist" side and 6 percent on the "devoted conservatives" side, according to one recent typology—wouldn't many people favor a middle course should the possibility arise in the form of a third party (Hare and Poole 2014; Hawkins et al. 2018)? Moreover, the credible danger that the emergence of a third party might pose to the two major parties could in principle act to limit the extreme partisanship and ideological polarization of the two majors: the party most disconnected from the center of the electorate would risk losing the most voters to a centrist third party.

And yet polarization (or perhaps better, party "sorting") is not new, even if it is increasing (Levendusky 2009). The process has spanned decades. If the incentive structure I have just sketched was truly in operation, shouldn't there have been a third party by now? Or at least, shouldn't the possibility of a serious third-party bid for the presidency have emerged as something more than the whim of self-financing billionaires?

Our chapter demonstrates why my initial presumption was off the mark. Yes, of course, *some* Americans would like a centrist alternative, just as *some* would prefer that their current party of choice be oriented more toward the center on some issues. But not enough. And largely missing from the discussion has been the genuine sentiment among liberal Democrats for a third (or fourth) party farther to the left of mainstream Democratic views and the sentiment of conservative Republicans for a third (fifth?) party farther to the right than mainstream GOP views.

The notion of a viable third-party candidate, let alone a viable and institutionalized third party, currently seems to be little more than a dream. What would have to change to create such third-party viability? Some propose electoral reform. Yet as our chapter also indicates, knowledge about possible reform measures is low, even among people who say they would favor reforms. We seem to be a long way from the adoption of reforms that would allow for the emergence of a third party.

Perhaps the establishment of a third party awaits only a political leader of sufficient charisma to found one. Here, the puzzle is why a leader possessing such charisma and desire for the highest public office would take the third-party route rather than seek the nomination of one of the two major parties. The Donald Trump example—from private citizen to president-elect in less than eighteen months—would seem to point in that direction.

Or perhaps some pressing issue will emerge to which neither of the two major parties will present an adequate answer. In Europe, fear of immigration seems to be such an issue—but then European parliamentary systems are generally multiparty in design.

It is famously the case that the US Constitution is silent on political parties and that the case for the Constitution outlined by Alexander Hamilton, James Madison, and John Jay in the *Federalist* likewise fails to anticipate the dominant role parties would play in American politics. Because of this failure—if, indeed, "failure" is the right word—they made no attempt to set constitutional strictures on the operation of political parties. In this respect, the establishment of political parties and their evolution over time can be construed as almost organic: the limitations imposed by the US Constitution plus the desire on the part of individuals to band together for the purpose of winning elections equals American politics.

It is not that the two-party character of American politics could not be anything other than what it is. But there are indeed compelling reasons why American politics is as it is. In this sense, what's rational is actual and what's actual is rational. From this vantage, a perspective I would describe as "critical political realism," we probably need to confront the prospect that the politics we have makes perfect sense in light of US constitutional strictures and human desire.

Parties, of course, used to encompass a variety of contradictory policy preferences, and at that time, perhaps, a strictly formal definition of political parties was apposite: a group that bands together to elect a slate of candidates to office. Post-"sorting" in the United States, however, one may reasonably speak of the substantive policy preferences of each party, not only in their own terms but in opposition to each other. It's possible that the falling away of substantive intraparty disagreements suggests that such points of division as the authors of the *Federalist* did discourse upon—faction, region, "opposite and rival interest," and so on—were mere placeholders. They were precursors for the sorting to come, which has produced an alignment of the two parties around the two (and only two) poles that shape contemporary democratic politics: the desire for equality that Democrats express so well and the desire for freedom that Republicans take as their touchstone.

Our politics will likely remain rancorous until each recognizes the other has a point.

Bill Galston

Our findings make it clear that Americans want—or to be precise, *say* they want—more than the two parties currently on offer. But contrary to the hopes of moderate reformers eager to heal today's polarized political system, Americans do not agree on the ideological orientation their preferred new party should espouse. Yes, some want a new party of the center. But large numbers also advocate new parties to the left of the Democrats and to the right of the Republicans. If the people had their way, the United States would have multiple parties along a spectrum as wide as in most European parliamentary systems.

Would this be a good thing? If so, good for what? I put the question in this form because hardly anyone thinks that political parties are ends in themselves. They exist to perform certain functions within constitutional democracies. If multiparty systems do this better than two-party systems, then there is a predicate (although not a decisive argument) for reforms that would move the United States toward additional parties.

We encounter an immediate difficulty: if parties are supposed to accomplish a range of functions, it is entirely possible that increasing the number of parties would improve the performance of the party system along some dimensions while worsening it along others.

And this is in fact the case. The more parties, the better the fit between each party and those who support it. In the most perfectly "representative" system, each citizen would be a party of one, with no need to compromise his or her views. But this is the reductio ad absurdum of the norm of representation, which in principle means that the represented somehow authorize representatives to speak on their behalf. A direct democracy might have factions, but it would not have parties.

Otherwise put, parties achieve representation through the aggregation of multiple individuals whose beliefs and objectives, though not identical, are in their view similar enough to warrant common action and make it possible. The representation parties give each individual member will be imperfect at best. When some come to see the gap between the party's stance and their own as unendurably wide, they may leave as individuals or, if the disagreement is along a single axis, they may act as a group to split the party.

This points to another tension. Parties do more than represent views; they serve as vehicles for attaining and exercising power. As parties in democracies become larger (which usually means more diverse), they become simultaneously more powerful and less representative, in that more members will have to coexist with, and perhaps even accept as the sentiments of their party's majority, positions with which they disagree.

There is no formula that tells us when the policy or moral costs of pursuing power in a diverse party coalition will come to be felt as unbearable. But history suggests that as parties change over time, many partisans will eventually face this question. Longtime Republicans who cannot accept President Trump's policies and conduct must choose between fighting to reclaim their party (with what appear to be scant prospects of success), joining forces with the Democrats, accepting political homelessness, or starting a new party. Their choice would be easier if a more traditional center-right party already existed, as is the case in most European countries that have experienced populist uprisings.

In times of political discontinuity, a two-party system makes divisive intraparty struggles all but inevitable. In 1952, Dwight Eisenhower asserted, and Robert Taft denied, that the Republican Party should make its peace with the New Deal. Eisenhower's victory redefined his party for decades. It also generated an unreconciled minority, helped spark the Goldwater insurgency, and eventually led to the overthrow of the Republican establishment in 1980.

In a multiparty system, these contending forces probably would have gone their separate ways in 1952. In a two-party system, however, a split in one party means victory for the other. In 1908, Republican William Howard Taft received 52 percent of the popular vote compared to 43 percent for Democrat William Jennings Bryan. In 1912, the Democratic nominee did a bit worse than Bryan had, garnering only 42 percent. But because Taft and Theodore Roosevelt split the Republicans' 52 percent of the vote almost evenly, Woodrow Wilson was elected and used the powers of incumbency to gain reelection four years later. Eight years in the political wilderness is a sobering price to pay for splitting a party to improve its fit with your faction's views.

Is it better to facilitate party exits, as multiparty systems do, or to impede them, as a two-party system does? I do not think that this question admits of a general answer. On the one hand, our system offers incentives to negotiate differences within a shared partisan framework, promoting what might be called the parties' integrative function. On the other hand, it forces members to choose between morally distasteful party stances and political irrelevance. If the Democratic Party had not begun moving toward civil rights in 1948, it might have been the Northern liberals who felt compelled to leave, not the Dixiecrats. Where would they have gone? And wouldn't their departure have left the field to their adversaries?

As we have learned over the past century, America's two-party system functions well in two very different contexts—when one party enjoys substantial and sustained dominance over the other (1933–1952, for example) and when the two parties are competitive but internally heterogeneous (1953–1980), guaranteeing a substantial overlap between them. By contrast, our system functions poorly when, as at present, our parties are both competitive and internally homogenous, with few areas of common ground across party lines. Because they are narrowly divided numerically, neither party can impose its agenda on the other. But because they are deeply divided substantively, they find it difficult to compromise across party lines. Party competition pulls in one direction, the imperatives of effective governance in the other. The result is policy stagnation coupled with public disaffection.

In circumstances like today's, it is tempting to believe that institutional change—such as moving toward multipartyism—is bound to be for the better. But as we have learned repeatedly, institutional reforms produce unanticipated consequences. We should proceed cautiously to examine the building blocks of multiparty systems, making full use of the flexibility inherent in America's federalism. Maine's experiment with ranked-choice voting bears watching. Congress should remove its prohibition on multimember districts, allowing states to test a range of procedures, including proportional representation and "bullet voting," when individual voters may bunch votes for a single candidate up to the number of their district's representatives.

Experimentation could conceivably build public support for a single set of national reforms. More likely, it would yield a patchwork quilt of electoral procedures, all well within the Constitution's guarantee to each state of a "Republican Form of Government." In a politically diverse continental nation, such a patchwork may be the closest approach to representation that our circumstances will permit.

APPENDIX A: IDEOLOGY AND PARTISANSHIP

Combining ideology *and* partisanship shows a more complex matrix with regard to support for a third party. Shading represents frequency in the overall population. Not surprisingly, independent moderates overwhelmingly want a third party.

As before, partisan asymmetries show up. Fifty percent of conservative/strong Republicans are satisfied with the two-party system, which is to say that even in the most satisfied group, half are *not* satisfied.

By contrast, 58 percent of liberal/strong Democrats want a third party, and 64 percent of very liberal/strong Democrats want a third party. The strongest support for a third party comes from those who call themselves "very liberal" and consider themselves weakly affiliated with the Democratic Party. Given the high support for a third party among Sanders voters, this is not surprising. But as the shading indicates, these voters are not numerous. Party affiliation and ideology are closely correlated, producing the darker squares along the diagonal from very liberal/strong Democrat to very conservative/strong Republican. Consider, however, the six lighter squares in the corners opposite the dominant ideological/party distribution—those represented by conservative Democrat-leaning voters and liberal Republican-leaning voters. The latter, in the lower right, are vanishingly small in terms of overall respondents. The former, in the upper left, are more numerous, with most falling in the cell for "conservative" and "not very strong" Democrat. Their support for a third-party candidate, at 66 percent, is about the same as the support of very liberal/strong Democrats for a third party (64 percent). Support for a third party among strong Democrats is weakest

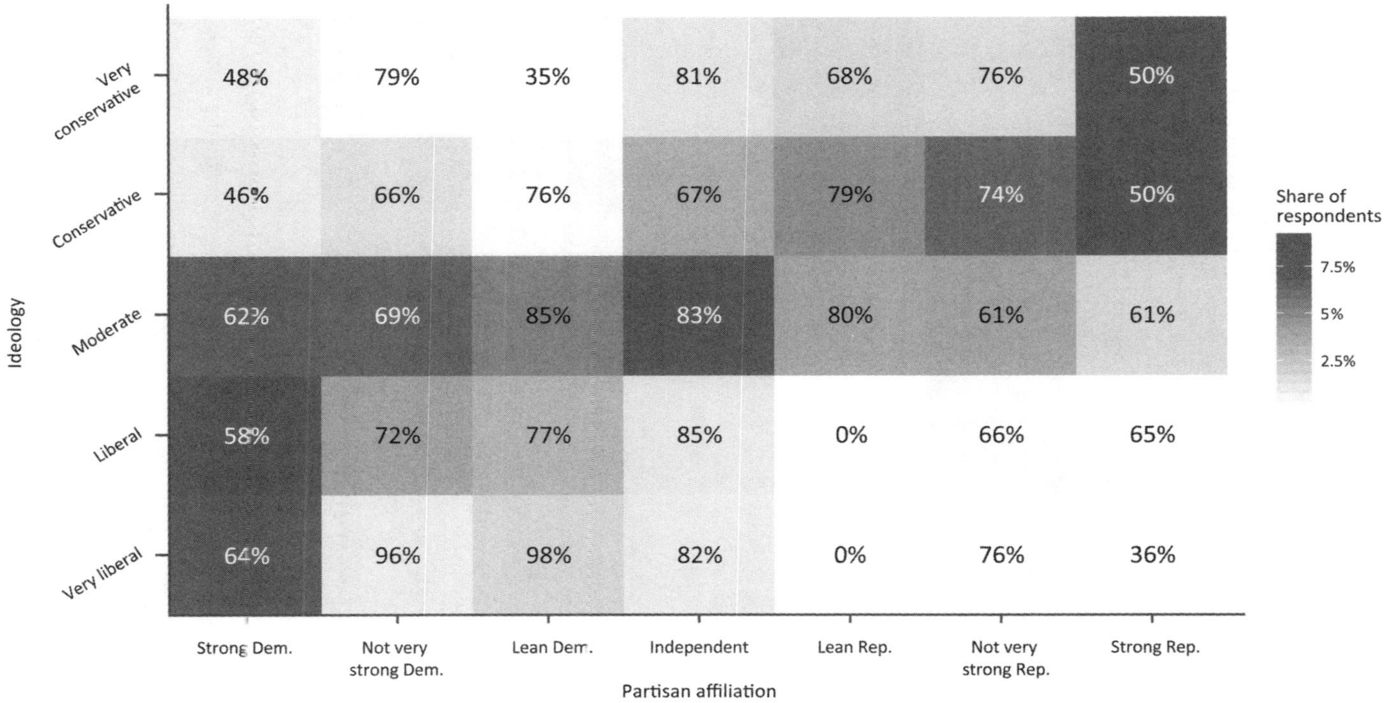

Figure 11.12: Support for a Third Party by Ideology and Partisan Affiliation. *Source*: Authors' computations.

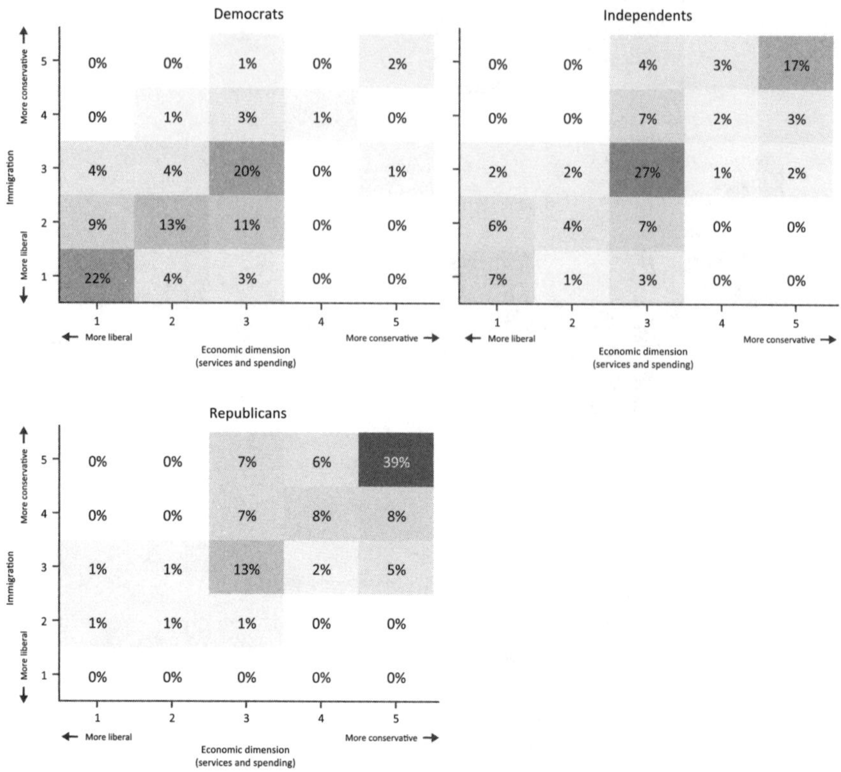

Figure 11.13: Where Should a Third Party Locate (by Partisan Affiliation). *Source:* Authors' computations.

among those who describe themselves as "conservative" or "very conservative"—a small but not trivial number of voters.

APPENDIX B: MORE ON WHERE A THIRD PARTY SHOULD LOCATE

Figure 11.13 shows the kinds of third parties that partisan subgroups would like to see, limiting the sample to those who actually want a third party. Almost 40 percent of Republicans who want a third party want it more conservative on both economic and immigration dimensions—about three times as many as those who would like a more centrist party. Democrats, on the other hand, are almost equally divided between those who would prefer a more centrist third party (20 percent) and those who are seeking a more liberal alternative (22 percent). Among independents, the largest group (27 percent) would prefer a more centrist third party, but a

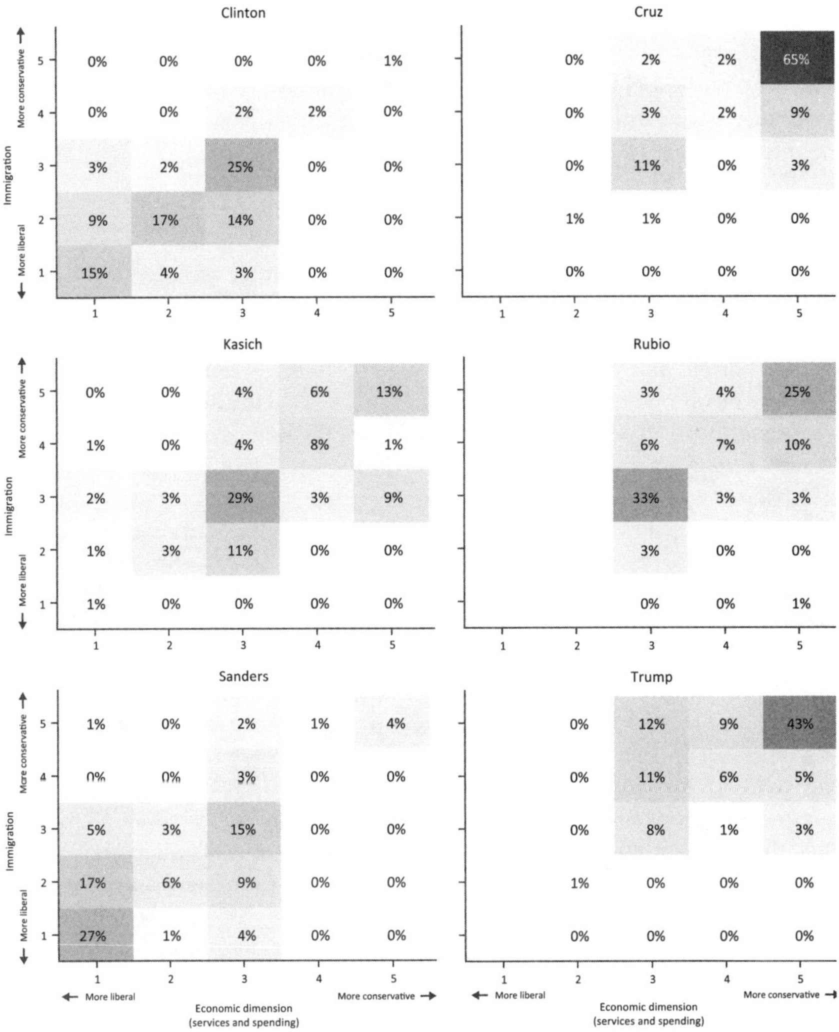

Figure 11.14: Where Should a Third Party Locate (by 2016 Primary Vote). *Source:* Authors' computations.

significant minority, 17 percent, want a more conservative third party. Few independents are seeking a more liberal alternative in a third party. Note: percentages for a question may not add up to 100 percent exactly due to rounding.

Figure 11.14 further breaks down respondents by whom they supported in the primaries. A party of the far left would appeal to Sanders supporters and some Clinton supporters. A party of the middle would appeal most to Clinton, Kasich, and Rubio supporters. A party of the far right would appeal to Trump and especially Cruz supporters. If there were a party moderate on economic issues and conservative on social issues, it might pull in some Trump supporters.

NOTES

1. Smaller numbers who say they want a third party either describe their desired party in ways that reflect the existing Democratic or Republican Party, or they describe a desired third party that blends Republican and Democratic positions, defying our ability to plot their preference on a simple liberal-to-conservative spectrum.

2. The survey question we asked was: "In your view, do the Republican and Democratic parties do an adequate job of representing the American people, or do they do such a poor job that a third major party is needed?" This is the same question Gallup has been asking since 2003.

3. Both Gallup and the VOTER Survey asked the question: "In your view, do the Republican and Democratic parties do an adequate job of representing the American people, or do they do such a poor job that a third major party is needed?" Pew Research Center asked a different variation: "Some people say we should have a third major political party in this country in addition to the Democrats and Republicans. Do you agree or disagree?"

4. Leaners are those who do not self-identify as partisans but vote as partisans.

5. Specifically, the 2018 VOTER Survey asked: "If you were to vote for a new third party, where would you like it to stand on economic issues—like how much the government spends and how many services it provides?" and "If you were to vote for a new third party, where would you like it to stand on the issue of immigration?" The VOTER Survey also asked about support for a third party on "social and cultural issues—like abortion and same-sex marriage?" Attitudes on this question were closely correlated with attitudes on the immigration questions, so including this dimension within the analysis did not add enough insight to justify the added complexity.

6. Third-party wins were rare and fleeting. Only in New York City, which used STV from 1937 to 1947, was there a persistently multiparty system. Even there, however, Democrats won a seat majority in all but the first STV election.

7. Instead of votes being aggregated up until a single candidate gets a majority, votes are aggregated to quotas. The quota is the number of votes a candidate needs to win a seat. As the number of seats in a district goes up, the size of the quota goes down. In a five-member district, for example, each winning candidate would need about 17 percent of votes—whether those were first-choice votes cast for that candidate, votes they got from eliminated candidates, or votes they got from other winners who had more votes than a quota. When voters of a certain party restrict their rankings to candidates of that party, the logic of quotas is how STV produces seats-to-votes proportionality.

8. Multimember districts were widely used in the United States prior to 1842, when the Whigs mandated single-member districts in an (unsuccessful) attempt to stave off midterm losses. However, the early multimember districting scheme allowed voters to choose a slate of candidates equivalent in size to the number of seats. This almost always meant one-party congressional delegations. This is not proportional representation, and it is very different from the single transferable vote system, which gives individual voters only one vote, albeit a transferable one. In 1967, Congress passed the Uniform Congressional Districting Act, which was intended to prevent Southern states from using the block vote to disenfranchise black people as a response to the Voting Rights Act and one-person, one-vote Supreme Court cases.

9. Among Democrats, those who supported Sanders are more supportive of these reforms than those who supported Clinton. Among Republicans, Kasich supporters are the most supportive of reforms.

REFERENCES

Abramowitz, Alan I. *The Great Alignment: Race, Party Transformation, and the Rise of Donald Trump.* New Haven, CT: Yale University Press, 2018.

Altman, David, Patrick Flavin, and Benjamin Radcliff. "Democratic Institutions and Subjective Well-Being." *Political Studies* 65, no. 3 (October 2017): 685–704. https://doi.org/10.1177/0032321716683203.

Amy, Douglas J. *Real Choices/New Voices: How Proportional Representation Elections Could Revitalize American Democracy.* New York: Columbia University Press, 2002.

Bowler, Shaun, and Bernard Grofman. *Elections in Australia, Ireland, and Malta under the Single Transferable Vote: Reflections on an Embedded Institution.* Ann Arbor: University of Michigan Press, 2000.

Cancela, João, and Benny Geys. "Explaining Voter Turnout: A Meta-Analysis of National and Subnational Elections." *Electoral Studies* 42 (June 2016): 264–275. https://doi.org/10.1016/j.electstud.2016.03.005.

Canon, David T. "Electoral Systems and the Representation of Minority Interests in Legislatures." *Legislative Studies Quarterly* 24, no. 3 (August 1999): 331–385.

Colomer, Josep M. "The More Parties, the Greater Policy Stability." *European Political Science* 11, no. 2 (June 2012): 229–243. https://doi.org/10.1057/eps.2011.34.

Converse, Philip E. "The Nature of Belief Systems in Mass Publics." In *Ideology and Discontent,* ed. David E. Apter, 206–261. New York: Free Press of Glencoe, 1964.

DeSilver, Drew. "US Trails most Developed Countries in Voter Turnout." *Pew Research Center.* May 21, 2018. https://www.pewresearch.org/fact-tank/2018/05/21/u-s-voter-turnout-trails-most-developed-countries/.

Diamond, Larry. "A Victory for Democratic Reform." *American Interest.* June 15, 2018. https://www.the-american-interest.com/2018/06/15/a-victory-for-democratic-reform/.

Ellis, Christopher, and James A. Stimson. *Ideology in America.* New York: Cambridge University Press, 2012.

Farrell, David M., and Richard S. Katz. "Assessing the Proportionality of the Single Transferrable Vote." *Journal of Representative Democracy* 50, no. 1 (May 2014): 13–26. https://doi.org/10.1080/00344893.2014.902212.

Farrell, David M., and Ian McAllister. "Australia: The Alternative Vote in a Compliant Political Culture." In *The Politics of Electoral Systems,* ed. Michael Gallagher and Paul Mitchell, 79–98. New York: Oxford University Press, 2005.

Free, Lloyd A., and Hadley Cantril. *The Political Beliefs of Americans: A Study of Public Opinion.* New Brunswick: Rutgers University Press, 1967.

Gallagher, Michael. "Ireland: The Discreet Charm of PR-STV." In *The Politics of Electoral Systems,* ed. Michael Gallagher and Paul Mitchell, 511–532. New York: Oxford University Press, 2005.

Geys, Benny. "Explaining Voter Turnout: A Review of Aggregate-Level Research." *Electoral Studies* 25, no. 4 (December 2006): 637–663. https://doi.org/10.1016/j.electstud.2005.09.002.

Gold, Howard J. "Third Party Voting in Presidential Elections: A Study of Perot, Anderson, and Wallace." *Political Research Quarterly* 48, no. 4 (December 1995): 751–773. https://doi.org/10.1177/106591299504800405.

Grossmann, Matt, and David A. Hopkins. *Asymmetric Politics: Ideological Republicans and Group Interest Democrats.* New York: Oxford University Press, 2016.

Hare, Christopher, and Keith T. Poole. "The Polarization of Contemporary American Politics." *Polity* 46, no. 3 (July 2014): 411–429. https://doi.org/10.1057/pol.2014.10.

Hawkins, Stephen, Daniel Yudkin, Míriam Juan-Torres, and Tim Dixon. "Hidden Tribes: A Study of America's Polarized Landscape." 2018. Accessed February 12, 2020. https://hiddentribes.us/pdf/hidden_tribes_report.pdf.

Kim, Heemin, Bingham Powell Jr., and Richard C. Fording. "Electoral Systems, Party Systems, and Ideological Representation: An Analysis of Distortion in Western Democracies." *Comparative Politics* 42, no. 2 (January 2010): 167–185.

Kinder, Donald R., and Nathan P. Kalmoe. *Neither Liberal nor Conservative: Ideological Innocence in the American Public.* Chicago: University of Chicago Press, 2017.

Klar, Samara, and Yanna Krupnikov. *Independent Politics: How American Disdain for Parties Leads to Political Inaction.* New York: Cambridge University Press, 2016.

Klein, Ezra. "Why Did the 2016 Election Look so Much Like the 2012 election?" *Vox.* June 5, 2017. https://www.vox.com/policy-and-politics/2017/6/5/15161442/2016-election-normalcy-democracy-realists-identity.

Levendusky, Matthew. *The Partisan Sort: How Liberals Become Democrats and Conservatives Become Republicans.* Chicago: University of Chicago Press, 2009.

"Party Affiliation." Gallup, accessed February 12, 2020, https://news.gallup.com/poll/15370/partyaffiliation.aspx.

Powell, G. Bingham, Jr. *Elections as Instruments of Democracy: Majoritarian and Proportional Visions.* New Haven, CT: Yale University Press, 2000.

Saad, Lydia. "Perceived Need for Third Major Party Remains High in US." Gallup, September 27, 2017. https://news.gallup.com/poll/219953/perceived-need-third-major-party-remains-high.aspx.

Santucci, Jack. "Party Splits, Not Progressives: The Origins of Proportional Representation in American Local Government." *American Politics Research* 45, no. 3 (November 2016): 494–526. https://doi.org/10.1177/1532673X16674774.

Selb, Peter. "A Deeper Look at the Proportionality-Turnout Nexus." *Comparative Political Studies* 42, no. 4 (April 2009): 527–548. https://doi.org/10.1177/0010414008327427.

Sides, John. "Most Political Independents Actually Aren't." *Washington Post.* January 8, 2014. https://www.washingtonpost.com/news/monkey-cage/wp/2014/01/08/most-political-independents-actually-arent/.

Tamas, Bernard. *The Demise and Rebirth of American Third Parties: Poised for Political Revival?* New York: Routledge, 2018.

Vavreck, Lynn. "The Ways That the 2016 Election Was Perfectly Normal." *New York Times.* May 1, 2017. https://www.nytimes.com/2017/05/01/upshot/the-ways-that-the-2016-election-was-perfectly-normal.html.

Voice of the People. "Public Supports Reforming How Members of Congress are Elected." Published April 12, 2018. http://vop.org/public-supports-reforming-how-members-of-congress-are-elected/.

Voice of the People and University of Maryland's Program for Public Consultation. "Government Reform: Ranked Choice Voting, Redistributing by Citizen Commission and Multi-Member Districts." Accessed February 12, 2020. http:// vop.org/wpcontent/uploads/2018/04/Elections_Redistricting_Slides041218.pdf.

PART FIVE

Donald Trump and the Evolution of American Politics

CHAPTER 12

Our "Undivided Support": Donald Trump, the Republican Party, and Executive-Centered Partisanship

Nicholas F. Jacobs and Sidney M. Milkis

Three years into the presidency of an iconoclastic businessman and bombastic reality television celebrity, the Republican Party has become the party of Trump.

Few scholars or pundits anticipated that an outsider, with no government experience, would so quickly and thoroughly rout the Republican establishment. Yet the evidence is difficult to deny. Eighty-nine percent of Republicans approve of President Trump's performance in office; indeed, his approval rating among GOP loyalists has been unwavering since he was anointed the party's standard bearer (Gallup 2019). The ranks of the "Never Trump" Republicans have thinned considerably; and the intellectual bulwark against Trump's "America First" conservativism, the *Weekly Standard*, closed shop following the 2018 midterm elections. Even after losing forty seats and control of the House during those elections, the Republican National Committee (2019) pledged its "undivided support" for the president nearly two years before Election Day—signifying an unprecedented merger between a president's reelection committee and the national party apparatus. Many of Trump's most ardent critics, including Senators Bob Corker (R-TN) and Jeff Flake (R-AZ), chose to resign rather than face hostile primary challenges from the wing of their party that displays staunch allegiance to the White House. Other former adversaries within the GOP have softened their tone. Senator Lindsey Graham (R-SC), who once labeled Trump the "the world's biggest jackass" and openly admonished the fact that "my party has gone batshit crazy," put a fine point on the Republican Party's new reality: "If we undercut the president, that's the end of his presidency and the end of our party, and we deserve to be punished if we give in now" (Hannity 2019; McCormack 2018).

As remarkable as Trump's domination of the Republican Party might seem, we argue that his conquest fits a pattern endemic to the modern presidency. Although there are many features of the Trump presidency that are novel, the president's partisan politics marks the culmination of a century-long development in American politics: the rise of an "executive-centered partisanship," with Democrats and Republicans alike relying on presidents and presidential candidates to pronounce party doctrine, raise campaign funds, campaign on behalf of their partisan brethren, mobilize grassroots support, and advance party programs (Milkis and Jacobs 2017; Milkis, Rhodes, and Charnock 2012).

Clearly, many actions taken during the first term of the Trump administration have not been deliberate and seem to exist outside the normal working arrangements of executive politics and party leadership. Nevertheless, as the stark partisan divide of the House impeachment and Senate trial of Trump highlights, amid all the travails and self-inflicted controversies, the president's support among Republicans has never faded. So, while it is tempting to focus on the never-ending tales of palace intrigue that constantly stream from the White House, a more challenging charge is to discern why Trump has maintained the loyalty of his party.

By placing Trump's relationship with the Republican Party in historical context, this chapter casts light on the causes and symptoms of presidential partisanship, which have come into full view since the 2016 election. From this perspective, Donald Trump is not an anomaly. In the hope of making good on campaign promises and succeeding at the ballot box, Republicans have embraced their president's aggressive use of administrative power, which has been a critical tool in forging a primordial relationship with the party's base. Moreover, building on, and even surpassing, his Republican predecessors, Trump has leveraged his atavistic connection to the GOP's most reliable and passionate supporters to remake the party organization in his own image—fully interjecting himself in the electoral fate of his co-partisans and imprinting his own brand of conservatism on Republican Party politics.

The displacement of party politics by executive administration has not made formal party organizations inconsequential. Rather, as Democrats and Republicans have come to rely on partisan administration to fulfill their collective goals, they have ceded greater authority to the White

House. In an era marked by vigorous party competition, divided government, and tribal struggles to control the judiciary (Lee 2018), Trump's influence on the course of American politics is likely to endure once he leaves office. Rather than triggering a revival of liberal norms and institutions, we fear that his political accomplishments will further encourage leaders who scorn the restraints that are a vital ingredient of constitutional government.

EXECUTIVE-CENTERED PARTISANSHIP IN AMERICAN POLITICAL DEVELOPMENT

Executive-centered partisanship in the United States sits at the crosscurrents of two related phenomena in American political development. First, the form of party contestation that allowed Trump to capture the Republican nomination is a consequence of organizational and electoral reforms that weakened the decentralized, patronage-based parties that dominated most of the nineteenth century. Throughout the twentieth century, both parties were pressured by insurgent movements to alter the rules governing their presidential nomination process—ostensibly to give more power to "the people" in selecting candidates for office and in determining party priorities. However, the pursuit of "participatory democracy" did not empower the Downsian median voter. Rather, the weakening of traditional party organizations enhanced the influence of donors, interest groups, and social activists who scorned the pragmatic politics and compromises hitherto credited with forging majority coalitions (Keller 2007).

The effect of those reforms has been enhanced by a second development: the creation of a presidential institution, formed in pursuance of the 1939 Executive Reorganization Act, and the development of an administrative state during Franklin Roosevelt's protracted presidency. With the Executive Office of the President, composed of the White House Office (the West Wing) and important staff agencies like the Office of Management and Budget—the president could form alliances with activists and outside groups who disdained the party "establishment," thus subordinating decentralized and pluralistic party coalitions to the more national and programmatic networks that shape contemporary partisan politics.

Roosevelt defended the centralizing biases of executive-centered government in terms that made it seem compatible with America's rights-based culture, redefining a social contract that privileged limited constitutional government, which the traditional party system nourished. As he argued in his iconic State of the Union message of 1941, traditional freedoms like speech and religion needed to be supplemented by two new rights: "freedom from want" and "freedom from fear." These new freedoms, representing for all intents and purposes the charter of the modern American state, were given institutional form by the welfare and national security states. While the defense of national administration infused reform during the Progressive era, as Daniel Carpenter (2002) has shown, the early architects of the administrative state, celebrating expertise and "independent" regulatory commissions, emphasized "bureaucratic autonomy." With the Executive Reorganization Act, Roosevelt and his political allies sought to strengthen the president's influence over the departments and agencies that sprawled during his first term, a consolidation of executive power that he insisted was necessary to secure the programmatic and human rights championed in the Four Freedoms address.

The consolidation of the modern executive was fiercely resisted, arousing a highly contentious, two-year battle between New Dealers and a conservative coalition of Southern Democrats and Republicans. Although the original legislation was compromised in important matters—for example, the independent regulatory commissions retained some of their autonomy—the reorganization act is appropriately viewed as the organic statute of the modern presidency. The Executive Office it formed was adopted and enlarged by FDR's successors. For a time, the modern presidency achieved a status above party conflict; as Roosevelt described this aspiration in his Commonwealth Club address, its cache was nonpartisan leadership, or "enlightened administration," tasked with the principal responsibility for managing the new "policy state" (Orren and Skowronek 2017).

With the swelling of executive authority, traditional decentralized party organizations lost influence. Gradually, the president became the depository of party responsibility, depriving leaders at the state and local level of the power to choose candidates, whip their party's membership into line, and control the policy agenda. Early in the twentieth century, Presidents Taft and Wilson used the presidency's growing prominence to insert themselves into divisive intraparty disputes. But with Franklin D. Roosevelt's interference in the 1938 primary elections—dubbed the "purge" campaign by the press—presidents became more active in shaping partisan politics. Most of the president's anointed candidates were defeated, but the purge campaign clarified the factional disputes in the Democratic Party and set the course for its future. As Roosevelt (1941) argued, "responsible" partisan debate and resolution "require[d] that one of its parties be the liberal party and the other be the conservative party." Only then could voters endow government with administrative power and hold it accountable. Going so far as to claim that he would prefer to have liberal Republicans than conservative Democrats elected, the president's purge campaign was a dramatic testament to the recognition that, as one Roosevelt aide, Ernest Cuneo (n.d.) put it, "the President, and not either party, was now the instrument of the people as a whole."

"Sixties Civics," as Hugh Heclo (2005) called it, gave rise to a new, more antinomian strain of executive-centered partisanship. The proliferation of social movements in the 1960s further exposed the Democrats and Republicans to social activism that disrupted their coalitions and intensified the assault on party organizations (Shafer 1983). Hoping to build a new progressive coalition in the vein of FDR, Lyndon Johnson deployed the tools of the administrative presidency in the service of the highly mobilized constituencies that became prominent during sixties uprisings: women, racial minorities, and immigrants. These constituencies were further strengthened by the antiwar movement, which imbued Great Society liberalism with a new form of globalism that promised to replace imperialist adventures like the Vietnam War with a renewed commitment to human rights. Together, these "new" liberals transformed the presidential selection process, affirming E. E. Schattschneider's (1935) insight that "new policies create new politics." Between the late 1960s and early 1970s, the old local and state party-based convention system was upended by a system of direct primaries and open caucuses. Ultimately, the new plebiscitary system exposed the rear guard of the New Deal establishment to the insurgent campaign of South Dakota's antiwar senator George McGovern, the Democratic presidential candidate in 1972.

In response to the momentous outpouring of energy on the left, Richard Nixon saw the potential to speak for the "Silent Majority" who felt marginalized in a country remade by the liberalization of racial, sexual, and religious mores and who sought to recover the image of America as a "City on a Hill" from an antiwar movement that denigrated patriotic values. Like Johnson, Nixon devoted the full arsenal of modern presidential powers—political, rhetorical, and administrative—on behalf of insurgent interests and demands. But Nixon's efforts to engage the forces of reaction marked the first effort by a Republican president to demonstrate that the modern executive office—designed to protect the commitments of New Deal and Great Society liberalism—could also be used to galvanize a national conservative offensive. Although liberal activists initiated the changes in party rules that established the system of direct primaries and open caucuses, the Republicans also accepted them. The bipartisan commitment to a media-churning, plebiscitary presidential selection process gave institutional form to campaigns that encouraged presidential candidates to denounce Washington, and promise, if elected, to seize the powers of the modern executive in the service of the policies that their most loyal supporters demanded.

Consequently, since the 1970s, both parties have relied on presidents to advance programmatic objectives and mobilize the base through the rhetorical and administrative powers of the modern executive office. Ronald Reagan extended these developments even as he posed a fundamental challenge to the liberal state. He enhanced the White House's ability to craft and amplify a principled message and mastered the art of using discretionary administrative authority in the service of conservative social movements. In a range of administrative initiatives, Reagan further welded presidential power to conservative activism—from issuing the Mexico City policy that prohibited funding for international NGOs that provided or counseled abortions, to preempting state-level regulations on business and environmental protections, to funding a secretive campaign to support anti-communist guerrillas in Nicaragua. Twenty years later, George W. Bush followed suit and mobilized conservative voters through executive decisions restricting the rights of LGBTQ individuals, banning funding for new stem cell research, and facilitating the provision of government services through faith-based organizations.

Eschewing the fiscal austerity championed by traditional conservatives such as Robert Taft and Barry Goldwater, Reagan and Bush drew on the considerable capacity presidents had accrued to implement supply-side economics, which tolerated large deficits in the cause of redistributing resources to traditional Republican constituencies. By the end of the Bush era, the Republican Party had built a militant conservative base, whose constituencies set their collective sights on the instruments of executive power. These new foot soldiers, most notably the sectarian Christian Right and Tea Party conservatives, determined to redeploy rather than roll back administrative power, rallied around their belief that liberalism had so corrupted the country that the national government had responsibility to support "family values," a view that permeates proposals to restrict abortion and undermine the Supreme Court ruling on same-sex marriage; to require work for welfare; and to impose standards on secondary and elementary schools (Jacobs, King, and Milkis 2019).

This form of presidency-led, movement politics prepared the ground for the election of America's first African American president. During his 2008 candidacy, Obama envisaged his campaign as a progressive crusade that marked a new stage in the fusion of executive power and partisan politics. Candidate-centered organizations had been a staple of American politics since the Kennedy administration, but Obama was the first president to keep his electoral machine intact as the vanguard of a movement that would free him from the constraints of the Democratic "establishment" and connect him directly to the new progressive coalition he envisioned. A former community organizer, Obama built an innovative information-age grassroots organization, "Obama for America" (OFA), dedicated to linking him directly with a widely scattered but potentially powerful "coalition of the ascendant," as the journalist Ron Brownstein (2015) has aptly termed it: millennials, environmentalists, racial minorities, feminists, and the LGBTQ community. After 2012, the OFA was spun off as a nonprofit social welfare agency called "Organizing for Action." Obama's "family," as OFA staff and volunteers referred to themselves, was critical not only to his two presidential campaigns but also to the enactment of major legislative reform including the 2010 Affordable Care Act. Significantly, just as Obama's attention shifted to executive action after the Democrats lost control of the House in the 2010 midterm elections, OFA's staff and volunteers shifted their attention to the president's administrative initiatives, touting with special urgency unilateral administrative actions that would advance climate change policy, LGBTQ rights, and immigration reform (Milkis and York 2017).

Obama's partisanship was a critical prelude to Trump's tactics and policies. Although Obama and Trump could not be more different in their underlying political philosophies and policy objectives, the style of politics they practice reflects two key features of contemporary executive-centered partisanship: a detachment from party organization and a vision of the White House as the vanguard of a movement. Trump's odds-defying ascendance to the presidency in 2016 appeared to complete the fusion of centralized administration and partisanship. As a candidate, Trump lacked an independent grassroots machine as institutionally sophisticated as OFA. Yet, he likewise chose to galvanize his base supporters by appealing to them directly through social media and the more than three hundred rallies held across the United States in the primary and general campaign season. These rallies were energizing spectacles that produced an image of the soon-to-be president as the leader of a movement. That campaign, Trump's campaign manager Kellyanne Conway (2016) recalled, "really mastered the art of putting Donald Trump where he was best, which was in these big rallies, these huge settings in swing states, in front of the people. . . . Donald Trump does best when he's with the people. He can take his message directly to the American people and cut through the noise or through the silence, whatever the case may be. It was a masterful way of doing it, . . . because it was low-cost; it was high-energy."

Obama saw himself as the leader of a new "coalition of the ascendant"; Trump and his strategists positioned him as the steward of a "coalition of restoration" composed of blue-collar, religiously devout, and nonurban white Americans who felt that traditional Republican politicians had forsaken their needs and demands. As president, Trump surpassed Obama in attending to his base (Brownstein 2015). From the first days in office, his efforts to mobilize support for his controversial plans to "Make America Great Again" have involved unrelenting appeals to core supporters. Despite pleas among fellow Republicans to act "more presidential," Trump relishes his administration's unapologetic support for, as one White House aide put it, the former businessman's most "loyal customers."[1]

The culmination of presidential partisanship has not made the president of the United States all-powerful. As the first term of the Trump administration has shown, the federal courts, the states, and Congress still offer resistance to executive aggrandizement. Yet, these checks on presidential power have become less reliable as the collective fate of party members has increasingly come to depend on the president's personal successes once in office—and as institutional loyalties have been severely challenged, if not displaced, by partisan priorities. Exacerbating polarized conflict, executive-centered partisanship has made it more difficult to pursue programmatic ambitions through the Congress or state legislatures, so the White House has increasingly come to be viewed as indispensable to the attainment of partisan objectives. The new style of campaigning gives presidential contenders the authority to command the party; administrative government gives them the power to advance its causes.

IMPRINTING THE TRUMP BRAND

As a candidate, Trump denounced the Obama administration's "major power grabs of authority." Yet as president, he has seized administrative power with more alacrity than his predecessor. Whereas Obama's resort to unilateralism became paramount after his party's losses in the 2010 midterm elections, Trump, with the complicity of the Republican majority in Congress, embraced partisan administration from the start. Trump, therefore, not only made use of many of the administrative strategies that Obama deployed, but his willingness to act unilaterally with congressional majorities in the House and Senate during his first two years testifies to the parties' increasing dependence on the White House to advance their causes.

America First

Trump promised to be a disruptive force, and many of the actions sponsored by the White House have upset the government's standard operating procedures. In policy areas where there was formerly broad public consensus among elected politicians, the instruments of modern administrative government have allowed Trump to transform inherited policy commitments without expanding support beyond his base. Theories of presidential behavior emphasize the need for a president, once ensconced in the office, to appeal to the median voter. Trump and his administration have defied the received wisdom, focusing obsessively on the mobilization of their most loyal supporters, a passionate but minority faction of the American electorate. With the president's daily job approval ratings consistently below 50 percent, it remains to be seen whether his defiance of public opinion (and conventional understandings) will produce a victorious coalition come next Election Day. There is not gainsaying, however, that the Republican Party has embraced much of Trump's America First agenda.

Trump's imprint on Republican partisanship has been most dramatically demonstrated in his battles with the GOP establishment over free trade. During the 2016 Republican primary contests, trade was a distinguishing position of then-candidate Trump. While Trump's positions on immigration (especially a proposed Muslim ban) received top media attention, his rhetoric on the debate stage emphasized the need to impose protectionist trade measures. Often, he was the only candidate speaking about the issue, indeed, more than any Republican candidate since the 1920s.[2]

Once in office, the Trump administration quickly imposed new protectionist measures on major imports such as steel, aluminum, lumber, and manufactured solar cells. Invoking seldomly used provisions of US trade law, the White House was able to impose tariffs without congressional authorization. The Trade Expansion Act of 1962 and the Trade Act of 1974 delegate broad authority to the president to investigate whether foreign imports represent a threat to US national security or are injurious to competing US industries. Although the Trump administration's tariffs emphasize the need to target unfair Chinese trading practices, with the stroke of a pen, the president also implicated imports from major US allies, such as Japan, South Korea, and Germany (Brown 2017). Consistent with the logic of executive-centered partisanship, the imports targeted for investigation were attuned to the coalition Trump forged during the 2016 campaign. The president's specific focus on agricultural products and goods manufactured primarily in Midwestern states confirms a consensus among academics that presidents are increasingly able to strategically distribute economic benefits—including trade protections—to areas needed in the next election (Lowande, Jenkins, and Clarke 2018; Kriner and Reeves 2015).

In addition to imposing tariffs, the administration notified Congress on May 18, 2017, of its intention to renegotiate the North American Free Trade Agreement (NAFTA), which the Clinton administration, with bipartisan support, pushed through the Congress in 1993. While the treaty with Canada and Mexico has been challenged from the left and right since its inception, Trump is the first president to denounce it. The president did not truly blow up the status quo as he promised. In fact, a year of negotiations produced a new trade deal—the United States-Mexico-Canada Agreement (USMCA)—that preserved many elements of the original treaty. Still, just replacing NAFTA with a new brand signals to Trump's base that he has fulfilled one of his most important campaign promises. Moreover, the new agreement, which Congress, in a rare display of bipartisanship, approved in late 2019, will marginally help farmers, by loosening Canadian protections of its dairy market; USMCA also might help American automakers by imposing a minimum wage requirement on manufactured goods and establishing stricter "rules of origin" requirements for assembled products.[3]

Regardless of economic effect, Trump has already declared a major victory for his America First platform. This is not merely rhetorical flourish. Its most important provision allows any of the participating countries to void the entire treaty if another successfully negotiates a free trade agreement with a "non-market country." Such a measure would limit China's ability to enter and influence the structure of Canadian and Mexican markets without US involvement.[4] The Trump administration, therefore, has managed to reach a deal with Canada and Mexico that enlists them in the president's most important objective: "an aggressive agenda of increasingly squeezing China out of global supply chains while pressing for structural change in Beijing" (Savage and Harris 2019).

Trump did not create a party divide on trade policy. Republican support for free-trade agreements, such as NAFTA, has declined since 2004. Nearly a decade ago, Democrats and Republicans showed no discernable difference in their attitudes toward the agreement. By the time President Trump took office, nearly 70 percent of Democrats supported NAFTA, while just above 20 percent of Republicans believed the agreement was "good for the US" (Swift 2017). However, elected leaders in the Republican Party remained impervious to these broader changes in the electorate until Trump's campaign and presidency gave them voice. It is not certain whether Trump reacted to public opinion or actively changed minds in the

2016 campaign, but his rhetoric and policies have further aggravated partisan conflict over trade. Recent Gallup polls indicate that 56 percent of Democrats believe that the tariffs will "make things worse" in the long run, while a supermajority of Republicans, 83 percent, reported that they thought the tariffs would either make things better or have little effect. The 2018 Cooperative Congressional Election Study (Schaffner and Ansolabhere 2019) showed even greater partisan splits: 85 percent of Republicans supported "$50 billion worth of tariffs on goods imported from China" (compared to 28 percent of Democrats), and 57 percent of Republicans supported "25% tariffs on imported steel and 10% on imported aluminum, even when imposed on Canada, Europe and Mexico" (compared to 17 percent of Democrats).

Trump's executive actions have defied lingering support among congressional Republicans for free trade—an important tenet of the Reagan "Revolution." This is partly a testament to the atavistic relationship he has formed with the GOP base. But the allure of executive-centered partisanship in a polity afflicted by partisan gridlock is no less important. In fact, Trump's ability to impose trade protections is a symptom of congressional deference to administrative fiat in a number of policy arenas. Even though the president's Republican allies often fret over how his trade policies will affect their constituencies—including key areas of rural America that helped Trump win the Electoral College—signs of institutional resistance have been sporadic. Senate Majority Leader Mitch McConnell led the effort to block a bill that would have given Congress the authority to approve tariff adjustments made under the national security provisions of the 1962 trade law, referred to as Section 232. "I don't think we need to be trying to rein in the president through legislation," McConnell said, following a closed-door meeting at the White House "Number one, it would be an exercise in futility" (Carney 2018).

Rallying the Base

Trump's partisan administration on immigration has been especially polarizing. For decades, no Republican candidate had been able to unite the party behind a comprehensive immigration plan. However, by constantly stoking his base, the president has rallied partisan support for his immigration policies. Again, Trump galvanized rather than created party differences. Republican voters had been trending toward nativist positions well before Trump's candidacy. But Trump made undocumented immigration a signature issue and a core commitment of Republican partisanship: just

10 percent of Americans in early February 2016 believed immigration to be the primary problem facing the country; by July 2019, immigration had risen to the top of the list of the most important issues in the country, with 22 percent of Americans—and 35 percent of Republicans—citing it as the major problem facing the nation.[5]

The Trump administration has taken advantage of a long-standing legal jurisprudence that has granted "broad discretion" to the executive in administering immigration laws.[6] Within days of taking office, the president issued a set of executive orders that clarified the new administration's priorities for national, state, and local officials who came into contact with unauthorized immigrants, threatening to withhold federal funds from "sanctuary cities" that refused to cooperate with federal immigration authorities. Trump also directed officials at the Department of Homeland Security to immediately suspend the United States Refugee Admissions Program (USRAP) for 120 days; suspend the entry of Syrian refugees indefinitely; and suspend entry, for at least 90 days, for travelers from Iran, Iraq, Libya, Somalia, Sudan, Syria, and Yemen.[7] The litany of court injunctions that followed from these controversial measures only hardened partisan lines. By the time the administration's revised order worked its way to the Supreme Court, Republicans in the Senate had approved the president's first nominee, Neil Gorsuch. With Gorsuch on the bench, the justices—in a contentious 5–4 decision—sustained the president's "ample power" in a policy area that, as they wrote, "exudes deference to the President in every clause."[8]

Operating with similarly wide latitude, the administration invented new schemes for making the Republican Party the party of "border security." Trump's decision to suspend President Obama's policy for the Deferred Action for Childhood Arrivals (DACA) jeopardized the immigration status of nearly eight hundred thousand undocumented individuals—the "Dreamers"—who came to the United States as minors. While rescinding DACA was a divisive measure that garnered extraordinary media coverage, the contours of the modern administrative state also created multiple, subtler avenues for the exercise of presidential power. Seemingly benign changes add up and seep through departments and agencies that hold secondary, and even tertiary, responsibility for policy change. Trump has thus deployed the full force of the executive branch to implement his desired immigration policy, from revising the rules that the Department of Housing and Urban Development uses to curtail rental assistance to unauthorized migrants to delaying and often suspending the enlistment of foreign-national military recruits (Kurta 2017). The White House also instructed Immigration and Customs Enforcement (ICE) officials to arrest unauthorized immigrants deep in the US interior, even targeting sensitive sites long viewed as off limits to immigration enforcement, such as courthouses and churches (Immigrant Defense Project 2019).

The defining issues of Trump conservatism—trade and immigration—were joined in the president's proposal to deploy tariffs as a weapon to stem the surge of Central American migrants coming to the United States through Mexico. Threatening to slap tariffs as high as 25 percent on all goods with Mexico unless it thwarted the transit of undocumented immigrants and refugees to the United States, Trump connected America First policies that cause unrest among the president's partisans in Congress, especially the Senate, but mobilize his base. In a resolution that the president's supporters heralded as an important victory for the "Disrupter-in-Chief," the Mexican foreign minister and the US secretary of state reached an agreement that obligated "Mexico [to] take unprecedented steps to increase enforcement to curb irregular migration," including the deployment of its national guard to its southern border. Mexico further guarantees that it will hold any migrants "while they await adjudication of their asylum claims" (Nakamura and Wagner 2019). Although some of Trump's supporters expressed skepticism that this deal would resolve the border crisis—and warned that the administration's weaponizing of tariffs would undermine a prosperous economy—the episode testified dramatically to how Trump's America First program has become an all-consuming dimension of conflict that will be a major issue in the 2020 election (Olorunnipa 2019a).

Indeed, Trump's resort to a fractious trade policy to control the border highlighted the president's Manichean struggle with Congress over his signature campaign promise: the construction of his "big beautiful Wall." Since his very first days in office, President Trump had requested additional funds for a new barrier along the US-Mexico border. Congressional Republicans—primarily in the Senate—frequently demurred, fearing that a special appropriation for the president's loudest campaign slogan would prompt a Democratic filibuster, end in a government shutdown, and produce a public-relations nightmare for the GOP. Yet following the 2018 midterm elections, and in the last remaining months of controlling both chambers of Congress, Republicans capitulated to their president's defiant stand against a stopgap funding bill that did not fund the wall—resulting in a thirty-five-day partial shutdown of the US federal government that is, to date, the longest in American history.

Shutdowns are, of course, not unique to Trump; such impasses are collateral damage in the partisan brinksmanship inherent to presidential party leadership. What is particularly noteworthy about the 2018–2019 government shutdown is that it began during a period of unified Republican control. When President Trump announced shortly after his party lost the House that he would be "proud to shut down the government for border security" (Werner and Wagner 2018), Republican leadership in the House and Senate successfully cobbled together a coalition to pass a spending bill that would have averted a shutdown and delayed negotiations over a border wall until the new Congress took power.[9] By most press accounts, Trump signaled that he was ready to sign the compromise bill, which denied the president's request for $5.7 billion in border wall funding. Yet, following a procedural vote in the Senate that advanced the bill, conservative pundits—especially on Fox News and talk radio—ridiculed the president's "Christmas present" to the Democratic Party (Johnson and Everett 2018). Overnight, the White House convened an impromptu meeting between the president and congressional Republican leaders, where Trump switched positions, charting a course that left his partisan allies with a Hobson's choice: they could either vote for a funding bill without a border wall and face his veto or give into the president's demands and risk a partial government shutdown. Congressional leaders left the White House knowing that Trump was determined to secure his alliance with the Republican base; moreover, facing a minority position in the House in just a few weeks, they recognized that advancing partisan causes prior to the 2020 election would depend on the institutional strength and prestige of the president. Caught in an intractable dilemma, Republicans sacrificed the spending package on the altar of Trump's presidential reputation.

When Democrats took over the House of Representatives in January 2019, the White House's posture took on a new, foreseeable dimension. Immigration reform, long seen as a divisive issue among Republicans, became the driving wedge the president hammered between liberals and conservatives. The day the new Congress started, Trump delivered a rare, unannounced press briefing in the White House. Standing alongside his directors of ICE and the Customs and Border Protection agency, the president launched what would become a recurrent refrain with the GOP—there was an emergency on the border, and if Democrats in Congress refused to act, the president would do so on his own (White House Press Office 2019a). Days later, in his first prime-time Oval Office address, Trump (2019) escalated the partisan acrimony: "How much more American blood must we shed before Congress does its job," he bluntly stated, "This is a choice between right and wrong." He might as well have said, between Republican and Democrat.

Against this background, Trump's decision to declare a national emergency and redirect nearly $3.6 billion in military construction appropriations for a border wall was neither a show of force nor a sign of institutional weakness.[10] It was a rational strategy for an institution that derives its power from exacerbating partisan divisions, energizing its most ardent supporters, and flouting constitutional restraints in the name of "the people." On February 15, 2019—the day the compromise measure reopening the government expired—the president had already secured $1.4 billion for additional border security. Together with other discretionary action—dipping into the Treasury's drug forfeiture fund ($601 million) and Defense's Support for Counterdrug Activities program ($2.5 billion)—Trump laid claim to nearly $8 billion to build the wall (White House Press Office 2019b).

By the time Congress exercised its statutory obligation, as established by the National Emergencies Act of 1976, to approve or disavow the president's emergency declaration, esoteric constitutional deliberation gave way completely to visceral presidential partisanship. As Trump threatened in an interview with Fox News several weeks before the vote, "I really think that Republicans that vote against border security and the wall . . . put themselves at great jeopardy" (Werner and John Wagner 2019). Not surprisingly, few Republicans challenged the president, and those who did risked the ire of his fiercely loyal supporters. Senator Thom Tillis (R-NC) witnessed the specter of a potential primary challenge after he disavowed the president's emergency declaration; so credible was the threat that even after Tillis authored a widely publicized op-ed against Trump, he switched his position and voted for the president's declaration (Wong and Bolton 2019). In the House of Representatives, just thirteen Republicans voted to overturn the president's declaration. In the Senate, a significantly higher proportion of the caucus—twelve members—broke party ranks. Noticeably, just one of those senators, Susan Collins of Maine, was up for reelection in 2020.

BUILDING A NEW REPUBLICAN (TRUMP) PARTY

Trump's administrative strategy has tested the boundaries of executive-centered partisanship, mobilizing his base of supporters and giving them an outsized influence on the direction of the Republican Party. The president and his base have also pursued a deliberate and effective plan to take command of the GOP's national and state organizations, further marginalizing a flagging Never Trump movement and possibly reshaping the contours of party competition for decades to come.

Trump's Ambiguous Electoral Legacy

Outside the nation's capital, the president has been an active presence in remaking the Republican Party through fundraisers, campaign rallies, and his Twitter account. Trump was determined to make the 2018 congressional elections all about him, and in doing so, he further established himself as the face of the Republican Party. On the campaign trail, he clearly defined the midterm election as a referendum on his presidency: "I'm not on the ballot," he acknowledged at one campaign rally. "But in a certain way, I'm on the ballot. So, please go out and vote" (Cadelago 2018).

To some extent, Trump's personalization of the midterm elections fits a pattern of twentieth-century presidential politics. Since Franklin Roosevelt first gave form to the modern executive office, presidents have become the repository of party responsibility. So positioned, however, few presidents have been able to prevent their party in Congress from suffering losses in the first midterm election (figure 12.1). Presidents Calvin Coolidge, Franklin D. Roosevelt, and George W. Bush are unique among modern presidents for seeing their party pick up seats in both chambers following their initial inauguration. Trump joins a larger class of presidents who expanded his majority in one chamber (the Senate, by one seat), although this is still a rare occurrence. The Republican Party lost forty seats and majority control of the House of Representatives following the 2018 midterm elections. Of the past twenty presidents, he ranks twelfth in this regard, outperforming his immediate predecessor, Barack Obama, who lost sixty-four seats in the 2010 "shellacking," but performing worse than Reagan did in 1982, when Republicans lost just twenty-six seats in the House.

Midterm elections are determined by many factors, including the president's performance in office, trends in economic growth, and the relative strength of each party when the president first takes office (Campbell 1997; Abramowitz 1985). But the constant flipping between Democratic and Republican majority control since the late 1960s is also a consequence of increasing party loyalty, straight-ticket voting, and the consolidation of national party messaging that focuses on presidential politics and popularity (Jacobson 2015). In essence, as Obama's two terms dramatically demonstrated, executive-centered partisanship tends to sacrifice the collective fortunes of the party brethren to the president's personal ambitions and programs.[11]

Given these historical trends, Trump's domineering presence in the 2018 elections followed a pattern endemic to executive partisanship; and, as history would suggest, his interventions had mixed results. In 2016,

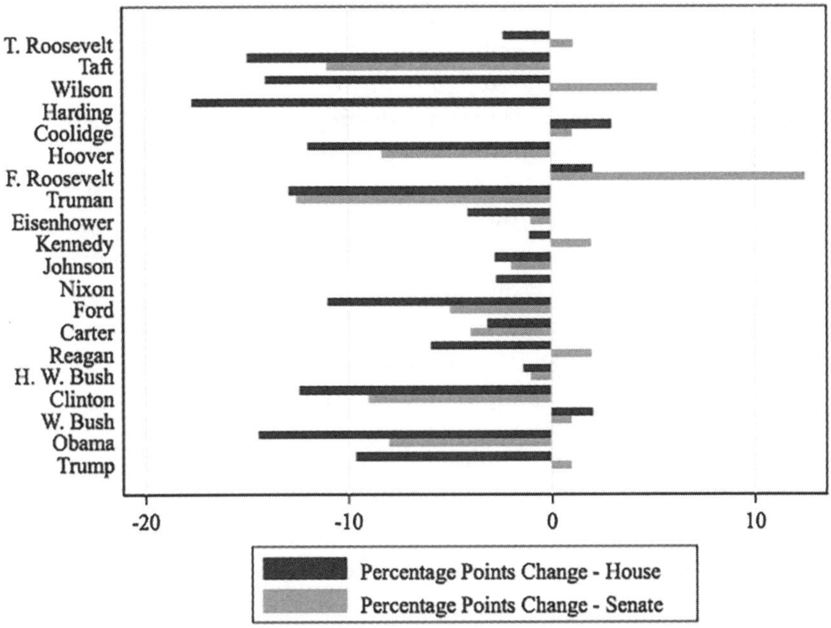

Figure 12.1: Presidential Losses in the First Midterm Election as a Percentage of the Chamber, 1902–2018. *Source*: Authors' calculations from US Congress data.

Trump outperformed the Republican candidate for the House seat in just 28 of the 211 contested races that a Republican won, or about 13 percent of races. Republican members were more electorally popular than their party leader in those contested races: Republican candidates won their district, on average, with 62.1 percent of the vote; Trump, in comparison, secured on average 56.5 percent of the vote in those same districts. Clearly, Republican voters in 2016 were much more supportive of the Republican congressional candidates than they were the Republican presidential nominee.[12]

Nevertheless, the outcome of the 2018 midterms suggests that the Trump campaign and the prerogatives of the modern presidency have forged a leaner and more united Republican Party. In effect, the Republican Party's support was increasingly confined to those places—rural and outer-ring suburban areas—where Trump performed well in 2016. Of the 170 contested races that a Republican won in the 2018 midterms, the president's 2016 numbers outperformed the Republican candidate in ninety-four districts, or 55.3 percent. Trump won those districts with an average 58.8 percent of the vote, while Republican congressional candidates averaged 59.1 percent of the vote. Trump has thus tied the fate of Republican candidates to his political fortunes.

Of course, numbers tell only part of the story—especially numbers taken from midterm returns, as compared to presidential election years. Still, Trump, more than his predecessors, leaned in heavily during the 2018 primary season, supporting Republican challengers in several high-profile races. It is difficult to systematically evaluate the president's influence in this process because incumbents have a choice when faced with a primary challenge. They can choose to run or retire. As already noted, two of the president's loudest critics in the Senate, Jeff Flake (AZ) and Bob Corker (TN), chose to retire rather than face primary opponents. In the fight to replace Corker, the open-seat contest between Marsha Blackburn (a Republican congresswoman) and Phil Bredesen (a Democratic two-time ex-governor) proved to be much closer than anticipated. About a month before the election, Trump visited Tennessee to campaign on behalf of Blackburn: "A vote for Marsha is really a vote for me," the president avowed, "and everything that we stand for. It's a vote for 'Make America Great Again'" (Korecki and Cadelago 2018). While Trump won Tennessee in 2016 with more than 60.7 percent of the vote, Blackburn took office with 54.7 percent of the vote cast. Whether this victory was because of Trump or in spite of him is an open conjecture; however, there is no question that he turned the contest into a referendum on his brand of conservatism.

Trump made similar appeals in Arizona during the general election, but there the Republican candidate, Martha McSally, lost to US Congresswoman Kyrsten Sinema (D). McSally faced a more competitive primary contest than did Blackburn, campaigning against two Republican contenders who styled themselves as the Trump-candidate: Joe Arpaio, the incendiary former sheriff of Maricopa County, whom Trump pardoned; and Kelli Ward, a former state senator who had tried to unseat Trump's nemesis John McCain in a 2016 primary contest. While Trump remained neutral in the primary contest, most political observers at the time acknowledged that McSally adopted a rhetorical style similar to Trump's and was careful not to criticize the president's administration, lest he endorse Arpaio or Ward (Associated Press 2018; Elliot 2018). McSally lost in a state that Trump previously won, while Ward won a divisive intraparty contest to chair the Arizona State Republican Party. Subsequently, the Republican governor of Arizona appointed McSally to the US Senate to fill the remainder of the late senator John McCain's term.

The Arizona race shows the power of Trump's endorsement, even in its absence. In two noteworthy cases, however, Trump's endorsement of a preferred Republican candidate in a primary contest proved futile. In Alabama's special election for US Senate in 2017, the president came out in support of Luther Strange—over the more "Trump-like" candidate running for the nomination. Strange took over Jeff Sessions's seat after Trump appointed Sessions attorney general, but he faced a strong challenge from the outspoken former state supreme court justice Roy Moore. Moore had earlier gained nationwide notoriety for his refusal to support the US Supreme Court's decision to legalize same-sex marriage and for his vocal support of Trump's racially tinged Birther Conspiracy, which denied that President Obama was a natural-born citizen. Moore won the primary; but despite gaining the president's support, he lost the general election.[13] In West Virginia—the only other Senate race where Trump made a clear intervention during a Republican primary—the most "Trump-like" candidate, Don Blankenship, also failed to secure the president's personal endorsement. Instead, Trump came out in support of the two other challengers, equivocating between the two in a last-minute tweet.[14] The ultimate victor, Patrick Morrisey, failed to beat out the Democratic incumbent, Joe Manchin, in a state where Trump garnered 68.5 percent of the vote in 2016. Manchin, nevertheless, has certainly felt the pressure from Trump's base. He has voted in line with President Trump's priorities in the Senate nearly 61 percent of the time, and he provided a critical vote to confirm Trump's second Supreme Court pick, Brett Kavanaugh.

Although the president's aggressive intervention in the 2018 contests was a mixed blessing for Republicans, he declared victory. As Trump (2018) proclaimed in a postelection press conference: "Candidates who embraced our message of low taxes, low regulations, low crime, strong borders, and great judges excelled last night. They excelled. . . . On the other hand, you had some that decided to 'let's stay away.' They did very poorly. . . . I feel just fine about it." The losses Republicans suffered in the House, as well as in many state and local races, cast serious doubt on the president's self-serving interpretation; nevertheless, his analysis did not prompt any vocal criticism from fellow Republicans, who seem to have accepted—even if reluctantly—the president's authority to weigh in on party contests and make Republican races all about him.

Transforming the Republican Party's Machinery

Trump has stifled most lingering resistance to his capture of the Republican Party with a well-conceived strategy to take over the party apparatus. To a point, he has followed a long-standing pattern of presidents transforming their parties' respective national committees (Galvin 2010); but he has gone further in his support of loyalists who have been engaged in contests to take over state party organizations. Seemingly indifferent, if not avowedly hostile, to the regular party apparatus, Trump and his strategists have proven to be surprisingly adept at mastering organizational politics—so much so that in the lead-up to his 2020 election, the president's reelection campaign preempted what once seemed inevitable: a prominent anti-Trump candidate entering the primary contests. Beyond squelching a challenge from within his party, the president has established a unified and well-funded party organization that will test the mettle of even the most formidable Democratic opponent.

Like Obama, Trump's initial campaign strategy was a mix of raw personality and energetic movement politics. And like Obama, Trump also maintained this strategy as he transitioned to the White House. Whereas Obama transformed his campaign organization, OFA, into a nonprofit advocacy group that advocated for the president's administrative positions, Trump returned to the campaign trail less than a month after his inauguration to sustain the momentum of his Make America Great Again crusade.[15] During his first year in office, Trump averaged about one campaign-style rally a month (complete with cable news coverage and live-feeds through his personal Twitter account). In the lead-up to the 2018 midterms, the president made forty-six separate appearances between March and November (almost one per week). The unmediated connection between the president and the people is a hallmark of the modern presidency, but with the tools of instant communication and the blurring of news and entertainment, Trump has given new meaning to the "permanent campaign" (Blumenthal 1980; Doherty 2012).

Yet, unlike Obama, Trump has pursued a carefully calculated strategy to transform the organization of his party. Obama constructed a parallel organization alongside the Democratic National Committee to advance his partisan objectives; Trump has decided to merge his reelection campaign and the RNC's election efforts, a tactic that might have a more enduring influence on his party. Rather than stand apart from the Republican apparatus, his objective is to remake its national and state committees in his own image.

President Trump set about this task on the very first day in office, becoming the first president in history to file reelection paperwork with the Federal Elections Commission on Inauguration Day. More than a symbolic gesture, the decision allowed Trump to maintain a separate campaign office (in Trump Tower), perpetually blurring the line between campaign functions and official presidential obligations. Dedicated to shoring up the campaign's data collection and fundraising efforts—especially among the mega-donors who were skeptical of Trump's 2016 candidacy—the extra time gave the president his desired advantage over potential Republican rivals and a head start to what is expected to be a hard-fought general election campaign. Nearly a year and a half before the 2020 election, Trump's principal campaign committee reported raising nearly $98 million, almost four times more than the leading Democratic fundraiser, Bernie Sanders. Barack Obama, in contrast, raised just $4.1 million in his first two years in office; George W. Bush raised $3.1 million during the same period.[16]

In one respect, the independent and aggressive fundraising efforts by Trump's personal campaign are the latest iteration of the candidate-centered campaign environment, by which modern presidents have tried to establish independence from the formal party organization once taking office. However, by strengthening the RNC and sealing its agenda to the White House's messaging strategy, Trump has been an attentive party-builder.

This is not to suggest that Trump has strengthened the Republican Party as a collective organization. Rather, he has recast it as an additional instrument of executive-centered partisanship. Beyond mere "branding," Trump's engagement with the RNC has been deliberate and unceasing. Successful presidential candidates are traditionally given the right to select their committee chairpersons; Trump followed suit by appointing Ronna Romney McDaniel as GOP chairwoman. The connection to Utah Republican senator Mitt Romney (her uncle and vocal Trump critic) is not nearly as important as the fact that McDaniel comes from Michigan—an essential battleground that Trump won in 2016 and that he will rely on come 2020. McDaniel has loyally overseen the reorganization of the RNC to strengthen the president's reelection chances. Despite the lack of a vocal opposition in the congressional rank and file for much of his first term, the iconoclastic president, registering the opposition of a shrinking but stubborn band of "Never Trumpers," recognized the possibility of a primary challenge. Several prominent Republican governors—most notably, Larry Hogan (MD) and former governor John Kasich (OH)—repeatedly raised the possibility. The RNC, however, sought to ensure that any possible primary challenge would be doomed from the start.

To accomplish this, the campaign staff in Trump Tower and the RNC orchestrated a state-by-state campaign to place Trump loyalists in powerful positions within the state party organizations, allowing them to more easily change party rules governing the selection of delegates for the national convention. McDaniel's experience as a state party chair proved invaluable in this respect, as the Trump machine succeeded even in states where the president performed poorly in 2016. For example, the Trump-backed candidate for state party chairman in Massachusetts, Jim Lyons, defeated the candidate supported by the vocal Trump critic and Republican governor, Charlie Baker. Once in charge of the state party, Lyon, with the active support of the Trump campaign, successfully pushed through a rule change that would make any presidential primary race a winner-takes-all contest—thus limiting the delegates that a primary challenger to the president might accumulate and making less likely a fractious convention (Murray 2019). Similar efforts took place in New Hampshire and Iowa.

Just how important these prophylactic measures are to the Trump administration became clear when Nick Trainer, a White House political operations director, left in December 2018 to head up an innovative "Delegates and Party Organization" branch of the campaign, with the goal of "organizing the state, county and local Republican parties; managing the delegate selection and ballot access process; and executing the national convention whip operation."[17] Trainer ably orchestrated the presidential campaign's direct intervention in state party leadership fights to control the Republican organizations in the key battlegrounds of Florida and Michigan. In other critical swing states, like Arizona and Colorado, the president's raw popularity, stoked by administrative action on polarizing issues such as immigration and trade, empowered Trump-loyalists to secure leadership positions by mobilizing grassroots support. With several successes already to his name, Trainer and his three regional directors have plans to ensure that no delegate at the 2020 Republican National Convention will be opposed to the president's reelection.

The optics of the 2020 Republican Convention in Charlotte, North Carolina (another important swing state) have motivated much of the party-building efforts thus far. If Trump's message to would-be supporters in 2016 was that he would shake up the Republican establishment, the theme of 2020 might be Trump's populist takeover of establishment organizations. The RNC hopes that a unified Republican convention, absent the internal dissent and personal squabbles that marred Trump's coronation at the 2016 Cleveland convention, will send precisely that message. While no incumbent president has failed to garner his party's nomination since the Democrat Franklin Pierce in 1856, modern electoral history suggests that drawn-out primary fights exacerbate existing divisions within the party and weaken the party's general election appeal. Ronald Reagan's challenge to Gerald Ford (1976), Ted Kennedy's run against Jimmy Carter (1980), and

Pat Buchannan's campaign to unseat George H. W. Bush (1992) were all reflective of the incumbent's vulnerability, and it is undeniable that efforts to overcome those nomination bouts weakened the incumbent's general election performance. To that end, Trainer and his aides are "diving into the rules that govern the state-by-state delegate allocations, keeping close tabs on the contests for the influential state chairmanship slots, and laying out plans to organize at local meetings where the convention-goers will be picked" (Isenstadt 2019a).

The incremental reforms across the various state party organizations complement the more ambitious efforts to restructure the Republicans' national organization. During the 2016 campaign, national committee staffers and novice Trump organizers routinely clashed on the campaign trail over small, but vital matters of campaign infrastructure: yard signs, phone bank volunteers, canvassers, and bumper stickers (Isenstadt 2016). To limit conflict and duplication, and to efficiently mobilize a cadre of necessary volunteers come 2020, the president's personal campaign organization formally merged with the RNC's campaign staff. The RNC and Trump fundraising arms joined efforts in 2016, creating the "Trump Victory Leadership Team," which raised an additional $108 million, independently of the president's personal campaign. But the most recent effort—simply "Trump Victory"—signifies the challenge of tying the president's highly personalized political style and reelection campaign to a collective partisan effort. It will unify the RNC's messaging strategy for other high-profile races in 2020 (Republicans will defend twenty-two of the thirty-four Senate races up for election) and provide Trump operatives with greater influence in directing national party resources to battleground states that are necessary for a Trump reelection. In the two-plus years following Trump's election, the joint fundraising committee raised $38.5 million to be used in Republican contests across the United States.[18]

The consolidation of the Republican Party's financial arrangements will further impress Trump's personal style of politics and his America First brand of conservatism on the party. Staffers for the joint RNC-Trump organization have rotated in and out of the White House, including top-level communications directors, who have made clear that the RNC views opposition to President Trump as a useless distraction. Campaign directors have even sought to limit the extent to which major donors can influence other Republican races and coordinate independent efforts with conservative organizations operating outside the party establishment. For example, the RNC has sought to distance itself from the Koch Network, a once-prominent organization in mainstream Republican politics that refused to endorse Trump in 2016; since then, the Kochs have openly clashed with the administration over its trade and immigration policies. After it was reported that the Koch network might openly support Democratic candidates in certain races, McDaniel made a personal appeal to key Republican donors to stop working with that organization, particularly as it related to the tradition of data-sharing between party organizations and outside conservative groups. "I want to be very clear," McDaniel wrote in a memorandum leaked by *Politico*, "the RNC proved in 2014 and 2016 that the Party is the only entity which can be trusted with the data Republican candidates need to win up and down the ballot—and this week proves why it is NECESSARY that the Party keep building on our successful operation" (Isenstadt 2018). While the RNC did not demand that Republicans refuse Koch donations in the future, the rift demonstrates the national committee's commitment to centralizing campaign operations in support of the president in an era marked by the proliferation of outside groups that compete with the party organization to provide services for candidates running for office.

The RNC's stated opposition to the Koch Network's independent efforts is not reflective of the Trump campaign's refusal to accept outside support. Formal coordination between campaigns and independent expenditures committees ("Super PACs") is legally forbidden; however, during the 2018 midterms, four of the ten largest organizations supporting conservative candidates self-identified as committees that formed specifically to support President Trump's agenda: America First Action, Restoration PAC, Future45, and the Committee to Defend the President spent a collective $51.36 million in the 2017–2018 midterm cycle. The largest of these, America First Action, targeted House races with clear implications for President Trump's Electoral College strategy, spending $7.4 million in Minnesota, $2.8 million Indiana, and $2.4 million in Michigan.

As a candidate, Trump abhorred outside fundraising, staking his reputation on the fact that he won a "populist" campaign in 2016 over Hillary Clinton, who, relying heavily on "independent" organizations, out-raised and outspent him in the election. As president, Trump has encouraged these organizations to raise and spend money in key legislative races. In addition to regular appearances on behalf of the Trump Victory fund (eleven separate appearances specifically for the RNC since taking office), the president often speaks before donors to these Super PACs, who have made it a regular occurrence to host events at the Trump International Hotel in Washington, DC, just blocks from the White House (Bykowicz and Colvin 2017). Just as the Trump administration has captured the party establishment, so it has fostered outside groups and cultivated mega donors who support the transformation of the Republicans into the Party of Trump.

Executive-Centered Partisanship, Impeachment, and the Future of American Constitutionalism

Although executive-centered partisanship has become an ingrained feature of American politics, Trump has engaged in aberrant behavior. The president's interference with independent counsel investigations, his refusal to comply with congressional subpoenas, and the condemnation of the press as "the enemy of the people" pose unprecedented dangers to the norms and institutions of liberal democracy. Yet, the raw factionalism of Trump's impeachment revealed that the transformation of the party system has severely weakened the ability of Congress to hold the president accountable for abuses of power. The American party system was formed during the first four decades of the nineteenth century to restrain presidential power. But over the course of the twentieth and twenty-first centuries, especially since the late sixties, partisanship has been weaponized in personalized political wars President Trump relishes.

As news broke that the president had withheld much-needed military assistance to Ukraine and made its release contingent upon a politically motivated investigation that would target his potential Democratic Party opponent in 2020, former vice president Joe Biden, the extraordinary events fit a predictable pattern. The president and his allies denounced the proceedings as a partisan "witch hunt"; Democrats closed ranks and relentlessly pursued the impeachment and trial of the president with virtually no support from Republicans. Many might have hoped that the calm presentation of facts and hours of deposition by respected foreign service officers might have persuaded at least a few minds. But, as it turned out, the drama peaked during a showdown vote in the Senate on whether to permit witnesses. Just two Republicans broke party lines: Susan Collins and Mitt Romney. Only Romney braved the threats of severe retribution to cast a guilty ballot—the first senator in history to vote to convict a president of his or her party.

The partisan fury of the Trump impeachment was not in itself irregular. As Alexander Hamilton warned in *Federalist 65*, "[Impeachment] will seldom fail to agitate the passions of the whole community. . . . [It] will enlist all their animosities, partialities, influence and interest on one side or on the other; and in such cases there will always be the greatest danger that the decision will be regulated more by the comparative strength of parties, than by the real demonstrations of innocence or guilt." The impeachment of Andrew Johnson and Bill Clinton seriously agitated the nation. Even Nixon's reckoning was a highly partisan affair until a "smoking gun" was discovered (Nevin 2017). Yet, Hamilton could not have envisioned how the fusion of presidential power and ritualized partisan combat would make the public, and its representatives, recklessly coarse to constitutional norms.

Indeed, the president's executive aggrandizement is a direct consequence of the political developments that have given rise to executive-centered partisanship. Trump and his Republican allies defended his machinations by invoking the progressive conceit—embraced by conservatives in the wake of the polarizing conflicts of the sixties—that the president embodies the national interest. The mystique of presidentialism led Congress to delegate immense power to the executive, with little oversight, further conflating the president's personal or partisan interest with the national interest. Trump has deployed the powers of the modern executive office with more impunity than his predecessors. Yet his indiscretions have exploited precedents set by Congress and the courts, which emboldened presidents to carry out a vast array of policies unilaterally, to withhold appropriated funds, to undertake major foreign policy initiatives secretly, and to direct intelligence and law enforcement agencies to do the president's bidding. Few defenders of the separation of powers will find consolation in the fact that the public, let alone members of Congress, were aware of Trump's Ukrainian actions only because of a single whistleblower and the decision of Michael Atkinson—inspector general of the intelligence community—to flout his White House superiors and take the report to the House Intelligence Committee.

Trump's usurpations were abetted by the subordination of institutional loyalties to partisan loyalties. In a political context where the political fate of Democrats and Republicans depend on the fortunes of their respective party's president, achieving bipartisan support for holding the White House accountable is highly unlikely. Given how deeply executive-centered partisanship is now rooted in American democracy, it is hardly surprising that reactions to the president's behavior fell along predictable party lines and that counterarguments from both sides fell on deaf ears. In the never-ending campaign season, Republican Senators stoked the president's base with "deep state" conspiracy theories promoted by FOX News and conservative talk radio. Determined not to let a good business opportunity go to waste, Trump's campaign used the impeachment proceedings to motivate Republicans to open their pocketbooks. Ads poured out of the RNC targeting the president's "most LOYAL supporters." Certain fundraising ads even permitted donors to jointly contribute to the accounts of Republican nominees in districts targeting vulnerable House Democrats who had voted to impeach the president (Isenstadt 2019b). During the last quarter of 2019, as the impeachment followed its predictable course, the president's campaign hauled in more than $46 million, including donations from six hundred thousand new donors (Dawsey and Lee 2020), exceeding any previous record. On the eve of the House's vote to impeach the first US president running for reelection, Trump's campaign manager celebrated the president's good political fortune: "That has put money in our bank. It has added volunteers to our field program. It's filled up the rallies easier" (Olorunnipa 2019b).

Nixon's pioneering and corrupt advance of executive-centered partisanship resulted in efforts to restore the "guardrails" of liberal democracy. One might hope that the Trump impeachment episode and its aftermath, which saw the White House take retribution against career diplomats and civil servants who testified in the impeachment investigations, might result in a renewed effort to restore constitutional norms and institutional constraints. But those who would seek to restore institutional restraints must face the imposing obstacle of a government that for years has sacrificed responsible leadership to aggressive and resolute partisan administration.

Indeed, Trump's bellicose partisanship seems to have influenced the Democratic Party almost as much as his own. With the approach of the 2020 campaign, most aspiring Democratic presidential nominees promised to fight fire with fire and to issue new executive orders that would rescind the incumbent's policies and advance progressive measures on a litany of issues ranging from climate change to immigration. Even though former vice president Joseph Biden—the early front-runner—promised to restore civility to American politics and celebrated his ability to broker legislative compromises with Congress, he found himself on the defensive as more ardent progressives such as Bernie Sanders, Elizabeth Warren, and Pete Buttigieg insisted that "there is no back to normal" (Siders 2019; Sullivan 2019).

Trump's disruptive presidency is testament to political developments that have fused executive power and fierce partisanship—and instilled in the country an obsession with the modern presidency's pseudo grandeur and the false hope that a single individual could ever truly serve as the sole steward of the public welfare. Until this misplaced faith in a presidency-centered democracy is decisively disabused, the hope of restoring the constitutional norms and institutions of the American republic will be a chimera.

NOTES

1. Interview with Nicholas Jacobs and Sidney Milkis, May 28, 2019, not for attribution.

2. For Trump, trade policy, especially with China, was the single most important indicator of the "serious trouble" America faced economically and in foreign policy. In the final debate featuring Trump and his remaining challengers, John Kasich, Marco Rubio, and Ted Cruz, all three contenders distinguished themselves from Trump first and foremost on the issue of free trade and the implication of Trump's victory on the global marketplace. See: Republican Candidates Debate in Miami, Florida, March 10, 2016. Full transcript available at: https://www.presidency.ucsb.edu/documents/republican-candidates-debate-miami-florida.

3. Although the USMCA was hammered out with Democrats in Congress, who succeeded in getting labor and environmental protections added to the agreement, no Democrat was invited to the signing ceremony (Stein 2020).

4. US-Mexico-Canada Agreement, Article 32.1: General Exceptions. https://ustr.gov/sites/default/files/files/agreements/FTA/USMCA/Text/32_Exceptions_and_General_Provisions.pdf.

5. The percentage of Americans indicating immigration as the most important problem was so small in 2016 that Gallup did not record a partisan differential. Information on 2016 and 2019 numbers were documented in the Internet Archive, www.gallup.com. See also: Frank Newport, "Immigration Surges to Top of Most Important Problem List," *Gallup*, July 18, 2018.

6. Arizona v. United States, 567 U.S. (2012).

7. "Protecting the Nation from Foreign Terrorist Entry into the United States," Executive Order 13769, January 27, 2017, Federal Registrar 82, no. 20: 8977–8982.

8. Trump v. Hawaii, 585 U.S. (2018).

9. H.R. 695, Department of Defense Appropriations Act, 2018, 115th Congress.https://www.congress.gov/bill/115th-congress/house-bill/695

10. "Declaring a National Emergency Concerning the Southern Border of the United States," Proclamation 9844, February 15, 2019, Federal Registrar 84, no. 34: 4949–4950.

11. Obama saw his party lose more support "down ballot" in Congress and the states than any president since Dwight Eisenhower.

12. Calculations derived from district-level data available at: David Leip, 2018, "US Presidential Election Data," *David Leip's Atlas of US Presidential Elections*. https://uselectionatlas.org/.

13. Trump backed Moore, even though he faced allegations of sexual abuse.

14. Donald Trump (@realDonaldTrump), "To the great people of West Virginia . . . ," Twitter, May 7, 2018.

15. Donald Trump's full remarks available at: "Read: Full Transcript of Trump's Rally Speech in Florida," February 18, 2017, *Palm Beach Post*: http://www.palm

beachpost.com/news/national/read-full-transcript-trump-rally-speech-florida /DeDCpoNEKLQmWcIKndWBoM/.

16. Calculations derived from data available at: Federal Election Commission, *Campaign Finance Data*, May 15, 2019, https://www.fec.gov/data/candidates/president/.

17. *Donald J. Trump for President*, "Donald J. Trump for President Announces Delegate and Party Organization Team for the 2020 Campaign," January 18, 2019.

18. Calculations derived from data available at: Federal Election Commission, 2019, "Trump Victory, PAC, Non-qualified, Joint-fundraising Committee," *Campaign Finance Data*, https://www.fec.gov/data/committee/C00618389/.

REFERENCES

Abramowitz, Alan I. "Economic Conditions, Presidential Popularity, and Voting Behavior in Midterm Congressional Elections." *Journal of Politics* 47, no. 1 (1985): 31–43.

Associated Press. "The Latest: McSally Embraces Trump in Arizona Senate Bid." *Washington Post*, January 12, 2018.

Blumenthal, Sidney. "The Permanent Campaign." Boston, MA: Beacon, 1980.

Brown, Chad. P. "Policy Brief 17-21—Steel, Aluminum, Lumber, Solar: Trump's Stealth Trade Protection." *Peterson Institute for International Economics*, 2017. www.pile.com.

Brownstein, Ronald. "The Clinton Conundrum." *Atlantic*, 2015. Last accessed September 12, 2017. https://www.theatlantic.com/politics/archive/2015/04/the-clinton-conundrum/431949/.

Bykowicz, Julie, and Jill Colvin. "Trump Trashes Media, Cheers Wins at $10 Million Fundraiser." Associated Press, June 29, 2017; Maggie Severns. "Trump Learns to Love Megadonors." *Politico*, June 8, 2018.

Cadelago, Christopher. "Trump's Midterm Pitch: Vote for Me." *Politico*, October 10, 2018.

Campbell, James E. *The Presidential Pulse of Congressional Elections*. Lexington: University Press of Kentucky, 1997.

Carney, Jordain. "Graham Downplays Need for Bill Reining in Trump on Tariffs after White House Meeting." *Hill*, June 6, 2018. https://thehill.com/home-news/senate/391087-graham-downplays-need-for-bill-reining-in-trump-on-tariffs-after-white-house.

Carpenter, Daniel P. *The Forging of Bureaucratic Autonomy: Reputations, Networks, and Policy Innovation, 1862–1928*. Princeton, NJ: Princeton University Press, 2002.

Conway, Kellyanne. "Transcript: Interview with Jim Gilmore on December 8, 2016." *Frontline*, 2016. Last accessed May 29, 2019: http://apps.frontline.org/trumps-road-whitehouse-frontline-interviews/transcript/kellyanne-conway.html.

Cuneo, Ernest. "The Eve of the Purge," 23, unpublished manuscript found in the Ernest Cuneo Papers, box 111, Franklin D. Roosevelt Library, Hyde Part, NY.

Dawsey, Josh, and Michelle Ye Hee Lee. "Trump and the RNC Raised almost Half a Billion Dollars Last Year—And Still Had Nearly $200 Million Heading into 2020." *Washington Post*, January 3, 2020.

Doherty, Brendan. *The Rise of the President's Permanent Campaign*. Lawrence: University Press of Kansas, 2012.

Edsall, Thomas B. "Trump Needs His Base to Burn with Anger, But Has He Raised the Political Temperature Too High for His Own Good? *New York Times*, July 3, 2019, https://www.nytimes.com/2019/07/03/opinion/trump-republican-base.html.

Elliott, Philip. "Martha McSally, Who Learned to Love Donald Trump, Wins Arizona Primary." *Time*, August 29, 2018.

Gallup. *Presidential Job Approval Center*. 2019. https://news.gallup.com/interactives/185273/r.aspx.

Galvin, Daniel. *Presidential Party Building: Dwight D. Eisenhower to George W. Bush*. Princeton, NJ: Princeton University Press, 2010.

Hannity, Sean. Interview with Lindsay Graham. January 8, 2019. *Fox News*, https://www.foxnews.com/transcript/mccarthy-trump-talked-about-the-facts-on-border-security.

Heclo, Hugh. "Sixties Civics." In *The Great Society and the High Tide of Liberalism*, ed. Sidney M. Milkis and Jerome Mileur. Amherst: University of Massachusetts Press, 2005.

Immigrant Defense Project. " Safeguarding the Integrity of Our Courts: The Impact of ICE Courthouse Operations in New York State." 2019. https://www.immigrantdefenseproject.org/wp-content/uploads/Safeguarding-the-Integrity-of-Our-Courts-Final-Report.pdf

Isenstadt, Alex. "Trump Campaign Moves to Stave Off Mayhem at 2020 Convention." *Politico*, January 7, 2019a.

———. "GOP Cashes in on Impeachment." *Politico*, September 25, 2019b.

———. "RNC Warns Donors to Steer Clear of Kochs." *Politico*, August 2, 2018.

———. "How Donald Trump Lost the Summer." *Politico*, August 17, 2016.

Jacobs, Nicholas F., Desmond King, and Sidney M. Milkis. "Building a Conservative State: Partisan Polarization and the Redeployment of Administrative Power." *Perspectives on Politics* 17, no. 2 (2019): 453–469.

Jacobson, Gary C. "It's Nothing Personal: The Decline of the Incumbency Advantage in US House Elections." *Journal of Politics* 77, no. 3 (2015): 861–873.

Johnson, Eliana, and Burgess Everett. "Pressure from Base Pushed a Flustered Trump into Shutdown Reversal." *Politico*, December 12, 2018. https://www.politico.com/story/2018/12/20/trump-budget-reversal-1071388.

Keller, Morton. *America's Three Regimes: A New Political History*. Oxford: Oxford University Press, 2007.

Korecki, Natasha, and Christopher Cadelago. "GOP Turns to Trump to Rescue Tennessee Senate Seat." *Politico*, October 1, 2018.

Kriner, Douglas L., and Andrew Reeves. *The Particularistic President: Executive Branch Politics and Political Inequality*. New York: Cambridge University Press, 2015.

Kurta, A. M. "Memorandum: Military Service Suitability Determinations for Foreign Nationals Who Are Lawful Permanent Residents." *Office of the Secretary of Defense*, October 13, 2017.

Lee, Frances. *Insecure Majorities: Congress and the Perpetual Campaign*. Chicago: University of Chicago Press, 2018.

Lowande, Kenneth S., Jeffery A. Jenkins, and Andrew J. Clarke. "Presidential Particularism and US Trade Politics." *Political Science Research and Methods* 6, no. 2 (2018): 264–281.

McCormack, John. "The Neo-Trumper." *The Weekly Standard*, 2018. https://www.weeklystandard.com/john-mccormack/the-neo-trumper.

McGovern, George. "Address Accepting the Presidential Nomination at the Democratic National Convention, Miami Beach, Florida, July 14." 1972. Retrieved January 3, 2018: http://www.presidency.ucsb.edu/ws/?pid=25967.

Milkis, Sidney M., and Nicholas F. Jacobs. "'I Alone Can Fix It': Donald Trump, the Administrative Presidency, and Hazards of Executive-Centered Partisanship." *Forum* 15, no. 3 (2017): 583–613.

Milkis, Sidney M., Jesse H. Rhodes, and Emily J. Charnock. "What Happened to Post-partisanship? Barack Obama and the New American Party System." *Perspectives on Politics* 10, no. 1 (2012): 57–76.

Milkis, Sidney M., and John W. York. "Barack Obama, Organizing for America, and Executive-Centered Partisanship." *Studies in American Political Development* 31, no. 1 (2017): 1–23.

Murray, Stephanie. "Massachusetts Republicans Move to Protect Trump in 2020 Primary." *Politico*, May 6, 2019: https://www.politico.com/story/2019/05/06/massachusetts-republicans-trump -2020-primary-1302875.

Nakamura, David, and John Wagner. "US and Mexico Sign Agreement, Avoid Tariffs." *Washington Post*, June 3, 2019, A1–A11.

Nevin, Mark. "Nixon Loyalists, Barry Goldwater, and Republican Support for President Nixon during Watergate." *Journal of Policy History* 29, no. 3 (2017): 403–430.

Olorunnipa, Toluse. "Trumps Frenetic Immigration Approach Becomes a Central Part of the 2020 Bid." *Washington Post*, June 3, 2019a, A2.

———. "'This Lit Up Our Base': Trump Campaign says Impeachment Will Help him Win Reelection." *Washington Post*, December 12, 2019b.

Orren, Karen, and Stephen Skowronek. *The Policy State: An American Predicament*. Cambridge, MA: Harvard University Press, 2017.

Republican National Committee. "Republican National Committee Resolution Supporting the Presidency of Donald J. Trump," January 26, 2019: https://prod-cdn-static.gop.com/media/documents/RNC_Resolution_Supporting_the_Presidency_of_Donald_J._Trump _1549555495.pdf.

———. "RNC & Donald J. Trump for President Announce 2016 Trump Victory Leadership Team." *Press Releases*, May 24, 2016.

Roosevelt, Franklin D. "Introduction." *Public Papers and Addresses* 7 (1938 volume), ed. Samuel I. Rosenman, xxviii–xxxii. New York: Macmillan, 1941.

Savage, Louisa, and John F. Harris. "Trump's Method on the Madness of Trade." *Politico,* June 6, 2019: https://www.politico.com/story/2019/06/06/donald-trump-trade-policy-global-translations-1355868.

Schaffner, Brian, and Stephen Ansolabhere. "2017 CCES Common Content." 2019. *Harvard Dataverse*: https://doi.org/10.7910/DVN/3STEZY.

Schattschneider, E. E. *Politics, Pressures and the Tariff.* New York: Prentice-Hall, 1935.

Shafer, Byron. *Quiet Revolution: The Struggle for the Democratic Party and the Shaping of Post-Reform Politics.* New York: Russell Sage, 1983.

Siders, David. "Democrats Preview Post-Trump Plan: Executive Orders." *Politico,* May 4, 2019.

Skowronek, Stephen. *Building a New American State: The Expansion of National Administrative Capacities, 1870–1920.* New York: Cambridge University Press, 1982.

Sparrow, James T. *Warfare State.* New York: Oxford University Press, 2013.

Stein, Jeff. "Trump Signs USMCA, Revamping North American Trade Rules." *Washington Post,* January 29, 2020.

Sullivan, Sean. "Liberals Take Biden to Task to Blunt Candidacy." *Washington Post,* June 3, 2019, A1, A4.

Swift, Art. "Americans Split on Whether NAFTA Is Good or Bad for US." Gallup, February 24, 2017: https://news.gallup.com/poll/204269/americans-split-whether-nafta-good-bad.aspx.

Trump, Donald. "Address to the Nation on the Crisis at the Border, January 8." White House Press Office. 2019: https://www.whitehouse.gov/briefings-statements/president-donald-j-trumps-address-nation-crisis-border/.

———. "Remarks by President Trump in Press Conference After Midterm Elections." *White House,* November 7, 2018.

Werner, Erica, and John Wagner. "GOP Opposition to Emergency Declaration Grows as Trump Warns Lawmakers." *Washington Post.* February 28, 2019.

———. "Trump Welcomes a Shutdown During Oval Office Squabble with Pelosi, Schumer." *Washington Post,* December 11, 2018.

White House Press Office. "Crisis at the Border." *Fact Sheets,* January 8, 2019a. https://www.whitehouse.gov/briefings-statements/congress-must-do-more-to-address-the-border-crisis/.

———. "President Donald J. Trump's Border Security Victory." *Fact Sheets,* February 15, 2019b. https://www.whitehouse.gov/briefings-statements/president-donald-j-trumps-border-security-victory/.

Wong, Scott, and Alexander Bolton. "GOP's Tillis Comes Under Pressure for Taking on Trump." *Hill,* March 13, 2019: https://thehill.com/homenews/senate/433929-gops-tillis-comes-under-pressure-for-taking-on-trump.

Conclusion: Reflections and Paths Forward

Eric M. Patashnik and Wendy J. Schiller

In this volume, we have drawn from a wide range of perspectives on the current state of the American democracy to explore the roles of key actors and forces that can produce a responsive government and those that diminish the government's capacity to serve the needs of its citizens. We have structured the chapters in this book to enable readers to consider the effects of these forces on their own and as they interact with each other in the ever-changing political environment. We have chosen not to focus in just one area, such as political parties or elections, but rather have highlighted new research in the wider set of areas that influences both political competition and policy outcomes. Here, we offer a synopsis of that work, as well as our own views on how rapid changes in the political environment will alter the internal workings of the American democracy in the coming decades.

AMERICAN POLITICS PAST AND PRESENT

In the introduction, we raised the classic political science question of whether political parties are a good foundation for the American democracy or whether they, as George Washington feared, would ultimately serve only as a continuous source of division and faction in the electorate. The earliest policy debates in the nation's history were framed as a dichotomous choice between two "sides," such as the debate between Federalists and anti-Federalists over the adoption of the Constitution. As the nation grew in population, geographic size, and wealth, the set of ideas and interests debated within the political sphere expanded as well. While the two major parties competed on a national stage, especially for control of the presidency, both federalism and the separation of powers prevented the parties from behaving like disciplined policy teams during much of the twentieth century. A Democrat from South Carolina and a Democrat from Massachusetts in 1950 might share support for the New Deal, but they would disagree on many other issues (Polsby 1997; Pierson and Schickler 2020). As we noted in the introduction, midcentury reformers were frustrated by this state of affairs and argued that more "responsible" parties were needed to promote effective government (American Political Science Association 1950).

Over the past thirty years or so, the American political system has undergone profound change. While the basic institutions of government remain in place, asymmetric polarization and party sorting have changed the way these institutions operate. As new issues like race, women's rights, LBGTQ rights, intervention in international conflicts abroad, climate change, and income inequality have emerged on the agenda, partisan divisions have increased among the electorate. These divisions are usually driven by elite actors, which include elected officials, party leaders, interest groups, media, and policy activists. Each of these sets of political actors promotes partisan messaging designed to clarify and reinforce their preferred stances on these issues among the electorate.

Elite-driven polarization runs counter to the traditional theoretical expectation that, in a democracy, voters hold their own preferences or views over policy outcomes and choose their elected officials based on their promises to carry out those policies. As much of the research presented in this volume shows, we live in a world where voters' preferences over policy are increasingly shaped by their allegiance to their political party or their "side," at times more than what their own individual circumstances would seem to require from government action. This condition yields two distortions to democratic governance. First, parties may cater to the intense demands of their bases and consequently fail to take stances that are responsive to the preferences of the broader public. Second, government may become much less responsive to constituents' needs because partisan disagreement prevents the necessary compromise to pass public policy. The result is a decline in the government's capacity to solve problems and promote the achievement of widely shared goals, such as rising living standards for all.

One of the contributions of this volume is to show how these political developments have unfolded over time. In their chapters, James A. Morone and Matt Grossmann illustrate how changes in the composition and behavior of the parties have weakened the prospects for effective democratic governance. In chapter 1, Morone argues that American politics has grown increasingly tribal. While the two parties were once "ideological cousins" who shared a lot of common ground, they now reflect "different worlds." To be sure, Morone observes that divisions over a fear of "aliens," moneyed elites, and the role of the national government are nothing new in American politics. However, Morone suggests that the current partisan alignment is unique. In the past, party policies diffused tribal conflicts because no party embraced both racial justice and immigrant rights. But today, for the first time, the parties are amplifying rather than dampening tribalism because the two parties now have distinct social identities and ideological commitments.

Matt Grossmann's work in chapter 2 provides a sweeping look at how a tacit bipartisan compromise over governance has broken down, making it increasingly difficult for the two parties to work together on behalf of the long-term policy interests of the country. Liberals and conservatives have long had different goals. Liberals have sought to use public policy to provide benefits to the diverse social groups within the Democratic Party coalition; Republicans have been wary of an expansion of government's domestic role. During the postwar era, the two parties worked out an implicit bargain that allowed slow and steady progress to be made on many issues. The expansion of national policy was built on a compromise in which Democrats would advance only a few issues at a time and Republicans would limit federal spending and preserve authority for the private sector and for state and local actors. This dynamic helps explain how the federal government grew dramatically between 1935 and 1975, even though the United States has never adopted a European-style welfare state. In an era of intense partisan polarization, however, the tacit compromise of using conservative means to address liberal policy goals is no longer viable. Rather than incremental policymaking, we now have sporadic bursts of liberal policymaking (such as the passage of the Affordable Care Act and economic stimulus legislation during the Obama administration) followed by sharp conservative backlashes. In sum, intense polarization is making government policymaking less consistent and effective. Grossmann argues that this is an acute challenge given the growing expectations of the federal government, made clear by the failure to adopt a national strategy on COVID-19.

Building on the exploration of how polarization arose over time, scholars Sarah A. Binder, Frances E. Lee, and Nolan McCarty each delve into the effect of polarization on congressional performance. In chapter 3, Binder shows that, over time, parties have become cemented in opposition to each other. She proposes that because of intense polarization, gridlock became the norm on Capitol Hill and created a condition whereby passing the most basic legislation, for example, to fund the government through congressional appropriations, can be obstructed because of conflict between the majority and minority parties. Gridlock is not only inefficient but also impedes the federal government's ability to address constituent needs. It also prevents the federal government from tackling emerging problems through policy innovation.

However, Frances E. Lee challenges that description of congressional policymaking in chapter 4. She documents that most legislation that passes Congress is still bipartisan and contends that bipartisan cooperation remains necessary for majority party success. In particular, she argues that having majority control of Congress and the White House, as the Republican Party did in the 115th Congress (2017–2019), is no guarantee of passing the party's agenda through legislation. Lee documents that the Republicans had what she calls "clear successes" on only four out of twelve items they considered their top policy agenda items, and they had five distinct failures from the same list. They had mixed success on the remaining agenda items. Lee attributes this mixed record under unified party government to disagreements within the Republican Party in Congress or between the congressional party and President Trump. Overall, Lee's work suggests that scholars and political observers rely too much on roll-call votes to judge the strength of the majority party and the extent of polarization in Congress; we should also assess the power of parties to enact their preferred policy agendas without the support of the other side.

In chapter 5, Nolan McCarty challenges the conventional wisdom that gridlock and polarization in Washington, DC, are necessarily detrimental for governance in American democracy. McCarty illustrates the extent of polarization in Congress and in state governments and argues that the gridlock that occurs at the federal level may in fact create an opening for states to craft policies more tailored to their constituents than to the nation as a whole. If and where the federal government does not act and state governments see a need to address a pressing issue, they can seize the initiative and move forward. However, McCarty notes that there are two limitations to this institutional corrective. First, the state legislatures are themselves becoming more polarized than in the past, albeit to a varying degree across regions and that has not reached congressional levels as yet. Second, as states become more uniformly partisan internally, they become increasingly different from each other. Consequently, we could see a country with greater inequality across states in terms of health care, education, and individual rights. In 2020, we saw just that with very different responses by states to the COVID-19 pandemic. Even with these different responses, though, many states were more responsive than Congress as a whole, bearing out McCarty's argument.

To understand how polarization is shaping politics and policymaking inside the halls of government, it is also important to investigate the political forces that influence voters' attitudes and behavior. In chapter 6, Kristin Kanthak examines public trust in government through the lens of negative partisanship, meaning here the tendency of voters to disapprove of government when the opposite party holds power. She uses survey data from the American National Election Studies to test whether individuals who felt strongly attached to a party had more or less trust in government compared with individuals who did not express a strong party affiliation. Controlling for party control of state government, she finds that respondents who label themselves strong partisans tended to have lower trust in government when their team is not in power. Respondents who have weaker partisan affiliations have higher trust in government.

In chapter 7, John Sides, Michael Tesler, and Lynn Vavreck extend our window into individual-level political attitudes by examining the interaction among gender, attitudes on gender-based issues, and partisanship. They find that people's attitudes on issues such as feminism, sexual harassment, and gender discrimination can, but do not always, produce different vote choices and that these issues may be stronger influences on women's vote choice than on men's. However, the gender gap is significantly mediated by party. In other words, how citizens feel about these issues is more strongly associated with their party affiliation today than in the past. The authors argue that differences in opinions on gender issues are yet another growing component of the divide between Democrats and Republicans.

The next two chapters bring the effects of social media into the larger picture of public opinion and voting behavior. In chapter 8, Samara Klar and Yotam Shmargad present the findings of a controlled experiment they conducted on how news feeds for individuals can shape their political views. By randomizing what people read on their social media pages and in what order, they find that items at the top of news feeds were more likely to receive likes from the respondent and that the closer the content of the news item was to the respondent's expressed ideology, the more likely there were to like it. This work strikingly illustrates the power of social media sources to influence and reinforce political opinions, as well as how the structure of news feeds can encourage echo chambers for particular political views.

In chapter 9, Deborah J. Schildkraut, Jeffrey M. Berry, and James M.

Glaser also demonstrate the effect of social media in their study of interaction among Twitter users who are identified as either liberal or conservative. The authors show that liberals are less willing than conservatives to engage in conflict over Twitter on postings that they disagreed with or opposed. Using an original dataset of Twitter postings, replies, and comments, they find that conservatives are more likely to take on the "other side" in their replies and comments. However, their research uncovers no evidence that ideology is associated with the tendency to use highly inflammatory or "toxic" language in Twitter engagement.

Part 4 includes two chapters that examine the prospect for increasing party competition from two different vantage points. In chapter 10, Katherine M. Gehl and Michael E. Porter propose a new theory of party competition centered around producing parties, and government, that would be more responsible and more responsive to constituent needs and concerns. They set forth the premise that much of the failure of present-day government lies in the fact that the two major parties do not face any serious competition and that there are few incentives for either party to produce policies that serve to improve government programs or people's daily lives. They attribute gaps in health-care insurance availability, the budget deficit, and even student loan debt to the failure of third parties to successfully challenge the dominance of the Democratic and Republican Parties. The authors propose eliminating party-based primaries, which California has already done, and implementing ranked-choice voting, as some states are trying to do.

But would such reforms actually work? Do scholars presume a demand or need for third parties that does not exist among the electorate? In chapter 11, Lee Drutman, William A. Galston, and Tod Lindberg tackle those questions in their study of several large public opinion survey questions about third parties. They find mixed levels of support for solutions of the sort offered by Gehl and Porter. Voters clearly want more alternatives to the Democrats and Republicans in modern American politics, but they do not necessarily want a specific third party, or even a specific type of third party. Instead, survey respondents say they want more choice in the candidates and policies put forth by candidates for elected office, and if that means another party is required, they would welcome it. However, that does not mean they would automatically switch parties, and the authors are careful to conclude that voters may not have the patience to change the structure of how campaigns are run in order to encourage additional political parties. Moreover, even if there were more party choices, it is not at all clear that voters would switch their vote to a third party, either temporarily or on a permanent basis. People get used to what party labels mean and how politicians speak about policies, and to break through that familiarity to affiliate with a lesser-known, new political party would clearly take time and energy that many voters do not have.

In the final chapter, Nicholas F. Jacobs and Sidney M. Milkis focus on the role of presidents in determining the direction of their political party while in office. The authors explore how President Donald Trump went from being an outsider challenging the establishment leadership of the Republican Party to having near complete control over the party at the national and state levels in a matter of four years. They argue that Trump's assertion of control over congressional Republicans is actually not surprising considering the rise in presidential power more generally over the past two decades. Congress has not necessarily ceded its power to the president willingly, but external foreign and military threats, budget deficits, and partisan gridlock have all combined to make Congress less effective relative to the executive branch. A president also has the major advantage of being a singular voice on politics and policy, which frequently rings louder than any of the collective voices in Congress. The authors demonstrate how all of these factors have given presidents the tools for control over their political party, with little internal party resistance in sight.

LOOKING TOWARD THE FUTURE OF AMERICAN DEMOCRACY

Can American democracy withstand extreme polarization, social media echo chambers, conflictual political discourse, legislative gridlock, and a president who breaks all the conventional rules? The research in this volume has tried to show how these developments have strained our politics and challenged expectations of effective and responsive governance. In the conventional model of democracy, voters have distinct interests and opinions, and they choose among candidates who run on two coherent party platforms based on promises they make to enact policy. After those candidates win elected office, voters are expected to judge them, and their parties, on the effectiveness of those policies in the next reelection cycle. This model breaks down if lawmakers focus on pleasing their party bases rather than the median voter, if the two parties do not work from a common set of facts, and if voters choose candidates not on the basis of their positions and performance but on tribal loyalty and dislike of the other side.

Does that mean democracy is no longer operative in the United States? There are certainly many reasons for concern about the health of our political process, but we would caution against excessive pessimism. The self-correcting mechanisms of American democracy have atrophied, but they still exist. As we noted, state governments can sometimes adopt policies that are better tailored to the preferences of voters, helping to offset partisan conflict and deadlock at the national level. In addition, voters have shown a willingness in recent years to vote against a majority party based on poor performance on the economy and foreign affairs or inattentiveness to constituent needs. Elected officials today are more loyal to their political party and less willing to cross the political aisle, but that just makes it easier for voters to identify where to place reward or blame. To say that voters are not in a position to make a clear choice is not accurate. Partisan polarization has costs, but it is not itself incompatible with democracy.

However, the constant seesaw of partisan competition, with majority party control of one or both branches of Congress changing hands more frequently than in the past, creates challenges for governance. Close party balance encourages policymakers to seek partisan advantage on every issue, because they perceive that control of government is at stake in every election cycle. This narrow focus on maximizing electoral advantage encourages posturing and position-taking rather than pragmatic problem-solving. In that case, the responsiveness part of the democracy equation remains unfulfilled. Effective government may be as simple as making sure that a student loan is processed or as complicated as testing millions of Americans for COVID-19; either way, there are real needs that government needs to meet in modern-day America. When elected officials cannot even agree on where and how to administer programs, government ceases to function efficiently. Far too many issues require effective government attention to accept politics as it is.

Rebuilding the capacity of American national government to solve major problems is an urgent priority. While administrative reforms such as reinvigorating the civil service, enhancing the capacity of public health agencies to manage future pandemics, and replacing the antiquated computer systems used to carry out social programs are necessary steps, they are insufficient ones. Americans will not achieve better government without a more robust democracy. To us, the key to renewing our democracy may lie in harnessing the creative energy of voluntary associations and social movements, fueled by the grassroots participation of citizens across lines of education, occupation, and wealth as well as by the power of social media, to propel the political system forward even when it appears hopelessly stalled. Even without Facebook, Twitter, WhatsApp, Instagram, and plain old email, activists throughout history have been able to accomplish enormous change using the basic rights of speech, assembly, and press. From the American

Revolution and abolitionism to the women's suffragette movement, the labor movement, the civil rights movement, and the movement to secure a constitutional right to same-sex marriage, American democracy, albeit still deeply flawed, has expanded the set of people who can exercise their constitutional rights. However, these struggles occurred in an age when politics was dominated by a single group: white men.

Today, the United States is struggling to become the first successful democracy in which no single ethnic or religious group is in the majority. In recent years, we have seen the upside of these changes, with the greater involvement and representation of previously unheard voices in politics and society. The massive nationwide protests against police brutality after the killing of George Floyd—a forty-six-year-old black man who died in police custody after a white officer knelt on his neck for almost nine minutes—may be a watershed moment. The protests not only signaled a dramatic increase in social movement activity but also demonstrated that millions of Americans support the simple yet radical idea of justice for all. As much as we have also seen the downside, as in the spread of hatred based on race, ethnicity, religion, and sexual orientation, America looks, feels, and sounds different than it ever has before. The deleterious effects of tribalism will not be easy to overcome, but there is no question in our minds that US political institutions will be forced to adapt to an ever-growing chorus of voters who want more responsive government. It is our hope that this volume has identified some of the political forces that will need to be harnessed to make that happen.

REFERENCES

American Political Science Association. "Toward a More Responsible Two-Party System: A Report of the Committee on Political Parties." *American Political Science Review,* Supplement 44, no. 3 (1950): v–96.

Pierson, Paul, and Eric Schickler. "Madison's Constitution Under Stress: A Developmental Analysis of Political Polarization." *Annual Review of Political Science* 23, no. 1 (2020): 37–58.

Polsby, Nelson W. "The American Party System." In *The New Federalist Papers,* ed. A. Brinkley, Nelson W. Polsby and Kathleen M. Sullivan, 37–44. Washington, DC: Brookings Institution, 1997.

About the Contributors

Jeffrey M. Berry is John Richard Skuse, Class of 1941, Professor of Political Science at Tufts University. Jeffrey Berry's research has focused on policy-making in Washington, interest groups, Massachusetts politics, nonprofits, and urban government. He is the author of many books, including *The Rebirth of Urban Democracy* (1993), which won the American Political Science Association's Gladys M. Kammerer Award, as well as *Lobbying and Policy Change* (2009) and *A Voice for Nonprofits* (2005), each of which received the Leon Epstein Outstanding Book Award. His book *The New Liberalism* (1999) was awarded the Aaron Wildavsky Award by the Policy Studies Organization. Other books include *The Outrage Industry* (2014), *The Oxford Handbook of American Political Parties and Interest Groups* (2010), *The Interest Group Society* (2008), and *Lobbying for the People* (1977). Berry is the recipient of the Samuel Eldersveld Career Achievement Award from the American Political Science Association and the Tufts Distinguished Scholar Award.

Sarah A. Binder is professor of political science at George Washington University and senior fellow in governance studies at the Brookings Institution. Professor Binder's most recent book is *The Myth of Independence: How Congress Governs the Federal Reserve*, coauthored with Mark Spindel (2017). Her previous books include *Advice and Dissent: The Struggle to Shape the Federal Judiciary*, coauthored with Forrest Maltzman (2009), *Stalemate: Causes and Consequences of Legislative Gridlock* (2003), *Minority Rights, Majority Rule: Partisanship and the Development of Congress* (1997), and *Politics or Principle? Filibustering in the United States Senate*, coauthored with Steven S. Smith (1997). Her work has also appeared in the *American Political Science Review*, *Journal of Politics*, *Legislative Studies Quarterly*, and elsewhere.

Lee Drutman is a senior fellow in the Political Reform Program at New America. He is the author of *The Business of America Is Lobbying* (2015), winner of the 2016 American Political Science Association's Robert A. Dahl Award for "scholarship of the highest quality on the subject of democracy."

In addition, he writes regularly for *Polyarchy*, a Vox blog. He is currently writing a book about the crisis of the two-party system in America. His areas of expertise include hyperpartisanship, Congress, lobbying, and money in politics. Drutman also teaches in the Center for Advanced Governmental Studies at Johns Hopkins University. He holds a PhD in political science from the University of California, Berkeley.

William A. Galston holds the Ezra K. Zilkha Chair in the Brookings Institution's Governance Studies Program, where he serves as a senior fellow. A participant in six presidential campaigns, he served from 1993 to 1995 as deputy assistant for domestic policy in the Clinton administration. Galston is the author of nine books and more than one hundred articles in the fields of political theory, public policy, and American politics. His most recent books are *Anti-Pluralism: The Populist Threat to Liberal Democracy* (2018), *Public Matters* (2005), and *The Practice of Liberal Pluralism* (2004). A winner of the American Political Science Association's Hubert H. Humphrey Award, Galston was elected a fellow of the American Academy of Arts and Sciences in 2004. Galston has appeared on all the principal television networks and is frequently interviewed on NPR. He writes a weekly column for the *Wall Street Journal.*

Katherine M. Gehl is the fourth-generation president and CEO of Gehl Foods. Katherine Gehl led an aggressive growth strategy, driving transformations across the company from management and processes to facilities and information systems. Gehl's background includes roles as vice president at Bernstein Investment Research and Management, special assistant for technology and economic development to Mayor Richard M. Daley, director of information technology services at Chicago Public Schools, and organizational development manager at Oracle.

James M. Glaser is professor of political science and dean of the School of Arts and Sciences at Tufts University. His research focuses on electoral politics and political behavior. His most recent book, coauthored with Timothy J. Ryan, is *Changing Minds, If Not Hearts: Political Remedies for Racial Conflict* (2013). Professor Glaser's previous books, *The Hand of the Past in Contemporary Southern Politics* (2005) and *Race, Campaign Politics, and the Realignment in the South* (1998) each received the Southern Political Science Association's V. O. Key Award, given to the year's best book on Southern politics. Professor Glaser has published articles in such periodicals as the *American Journal of Political Science, Journal of Politics, British Journal of Political*

Science, Political Behavior, PS: Political Science and Politics, Public Opinion Quarterly, Electoral Studies, and *Political Research Quarterly.*

Matt Grossmann is the director of the Institute for Public Policy and Social Research (home of the Michigan Political Leadership Program and Policy and Survey Research Programs) as well as associate professor of political science at Michigan State University. He received his PhD from the University of California, Berkeley. His research concerns American politics and policymaking, especially interest-group representation and influence, political parties, political networks, campaigns, and policy change. He is the author of *Asymmetric Politics: Ideological Republicans and Group Interest Democrats* with David Hopkins (2016), *Artists of the Possible: Governing Networks and American Policy Change Since 1945* (2014), *New Directions in Interest Group Politics* (2013), and *The Not-So-Special Interests: Interest Groups, Public Representation, and American Governance* (2012).

Nicholas F. Jacobs is a political scientist and faculty fellow in the Department of Government at Colby College. He has research interests in executive branch policymaking and intergovernmental politics. His scholarly work has appeared or is forthcoming in *Perspectives on Politics, Publius: The Journal of Federalism, Studies in American Political Development, Journal of Policy History, Presidential Studies Quarterly, Political Research Quarterly, Education and Urban Society,* and the *Forum.* He received his PhD from the Department of Government at the University of Virginia.

Kristin Kanthak is associate professor of political science at the University of Pittsburgh and coeditor of *State Politics and Policy Quarterly.* Her research focuses on the effects on political representation of exogenous constraints such as political institutions. She is the author, with George Krause, of *The Diversity Paradox: Political Parties, Legislatures, and the Organizational Foundations of Representation in America* (2012), and she has published articles in the *American Political Science Review,* the *American Journal of Political Science,* the *British Journal of Political Science,* the *Journal of Law, Economics, and Organization, State Politics and Policy Quarterly,* and other outlets.

Samara Klar is associate professor in the School of Government and Public Policy at the University of Arizona. Her book *Independent Politics* (2016), coauthored with Yanna Krupnikov, received the Best Book Award from the American Political Science Association's Experimental Politics Section and the Robert E. Lane Award for Best Book from the American Political Science Association's Political Psychology Section in 2017. Klar has received a variety of other awards for her research, including the Emerging Scholar Award from the American Political Science Association section on Elections, Public Opinion, and Voting Behavior (2018) and the Emerging Scholar Award from the American Political Science Association section on Political Organizations and Parties (2016). She has received both the Burns Roper Fellowship from the American Association of Public Opinion Research and the Distinguished Junior Scholar Award from the American Political Science Association's Political Psychology Section. In 2016, she founded WomenAlsoKnowStuff, a website that promotes women in political science. She also serves on the board of Social Science Data Initiative, Social Science One. Her research has been supported by numerous grants, including funding from the National Science Foundation, and she has published her work in more than a dozen journals, including the *American Journal of Political Science*, the *Journal of Politics*, *Public Opinion Quarterly*, and *Political Psychology*.

Frances E. Lee is professor of politics and public affairs at Princeton University. Lee has broad interests in American politics, with a special focus on congressional politics, national policymaking, party politics, and representation. She is the author of *Insecure Majorities: Congress and the Perpetual Campaign* (2016) and *Beyond Ideology: Politics, Principles, and Partisanship in the U.S. Senate* (2009). She is also coauthor of *Sizing Up the Senate: The Unequal Consequences of Equal Representation* (1999) and a textbook, *Congress and Its Members* (2019). Her research has appeared in the *American Political Science Review*, *American Journal of Political Science*, *Perspectives on Politics*, *Journal of Politics*, *Legislative Studies Quarterly*, and other outlets. Lee is editor of the Cambridge Elements Series in American Politics and a series editor for Chicago Studies in American Politics. She was coeditor of *Legislative Studies Quarterly* from 2014 to 2019. Lee earned her BA from the University of Southern Mississippi and her PhD from Vanderbilt University. She is a fellow of the American Academy of Arts and Sciences.

Tod Lindberg is a senior fellow at Hudson Institute specializing in national security issues and the role of US leadership. He writes widely on US foreign policy and national security as well as on American politics and philosophical topics. He is the author of *The Heroic Heart: Greatness Ancient and Modern* (2015), a philosophical investigation of changing ideas about heroism and its connection to political order and change, and *The Political Teachings of Jesus* (2007), a study of Jesus's Gospel teachings about worldly affairs. He is coauthor with Lee Feinstein of *Means to an End: U.S. Interest in the International Criminal Court* (2009). He is the editor of *Beyond Paradise and Power: Europe, America, and the Future of a Troubled Partnership* (2005) and coeditor with Derek Chollet and David Shorr of *Bridging the Foreign Policy Divide* (2007). He studied political philosophy and literature at the University of Chicago.

Nolan McCarty is the Susan Dod Brown Professor of Politics and Public Affairs and former chair of the Department of Politics at Princeton University. He was formerly the associate dean at the Woodrow Wilson School of Public and International Affairs. His research interests include US politics, democratic political institutions, and political game theory. He is the recipient of the Robert Eckles Swain National Fellowship from the Hoover Institution and the John M. Olin Fellowship in Political Economy. His most recent book is *Polarization: What Everyone Needs to Know* (2019), and he has coauthored three books: *Political Game Theory: An Introduction* with Adam Meirowitz (2007), *Polarized America: The Dance of Ideology and Unequal Riches* with Keith Poole and Howard Rosenthal (2006), and *Political Bubbles: Financial Crises and the Failure of American Democracy* with Keith Poole and Howard Rosenthal (2013). In 2010, he was elected a fellow of the American Academy of Arts and Sciences. He earned his AB from the University of Chicago and his PhD from Carnegie Mellon University.

Sidney M. Milkis is the White Burkett Miller Professor and the Cavaliers' Distinguished Teaching Professor in the Department of Politics and a faculty associate at the University of Virginia's Miller Center. His books include *The President and the Parties: The Transformation of the American Party System since the New Deal* (1993), *Political Parties and Constitutional Government: Remaking American Democracy* (1999), *Presidential Greatness*, coauthored with Marc Landy (2000), *The American Presidency: Origins and Development, 1776–2018*, 8th ed., coauthored with Michael Nelson (2019), *Theodore Roosevelt, the Progressive Party, and the Transformation of American Democracy* (Kansas, 2009), and *Rivalry and Reform: Presidents, Social Movements, and the Transformation of American Politics*, coauthored with Daniel J. Tichenor (2018). He is the coeditor, with Jerome Mileur, of three volumes on twentieth-century political reform: *Progressivism and the New Democracy* (1999), *The New Deal and the Triumph of Liberalism* (2002), and *The Great Society and the High Tide of Liberalism* (2005). His articles on American government and political history have appeared in *Perspectives on Politics, Political Science Quarterly, Studies in American Political Development, PS: Political Science and Politics*, the *Journal of Policy History, Antitrust Law Journal, Presidential Studies Quarterly, Journal of*

Supreme Court History, and several edited volumes. In addition to teaching graduate and undergraduate students, he regularly gives public lectures on the historical roots of contemporary developments in American politics. He has a BA from Muhlenberg College and a PhD in political science from the University of Pennsylvania.

James A. Morone is the John Hazen White Professor of Public Policy and professor of political science and urban studies. Morone has written ten books and more than 150 articles, reviews, and essays on American political history, health-care policy, and social issues. His first book, *The Democratic Wish* (1991), won the American Political Science Association's Gladys M. Kammerer Award for the Best Book on US National Policy. His *Hellfire Nation: The Politics of Sin in American History* (2003) was nominated for a Pulitzer Prize and named a top book of 2003 by numerous newspapers and magazines. His *The Heart of Power: Health and Politics in the Oval Office* (coauthored with David Blumenthal, MD; 2009) was featured on the cover of the *New York Times Book Review.* Morone's latest book, *The Devils We Know*, was published by the University Press of Kansas in 2014. He received his BA from Middlebury College and his PhD from the University of Chicago.

Eric M. Patashnik is Julis-Rabinowitz Professor of Public Policy, professor of political science, and director of Brown University's Master of Public Affairs Program. Patashnik is also nonresident senior fellow at the Brookings Institution and an elected fellow of the National Academy of Public Administration. Patashnik is the author and editor of several books, including *Unhealthy Politics: The Battle over Evidence-Based Medicine*, with Alan Gerber and Conor Dowling (2017) and *Reforms at Risk: What Happens after Major Policy Changes Are Enacted* (2008). He has twice won the Louis Brownlow Book Award of the National Academy of Public Administration and has also won the Don K. Price Book Award of the American Political Science Association. He was a research fellow at the Brookings Institution from 1995 to 1996, served as president of the Public Policy Section of the American Political Science Association from 2017 to 2018, and was the editor of the *Journal of Health Politics, Policy and Law* from 2016 to 2019. Patashnik received his PhD from the University of California, Berkeley.

Michael E. Porter is the Bishop William Lawrence University Professor at Harvard Business School. Professor Porter is a leading authority on competitive strategy; the competitiveness and economic development of nations, states, and regions; and the application of competitive principles to social problems such as health care, the environment, and corporate responsibility. Professor Porter is generally recognized as the father of the modern strategy field and has been identified in a variety of rankings and surveys naming him the world's most influential thinker on management and competitiveness.

Deborah J. Schildkraut is professor and chair of political science at Tufts University. She is the author of *Americanism in the Twenty-First Century: Public Opinion in the Age of Immigration* (2011), *Press "One" for English: Language Policy, Public Opinion, and American Identity* (2005), and, with Kenneth Janda, Jeffrey Berry, Jerry Goldman, and Paul Manna, *The Challenge of Democracy: American Government in Global Politics* (2015). Her research examines the implications of the changing ethnic composition of the United States on public opinion in a variety of domains. She has also published articles in the *Journal of Politics, Political Behavior, Political Psychology, Political Research Quarterly, Politics, Groups, & Identities, American Politics Research,* and *Perspectives on Politics.* Professor Schildkraut received her PhD from Princeton University and her BA from Tufts University.

Wendy J. Schiller is Royce Family Professor of Teaching Excellence in Political Science, professor of international and public affairs, and chair of the Department of Political Science at Brown University. She did her undergraduate work in political science at the University of Chicago, served on the staffs of Senator Daniel Patrick Moynihan and Governor Mario Cuomo, and then obtained her PhD from the University of Rochester. After fellowships at the Brookings Institution and Princeton University, she came to Brown University in 1994, where she teaches popular courses titled The American Presidency, Introduction to the American Political Process, and Congress and Public Policy. Among books she has authored or coauthored are *Electing the Senate: Indirect Democracy before the Seventeenth Amendment* (2014), *Gateways to Democracy: An Introduction to American Government,* Enhanced Fourth Edition (2019), *The Contemporary Congress* (2018), and *Partners and Rivals: Representation in U.S. Senate Delegations* (2000). She has also published articles in the *American Journal of Political Science, Legislative Studies Quarterly, Studies in American Political Development,* and the *Journal of Politics.* She regularly provides political commentary for national and local news outlets.

Yotam Shmargad is assistant professor in the School of Government and Public Policy at the University of Arizona. His research focuses on virtual experiments and analyzing large online datasets to study how digital media shape social and political behaviors. His recent projects look at Twitter and electoral competitiveness, algorithmic sorting and political polarization, and social feedback and incivility. His work has been published in the *International Journal of Communication, Journal of Political Marketing,* and *Journal of Politics,* as well as other outlets.

John Sides is professor of political science at Vanderbilt University, and he studies political behavior in American and comparative politics. He is coauthor of *Identity Crisis: The 2016 Presidential Campaign and the Battle for the Meaning of America* (2018), *The Gamble: Choice and Chance in the 2012 Election* (2014), and *Campaigns and Elections: Rules, Reality, Strategy, Choice* (2011). He has published articles in various scholarly journals, including the *American Political Science Review, American Journal of Political Science, British Journal of Political Science,* and *Journal of Politics.* His current book project focuses on fiscal politics in the United States. He helped found and serves as editor-in-chief of the *Monkey Cage,* a blog about political science and politics at the *Washington Post.* He received his BA from the University of North Carolina–Chapel Hill and his MA and PhD from the University of California, Berkeley. Before coming to Vanderbilt, he taught at the University of Texas at Austin and George Washington University.

Michael Tesler is associate professor of political science at the University of California, Irvine, where he teaches courses on public opinion, racial politics, elections, political psychology, American government, and quantitative research methods. He is author of *Post-Racial or Most-Racial? Race and Politics in the Obama Era* (2016), and coauthor, with David O. Sears, of *Obama's Race: The 2008 Election and the Dream of a Post-Racial America* (2010). His latest book, coauthored with John Sides and Lynn Vavreck, *Identity Crisis: The 2016 Presidential Campaign and the Battle for the Meaning of America,* was published in 2018. Tesler's research has been funded by the National Science Foundation, featured in several prominent media outlets, and published in such scholarly journals as the *American Journal of Political Science* and the *Journal of Politics.* As a contributing editor for the *Washington Post*'s *Monkey Cage,* his work has received recognition from both popular and academic sources. Before arriving at the University of California, Irvine, he earned a PhD in political science from the University of California, Los Angeles, in 2011 and was on the faculty at Brown University from 2011 to 2014.

Lynn Vavreck is the Marvin Hoffenberg Professor of American Politics and Public Policy at the University of California, Los Angeles, a contributing columnist to the *Upshot* at the *New York Times,* and coauthor of *Identity Crisis:*

The 2016 Presidential Campaign and the Battle for the Meaning of America (2018). Her 2012 award-winning campaign book, *The Gamble: Choice and Chance in the 2012 Presidential Election,* was described by Nate Silver as the "definitive account" of the 2012 election, and political consultants on both sides of the aisle refer to her work on political messaging as "required reading." In 2015, she was awarded an Andrew F. Carnegie Fellowship to investigate the influence of political advertising. Her research has been supported by the National Science Foundation and she has served on the advisory boards of both the British and American National Election Studies. At the University of California, Los Angeles, she teaches courses on campaigns, elections, and public opinion. Vavreck holds a PhD in political science from the University of Rochester and held previous appointments at Princeton University, Dartmouth College, and the White House.

Index